CLARENDON ANCIENT HISTORY SERIES

General Editors

Brian Bosworth   Miriam Griffin
David Whitehead   Susan Treggiari

The aim of the CLARENDON ANCIENT HISTORY SERIES is to provide authoritative translations, introductions, and commentaries to a wide range of Greek and Latin texts studied by ancient historians. The books will be of interest to scholars, graduate students, and advanced undergraduates.

Asconius
Commentaries on
Speeches of Cicero

Translated with Commentary by R. G. Lewis

(REVISED BY JILL HARRIES,
JOHN RICHARDSON, CHRISTOPHER SMITH,
AND CATHERINE STEEL)

with Latin text
edited by A. C. Clark

OXFORD
UNIVERSITY PRESS

OXFORD

UNIVERSITY PRESS

Great Clarendon Street, Oxford OX2 6DP

Oxford University Press is a department of the University of Oxford.
It furthers the University's objective of excellence in research, scholarship,
and education by publishing worldwide in

Oxford New York

Auckland   Cape Town   Dar es Salaam   Hong Kong   Karachi
Kuala Lumpur   Madrid   Melbourne   Mexico City   Nairobi
New Delhi   Shanghai   Taipei   Toronto
With offices in
Argentina   Austria   Brazil   Chile   Czech Republic   France   Greece
Guatemala   Hungary   Italy   Japan   South Korea   Poland   Portugal
Singapore   Switzerland   Thailand   Turkey   Ukraine   Vietnam

Oxford is a registered trade mark of Oxford University Press
in the UK and in certain other countries

Published in the United States
by Oxford University Press Inc., New York

ISBN 978-0-19-929053-6

Printed in the United Kingdom by
Lightning Source UK Ltd., Milton Keynes

Preface

THIS book has been compiled to meet the perceived needs of those who have little or no knowledge of Latin but are studying the Roman Republic of the Ciceronian age from original sources in translation. While Cicero himself is very much the most important of them, what survives from Asconius' learned commentaries on just five of his orations, only two of them fully extant, is an indispensable supplement. The Latin text is still readily available in the Oxford Classical Text of A. C. Clark, regarded by Anglophones at least as the standard edition for purposes of citation, but it is curious— indeed astonishing—that in this day and age there exists no comparably accessible version in English which incorporates commentary and helpful indices. I have sought to provide one.

I also thought it useful to add a short introduction on the author and his sources; and a glossary of those Latin technical terms which it seems better to leave untranslated rather than to risk misleading readers by offering approximations in English. The other features are a list of Laws and Rogations mentioned by him and an Index of Personal Names. The commentary offers some limited annotation on the translated text, including a few bibliographic items for those who wish or need to pursue matters further. It is by no means comprehensive, even on purely historical matters, much less on literary or linguistic questions; and only in one or two places have I considered the textual problems posed by the manuscripts. Since specialist students of the Ciceronian age are unlikely to be beginners, I have assumed a basic historical knowledge of the late Roman Republic and its institutions. It will be obvious from the Notes how very much I owe to the remarkable industry and scholarship of Bruce A. Marshall in his much further-ranging *Historical Commentary on Asconius* (University of Missouri Press, Columbia, 1985), which I have consulted constantly, and always to my pleasure and profit, if not always in complete agreement.

It remains for me to thank colleagues at Edinburgh for encouragement, advice, and salvation from error on various matters, most especially Dr Edward Bispham and Professor John Richardson. They bear no blame for surviving faults.

R. G. L.

Edinburgh
December 1999

Preface by the Revisers

WHEN Geoffrey Lewis died in 2001, he left his translation and commentary on Asconius all but completed. Four of his colleagues in the Scottish universities, with the encouragement of his widow, Mrs Sheila Lewis, have undertaken final revision of Lewis's work which he had been unable to complete, and have supplied two short sections to the Introduction, which we felt sure he would have wished to add. We would also wish to express our thanks to Peter Wiseman for his advice on a number of points. The book remains essentially as Geoffrey left it, and represents his views and his approach to Asconius and the period for which he is so valuable a source. It is our hope that it will stand as a fitting memorial to a scholar who devoted his life to the exposition of Roman history and to the communication of his understanding and enthusiasm to generations of students.

Although the original intention had been to publish a translation and commentary only, the General Editors of the series suggested, much to our delight, that it would be useful to add the Latin text, in A. C. Clark's edition of 1907, which is presently out of print. We have no doubt that Geoffrey Lewis, who has at several points commented on the manuscript tradition, would have been as glad of this as we are.

J. D. H.
J. S. R.
C. J. S.
C. E. W. S.

May 2006

Contents

Introduction

THE AUTHOR

Q. Asconius Pedianus most probably hailed from Patavium (Padua), and was thus a fellow-townsman of Livy, to whom he refers as 'our friend' (77C) and whose diction he criticized (Quintilian 1.7.24). According to the entry in the chronicle of the fourth-century Christian writer Jerome for AD 76, which he derived from Suetonius' *Lives of Famous Men*, Asconius, 'a distinguished historical writer', became blind at the age of seventy-three and lived for twelve more years as a universally respected figure. He was thus born in 9 BC, lived for eighty-five years to AD 76 but went blind in AD 64. He moved in exalted circles: a late authority (the *Suda*, s.v. Apicius) has him attending a banquet as the fellow-guest of consuls and ex-consuls in AD 28, 'towed along uninvited like a dinghy'; another late tradition (Servius' commentary on Vergil's *Eclogues*, 4.11) records that, later in life, he heard C. Asinius Gallus, an obstreperous senator under Tiberius who died in AD 33, boasting that he was the Wonderchild prophesied in Vergil's *Fourth Eclogue*.

Asconius will almost certainly have been of equestrian birth and possibly a senator himself. He was familiar with Roman political processes and senatorial procedure, which he explains to his sons, the purported beneficiaries of these Commentaries, because they are supposed to be too young to be aware of such niceties (43C). He may also have been a magnate of his native community (Silius Italicus, *Punica* 12. 212–14, 218–22).

THE WORKS

Many of Asconius' works have been lost. They may have included a treatise on longevity: the elder Pliny (*NH* 7.159) mentioned a man of 110 years old, whose age was recorded by Asconius. He also wrote a biography of the historian and politician Sallust, who was active in politics in the 50s and later a follower of Caesar. However, Sallust's account of the conspiracy of Catiline (*Bellum Catilinae*) has little apparent impact on Asconius' commentary on the *In Toga Candida*. Another lost work was a counterblast to critics of Vergil, still extant and known to writers in the fourth century such as the grammarian Donatus (*Vit. Verg.* 57), and the antiquarian Macrobius (*Saturnalia* 5.3.16).

Some further *Commentaries on the Speeches of Cicero* have also perished and even the surviving text may be incomplete. There is a reference to one commentary on Cicero's speech in defence of Roscius of Ameria (delivered in 80 BC) in the second-century man of letters Aulus Gellius (*Attic Nights* 15.28.4), who cites Asconius in criticism of Fenestella for getting Cicero's age wrong. A reference by a fifteenth-century cleric to the discovery of a manuscript of commentaries by Asconius on eight speeches, if not a slip, may point to some loss in transmission. Moreover, internal evidence from the extant commentaries suggests that Asconius may have commented also on a number of other speeches, including the two for the tribune Manilius in 66 BC, the Catilinarian speeches of 63 BC, the *Pro Sestio* of 56 BC and others (see Marshall (1985*b*), 1–25).

The Commentaries on the five speeches that are extant can be dated to between AD 54 and 57 (Clark, OCT Preface, v–vi). In his commentary on *The Defence of M. Scaurus* (27C) Asconius notes that at the time of writing the defendant's house was owned by Caecina Largus 'who was consul with Claudius' (AD 42). Such language referring to the Emperor could be used only after his death in AD 54; and Caecina, still alive in the context, was a constantly active member of the priesthood of the *Fratres Arvales*, as is evident in their extant records, from which he disappears in AD 57, presumably deceased.

THE TRANSMISSION OF THE TEXT

A text of Asconius, with commentary on eight speeches, was discovered at St Gallen in modern Switzerland in 1416 by the scholar Poggio Bracciolini, along with C. Valerius Flaccus' *Argonautica* and a manuscript of Quintilian. From this somewhat tattered manuscript of Asconius were derived two copies, one a transcription authorized but not carried out in person by Bartholemaeus de Montepolitiano (M) and the other by one Sozomenus (S), both in 1417. See further, Reeve (1983).

ASCONIUS AND HIS AGE

There is no doubt of Asconius' acutely critical scholarship and widely learned curiosity over details, nor of his reputation for these attributes in an age which had no lack of similar figures. He was cited by name by Quintilian, the writer on oratory (*Inst. Or.* 1.7.24, 5.10.9) and the elder Pliny, polymath and writer of the encyclopedic *Natural History* (*NH* 7.9) and in addition shared the cultural preoccupations of Silius Italicus, Valerius Maximus, and Valerius Probus. Probus and Quintilian at least, like Asconius and two luminaries of the next two generations, the younger Pliny and Suetonius, were much concerned, in reaction to the excesses of the younger Seneca and his acolytes, to revive the study and indeed imitation of the classical Latin writers of the Golden Age of Cicero and Augustus.

In writing these *Commentaries* Asconius' professed intention is to guide his young sons through their reading of Cicero's speeches. There seem to have been a few remarks on diction, style, and rhetorical technique, but the exposition is chiefly concerned with historical background and with minutiae of prosopography, topography, constitutional and legal practice, conduct and results of the processes involved, explanation of perceived obscurities. Unsurprisingly, this material does not greatly lend itself to literary elegance: the Latin, while generally correct and for the most part painstakingly lucid, almost never rises above the ponderously plain and pedestrian. Since it contains a good deal of technical terminology which in translation is best rendered with as much consistency as possible, anyone attempting an English version is fettered by it and from the literary viewpoint under serious limitations in any effort to render the style more attractive. At best one may seek to offer something tolerably readable.

For these aesthetic shortcomings, however, there is compensation in Asconius' intellectual virtues. The extant text does exhibit a number of errors and confusions, but this author is honest enough to admit when appropriate both puzzlement and occasional failures—to date—to ascertain the truth to his own satisfaction. They are never for want of application. He gathers evidence with avidity, skill, and for the most part a discriminating eye for relevance to the point at issue, and normally evaluates it with persuasive argumentation and critical acumen. True, the questions that he raises are not always those which modern students want answered, nor is his coverage even of Cicero's orations as comprehensive as we might wish. Nevertheless he offers a particularly rich store of information not only on the orations, but on very many other features and events of the age in which they were delivered—and for that matter in places also on earlier times. For breadth and volume of reading, if not perhaps range of interests, he bears comparison not, one must admit, with Varro or the elder Pliny, and possibly not with later scholars like Suetonius or Gellius, but certainly with Atticus, Nepos, or Cicero himself.

THE COMMENTARY FORM

The title, *Enarratio*, attached to Asconius' work implies an expository narrative, designed for guidance and education, perhaps sometimes on a fairly basic level. The word *enarratio* occurs in the *Rhet. ad Herenn.* (4.55.69) meaning 'narrative of events' and in Varro, as 'explanation of a text'. Both Varro and Quintilian state that *enarratio* in the sense of explanation of a text is a duty of the grammarian, and Quintilian (2.1.5) extends the duty to the teacher of rhetoric as well. As 'exponent' of Cicero's text, Asconius was therefore acting in accordance with the principles of teaching as enunciated by Varro and Quintilian. Annotation and commentary upon major literary figures was a well-established form of scholarly activity at Rome by the time Asconius wrote. Suetonius places the origins of a critical interest in the interpretation of poetry in the lectures given at Rome by Crates of Mallos in 168 BC (Suetonius, *Gram.* 2), and the writing of commentaries on poetic texts in Latin is well attested by the first century BC.[1] There were also by this time commentaries in Greek on some of Demosthenes' speeches by Didymus (who may possibly have visited Rome) which consider historical questions as well as those of language.[2] Less certain, but perhaps relevant to the development of the lemma form of commentary employed by Asconius, is the existence and format of commentaries on legal texts. Sex. Aelius Paetus Catus, consul in 198, appears to have edited and commented on the Twelve Tables (*OCD* 19). It is possible that the format adopted by Cicero's *De Legibus*, Books 2 and 3 of a complete text of the 'law codes' followed by a separate commentary, clause by clause, owes its structure to Sex. Aelius, whose work Cicero knew. An attack on Q. Mucius Scaevola's major treatise on civil law by the jurist Servius Sulpicius Rufus, consul 51, is entitled *Reprehensa Scaevolae Capita*. It is known primarily from the second-century writer Aulus Gellius (*Attic Nights* 4.1.17 and 20) and may have been in lemma form, with a series of extracts from Scaevola (*capita*) accompanied in each case by Servius' presumably critical commentary (*Digest* 17.2.30 and 33.9.3.6). It is certain that in the second century AD Mucius did receive the lemma treatment in the commentary *Ad Q. Mucium* by the legal historian and jurist, Pomponius.

Asconius' work can also be understood in a different context, that of works of advice to a son. Cato the Elder wrote an *Ad Filium*, the second-century jurist M. Brutus wrote at least three books on law addressed to his son, and one can note also Cicero's catechistic *Partitiones Oratoriae* and the *De Officiis*, both directed at his son Marcus.[3] Asconius' concern in his commentaries with historical context and political procedure rather than language or style (the comment on conjunctions at 21C is almost certainly not Asconius') fits into this framework rather better than into that of the grammarians, and it is surely right to see his aim in writing to be the instruction of his sons through the exposition of some important political texts (Marshall (1985*b*), 32–8); this aim does not preclude

---

[1] Rawson (1985), 268–70.
[2] Gibson (2002), 26–50.
[3] Dyck (1996), 10–16.

his envisaging a wider audience for his work from the time of composition.

Asconius' commentaries as we have them are clearly intended to be read alongside the text of Cicero's speeches. This is the reason for the remarks which occur at the beginning of each section of his exposition of each of the speeches, indicating how far from the beginning or ending of the roll (*volumen*) containing the speech this section is to be found.

SOURCES

For the Ciceronian Commentaries Asconius' attested sources, besides the Orations themselves, with which he was plainly intimately familiar, make an impressive list.

Official documents

The *Acta*—that is, the official record of transactions of the Roman senate, as well as records or events outside the senate, were regularly published under a measure instituted by C. Iulius Caesar in his first consulship of 59 BC (Suet. *Div. Iul.* 20; cf. 24.3, 74.2, *Aug.* 66). They are cited more frequently than any other source (five out of six occur in the Milo speech commentary) and Asconius may have prided himself on his attention to this source.

Cicero (besides the Orations and other extant works on rhetoric and philosophy)

(i) Notes (*commentarii*) of various speeches, edited by his freedman secretary Tiro (87C; Quintil. 10.7.31).

(ii) 'Explanation of his political calculations' (*Expositio consiliorum suorum*)—an account of his political decisions at various junctures, started in 59, and suppressed until after his death (83C; cf. Cic. *Att.* 2.6.2; Dio 39.10.3).

(iii) *Pro Milone*—the original speech actually delivered in court in 52 BC, markedly different and much less effective than the published, extant version (47C).

Historians (etc.)

Antias (Valerius) (13C, 69C). Wrote sometime in the first century BC, but his exact date is disputed. His historical work, known only from quotations in other authors, covered the history of Rome from its foundation down to at least 91 BC; its scale expanded as it approached his own time. Livy often cites him, usually to express disagreement.

Atticus (13C, 77C). T. Pomponius Atticus, born in 110 BC, is best known as the close friend and literary adviser of Cicero but his network of political contacts was extensive. He wrote a *Liber Annalis*, a chronological summary of world and Roman history, which is cited by Asconius. Atticus was celebrated in a biography by Cornelius Nepos, and died in 32 BC.

Fenestella (5C, 31C, 85C, 86C). Born in 52 BC (possibly 35 BC), he wrote an annalistic history of Rome in at least twenty-two books down to 57 BC. He had wide antiquarian interests and wrote in the Varronian tradition. Asconius' references to him are usually to state opposition to his views.

Hyginus, *De Viris Claris* (13C). C. Iulius Hyginus, a freedman of Augustus and librarian of the Palatine Library (Suet. *Gram.* 20), wrote extensively on a wide range of topics including agriculture, Vergil, history and archaeology (e.g. on Trojan families and the origins of Italian cities) and on religion. His works are now lost.

Livy (66C, 77C). Born 59 BC, died AD 17, he came from Padua, also Asconius' home town, and was on good terms with Augustus. His history of Rome from the origins of the city to 9 BC extended to 142 books, of which only 1–10 and 21–45 survive, the latter with lacunae; most of the rest are preserved in summary (*epitome*) form. Asconius cited Livy twice by name but may have used him more extensively.

Sallust (66C). C. Sallustius was one of the Ten Tribunes in 52 BC, later governor of Africa and a follower of Caesar. After Caesar's death he wrote monographs on the conspiracy of Catiline (apparently not

xviii   *Introduction*

much used by Asconius) and the *War with Jugurtha*. His main work, the *Histories*, consulted by Asconius, survives in fragmentary form.

C. Sempronius Tuditanus (77C). He was consul in 129 BC and an opponent of the Gracchan land reforms. He wrote a work entitled by one authority *Commentarii*, on the authority and hierarchy of magistrates, perhaps as an offshoot from augural law. It comprised at least thirteen books.

M. Tullius Tiro, *Vita Ciceronis* (48C). This is the faithful freedman and secretary of Cicero, responsible for editing and circulating his work.

Varro, *De Vita Populi Romani* (13C). M. Terentius Varro (116–27 BC), from Reate in the Sabine country, had a public career as praetor and supporter of Pompey. Pardoned by Caesar, he was proscribed by Mark Antony and retired. A prolific and learned author, two of his works survive in part, the *De Lingua Latina*, on Latin language in twenty-five books, and the *De Re Rustica* in three books. Among his many lost works (he wrote nearly seventy-five different works totalling 620 books), the *Antiquitates* in forty-one books, is the most significant. Varro was arguably the most influential of all the writers of antiquity.

A group called 'Writers on the Second Punic War' (3C) may have included Coelius Antipater, perhaps others too.

Orators (other than Cicero)

These are surprisingly few:

M. Iunius Brutus (85–42 BC), one of the assassins of Julius Caesar; after Milo's conviction he wrote an alternative defence speech (41C), which appears to have relied heavily upon the argument that Clodius' death was in the public interest.

C. Iulius Caesar (100–44 BC), the dictator; his prosecution, at the age of twenty-three, of Cn. Cornelius Dolabella for extortion whilst governor of Macedonia (26C) was unsuccessful—Dolabella was acquitted—but made Caesar's name as a speaker, and the speech itself gained lasting fame.

P. Cominius, from Spoletium in Umbria; he seems, with his brother Lucius, to have engaged regularly in prosecution cases; the prosecutor, with his brother, of Cornelius in 65 BC (59–61C).

L. Lucceius, politician41 (praetor at some point in the 60s, unsuccessful consular candidate for 59), friend and correspondent of Cicero, and historian; no references survive outside Asconius' text to his speeches against Catiline (92C).

Poets

Lucius Accius (16C), 170–*c*.86 BC, a freedman from Umbria, who produced tragedies (forty titles survive) and a variety of poems in a rather grand style. Cicero heard him lecture in the early 80s. None of his work survives complete, but there are substantial fragments, some of which are quoted by Cicero himself.
    Philodemus (16C), *c*.110–40/35 BC. Born in Syria at Gadara, Philodemus came to Rome around 75 BC and enjoyed the patronage of the Calpurnii Pisones, and through them attained a position in a villa in Herculaneum, whence most of his work was recovered on papyri. He wrote poetry which was fashionable among the literary elite, and popularized Greek philosophy for a learned Roman audience—he was himself an Epicurean.
    L. Iulius Caesar Strabo Vopiscus (25C), a tragic poet and orator, aedile in 90 BC, who died in 87 BC, in the massacres when Cinna and Marius entered Rome. Accius refused to stand in his presence, because he was an inferior poet (Val. Max. 3.7.11), but Cicero makes him one of the characters in *De Oratore*. His work is almost entirely lost.
    C. Licinius Calvus (93C), born 82, dead by 47 BC; son of the annalist C. Licinius Macer, he was a lively orator, admired by Cicero (*Fam.* 15.21.4; *Brut.* 279), and his speeches were still read in Tacitus' day (*Dial.* 21.4). He was a close friend of Catullus the poet (Catull. 14, 50, 53, 96); later writers often paired the two poets. Only fragments survive of both poetry and oratory.

    These are merely the sources which the extant Commentaries cite by name (Marshall (1985*b*), 39–61). There were probably many more. The one glaring omission is the collection of Cicero's *Letters to Atticus*. Cornelius Nepos had seen them, or some of them (Nepos, *Att.* 16), but it is generally still believed that they were not definitively edited and published until *c*. AD 60, when Seneca is the first to cite them (*Ep.* 97.6). Most unfortunately, therefore, it would seem, they were not available to the greatest Ciceronian scholar since M. Tiro and before Quintilian—and superior to either in his intimate knowledge of political history in the late Republic.

ASCONIUS AND THE CITY OF ROME

We learn relatively little from Asconius about the city of Rome, and there are only a few instances where his commentary is largely concerned with a matter of urban topography. Thus, although Squires argues that 'he writes at least partly for readers who were like himself provincials',[4] his interest is not in explaining the topographical landscape of the relevant speeches, and it certainly either assumes a degree of knowledge of the city, or assumes that the details are not important to the reader. Asconius shows none of the topographical sensitivity which Vasaly recently attributed to Cicero; this is particularly evident in the commentary on the *Pro Scauro*, where Cicero's claims for the family's impact on the Forum is covered by the terse identification of the Temple of Castor and Pollux rebuilt by L. Metellus (27C). There is little said about the physical topography of the city; Asconius mentions the Palatine, Capitoline, and Janiculan hills, and the Mons Sacer, to which the plebeians seceded. The larger number of his references to the city topography relate to private houses, and Asconius reminds us of the extraordinary significance of the residences of the key players in Roman politics. One house which inevitably is mentioned is Cicero's own (10C). Cicero's house on the Palatine Hill overlooking the Via Sacra and opposite the Velia was part of a substantial area of residential housing, some of which dated back to the sixth century BC. After Cicero's exile, Clodius demolished the house, enlarged the adjacent portico of Catulus, and turned the plot into a temple of Libertas, but all these actions were reversed when Cicero was allowed to return (*LTUR* 2. 202–4). Asconius has nothing much to say about all this (it may have been covered elsewhere), but he does digress on houses built at public expense (13C). Another famous house is that of M. Aemilius Scaurus, which Asconius located with unusual certainty, and which it

---

[4] Squires (1990), p. vii.

is claimed has recently been identified (27C; *LTUR* 2. 26).[5] The house was sold to P. Clodius Pulcher and it was there that Clodius' body was taken and displayed after his murder (32C). The house was famously expensive in its time, and the four Hymettan marble columns of its atrium, which had been used by Scaurus in his temporary theatre, were transferred to the Theatre of Marcellus, as Asconius notes (27C).[6]

Another key *domus* is that of Pompey. In 58 BC, his life apparently having been threatened, Pompey retreated to his home, and this must be a house on the Carinae near the Temple of Tellus (46C). In 52 BC, allegedly in fear of Milo, after Clodius' death, Pompey again retreated, this time not to his house but to his upper gardens (*horti superiores*). The location of these has never been satisfactorily settled, though it is from these passages that *horti inferiores* are inferred and identified with gardens near the Theatre of Pompey (completed 55 BC) in the Campus Martius, which passed to Antony and then to Agrippa. Nevertheless, the *horti superiores* must be somewhere near the theatre since at the time that Pompey was guarded there, the senate met in his portico, so that he could attend (52C). Pompey's portico was attached to his theatre, directly behind the stage building and adjoining the *scaena* (*LTUR* 4. 148–9). The theatre itself in the Campus Martius was inaugurated around the time that the speech *In Pisonem* was delivered, with huge games (16C).

Asconius mentions a number of other houses; he explains Cicero's oblique reference to a meeting of Catiline and his supporters in the house of a certain nobleman as meaning either Caesar, who had a house in the Subura, though whether he lived there in 64 BC is unclear (Suetonius, *Div. Jul.* 46), or Crassus (Cicero bought this house in 62 BC). After the death of Clodius, the mob attacked the house of Milo (on the *clivus Capitolinus*, though it is Cicero not Asconius who tells us that); and that of the *interrex* M. Lepidus (33C; Cic. *Pro Milone* 64). Finally, in his account of houses built at public expense, Asconius mentions M. Valerius Maximus' house on the Palatine, built for the dictator of 494 BC, with doors that opened outwards, and the house of Valerius Publicola on the Velia, currently a temple of Victory,

---

[5] Haselberger (2002), 104.
[6] Pliny, *NH* 17.5–6, 24.106, 36.5–6; Asconius (27C) also tells us that the owner in his time was Caecina Largus (cos. AD 42).

according to Asconius, but more accurately Vica Pota (13C). A house was built for Antiochus III's son when he was kept as a hostage, and another for the people of Mutina.

In terms of temples, Asconius mentions the temple of Castor, in the Forum, which was restored by L. Caecilius Metellus in 117 BC, but damaged in the aftermath of Catiline's conspiracy. He is careful to point out that when Cicero recounts how Catiline carried the severed head of Marius Gratidianus from the Janiculum to the Temple of Apollo, he means the temple in the Forum Holitorium, not the Augustan temple on the Palatine. This temple was vowed in 433 and dedicated in 431 BC, and probably underwent major refurbishment in the early second century, as well as a complete rebuilding by C. Sosius in the late 30s BC (90C). Asconius also mentions in passing the grove of Libitina (33C) but fails to add the crucial explanatory note that we find in Plutarch, *Roman Questions* 23 that the grove was the headquarters of the *libitinarii* or undertakers, and thus well equipped to provide material for a funeral. Some references are so obscure as to defeat us; the *monumentum Basilii* on the Appian Way for instance, or the otherwise unknown house of Hypsaeus (50C, 33C). Yet Asconius does give us a glimpse into the complexity of the urban fabric of Rome. After the events surrounding Clodius' death, perhaps the most vivid moment in Asconius relates to events in 66 BC in his commentary on the speech *Pro Cornelio*. The Cominii laid a charge against Cornelius, but in front of the tribunal gangleaders intimidated them, and they fled up some stairs and out of the city by night across the rooftops (59–60C). Asconius here, and in his account of the trial of Milo (50C, 33C), reminds us that the whole business of law at Rome happened in a very exposed way in the Forum, with the praetor's tribunal near the Comitium and Rostra (*LTUR* 5. 88–9). The courts too were located in the Forum, the magistrate on a low bench, with the jurors, defendant, and the orators ranged on either side. The influence of the crowd, or the *corona* of spectators, is never clearer than in relation to the *Pro Milone*, but that was merely an extreme case. Reading the commentaries, we gain an even greater sense of the remarkably public nature both of legal process, and of domestic buildings.[7]

---

[7] On the courts see Millar (1998), 38–43 with a useful map and references to previous bibliography.

Abbreviations used in the Commentary

CAH VII.2²   F. W. Walbank, A. E. Astin, M. W. Frederiksen, R. M. Ogilvie, and A. Drummond (eds.), *The Cambridge Ancient History*, 2nd edn., vol. VII. 2 (Cambridge, 1989)

CAH IX²   J. A. Crook, A. W. Lintott, and E. D. Rawson (eds.), *The Cambridge Ancient History*, 2nd edn., vol. IX (Cambridge, 1994)

CIL   *Corpus Inscriptionum Latinarum* (Berlin, 1863–)

HRR   H. Peter, *Historicorum Romanorum Fragmenta*, 2 vols. (repr. Stuttgart, 1957)

IGRR   *Inscriptiones Graecae ad res Romanas pertinentes*, ed. R. Cagnat (Paris, 1911–27)

ILLRP   A. Degrassi, *Inscriptiones Latinae Liberae Rei Publicae* (Florence, vol. 1 (1957), vol. 2 (1963), vol. 1² (1965))

ILS   *Inscriptiones Latinae Selectae*, ed. H. Dessau (Berlin, 1892–1916)

LTUR   E. M. Steinby (ed.), *Lexicon Topographicum Urbis Romae*, 6 vols. (Rome, 1993–2000)

MRR   T. R. S. Broughton, *Magistrates of the Roman Republic* (vols. 1–2, New York, 1951–2; vol. 3, Atlanta, 1986)

OCD   S. Hornblower and A. Spawforth (eds.), *The Oxford Classical Dictionary*, 3rd edn. (Oxford, 1996)

OGIS   *Orientis Graeci Inscriptiones Selectae*, ed. W. Dittenberger (Leipzig, 1903)

ORF   E. Malcovati, *Oratorum Romanorum Fragmenta*, 4th edn. (Turin, 1976–9)

RE   Pauly–Wissowa, *Real-Encyclopädie der klassischen Altertumswissenschaft*

SIG   *Sylloge Inscriptionum Graecarum*, 3rd edn., ed. W. Dittenberger *et al.* (Leipzig, 1915)

St.   T. Stangl, *Ciceronis Orationum Scholiastae* (Vienna, 1912)

Sigla

S = Pistoriensis, Forteguerri 37, a Sozomeno scriptus
P = Matritensis x. 81 a Poggio scriptus
M = Laur. liv. 15 ex apographo Bartolomaei de Montepolitiano descriptus
Σ = codd. *SPM* consensus
π = correctiones a m. 2 vel 3 in P factae
ς = coniecturae in recentioribus libris (vel libro) inventae
KS = Kiessling-Schoell

The numbers of the sections in the text, translation and commentary (given with C) are those of the pages in Clark's edition.

In the translation and commentary, Asconius' quotations from Cicero are printed in *italics*. In the Latin text, these are printed o u t s p a c e d.

In the translation, round brackets ( ) are used to enclose additional words provided by the translator to fill out the sense, and square brackets [ ] for additional information, such as dates and translations of some Latin terms.

TEXTS AND TRANSLATIONS

In Senatu Contra
L. Pisonem

HAEC oratio dicta est Cn. Pompeio Magno II M. Crasso II coss. ante paucos dies quam Cn. Pompeius ludos faceret quibus theatrum a se factum dedicavit. Hoc intellegi ex ipsius Ciceronis verbis potest quae in hac ora-
5 tione posuit. Dixit enim sic: Instant post hominum memoriam apparatissimi magnificentissimique ludi. ...... quidem posuit hanc inter eas orationes quas dixit Cicero L. Domitio Appio Claudio coss. ultimam. Sed ut ego ab eo dissentiam facit primum quod Piso reversus est ex pro-
10 vincia Pompeio et Crasso consulibus, Gabinius Domitio et Appio: hanc autem orationem dictam ante Gabini reditum ex ipsa manifestum est. Deinde magis quidem naturale est ut Piso recenti reditu invectus sit in Ciceronem responderitque insectationi eius qua revocatus erat ex
15 provincia quam post anni intervallum. Apparet autem Ciceronem respondisse Pisoni. In summa, cum dicat in ipsa oratione Cicero instare magnificentissimos apparatissimosque ludos, non video quo modo hoc magis Domitio et Appio coss. dictum sit, quibus consulibus nulli notabiliores

---

Tit. IN SENATV CONTRA L. PISONEM *SP*: Q. ASCONII EPEDIANI
// //
IN SENATV C͠NT. L PISONEM *M*   4 uerbis Ciceronis *P* (uerbis *om.* S)
6 ludi...... (4 *litt.* P) Σ: Fenestella *suppl.* ς, *ed. Ven.*: Tiro (*vel*
Nepos) *suppl. KS*   9 ab eo *P*: habeo *SM*   12 quidem
scripsi: quod Σ: quoque *Orelli* (quod magis ς)   13 ut *ed. Iunt.*:
in Σ   Piso *Rinkes*: ipso Σ   14 quare uocatus *P*: ante (*post*
quare) *add. in mg.* π   15 *in voc.* interuallum *finitur paragraphus in*
SP, sequitur proximo versu APPARET   16 in summa Σ: in senatū
P sup. lin. m. 1   dicat in ς, *Manutius*: dicens Σ: diceret *Poggius*

This speech was delivered in the second consulship of Cn. Pompeius Magnus and M. Crassus [55 BC], a few days before Cn. Pompeius held the games at which he dedicated the theatre which he had constructed. This may be inferred from Cicero's own wording which he deployed in this speech. For he spoke as follows: '*The most lavish and most magnificent games in human memory are imminent.*'

... 'X', certainly, identified this speech as the last which Cicero delivered in the consulship of L. Domitius and Appius Claudius [54 BC]. But what leads me to disagree with him is firstly the fact that Piso returned from his province in the consulship of Pompeius and Crassus, and Gabinius in that of Domitius and Appius; and that this speech was delivered before the return of Gabinius is manifest from the text itself. Secondly, it is surely more natural for Piso to have attacked Cicero, and to have replied to the polemics from him which had occasioned his recall, shortly after his return from his province rather than after a year's interval. And it is clear that Cicero made his reply to Piso. In sum, when Cicero declares that the most magnificent and lavish games are imminent, I do not see how this can have been uttered in the consulship of Domitius and Appius, when there were no games of much distinction,

2C ludi fuerunt, quam Pompeio et Crasso, quo anno Pompeius
exquisitissimis magnificentissimisque omnis generis ludis
theatrum dedicavit. Argumentum orationis huius breve admodum est.

5 Nam cum revocati essent ex provinciis Piso et Gabinius sententia Ciceronis quam dixerat de provinciis consularibus Lentulo et Philippo consulibus, reversus in civitatem Piso de
insectatione Ciceronis in senatu conquestus est et in eum
invectus, fiducia maxime Caesaris generi qui tum Gallias
10 obtinebat. Pisoni Cicero respondit hac oratione.

ENARRATIO

CIRCA VERS. A PRIMO ✱✱✱

Quod minimum specimen in te ingeni? Ingeni
autem? immo ingenui hominis ac liberi : qui colore
15 ipso patriam aspernaris, oratione genus, moribus
nomen.

Tametsi haec oratio sic inscribitur : In L. Pisonem;
tamen non puto vos ignorare hunc Pisonem ex ea familia
esse quae Frugi appellata sit : et ideo dicit aspernari eum moribus
20 nomen.

CIRCA VERS. LXXX

Hoc non ad contemnendam Placentiam pertinet
unde se is ortum gloriari solet : neque enim hoc
mea natura fert, nec municipi, praesertim de me
25 optime meriti, dignitas patitur.

Magnopere me haesitare confiteor quid sit qua re Cicero

1 Pompeii et Crassi Σ: *corr. Poggius*   2 -que *om. P*   4
ARGVMENTVM *P: tum versu seq.* Argumentum huius orationis *etc.*
5 Gabinius *PM* : Gabinus *S*   8 consecutus *S*   11 Enarratio
(*litt. min.*) *prioribus continuant PM*   12 *om. SM*   13 specimen
P : speciē ēm *SM*   ingenii *semel hab. S*   14 ingenii *S*[1]
colore *M, ed. Ald.* : colorore *S*: color. colore *P*[1] : color. Ore *Poggius*
21 *om. SM*   23 is *P* : his *SM*

rather than in that of Pompeius and Crassus, the year in which   2C
Pompeius dedicated his theatre—with games of the choicest mag-
nificence of every kind. To provide an explanatory preface for this speech is no lengthy
matter at all. For when Piso and Gabinius were recalled from their
provinces in accordance with the views of Cicero which he declared
in his speech *On the Consular Provinces*, in the consulship of Lentulus
and Philippus, Piso on his return to the city complained of Cicero's
polemics and inveighed against him, especially confident of support
from his son-in-law Caesar, who at that time held the Gallic provinces. Cicero replied to Piso in the present oration.

Commentary

Around line ... from the beginning
*Do you have in you even the least semblance of mental capacity?—
Mental capacity? Ha! For that matter of free birth and status—a man
who in your very complexion give the lie to Roman provenance, in
speech to your family, in way of life to your name.* Although this speech
is entitled as follows: 'Against L. Piso', all the same I think you will not
be unaware that this Piso was from the family which bore the name
Frugi ('morally sound'), and for that reason he says that he repudi-
ates his name by his way of life.

Around line 80
*This is not meant to express contempt for Placentia, which he is given to
boast as his birthplace: for neither does my own natural disposition
allow such a thing, nor does its high rank as a municipium, especially
one which has deserved so well of me, permit it.* I confess that I am in a
great quandary as to what reason Cicero could possibly have for

3C   Placentiam municipium esse dicat. Video enim in annali-
       bus eorum qui Punicum bellum secundum scripserunt tradi
       Placentiam coloniam deductam pridie Kal. Iun. primo
       anno eius belli, P. Cornelio Scipione, patre Africani prioris,
    5 Ti. Sempronio Longo coss. Neque illud dici potest, sic
       eam coloniam esse deductam quemadmodum post plures
       aetates Cn. Pompeius Strabo, pater Cn. Pompei Magni,
       Transpadanas colonias deduxerit. Pompeius enim non
       novis colonis eas constituit sed veteribus incolis manenti-
   10 bus ius dedit Latii, ut possent habere ius quod ceterae
       Latinae coloniae, id est ut petendo magistratus civitatem
       Romanam adipiscerentur. Placentiam autem sex milia
       hominum novi coloni deducti sunt, in quibus equites
       ducenti. Deducendi fuit causa ut opponerentur Gallis
   15 qui eam partem Italiae tenebant. Deduxerunt III viri
       P. Cornelius Asina, P. Papirius Maso, Cn. Cornelius Scipio.
       Eamque coloniam LIII ...... deductam esse invenimus:
       deducta est autem Latina. Duo porro genera earum colo-
       niarum quae a populo Romano deductae sunt fuerunt, ut
   20 Quiritium aliae, aliae Latinorum essent. De se autem
       optime meritos Placentinos ait, quod illi quoque honora-
       tissima decreta erga Ciceronem fecerunt certaveruntque in
       ea re cum tota Italia, cum de reditu eius actum est.

3 Ian. Σ, *corr. Madvig*   4 P. *Manutius : om.* Σ   8 colonias
(-ia *M*) Σ: colonos *Sozomenus* ⁀deduxerat Σ, *corr. Manutius*
9 ea Σ, *corr.* π   10 habere] *hic P*   11 petendo *scripsi*:
petendi (peti *S*) Σ: gerendo *A. Augustinus*   12 Placentiam
S: Placentia *PM*   14 ducenti *KS*: ducendi *S: om. PM* dedu-
cendit *P¹*   15 III uiri *S*: triumuiri *PM*   16 Maso *S, Perizonius:*
Maso, Cn. Pompeius *PM*   17 LIII] *seq. lac.* (3 *litt. P,* 5 *S,* 8 *M*)
deducta messe (me messe *M*) Σ, *corr. Poggius*   19 ut Quiritium aliae *Baiter:* itaque Σ   22 certaueruntque *S* : certauerantque
PM   23 reditu eius *PM:* re.... *S*

calling Placentia a *municipium*. For I note in the Annals of those who   3C
wrote on the Second Punic War the tradition that Placentia was
founded as a *colonia* on 31 May in the first year of that war, in the
consulship of P. Cornelius Scipio, father of the elder Africanus, and
Ti. Sempronius Longus [218 BC]. Nor can the point be made that this
colony was founded in the manner in which several generations later
Cn. Pompeius Strabo, father of Cn. Pompeius Magnus, founded
Transpadane colonies. For Pompeius established them not with
new colonists, but granted the Latin Right to the old inhabitants
who remained there, so that they might enjoy the rights held by the
rest of the Latin colonies—that is, that by standing for magistracies
they might attain Roman citizenship. But at Placentia six thousand
men were installed as the original colonists, among them two hundred *equites*. The purpose of their installation was that they should
confront the Gauls who were in possession of that part of Italy.
A Board of Three, P. Cornelius Asina, P. Papirius Maso, and Cn.
Cornelius Scipio, founded it. And we have discovered that this colony
was founded ... fifty-three... ; and it was founded as one of Latin
status. There were, of course, two kinds of *coloniae* which were
founded by the Roman people, so that some were of full Roman
citizens, others of Latins. He states that the Placentines had deserved
extremely well of him, since they had passed decrees paying him the
highest honours, and had in this respect vied with all Italy when
action was taken to secure his recall from exile.

PAVLO POST

d e   a v o   P i s o n i s   m a t e r n o :
H i c   c u m   a   d o m o   *p r o f e c t u s*   P l a c e n t i a e   f o r t e
c o n s e d i s s e t   p a u c i s   *p o s t   a n n i s*   i n   e a m   c i v i t a t e m—
5 n a m   t u m   e r a t . . . .—a s c e n d i t .   P r i u s   e n i m
G a l l u s ,   d e i n   G a l l i c a *n u s* ,   e x t r e m o   P l a c e n t i n u s
h a b e r i   *c o e p t u s*   e s t .
Hoc quod dicit civitatem fuisse *Placentiam*, ab eadem
persuasione ponit municipium fuisse. Avum autem *mater-*
10 *num* Pisonis primo Gallum fuisse ideo ait quod venisse
eum in Italiam dicit trans Alpis, *dein Gallicanum*, quod in
Italia consederit, Placenti*num denique*, postquam adscitus
sit a Placenti*nis*. *Sed Pisonis* avus multo post ea tempora
fuit quibus Placentia colonia est deducta.

15   CIRCA VERS. A PRIMO***

L a u t i o r e m . . . . p a t e r   t u u s   s o c e r u m   q u a m   C .
P i s o . . . . i n   i l l o   l u c t u   m e o .   E i   e n i m
f i l i a m   m e a m   c o l l o c a v i   q u e m   e g o ,   *s i   m i h i*   p o t e s t a s
t u m   o m n i u m   f u i s s e t ,   u n u m   p o t i s s i m u m   d e l e-
g i s s e m .

1 *prioribus continuat* S, *om.* M   3 a domo profectus *KS:*
ad *om.* . . . (6 *litt.* M) Σ   foret Σ, *corr. Manutius*   4 consedit et
Σ, *corr. Manutius*   paucis post annis *Manutius :* pauci . . . .
Σ   erat . . . . Σ :   civitas *suppl. Manutius:*   incola *suppl.*
Mommsen   6 Gallica . . . (7 *litt.S)* *SP:* Gallica *M, corr. Manutius*
extremus Σ,   *corr. Manutius*   7 coeptus *Manutius:* . . . .
(12 *litt.* S) Σ   8 quod *KS:* quoque Σ : quoque quod *Mommsen*
Placentiam *KS:* . . . . Σ   9 ponit S: ponit placentiam *PM* maternum *KS:* . . . . S: *om. PM*   10 uenisse
P: inuenisse *SM*   11   dein Gallicanum *Sigonius:* . . . .
(5 *litt.* S) Σ   12 placenti . . . . S: placentiae . . . . .
(*sine lac. P*) *PM: suppl. Bücheler*   adaccitus (-aci- M) *PM:*
ad acciatus S, *corr. Manutius*   13 placenti . . . .
(12 *litt.* S, 10 M, 7 P) Σ : *suppl. Bücheler*   15 *om.* M (*ita fere semper*)
16 lautiorem . . . . *PM:* *lac. om.* S   17 Piso . . . . (12
litt. P) Σ   meo. Ei enim *scripsi :* non enim *SM :* non ei *P*   18
colloca . . . S : colloca *PM, corr. ed. Ven.*   si mihi *supplevi:*
. . . . (9 *litt.* S) Σ

A little further on   4C
On Piso's maternal grandfather: *This fellow, on leaving his home,*
chanced to take up residence at Placentia, a few years later—for at
that time he was ... *rose to membership of this political community.*
For he was originally reckoned a Gaul, then a Gallic inhabitant of the
province, and ultimately a Placentine. When he calls Placentia a
'political community', by that very conviction he posits that it was
a *municipium*. But he claims that Piso's maternal grandfather was
originally a Gaul for the reason that he declares that he came into
Italy over the Alps; then a Gallic inhabitant of the province because
he took up residence in Italy; and finally a Placentine because he was
enrolled by the Placentines. But Piso the grandfather lived long after
those times in which Placentia was founded as a *colonia*.

Around line ... from the beginning
Did your father get a father-in-law ... *of greater distinction than did*
C. Piso? ... [lacuna] ... *at the time of that great sorrow of mine.*
... [lacuna?] ... *For I bestowed my daughter upon the one man who,*
even had I had at that time the choice of all men, would have been my
first preference.

5C　　Quis fuerit socer Pisonis patris ipse supra dixit his
verbis:
　　　Insuber quidam fuit, idem mercator et praeco:
　　is cum Romam cum filia venisset, adulescentem
5　nobilem, Caesonini hominis furacissimi filium,
　　ausus est appellare, *eique* filiam collocavit. Cal-
　　ventium aiunt eum appellatum.
　　Ipsius Pisonis contra quem haec oratio est socerum
　　Rutilium Nudum Fenestella tradit. Cicero filiam post
10　mortem Pisonis generi P. Lentulo collocavit, apud quem
　　illa ex partu decessit.

CIR. VER. A PRIMO CCLXX

　　(§ 4.) Ego in C. Rabirio perduellio*nis reo* xxxx annis
ante me consulem interpositam senatus auctoritatem sustinui
15　contra invidiam atque defendi.
　　Possit aliquis credere *errare* Ciceronem, quod dicat
quadraginta annis factum esse *ut* ex S. C. *arma ad*versus
L. Appuleium Saturninum tribunum plebis sumerentur.
C. enim Mario L. *Valerio* coss. id senatum decre*visse, qui*
20　coss. *annis* ante consulatum Ciceronis xxxvii *fuerint*. Sed
hic non subtilis computatio annorum facta est verum sum-

1 pater Σ, *corr. Manutius* ipse *om.* S　3 intuber Σ, *corr. ed.*
Ven.　4 filio Σ, *corr. Manutius*　5 caesoniani Σ, *corr. Mommsen*
frugalissimi *Rinkes*　6 eique *Rinkes*: *om.* Σ　caluentinum Σ,
corr. ed. Ald. (Calventium … appellatum *Ciceroni reddidit Rau*)　8
ipsius *Madvig*: sepius Σ　9 Rutilium] Atilium *add.* Σ, *del.*
Perizonius tradit P : tradi *SM*　11 decessit P: discessit *SM*
13 perduellio . . . . . . Σ, *suppl.* π *ex Cicerone*　14 interpositam
(-ta *SM*) . . . . (7 *litt.* P) Σ *contra Ciceronem*　15 invidiam
Cic.: . . . . (5 *litt.* P) invidiam Σ　16 errare *KS* : . . . . . . Σ
17 annis *PM*: . . . . . . S ut *Poggius*, M : *om.* SP[1]　arma
adversus *KS*: . . . . (5 *litt.* M) *PM*: uersus S　18 Appul.
P: apul. *SM*　tr. pl. P : . . . . plebis S: num tr. pl . . . . plebis M
numerentur Σ, *corr. KS*　19 ario P[1]M: . . . . S, *corr. Poggius*
L. Valerio *Lodoicus*: cn (n S) . . . . . . (10 *litt.* S) Σ　19–20 ad
senatum decre . . . . eos . . . añ consuetum ciceronis . . . .
S : *om. PM* : *suppl. KS*　21 annorum *PM*: . . . . . . S

The identity of the elder Piso's father-in-law he himself declared   5C
above, in the following words: *There was some Insubrian, both trader
and auctioneer. When he arrived in Rome with his daughter, he had the
nerve to approach a young noble, son of that kleptomaniac individual
Caesoninus, and bestowed his daughter upon him. They say that he was
known as Calventius.* The father-in-law of the actual Piso who is the
target of this speech Fenestella records as Rutilius Nudus. Cicero,
after the death of [C.] Piso, his (own) son-in-law, bestowed his
daughter upon P. Lentulus, in whose house she died in childbirth.

Around line 270 from the beginning

In Pis. 4: *In the case of C. Rabirius, charged with* perduellio, *it was I
who despite resultant political hostility upheld the authority of the
senate, which had been asserted forty years before my consulship, and
I who defended it.* It is possible that a person might suppose that
Cicero is wrong in saying that it was forty years since the episode in
which by senatorial decree arms were taken up against L. Appuleius
Saturninus, tribune of the plebs. For (he might say), the senate made
this decree in the consulship of C. Marius and L. Valerius [100 BC],
who were consuls thirty-seven years before the consulship of Cicero.
But here the reckoning of the years is not made with precision, but

matim tempus comprehensum est, ut proinde *debeamus*
accipere ac si dixerit: prope xxxx annis. Haec consuetudo
in ipsis *orationibus est*: itaque idem Cicero in ea quoque
quam habuit in Catilinam in senatu, †ait.. octavus deci-
5 mus dies esset postea quam factum *est* senatus consultum
ut viderent consules ne quid res publica detrimenti caperet,
dixit vicesimum diem habere *se* S. C. tamquam *in vagina*
reconditum.

CIR. VERS. A PRIMO CCC

10 (§ 6.) Ego cum in contione abiens magistratu
dicere a tribuno plebis prohiberer quae consti-
tueram, cum is mihi tantum modo iurare permit-
teret, sine ulla dubitatione iuravi rem p. atque
hanc urbem mea unius opera esse salvam.
15   Diximus iam antea a Q. Metello Nepote tr. pl. Ciceronem consulatu abeuntem prohibitum esse contionari de
rebus quas in eo magistratu gessit.

CIR. VER. A PRIMO CCCXX

dicit de ludis Compitaliciis:
20 (§ 8.) Quos Q. Metellus—facio iniuriam fortis-

1 tempus *P*: .... *SM*   proinde (perinde *P*) ......
(10 *litt. M*) Σ: *suppl. KS*   2 vixerit Σ, *corr. Lodoicus* annis.
Haec *PM*: .... *S*   3 ipsius Σ, *corr. KS* orationibus est *Baiter*: .... (7 *litt. S*) Σ   quoque quam
habuit *PM*: quoll ..... *S*   4 ait..(6 *litt. M*) *PM*: .... *S*:
cum *Lodoicus*   5 est Σ, *corr. Lodoicus* postea quam
PM: ..... *S*   facto *S*: facta *F¹*: sciuit *M, corr. Poggius* est
supplevi   6 uiderent *P*: uideret *SM*   7 diem *PM*: .....
S   se *Rinkes*: *om.* Σ   in vagina reconditum *Cic.*: *om.*
Σ (12 *litt. P,* 20 *M, sine lac. S*)   9 CIRCA *P*   10 abiens *P*
et Cic.: abiens (-en *S*) .... *SM*   11 dicere a tr. pl. *S, Cic.*:
a tr. pl. dicere *P*: a tr. pl. dicere a tribus plebis *M*   prohibere *P, Cic.*:
prohibere *SM*   quae *S, Cic.*: ea quae *PM*   12 cum Σ: cumque
Cic.   iurare Σ: ut iurarem *Cic.* ς   13 rem p .....
M   15 ante *KS*   16 cos. consulatu hñtem *S* con-
tionā *S*   20 quos Q. *P, Cic.*: quosque *SM*   Metellus *Cic.*:
fieri uetuit *add.* Σ, *del. Rau*

the dating is encompassed in round figures, so that we ought to take   6C
it as the virtual equivalent of his saying 'around forty years'. This is
normal practice in actual speeches—so that it is Cicero also who, in
the speech which he delivered against Catilina in the senate, when it
was in fact the eighteenth day after the passing of a senatorial decree
that the consuls should see to it that the state take no harm, said that
for twenty days he had the senate's decree, as it were, still not
unsheathed.

Around line 300 from the beginning
In Pis. 6: *I, when at the* contio *on vacating my magistracy I was being
forbidden by a tribune of the plebs to say what I had meant to say, when
he would allow no more than the oath, without the least hesitation I
swore that the state and this city had attained its salvation by my efforts
and mine alone.* We have already said earlier that Cicero on vacating
his consulship was forbidden by Q. Metellus Nepos, tribune of the
plebs, to address the *contio* on his achievements in that magistracy.

Around line 320 from the beginning
He is speaking of the Games of the Compitalia: *In Pis.* 8: *Those
games Q. Metellus—I do wrong to so gallant a man,*

simo viro mortuo, qui illum cuius paucos pares
haec civitas tulit cum hac importuna belua con
feram—, sed ille designatus consul, cum quidam
tr. pl. suo auxilio magistros ludos contra S. C.
5 facere iussisset, privatus fieri vetuit.—Tu cum
in Kal. Ian. Compitaliorum dies incidisset, Sex.
Clodium, qui numquam ante praetextatus *fuisset*,
ludos facere et praetextatum volitare passus *es*.
L. Iulio C. Marcio consulibus quos et ipse Cicero supra
10 memoravit senatus consulto collegia sublata sunt quae
adversus rem publicam videbantur esse *constituta*. Solebant autem magistri collegiorum ludos facere, sicut magistri
vicorum faciebant, Compitalicios praetextati, qui ludi subla-
tis collegiis discussi sunt. Post VI deinde annos quam
15 sublata erant P. Clodius tr. pl. lege lata restituit collegia.
Invidiam ergo et crimen restitutorum confert in Pisonem,
quod, cum consul esset, passus sit ante quam lex ferretur
facere *Kal. Ianuar.* praetextatum ludos Sex. Clodium. Is
fuit familiarissimus Clodii et operarum Clodianarum dux,
20 quo auctore postea illato ab eis corpore Clodii curia cum
eo incensa est. Quos ludos tunc quoque fieri prohibere
temptavit L. Ninnius tr. pl. Ante biennium autem quam
restituerentur collegia, Q. Metellus Celer consul designatus
magistros vicorum ludos Compitalicios facere prohibuerat,
25 ut Cicero tradit, quamvis auctore tribuno plebis fierent
ludi; cuius tribuni nomen adhuc non inveni.

3 sic ille (sicilie *S*) desicco si cum Σ, *corr.* π *ex Cic.*   4 magistros *Cic.*: magis *S*: magnos *PM*   5 tu cum in *Cic.*: tum cum Σ
6 incidissent *codd. Ciceronis*   7 praetextato ludos faceret et Σ:
corr. ς, *Beraldus ex Cic.*   8 es *om.* Σ, *suppl.* ς, *ed. Ald. ex Cic.*   9
Mario Σ, *corr. Lodoicus*   11 constituta *KS*: ea ...... (6 *litt. S*,
8 *P*, 10 *M*)   13 vicorum *PM*: ludorum *S*   14 VI *Rinkes*:
novem Σ: v *Rau*   16 et crimen *om. S*   18 Kal. Ian. *KS*:
.... Σ   praetextatum *om. M*   cloelium *PM* : proclium
    //   //
S, corr. ed. Ven.   20 inlato postea *P*   his Σ, *corr. Manutius*
duria *S*   22 autem] ante *add.* Σ, *del. Manutius*   24 uicorum
ς: ludorum Σ (*cf. v.* 13)

now dead, in comparing him, when this state has produced so few of his 7C
like, with this savage monster—he, anyhow, as consul designate, when a
certain tribune of the plebs pressed the magistri *to hold the games in*
defiance of a senatorial decree relying upon his protection, even as a
private citizen forbade their celebration. You, when the day of the
Crossroads Festival fell on the first of January, allowed Sex. Cloelius,
who had never before been entitled to a stripe-edged toga, to hold games
and flit around in one.

In the consulship of L. Iulius and C. Marcius [64 BC], whom
Cicero himself mentioned above, the *collegia* which were deemed to
be against the public interest were suppressed by senatorial decree.
Now the *magistri* of the *collegia* usually gave the games for the
Compitalia, just as the *magistri* of the city wards used to do, dressed
in the stripe-edged toga—and these games were scrapped with the
suppression of the *collegia*. Then six years after their suppression
P. Clodius, as tribune of the plebs, carried a law to restore the *collegia*.
For this reason he heaps resentment and recriminations upon Piso
for having, despite his powers as consul, before the passage of the law,
allowed Sex. Cloelius to hold these games on 1 January dressed in the
striped toga. (This person was a very close associate of Clodius and a
leader of his gangs, and it was at his instigation later that when they
brought in Clodius' corpse the senate house was burnt down with it.)
The holding of these games on that occasion also L. Ninnius, tribune
of the plebs, tried to forbid. Further, two years before the restoration
of the *collegia*, Q. Metellus Celer, as consul designate, had forbidden
the *magistri* of the wards of the city to hold the Compitalia, as Cicero
records, even though the games were being held on the authority of a
tribune of the plebs—whose name I have not yet been able to
discover.

PAVLO POST

8C

(§ 9.) Ergo his fundamentis positis consulatus
tui, triduo post, inspectante te et tacente, a fatali
portento prodigioque rei publicae lex Aelia et
5 Fufia eversa est, propugnacula murique tranquil-
litatis atque oti; collegia non ea solum quae
senatus sustulerat restituta, sed innumerabilia
quaedam ex omni faece urbis ac servitio concitata. Ab eodem homine in stupris inauditis ne-
10 fariisque versato vetus illa magistra pudoris et
modestiae censura sublata est.
Diximus L. Pisone A. Gabinio coss. P. Clodium tr. pl.
quattuor leges perniciosas populo Romano tulisse: anno-
nariam, de qua Cicero mentionem hoc loco non facit—fuit
15 enim summe popularis—ut frumentum populo quod antea
senis aeris ac trientibus in singulos modios dabatur gratis
daretur: alteram ne quis per eos dies quibus cum populo
agi liceret de caelo servaret; propter quam rogationem ait
legem Aeliam et Fufiam, propugnacula et muros tranquilli-
20 tatis atque otii, eversam esse;—obnuntiatio enim qua perni-
ciosis legibus resistebatur, quam Aelia lex confirmaverat,
erat sublata—: tertiam de collegiis restituendis novisque
instituendis, quae ait ex servitiorum faece constituta:
quartam ne quem censores in senatu legendo praeterirent,
25 neve qua ignominia afficerent, nisi qui apud eos accusatus
et utriusque censoris sententia damnatus esset. Hac ergo

3 te et tacente Σ: et tacente te *Cic.*   4 Aelia et Fusia (Fufia *Cic.*)
P, Cic.: Aliae (elie *M*) Fusia *SM*   5 eversae sunt *Pighius* (*contra
Cic.*)   7 tulerat Σ, *corr.* 𝔰, *Lodoicus*   8 quaedam nova ex *Cic.*
ac] atque *S*   9 in] ut Σ, *corr.* 𝔰, *Beraldus*   11 censura Σ:
severitas *Cic.*: censoria severitas *ed. Ald.*   12 A. KS: et Σ: et A.
Manutius   13 annonianam Σ, *corr. Graevius*   16 senis
Σ: semis 𝔰, *Manutius* : semissibus *Turnebus*   ac trientibus 𝔰:
acirientibus *PM* : arientibus *S*   grauis *S*   19 aliam et
fusiam *SM*: fusiam et eliam *P*   20 euersa Σ, *corr. Manutius*:
eversas *Madvig*   pernicio *M*   23 quam ait ex *P*: quam
ut (ēt *S*) et *SM, corr. Manutius*   constitutam Σ, *corr. Manutius*

A little further on   8C

In Pis. 9: *Thus having laid these foundations for your consulship, three days later, while you looked on and held your peace, at the hands of that monstrous harbinger of doom for our state the Aelian and Fufian laws were overthrown, which afforded the very bastions and defence-walls of internal peace and stability; and not only were the* collegia *restored which the senate had suppressed, but various others without number were raised from all the filth of the city and its servile population. By this same person, so well practised in unspeakably foul sexual vices, that ancient guardian of morals and modesty, the censorship, was eliminated.* We have said that in the consulship of L. Piso and A. Gabinius [58 BC] P. Clodius, tribune of the plebs, passed four laws which endangered the Roman people: (1) a corn law, of which Cicero makes no mention in this passage—for it was extremely attractive to the people—to provide for distribution to the people free of charge of corn which previously had been distributed at a price of six-and-one-third *asses* for each *modius*; (2) to ban survey of the heavens (for omens) on days on which it was legal to transact business with the people—on account of which rogation he declares that the Aelian and Fufian laws, bastions and defence-walls of internal peace and stability, had been overthrown—since the practice of *obnuntiatio*, which the Aelian Law had consolidated, was removed; (3) for the restitution of *collegia* and the institution of new ones, which he says were made up of the filth of the servile population; (4) to prevent the censors in selecting the senate from passing over or branding with any mark of ill-repute any man who had not been charged before them and condemned by the declared verdict of both censors.

9C   eius lege censuram, quae magistra pudoris et modestiae est,
           sublatam ait.

PAVLO POST

           (§ 11.) Persequere continentis his funeribus
     5 dies. Pro Aurelio tribunali ne conivente quidem
           te, quod ipsum esset scelus, sed etiam hilarioribus
           oculis quam solitus eras intuente, dilectus servo-
           rum habebatur ab eo qui nihil sibi umquam nec
           facere nec pati turpe duxit.
    10   Profecto intellegitis P. Clodium significari.

CIR. VER. A PRIMO *DC*

           dicit de Castoris templo:
           (§ 23.) Id autem templum sublato aditu, revolsis
           gradibus, a coniuratorum reliquiis atque a Cati-
    15 linae praevaricatore quondam, tum ultore, armis
           teneretur.
           Catilinam lege repetundarum absolutum esse accusante
           P. Clodio iam supra dictum est.

STATIM

    20 Cum equites Romani relegarentur, viri boni
           lapidibus e foro pellerentur.
           L. Lamiam a Gabinio consule edicto relegatum esse iam
           diximus.

1 censura *S*   2 adit *SM* : addit *P, corr. Manutius*   4 continentes
Σ: connexos *Cic.,* π   5 tribunali *Poggius, Cic.*: tribuno (tr. *S*) Σ
nec (ne *M*) an ueniente *SM*: nec annuente *P, corr.* π *ex Cic.*   8
habebantur *S* (*contra Cic.*)   9 turpe *om. M*: turpe esse *Cic.* dixit
SM, Cic. cod. E   10 intellegitur Σ, *corr. Rinkes*   11 *DC KS*:
om. SP (*v.* 10 *om. M ut semper*)   14 reliquis *S, corr. Beraldus
ex Cic.*   atque a *P¹, Cic.*: atque *SM, Poggius*   15 tum ultore
armis π *ex Cic.*: tumultuarum is (is *sup. lin. in P*) Σ   16 teneretur
S, Cic.: tenetur *PM*   18 supra *om. P*   20 rogarentur *S*: nega-
rentur *M*: necarentur *P, corr.* ς, *ed. Iunt. ex Cic.*   22 t. clamiam Σ,
corr. ς, *Lodoicus* (*cf. Sest.* 29)   relegatum *S*: religatum *PM*

Thus by this law of his, the censorship, guardian of morals and   9C
modesty, he says was abolished.

A little further on
In Pis. 11: *Review one by one the days subsequent to these death-rites.
Before the Aurelian tribunal, you did not so much turn a blind eye,
which of itself would have been criminal, but actually looked on with
more gladness in your countenance than usual, while a levy of slaves
was held by the man who never regarded anything as beneath him,
whether to do it or have it done to him.* You are of course well aware
that P. Clodius is meant.

Around line 600 from the beginning
He is speaking of the Temple of Castor. *In Pis.* 23: *And this temple, its
access removed, its steps torn up, was being held under force of arms by
the remnants of the conspirators and the sometime collusive prosecutor
of Catilina, latterly his avenger.* It has already been said above that
Catilina was acquitted under the law *de repetundis*, with Clodius the
prosecutor.

Immediately thereafter
While Roman equites *were being banished from the city and respectable
men driven from the Forum by stoning* ... We have already said that
L. Lamia was banished from the city by edict of the consul Gabinius.

CIR. VER. A PRIMO DCXX

(§ 24.) Seplasia me *hercule*, te ut primum aspexit, Campanum consulem repudiavit.

Dictum est in dissuasione legis agrariae apud populum
5 plateam esse Capuae quae Seplasia appellatur, in qua unguentarii negotiari sint soliti. Ergo eos quoque qui in ea platea negotiarentur dicit invitos Pisonem vidisse, cum Capuam consul venit, quod eos a quibus ipse expulsus erat adiuvisset.

10 ## CIR. VER. A PRIMO DCXL

(§ 26.) Ecquod in hac urbe maius umquam incendium fuit cui non consul subveniret? At tu illo ipso tempore apud socrum tuam cuius domum ad meam exhauriendam patefeceras sedebas.
15 Post profectionem ex urbe Ciceronis bona eius P. Clodius publicavit; postquam direpta sunt omnia quae aut in domo aut in villis fuerunt, et ex eis ad ipsos consules lata complura, domus direpta primum, deinde inflammata ac diruta est. Socrus Pisonis quae fuerit invenire non potui,
20 videlicet quod auctores rerum non perinde in domibus ac familiis feminarum, nisi illustrium, ac virorum nomina tradiderunt.

1 PRINCIPIO S   DCXX P: DCCC S   2 selapsia P (*ita mox*) mehercule *ed. Ven.* : he . . . . Σ : mehercule ut dici audiebam *Cic.*, π   uti *ed. Ven.* (*contra Cic.*)   7 negotiantur S   dicat S 8 ipse *Bücheler* : ille Σ   10 CIRCA VER. A PR. P   DCXX SP, *corr. ed. Ald.*   11 et quod Σ, *codd. Ciceronis, corr. Lodoicus* 12 subvenerit *Cic.*   13 illo ipso P, *Cic.* : illos ipsos SM   tuam Σ : tuam prope a meis aedibus *Cic.* 5   cuius domum ad *Hotoman ex Cic.* : cui domum Σ   14 meam Σ : meam domum *Cic.*   17 ipsos collata Σ, *corr. Manutius*   18 domū SP¹ : domos M, *corr. Poggius* diruta P : duruta M : durata S   19 potui P : potuit SM¹

Around line 620 from the beginning

In Pis. 24: *Even the Seplasia, heaven knows, when it first got a sight of you, disowned you as Campanian consul.* It was noted in the speech against the agrarian law before the people that there is a square in Capua which is called the Seplasia, where the perfumers normally conducted their business. So then he is saying that even those who were trading in that square took no pleasure at the sight of Piso on his visit to Capua as consul because of the assistance he had given to those by whom he [Cicero] had been ejected.

Around line 660 from the beginning

In Pis. 26: *Now what fire of any magnitude ever broke out in this city at which the consul did not seek to give assistance? Yet you at that very time sat at ease in your mother-in-law's house, which you had opened up in order completely to strip mine bare.* After Cicero's departure from the city, P. Clodius confiscated his property. After everything had been looted that was in his town-house or his country villas, and much of it had been passed to the consuls themselves, his house was first taken apart and then set on fire and destroyed. I have not been able to find out who was Piso's mother-in-law—obviously because the historians have not paid as much attention to recording among households and families the names of women, except those of high rank, as those of men.

PAVLO POST

(§ 27.) Ac ne tum quidem emersisti, lutulente
Caesonine, e miserrimis naturae sordibus cum
experrecta tandem virtus celeriter et verum ami-
5 cum et optime meritum civem et suum pristinum
morem requisivit.
Profecto Cn. Pompeium significari intellegitis.

CIR. VER A PRIMO DCCC

(§ 35.) De me cum omnes magistratus promul-
10 gassent praeter unum praetorem a quo non fuit
postulandum, fratrem inimici mei, praeterque
duos de lapide emptos tribunos, legem comitiis
centuriatis tulit P. Lentulus consul.
Frater ille inimici mei, id est P. Clodi. Ap. Claudius,
15 sicut iam saepe significavi, tum fuit praetor. Duos tribunos
de quibus ipsis quoque iam diximus, quos de lapide emptos
ait, quia mercede id faciebant, Sex. Atilium Serranum et
Q. Numerium significat.

CIR. MEDIVM

20 (§§ 38, 39.) Appellatus est hic volturius illius provinciae, si dis placet, imperator. Ne tum quidem,
Paule noster, tabellas cum laurea Romam mittere
audebas?

2 tu *S*   3 caesone *S* : ceso *PM, codd. Ciceronis, corr. Manutius*
e Σ : ex *Cic.*   naturae tuae *Cic.*   4 experta *codd. Ciceronis*
uirtus Σ : uirtus clarissimi viri *Cic.*   7 intelligis Σ, *corr. Lodoicus*
9 omnes (-is *P*) *P et Cic.* : añis *SM*   promulgasset *S*   10 praetorem *Cic.* : praet. *P*: pr. et *M* : praeci *S*   non fit *S*   11–14
praeterque... mei *om. S*   15 significavi tum *Mommsen* : signifi-
cabitur Σ : significavimus *Manutius*   praetor *Orelli* : frater Σ   16
quoque *Poggius* : q̄q̄ *S*: queq; *M* : ṣẹp̣ẹ *P*   17 Sex. *P* : sed *SM*
statilium Σ, *corr. Manutius*   et Q. *P´* : etq' *M*: eq ecq̄ *S*   18 Numerium *P*: numerum *SM*   19 CIRCA *P*   20 hic ueteris Σ, *corr.
Beraldus ex Cic.*   22 tabellas cum laurea (lausea *SP¹*) Romam Σ :
tabulas Romam cum laurea *Cic.*

A little further on

In Pis. 27: *And not even then, Caesoninus, wallowing in your pig-dirt, did you rise above your utterly wretched innate squalor, when in the end Sterling Worth was bestirred and swiftly took action to reclaim a true friend and thoroughly deserving fellow-citizen, and its own time-honoured traditions.* Of course, you realize that Cn. Pompeius is meant.

Around line 800 from the beginning

In Pis. 35: *I was the subject of a Law promulgated by all the magistrates, with the exception of a single praetor, from whom it was not to be demanded, my enemy's brother, and of two tribunes bought off the block (in the slave market)—and it was passed in the centuriate assembly by P. Lentulus the consul.* 'Brother of my enemy'—that is, of P. Clodius. Ap. Claudius, as I have already often indicated, was praetor at the time. By the two tribunes, on whose own persons we have also had something to say, whom he claims were bought in the slave market because they did it for a price, he means Sex. Atilius Serranus and Q. Numerius.

Around the mid-point

In Pis. 38–9: *This vulturine scavenger of his province, was hailed, would you believe it, as Imperator! Did you not even then, our heroic Paulus, have the nerve to send in to Rome your accounts along with your laurels?*

12C   Confido vos intellegere L. Paulum hunc significari qui
fuit pater naturalis Africani posterioris, de Macedoniaque
ultimum et Perse rege triumphavit. Macedoniam autem
Piso in quem haec oratio est obtinuit; propter quod Paulum
5 eum appellat, irridens eum quod ibi rem non prospere
gessit.

CIR. MEDIVM

(§ 44.) *M.* Marcellus qui ter consul fuit summa
virtute, pietate, gloria militari, periit in mari: qui
10 tamen ob virtutem *in* gloria et laude vivit.
Fortasse quaeratis quem dicat Marcellum. Fuit autem
nepos M. Marcelli eius qui bello Punico secundo Syracusas
vicit et quinque consulatus adeptus est. Hic autem Marcellus de quo Cicero dicit naufragio ad ipsam Africam
15 periit paulo ante coeptum bellum Punicum tertium. Idem
cum statuas sibi ac patri itemque avo poneret in monu-
mentis avi sui ad Honoris et Virtutis, decore subscripsit:
III MARCELLI NOVIES COSS. *Fuit enim ipse ter consul,* avus
quinquies, pater semel: itaque neque mentitus est et apud
20 imperitio
res patris sui splendorem auxit.

CIR. VER. A NOV. DCCCC

(§ 52.) Me consequentibus diebus in ea ipsa
domo qua tu me expuleras, quam incenderas,

2 Macedonia atque Σ, *corr. Madvig* 3 et Perse *Madvig*: eius
de Σ 4 palum P¹: palam *M, corr. Poggius (lectio cod. S evanuit)*
5 eum] etiam *Bücheler* rem *Broukhusius*: se Σ 8 M. *add.*
Lodoicus ex Cic. 9 virtute *add.* ς, *Beraldus ex Cic.* perit Σ,
corr. Beraldus 10 in (*om.* in Σ) gloria et laude, *Cic. cod. V,* Σ:
gloriae laude *Cic. codd. cett.* 15 periit P: perit SM idem P:
item SM 17 decorem Σ, *corr. Baiter* 18 III *Manutius*: hi (hic
M) Σ cos. Σ, *corr. Manutius* Fuit…consul *add. Bücheler*
19 neque *om.* M 21 DCCCC *Bücheler*: DCCC SP 23 expu-
leras] quam expilaras *add. Cic.* incenderat S

I am sure that you are well aware that by this man is meant the
L. Paulus who was the natural father of the younger Africanus and
held his last triumph over Macedonia and King Perseus. And
Macedonia was the province held by Piso, the target of this
speech—so that on this account he calls him 'Paulus', mocking him
for his failure there.

Around the mid-point

In Pis. 44: *M. Marcellus who was three times consul, a man of the
highest sterling worth, moral scruple, and military renown, was lost at
sea; yet on account of that sterling worth lives on in renown and repute.*
You might ask which Marcellus he means. In fact he was the grandson of the M. Marcellus who in the Second Punic War conquered
Syracuse and won five consulships. Now this Marcellus of whom
Cicero speaks perished in a shipwreck off Africa itself shortly before
the start of the Third Punic War. This same man on erecting statues
to himself, his father, and his grandfather, added with propriety on
the memorials for his grandfather close by the Temple of Honour and
Virtue the further words 'Three Marcelli held nine consulships'. For
he was himself three times consul, his grandfather five times, and his
father once. Thus he told no lies and enhanced his father's repute in
the eyes of the less well informed.

Around line 900 from the end

In Pis. 52: *In the days that followed the pontifices, the consuls and
Conscript Fathers installed me in that home from which you had
expelled me and which you had set afire,*

13C

pontifices, consules, patres conscripti conlocarunt,
mihique, quod antea nemini, pecunia publica aedi-
ficandam domum censuerunt.

Hoc Cicero oratorio more, non historico, videtur posuisse:
5 nam multis aetatibus ante Ciceronem nulli id contigisse verum est, nemini vero umquam antea videamus ne parum
caute dicat. Antiquis enim temporibus pluribus idem contigit; nam *M.* Valerio Maximo, ut Antias tradidit, inter
alios honores domus quoque publice aedificata est in Palatio,
10 cuius exitus quo magis insignis esset in publicum versus
declinaretur hoc est, extra privatum aperiretur. Varronem
autem tradere M. Valerio, quia Sabinos vicerat, aedes in
Palatio tributas, Iulius Hyginus dicit in libro priore de viris
claris, *et* P. Valerio Volesi filio Publicolae aedium pub*lice*
15 *lo*cum sub Veliis, ubi nunc aedis Victoriae est, populum ex
lege quam ipse tulerat concessisse. Tradunt et Antiochi
regis filio obsidi domum publice aedificatam, inter quos
Atticus in annali: quae postea dicitur Lucili poetae fuisse.
Varro quoque in libro III de vita populi Romani, quo loco
20 refert quam gratus fuerit erga bene meritos, dicit Mutinae,
quod in Sicilia cum equitatu suo transierat ad nos, civitatem
Romae datam aedesque et pecuniam ex aerario. Videamus
tamen num ideo Cicero dicat sibi, quod antea nulli, domum
pecunia publica ex aerario aedificatam, quia illis aut locus
25 publice datus sit, aut domus quae non fuerant eorum propter illos publico sumptu aedificatae: Ciceroni domus quae

---

1 patres conscripti *Baiter ex Cic.* : patres *SM* : praetor *P*   conlo-
caverunt *Cic.*   2 antea Σ : ante me *Cic.*   pecuniam publicam ad
Σ, *corr.* ς, *Beraldus ex Cic.*   7 dicamus Σ, *corr. KS: fort.* dicatur
8 M. *add. KS*   10 esset et in Σ, *corr.* ς, *Lodoicus*   12 Sabinos
Schwegler : saepius Σ   13 L. Hyginus (hyginius *M* : higinius *P*) Σ,
corr. Popma   14 et *add. Garatoni*   aedilium *S*   publice locum
Rinkes: repul . . . . . . (3 *litt. S*) cum Σ   15 uelis Σ, *corr. KS:*
Velia ς   16 addunt et *S*   17 obsidem *S*   18 annale
(and- *S*) Σ, *corr. ed. Iunt.* Lucii (L. *S*), *corr. Manutius*   20 Mutinae
S: murtinae *M¹*: murrinae *P¹M²*: muttinae *P³*   21 ad noc *P¹*
25 fuerant *S*: fuerat *PM*   propter *Beraldus*: qua propter Σ   26
illo *S*   Ciceronis Σ, *corr.* ς

and passed a vote that a house should be built for me from public funds,   13C
a grant made previously to no one else. This point Cicero appears to
have made in accord with rhetorical rather than historical practice.
For that this happened to nobody for many generations before
Cicero is true, but previously to nobody ever at all is a proposition
that requires us to consider whether he may be speaking somewhat
carelessly. You see, in ancient times the same thing happened to quite
a number of men. For, as Antias records, among many other honours
in addition a house was built at public expense for M. Valerius
Maximus on the Palatine, the exit of which, to enhance its distinction, was turned at an angle to face onto public space—that is, it
opened onto non-private ground. Iulius Hyginus, in the first book
On Famous Men, says that Varro recorded that a dwelling on the
Palatine was assigned to M. Valerius because he had defeated the
Sabines, and that the people granted to P. Valerius Publicola, son of
Volesus, by a law that he himself carried, a site for a dwelling, at
public expense, under the Velia, where the Temple of Victoria now
stands. Authors, among them Atticus in his *Book of Years*, record that
a house was built at public expense for the son of King Antiochus, a
hostage—which is said to have belonged later to Lucilius the poet.
Varro also, in book 3 of his *Lifestyle of the Roman People*, where he
refers to its gratitude towards those who deserved well of it, says that
the citizenship was granted to Mutina for having come over with his
cavalry to our side in Sicily, and with it a house and money from the
Treasury. However, we might consider whether the reason that
Cicero says that a house was built for him with public funding
from the Treasury, as for no one else before him, might be this—
that in those (former) cases either the *site* was given at public
expense, or the house which was built on their account at public
cost had not previously belonged to them; whereas in Cicero's case
the house that was built at

14C fuerat ipsius et diruta atque incensa erat et consecrata publico sumptu aedificata sit: quod novum et huic primo et
adhuc etiam soli contigit.

CIR. VER. A NOVIS. DCCCXX

5 (§ 58.) O stultos Camillos, Curios, Fabricios, Ca-
latinos, Scipiones, Marcellos, Maximos! o amentem Paulum, rusticum Marium, nullius consili
patres horum amborum consulum qui triumpha-
runt!
10 Diximus hanc orationem esse dictam Cn. Pompeio
Magno ii M. Crasso ii coss. Pompeii pater bello Italico
de Picentibus, M. Crassi pater P. Crassus ante bellum
Italicum de Hispanis triumphavit.

CIR. VER. A NOV. DCLX

15 (§ 62.) Eadem cupiditate vir summo ingenio
praeditus, C. Cotta, nullo certo hoste *flagravit.*
Eorum neuter triumphavit, quod alteri illum
honorem collega, alteri mors peremit.
Credo vos quaerere et quis hic Cotta et quis ille collega
20 Crassi fuerit. Fuit autem C. Cotta orator ille compar
P. Sulpici qui est in dialogis Ciceronis de Oratore scriptis.
Cum decretus illi esset triumphus, mortuus est ante diem
triumphi, cum cicatrix vulneris eius quod ante plures annos
in proelio acceperat rescissa esset repente. L. autem Crasso
25 collega fuit Q. Scaevola pontifex qui, cum animadverteret

2 aut adhuc Σ, *corr. Manutius* 4 CIRC. VERS. *P* 5 Furios
Σ, *corr. ed. Ald. ex Cic.* 6 Marcellum Σ, *corr.* π *ex Cic.* O amen-
tem π: so ornamentum *SP¹* : ornamentum *Poggius, M* : amentem
Cic. 7 ruscium Σ, *corr.* ς, *Beraldus ex Cic.* 8 auorum Σ, *corr.* π
ex Cic. triumpharint *Cic. cod. V* 16 C. *add. ed. Ald. ex
Cic.* flagravit π *ex Cic.*: . . . . (5 *litt. S)* Σ 18 peremit
S, Cic. cod. V : ademit (ed-*M) PM, Cic. codd. plerique*: praeripuit
Cic. pal. T 20 C. *P.*: o *S: om. M* 22 ille *SM* triumphos
mortuos *P¹, corr. Poggius* 22–24 triumphus . . . esset *om. S* 24
L. *S: om. PM* 25 Q. *om. M*

public cost had previously been his own, and had been demolished,   14C
burned, and declared sacred land—and that *was* a novelty and to
date he had been the first and only person to have this happen to
him.

Around line 820 from the end

In. Pis. 58: *How stupid were Camillus, Curius, Fabricius, Calatinus, the
Scipios, Marcelli, and (Fabii) Maximi! How witless was Paulus, what a
bumpkin was Marius, how ill-advised the fathers of both our present
consuls, in holding their triumphs!* We have already said that this
speech was delivered in the second consulship of Cn. Pompeius
Magnus and M. Crassus. Pompeius' father triumphed in the Italic
War over the Picentes, and P. Crassus, father of M. Crassus, before the
Italic War, over Spaniards.

Around line 660 from the end

In Pis. 62: *A man endowed with very great talent, C. Cotta, was
inflamed with yearning for the same thing—without any clearly identifiable foe. Neither of these two actually triumphed, since his colleague
ruled out the honour for the first, as did death for the second.* I suppose
you are wondering both who this Cotta was and who was that
colleague of Crassus. Well, that C. Cotta was the orator coeval with
P. Sulpicius who appears in the books of dialogue written by Cicero
On the Orator. When a triumph was decreed for him, he died on the
day before it, when the scar of a wound which he had received several
years before suddenly opened up again. And L. Crassus' colleague
was Q. Scaevola the *pontifex*, who on observing

15C

Crasso propter summam eius in re publica potentiam ac
dignitatem senatum in decernendo triumpho gratificari, non
dubitavit rei publicae magis quam collegae habere rationem
ac ne fieret S. C. intercessit. Idem provinciam, cuius cupi-
5 ditate plerique etiam boni viri deliquerant, deposuerat ne
sumptui esset †oratio.

STATIM

(§ 62.) Inrisa est a te paulo ante M. Pisonis cu-
piditas triumphandi a qua te longe dixisti abhor-
10 rere: qui etiam si minus magnum bellum gesserat,
istum honorem omittendum non putavit. Tu
eruditior quam Piso.
Quis hic M. Piso fuerit credo vos ignorare. Fuit autem,
ut puto iam nos dixisse, Pupius Piso eisdem temporibus
15 quibus Cicero, sed tanto aetate maior ut adulescentulum
Ciceronem pater ad eum deduceret, quod in eo et antiquae
vitae similitudo et multae erant litterae: orator quoque
melior quam frequentior habitus est. Biennio tamen serius
quam Cicero consul fuit; triumphavit procos. de Hispania
20 Q. Hortensio Q. Metello Cretico coss. ante Ciceronis
consulatum.

PAVLO POST

(§ 65.) Instant post hominum memoriam apparatissimi magnificentissimique ludi, quales non

---

4 idem *Bücheler*: sed idem Σ   5 deliquebant (-linq- *M*) Σ, *corr.*
KS   6 oratio (o͠ro *P*) Σ: aerario *Manutius: fort.* populo Romano
8 a Σ: abs *Cic.*   10 gesserat Σ: ut abs te dictum est tamen *add.*
Cic. ϛ   11 omittendum Σ: contemnendum *Cic.*   tu *Cic.* ϛ:
puer Σ   12 Piso *Cic.* ϛ: ipso *S*: ipse *PM*   14 P. Piso Σ, *corr.*
Manutius   16 eo etiam quae Σ, *corr.* ϛ, *Manutius*   18 secius
S   22 *add.* *KS*   23 paratissimi *plerique codd.* *Cic.*

that the senate was doing a favour to Crassus in decreeing him a
triumph on account of his enormous power and ranking in the state,
did not hesitate to take more account of the state than of his
colleague, and vetoed the passage of the senatorial decree. This
same man had set aside a province which had made many men—
even men of sound principles—do wrong in their eagerness to hold
it, lest his †officially sanctioned expense allowance† should occasion
costs.

Immediately afterwards

*In Pis. 62: Not long before the eagerness of M. Piso to hold a triumph
was subjected to your mockery—a desire from which you claimed to be
very much disinclined. But he, even if his was a war of no great significance, at least thought that he ought not to dispense with the honour.
Are you any better read than Piso?*

    I believe you will not know the identity of this Piso. Well there was,
as I think we have already said, a Pupius Piso in the same era as
Cicero, but sufficiently his senior for Cicero's father to have placed
the young Cicero in his care, since there was in him some semblance
of the ancient way of life and a wide knowledge of literature—and
he was also reckoned a good rather than frequent practitioner of
oratory. Yet he was consul two years later than Cicero. He triumphed
as proconsul over Spain in the consulship of Q. Hortensius and
Q. Metellus [69 BC], before the consulship of Cicero.

A little further on

*In Pis. 65: The most lavish and most magnificent games in human
memory are imminent, in kind not*

16C

modo numquam fuerunt, sed ne *quo* modo fieri quidem posthac possint possum ullo pacto suspicari.

 Cn. Pompeii ludos significat quibus theatrum a se factum
5 dedicavit, quibus ludis elephantorum pugnam primus omnium dedit in Circo.

VER. A NOVIS. DLX

 (§ 68.) Est quidam Graecus qui cum isto vivit, homo, vere ut dicam—sic enim cognovi—huma-
10 nus, sed tam diu *quam diu* aut cum aliis est aut ipse secum.

 Philodemum significat qui fuit Epicureus illa aetate nobilissimus, cuius et poemata sunt lasciva.

CIR. VER. A NOVIS. CCCXX

15 (§ 82.) Quamquam, quod ad me attinet, numquam istam imminuam curam infitiando tibi.

 Prope notius est quam ut indicandum sit hunc versum esse L. Acci poetae et dici a Thyeste Atreo.

CIR. VER. A NOVIS. CC

20 (§ 89.) Quod populari illi sacerdoti sescentos ad bestias socios stipendiariosque misisti.

 Manifestum est P. Clodium significari.

---

1 unquam *P* quo *om.* Σ, *suppl. Poggius ex Cic.* quidem fieri *P*
2 possum] possunt *S* pacto] modo *P¹, corr. Poggius* 7 A VISS.
SP 8 quidem *PM* 9 uere ut Σ: ut vere *Cic. cod. V* 10 quam.
diu *add. ed. Ald. ex Cic.* aut cum Σ *Cic. cod. V teste Ströbel* : cum
cett. codd. Cic. 12 filodemum *P*: filio demum *SM* 13 lascivia
S 14 ANVOS *SP* 16 in faciendo *S* 17 iudicandum Σ,
corr. Beraldus 19 NOVIS. *ed. Iunt.* : NO *SP* 21 socios
stipendarios quoque Σ, *corr. ed. Ven.* : amicos sociosque *Cic.*

only unprecedented, but such as I cannot even guess any means at all   16C
whereby they might be celebrated hereafter. He alludes to the games of
Cn. Pompeius at which he dedicated the theatre which he had
constructed. At these games he was the first of all to put on show a
battle of elephants in the Circus.

Line 560 from the end

In Pis. 68: *There is a Greek who lives with him, a person, to tell the
truth—for so I have ascertained—of civilized instincts, but he has done
so for no longer than he has with others or else by himself.* He alludes to
Philodemus, who was an Epicurean of the greatest repute at that
time. There are also extant some salacious poems of his.

Around line 320 from the end

In Pis. 82: *Even so, so far as I am concerned, 'I'll never ease that care of
yours by going back on promises.'* It is almost too well known to be
worth indicating that this is a line of the poet L. Accius, and is spoken
by Thyestes to Atreus.

Around line 200 from the end

In Pis. 89: *(What of) the fact that you sent to that populist priestling six
hundred allies and tribute-payers for his beast-hunts?* It is obvious that
P. Clodius is meant.

CIR. VER. A. NOVIS. CXX

(§ 94.) Ecquid vides, ecquid sentis, lege iudiciaria
lata, quos posthac iudices simus habituri?

Legem iudiciariam ante aliquot annos quibus tempori-
5 bus accusatus est Verres a Cicerone tulit L. Aurelius Cotta
praetor, qua communicata sunt iudicia senatui et equitibus
Romanis et tribunis aerariis. Rursus deinde Pompeius in
consulatu secundo, quo haec oratio dicta est, promulgavit
ut amplissimo ex censu ex centuriis aliter atque antea lecti
10 iudices, aeque tamen ex illis tribus ordinibus, res iudicarent.

CIR. VER. A NOVIS. LXXXX

(§ 95.) L. Opimius eiectus patria est qui et post
praeturam et consul maximis periculis rem publicam liberarat. Non in eo cui facta iniuria est sed
15 in eis qui fecerunt sceleris et conscientiae poena
permansit.

Notum est Opimium in praetura Fregellas cepisse, quo
facto visus est ceteros quoque nominis Latini socios male
animatos repressisse, eundemque in consulatu Fulvium
20 Flaccum consularem et C. Gracchum tribunicium oppres-
sisse, ob quam invidiam postea iudicio circumventus est et
in exsilium actus.

---

2 et quid ... et quid Σ, *corr. ed. Ald.*   3 quod Σ, *corr.*
Manutius   iudices *om.* P   sumus P   5 est *om.* S
L.   S : *om.* PM   9 atque SM : que P   11 A NOVIS *ed.*
Iunt.: A NIIO S : ANVO P   12 patria *Poggius in mg.* : p̄rio S :
...... P¹M (est e patria *Cic.*)   post praeturam Σ : praetor
Cic.   13 rem p. periculis *Cic.*   14 in eum cui Σ, *corr. Lodoicus ex*
Cic.   est iniuria *Cic.*   16 permansit *Cic.* cod. E: remansit Σ, *Cic.*
codd. dett.   17 ex praetura *Rau*   18 pacto Σ, *corr. Madvig*
19 Fulvium Flaccum *om.* S

Around line 120 from the end

In Pis. 94: Do you see at all, have any inkling, once the law on the courts is passed, what jurymen we are going to get henceforth?

A law on the courts was passed by L. Aurelius Cotta as praetor some years before, when Verres was prosecuted by Cicero, by which the courts were shared among the senate, Roman knights, and *tribuni aerarii*. Then once more, in his second consulship, in which this speech was delivered, Pompeius promulgated a measure to the effect that jurymen should be chosen from the highest property-rating from the centuries in a manner different from previous practice, but in equal numbers from those three orders, and these should be jurors in court-cases.

Around line 90 from the end

In Pis. 95: L. Opimius was thrown out of his native land, a man who both after his praetorship and as consul had freed the state from the gravest perils. The taint of criminal conduct and sense of guilt for it has remained attached not to him on whom this outrage was perpetrated, but to those who perpetrated it. It is known that Opimius in his praetorship captured Fregellae, and thereby appeared to have checked the rest of the allies of Latin status who were disaffected; and that the same man in his consulship suppressed the consular Fulvius Flaccus and the ex-tribune C. Gracchus, and on account of the resultant political hostility was the victim of judicial conspiracy and driven into exile.

Q. Asconi Pediani
Pro M. Scauro

HANC quoque orationem eisdem consulibus dixit quibus
pro Vatinio, L. Domitio Ahenobarbo et Appio Claudio
Pulchro coss. Summus iudicii dies fuit a. d. IIII Nonas
Septemb.

5   ARGVMENTVM HOC EST

M. Scaurus M. Scauri filius qui princeps senatus fuit
vitricum habuit Sullam: quo victore et munifico in socios
victoriae ita abstinens fuit ut nihil neque donari sibi vo-
luerit neque ab hasta emerit. Aedilitatem summa magnifi-
10 centia gessit, adeo ut in eius impensas opes suas absumpserit
magnumque aes alienum contraxerit. Ex praetura provinciam Sardiniam obtinuit, in qua neque satis abstinenter
se gessisse existimatus est et valde arroganter: quod genus
morum in eo paternum videbatur, cum cetera industria
15 nequaquam esset par. Erat tamen aliquando inter patronos causarum et, postquam ex provincia redierat, dixerat
pro C. Catone, isque erat absolutus a. d. IIII Nona Quint.
Ipse cum ad consulatus petitionem a. d. III Kal. Quint.
Romam redisset, querentibus de eo Sardis, a P. Valerio
20 Triario, adulescente parato ad dicendum et notae industriae

Tit. Q. ASCONI PEDIANI IN L. PISONEM. PRO (Q. PRO S) SCAVRO
SP : om. M   2 batinio S   et del. KS (cf. 7.22, 72.6)   3 a.d.
Beier: a Σ : ad ed. Ald.   7 uictricum Σ, corr. Manutius   syllam
Σ, ita semper   16 et Madvig : sed Σ : scilicet Baiter   17 co
catone isque S : eo catone cisque P¹, corr. Poggius, M   ad IIII (III P)
Σ, corr. Beier (ita mox)   18 ipse SP¹ : inde Poggius : inde
ipse M   Quinto S   19 eo] quo S   20 Triario om. S

Commentary of Q. Asconius Pedianus on *On Behalf of Scaurus*

This speech too he delivered in the same consulship as the one for Vatinius, that is, in the consulship of L. Domitius Ahenobarbus and Appius Claudius Pulcher [54 BC]. The last day of the trial was 2 September.

This is the explanatory preface

M. Scaurus, son of the M. Scaurus who was *princeps senatus*, had Sulla for a stepfather. When the latter emerged victorious and showed generosity to those who had assisted his victory, he (Scaurus) was so little motivated to profit that he desired no gifts for himself, nor did he purchase anything at auction. He ran his aedileship with such outstanding extravagance that he exhausted his own resources and contracted huge debt. After his praetorship he was governor of Sardinia, in which he was reckoned to have conducted himself with insufficient regard for others' property and with particular arrogance. This sort of behaviour he appeared to have inherited from his father, although his application to hard work was in other respects at nothing like the same level. However, he did sometimes act as an advocate, and after he returned from his province had defended C. Cato, who was acquitted on 4 July. He himself returned to Rome on 28 June to stand for the consulship, but on 6 July, as is written in the *Acta*, the third day after C. Cato's acquittal, he was indicted in the court of M. Cato, the praetor presiding over cases *de repetundis*, on the complaint against him of the Sardinians. The prosecutor was P. Valerius Triarius, a young man of ready eloquence and well-known application,

—filio eius qui in Sardinia contra M. Lepidum arma tulerat
et post in Asia legatus Pontoque L. Luculli fuerat, cum is
bellum contra Mithridatem gereret—postulatus *est* apud M.
Catonem praetorem repetundarum, ut in Actis scriptum
5 est, pridie Nonas Quintil. post diem tertium quam *C.* Cato
erat absolutus. Subscripserunt Triario in Scaurum L. Marius L. f., *M.* et Q. Pacuvii fratres cognomine Claudi. Qui
inquisitionis in Sardiniam itemque in Corsicam insulas dies
tricenos acceperunt neque profecti sunt ad inquirendum:
10 cuius rei hanc causam reddebant, quod interea comitia consularia futura essent; timere ergo se ne Scaurus ea pecunia
quam a sociis abstulisset emeret consulatum et, sicut pater
eius fecisset, ante quam de eo iudicari posset, magistratum
iniret ac rursus ante alias provincias spoliaret quam ratio-
15 nem prioris administrationis redderet.   Scaurus summam
fiduciam in paterni nominis dignitate, magnam in necessitudine Cn. Pompeii Magni reponebat.   Habebat enim filium
liberorum Cn. Pompeii fratrem: nam Tertiam, Scaevolae
filiam, dimissam a Pompeio in matrimonium duxerat. M.
20 Catonem autem qui id iudicium, ut diximus, exercebat
metuebat admodum propter amicitiam quae erat illi cum
Triario: nam Flaminia, Triarii mater, et ipse Triarius soro-
rem Catonis Serviliam, quae mater M. Bruti fuit, familiariter diligebat; ea porro apud Catonem maternam obtinebat
25 auctoritatem.   Sed in eo iudicio neque Pompeius propen-
sum adiutorium praebuit—videbatur enim apud animum

---

3 est *add. Baiter*   5 non. quint. *P* : nonis quintio *SM*
C. add. Heinrich   6 in] m *S*   Q. Marius Σ, *corr. Lodoicus*   7
M. add. Manutius   pacuuii *S* : pacuijii *P*: pacuii *M*   Claudii Σ,
corr. Manutius: Caldi *Pighius* (*cf. C.I.R.* 2451)   8 inquisitiones
SM : inquisitionem *P, corr. KS*   corsicas *S*   10 quod *P* :
quoad *SM*   11 essent *S* : erant *PM*   12 ab sociis *P*   consulatum *P* : consulatus *SM*   14 iniret *P* : inire *M* : in re *S*
ante] in *S*   spoliare *S*   16 necessitudine (-ē) *SM*: *om. P*
19 filium Σ, *corr.* ς, *ed. Ven.*   22 Triarii] Triaria Σ, *corr.* ς, *ed.*
Iunt.   24 diligebant *KS*   mater nam *SP*[1], *corr. Poggius, M*
25 in eo π : in et *SP*[1] : in *M* : ei in *KS*

son of the man who had borne arms against M. Lepidus in Sardinia   19C
and later had been legate to L. Lucullus in Asia and Pontus during the
latter's war against Mithridates. Triarius' accusation of Scaurus was
assisted by L. Marius, son of Lucius, and the brothers M. and Q.
Pacuvius surnamed Claudus. These men were each granted thirty
days for investigations in the islands of Sardinia and also Corsica, but
did not leave to conduct them, and offered as their reason for this
that the consular elections were due to take place in the interim:
consequently, they were apprehensive, they said, that Scaurus would
purchase the consulship with the money that he had stolen from the
allies, and, as his father had done, before a verdict in the courts could
be reached on him would enter his magistracy, and once again
despoil other provinces before giving due account for his previous
administration. Scaurus reposed the utmost confidence in the standing of his father's name, and a good deal in his connection with Cn.
Pompeius Magnus. For he had a son who was half-brother to the
children of Pompeius, since he had married Tertia, daughter of
Scaevola, after Pompeius had divorced her. But he particularly
dreaded M. Cato, who, as we said, was running this trial, on account
of his friendship with Triarius—for Flaminia, Triarius' mother, like
Triarius himself, was on closely affectionate terms with Cato's
half-sister Servilia, mother of M. Brutus—and she in turn enjoyed
virtually a mother's influence with Cato. But in that trial Pompeius
failed to extend him any enthusiastic support: Scaurus appeared,

20C

eius non minus offensionis contraxisse, quod iudicium eius in Muciam crimine impudicitiae ab eo dimissam levius fecisse existimaretur, cum eam ipse probasset, quam gratiae adquisisse necessitudinis iure, quod ex eadem uterque liberos 5 haberet—neque Cato ab aequitate ea quae et vitam eius et magistratum illum decebat quoquam deflexit. Post diem autem quartum quam postulatus erat Scaurus Faustus Sulla tum quaestor, filius Sullae Felicis, frater ex eadem matre Scauri servis eius vulneratis prosiluit ex lectica et questus 10 est prope interemptum esse *se a* competitoribus Scauri et ambulare cum ccc armatis seque, si necesse esset, vim vi repulsurum.

Defenderunt Scaurum sex patroni, cum ad id tempus raro quisquam pluribus quam quattuor uteretur: at post bella 15 civilia ante legem Iuliam ad duodenos patronos est perventum.   Fuerunt autem hi sex: P. Clodius Pulcher, M. Marcellus, M. Calidius, M. Cicero, M. Messala Niger, Q. Hortensius.   Ipse quoque Scaurus dixit pro se ac magnopere iudices movit et squalore et lacrimis et aedilitatis 20 effusae memoria ac favore populari ac praecipue paternae auctoritatis recordatione.

ENARRATIO

CIRCA VER. *A* PRIM. XXXX

Cum enumerat iudicia quae pater Scauri expertus 25 est:

---

1 contradixisse *S*   5 ea quam Σ, *corr. Beraldus*   7 quartum *ed. Iunt.* : iiii Σ : quartam *ed. Ven.*   9 servus eius vulneratus Σ, *corr. Heinrich*: cum servus eius esset vulneratus *Halm*   lecticiis Σ, *corr. Heinrich* : lecticariis *Rau*   10 pro interempto esse Σ, *corr. Lodoicus*   11 necesset uiuum *S*   13 defenderent *S*   14 ac Σ, *corr. Hotoman*   15 ad π : ante Σ   16 sex *P*: et *S*: se et *M*, *del. Manulius*   18 magnopere iudices *P* : magno per iudices *S* : magnopere i....*M*   20 effusa Σ, *corr. Heinrich*   23 A *add. ed. Ald.*   24 enumeraret Σ, *corr. ed. Lugd.*

to have given offence to Pompeius because he was thought to have made light of Pompeius' judgment in divorcing Mucia for unfaithfulness, inasmuch as he had shown approval of her himself. This seemed to outweigh any favourable influence he might have acquired with him through the family connection, that both of them had children by the same woman. Nor did Cato in any way deviate from the standard of fairness required of him by his own way of life and that office which he held. On the third day after Scaurus was indicted, Faustus Sulla, at that time quaestor, son of Sulla Felix and maternal half-brother to Scaurus, leapt out of his litter when some of his slaves had been wounded and protested that he had nearly been murdered by Scaurus' electoral rivals, and was proceeding on foot with an armed escort of three hundred, and that he would, if necessary, repel violence with violence.

In defence of Scaurus there were six advocates, though at that time it was rare for anyone to engage more than four—but after the civil wars before the Lex Iulia the number went as high as twelve advocates. Well, these were the six: P. Clodius Pulcher; M. Marcellus; M. Calidius; M. Cicero; M. Messalla Niger; Q. Hortensius. Scaurus himself also spoke on his own behalf, and greatly moved the jurors by his dishevelled appearance and tears, the remembrance of his lavish aedileship and his resultant popularity, and above all by the recollection of his father's position.

Commentary

Around line 40 from the beginning
When he lists the judicial indictments which Scaurus' father experienced:

Subiit etiam populi iudicium inquirente Cn.
Domitio tribuno plebis.
     Cn. Domitius qui consul fuit cum *C.* Cassio, cum esset
tribunus plebis, iratus Scauro quod eum in augurum colle-
5 gium non cooptaverat, diem ei dixit apud populum et
multam irrogavit, quod eius opera sacra populi Romani
deminuta esse diceret. Crimini dabat sacra publica populi
Romani deum Penatium quae Lavini fierent opera eius minus recte casteque fieri. Quo crimine absolutus est Scaurus
10 quidem, sed ita ut a tribus tribubus damnaretur, a xxxii
absolveretur, et in his pauca puncta inter damnationem et
absolutionem interessent.

IBIDEM

Reus est factus a Q. Servilio Caepione lege
15 Servilia, cum iudicia penes equestrem ordinem
essent et P. Rutilio damnato nemo tam innocens
videretur ut non timeret illa.
     Q. Servilius Caepio Scaurum ob legationis Asiaticae in-
vidiam et adversus leges pecuniarum captarum reum fecit
20 repetundarum lege quam tulit Servilius Glaucia. Scaurus
tanta fuit continentia animi et magnitudine ut Caepionem
contra reum detulerit et breviore die inquisitionis accepta
effecerit ut ille prior causam diceret; M. quoque Drusum
tribunum plebis cohortatus sit ut iudicia commutaret.

1 subit Σ, *corr. Mai*   anquirente *Mommsen*   3 C. *add. Manu-*
tius   4 collegium *P* : collegio *SM*   6 multam *M* : mulctam *SP*
multa *add. post* sacra Σ, *ego delevi* (*cf.* 26. 11, 27. 8 *et* 9, 48. 5)   7
deminuta *S* : diminuta *PM*   8 lauini *P* : labini *SM*   fuerunt Σ,
corr. Manutius   10 xxxii *S* : xxxvii *PM*   11 eis Σ, *corr.*
Bücheler   12 essent *P*¹   17 timeret *P* : timere *SM*   18
Q. *Poggius* : que Σ   19 et *del. Mommsen*   reum *P* : rerum *SM*
20 Glaucia] claudia gracchia Σ, *corr. Lodoicus*   22 contrarium Σ,
corr. Manutius   24 sit] fuit *S*

He also faced trial before the people with Cn. Domitius tribune of the plebs, as inquisitor [104 BC]. Cn. Domitius, who was consul with C. Cassius, when he was tribune of the plebs, in anger against Scaurus for failing to co-opt him into the College of Augurs, set him a day for trial before the people and imposed a fine on him, on the grounds that by his agency the sacred rites of the Roman people had been degraded. He entered as a criminal charge the allegation that by his agency the sacred rites of the Roman people for the Di Penates held at Lavinium were being conducted without due form and regard for purity. On this charge Scaurus was indeed acquitted, but not without being condemned by three tribes, and while thirty-two voted for acquittal, among these there was little difference in the number of marks for condemnation and acquittal.

In the same passage
He was indicted by Q. Servilius Caepio under the Lex Servilia at a time when the courts were in the hands of the equestrian order, and after the condemnation of P. Rutilius no one appeared blameless enough not to fear it. Q. Servilius Caepio indicted Scaurus on account of political resentment from his Asian posting and for taking monies contrary to law, and did so under the statute on extortion carried by Servilius Glaucia. Scaurus was cool-headed and spirited enough to enter a counter-accusation against Caepio, and by obtaining an earlier date for the trial contrived that the latter should plead his case first—and he also urged M. Drusus, tribune of the plebs, to reform the courts.

IBIDEM

Ab eodem etiam lege Varia custos ille rei
publicae proditionis est in crimen vocatus: vexatus a Q. Vario tribuno plebis est.
5 Non multo ante, Italico bello exorto, cum ob sociis nega-
tam civitatem nobilitas in invidia esset, Q. Varius tr. pl.
legem tulit ut quaereretur de iis quorum ope consiliove socii
contra populum Romanum arma sumpsissent. Tum Q. Caepio
vetus inimicus Scauri sperans se invenisse occasionem
10 opprimendi eius *egit* ut Q. Varius tribunus plebis belli con-
citati crimine adesse apud se Scaurum iuberet anno LXXII.
Ille per viatorem arcessitus, cum iam ex morbo male solveretur, dissuadentibus amicis ne se in illa valetudine et
aetate invidiae populi obiceret, innixus nobilissimis iuvenibus
15 processit in forum, deinde accepto respondendi loco dixit:
'Q. Varius Hispanus M. Scaurum principem senatus socios
in arma ait convocasse; M. Scaurus princeps senatus negat;
testis nemo est: utri vos, Quirites, convenit credere?' Qua
voce ita omnium commutavit animos ut ab ipso etiam tri-
20 buno dimitteretur.
    Dicit iterum de patre M. Scauri:
Non enim tantum admiratus sum ego illum
virum, sicut omnes, sed etiam praecipue dilexi. Primus enim me flagrantem studio laudis in spem
25 impulit posse virtute me sine praesidio fortunae
quo contendissem labore et constantia pervenire.

---

2 castos Σ, *corr.* ς, *ed. Iunt.* rłip Σ, *corr. ed. Iunt.* 3 vexatus
om. S 5 non multo (-tum *S*) antea *Asconio reddidit Patricius*
ab Σ, *corr. Poggius* 6 in *om. S* 9 se inuenisse se questionem
S: inuenisse se (se se *M*) quaestionem *PM*, *corr. Manutius*: se
inuenisse sequestrem *KS*: *fort.* se inuenisse ea quaestione rationem
10 egit *om. SP*[1], *suppl. Poggius, M* uapius *SP*[1], *corr. Poggius, M*
11 iubere *S* annorum *KS* 12 arcess. *PM*: accers. *S* (*ita* 23. 16)
16 senatus (t' *M*) *PM*: senatorem *S* 25 intulit *S* uirtutem sine
Σ, *corr. Mommsen* 26 contendisset *Manutius*

In the same passage   22C
That guardian of the state was also summoned by the same man under
the Lex Varia on a charge of high treason: he was harried by Q. Varius,
tribune of the plebs. Not long before, when the Italic War broke out,
the nobility were the target of resentment for denying the allies
citizen-rights and Q. Varius, tribune of the plebs, passed a law to
hold inquisitions into persons by whose aid or counsel (any) allies
had taken up arms against the Roman people. Then Q. Caepio, an
old enemy of Scaurus, hoping that he had found an opportunity to
crush him, arranged for Q. Varius, as tribune of the plebs, to order
Scaurus, at the age of seventy-two, to appear before him on a charge
of having stirred up the war. Scaurus was then scarcely recovered
from an illness and his friends advised him not to expose himself in
that state of health and at his age to the hostility of the people; but
when he was summoned by the official attendant he made his way
into the Forum, supported by young men of the highest rank, and
when the time came to reply he said : 'Q. Varius the Spaniard alleges
that M. Scaurus, *princeps senatus,* summoned the allies to arms.
M. Scaurus, *princeps senatus,* denies it. There is no witness. Which
of the two of them, citizens of Rome, is it fitting for you to believe?'
By this utterance he caused all present to change their minds—so
much so that he was allowed to go free by even the tribune himself.

On the elder Scaurus again he says: *For I did admire that man very*
much indeed, as did all. Not only that, but I was also particularly fond
of him. He was, you see, the first to inspire me, fired as I was with
eagerness to win plaudits, to hope that by my own prowess and without
the protection of Fortune I might reach my goal by single-minded effort.

23C   Possit aliquis quaerere cur hoc dixerit Cicero, cum Scaurus patricius fuerit: quae generis claritas etiam inertes
homines ad summos honores provexit. Verum Scaurus
ita fuit patricius ut tribus supra eum aetatibus iacuerit
5 domus eius fortuna. Nam neque pater neque avus neque
etiam proavus—ut puto, propter tenues opes et nullam vitae
industriam—honores adepti sunt. Itaque Scauro aeque ac
novo homini laborandum fuit.
     Si, me hercule, iudices, pro L. Tubulo dicerem
10 quem unum ex omni memoria sceleratissimum et
audacissimum fuisse accepimus, tamen non time-
rem, venenum hospiti aut convivae si diceretur ce-
nanti ab illo datum cui neque heres neque iratus
fuisset.
15   L. hic Tubulus praetorius fuit aetate patrum Ciceronis.
Is propter multa flagitia cum de exsilio arcessitus esset ut
in carcere necaretur, venenum bibit.

CIRCA TERTIAM PARTEM A PRIMO

     Illa audivimus; hoc vero meminimus ac
20 paene vidimus, eiusdem stirpis et nominis P. Crassum, ne in manus incideret inimicorum, se ipsum
interemisse.
     Hic Crassus fuit pater Crassi eius qui aemulus potentiae
Cn. Pompeii fuit. Periit autem in dominatione L. Cinnae,
25 cum ille et alios principes optimatum et collegam suum Cn.
Octavium occidit.

---

2 caritas Σ, *corr.* π   5 nam neque] nanque S   6 proauus etiam
P   9 tubulē S   10 quem unum P : q̄. in unum S : q̄; munum M
et omni Σ, *corr. Lodoicus*   et audacissimum *om.* S   16 ut SM :
ne P   17 carcere S : carcerem PM (in carcerem duceretur *Rau*)
18 CIRC. P   19 illa *add. Manutius*   audiuimus S : audimus PM
21 supsum S¹   24 periit S : perit PM

Some person might inquire why Cicero should have said this, since Scaurus was a patrician, and that distinction of birth has propelled even idle men to the highest offices. In fact, though, Scaurus may have been patrician, but for three generations before him the fortunes of his house had been at low ebb. For neither his father nor his grandfather nor even his great-grandfather—I surmise because of slender resources and lack of application in their lifestyle—had attained offices. And so Scaurus needed to work just as hard as any *novus homo*.

Heaven knows, gentlemen of the jury, if I were speaking for L. Tubulus, who was, we are told, the most utterly uninhibited criminal on record, still I should not fear any allegation that he had administered poison at table to a guest or fellow-diner to whom he was neither heir nor roused to hostility. This L. Tubulus was of praetorian rank in the time of earlier generations of Cicero's family. When on account of his many outrages he was summoned from exile to be executed in prison, he drank poison.

Around one-third from the beginning
We have heard all that; but we do remember, in fact all but saw it, that P. Crassus, of the same stock and name, to avoid falling into the hands of his enemies, slew himself. This Crassus was the father of the Crassus who was Cn. Pompeius' rival for power. He perished in the period of L. Cinna's domination, when Cinna slew among other leading figures of the *optimates* his colleague Cn. Octavius.

24C

[STATIM

Ac neque illius Crassi factum superioris isdem
honoribus usus, qui fortissimus in bellis fuisset,
M'. Aquilius potuit imitari.
5 Haec verba quibus Cicero nunc utitur, ac neque, eam
videntur habere naturam ut semel poni non soleant; quia
est coniunctio disiunctiva et semper postulat ut rursus infe-
ratur neque, ut cum dicimus neque hoc neque illud.
Quo autem casu acciderit quave ratione ut hoc loco Cicero
10 hoc verbo ita usus sit, praesertim cum adiecerit illam apposi-
tionem, ut non intulerit postea alterum, neque perspicere
potui et attendendum esse valde puto: moveor enim merita
viri auctoritate. Neque ignoro aliquando hoc verbum neque
vel semel poni, ut in eadem hac oratione ante ipse Cicero
15 posuit: Sic, inquam, se, iudices, res habet; neque hoc
a me novum disputatur sed quaesitum ab aliis est.
Sed hoc loco et sine praepositione illius verbi videmus esse
positum, et tamen quasi secundum aliquid inferri. Nam
cum dixerit neque hoc a me novum disputatur, infert
20 sed quaesitum ab aliis est.]

PAVLO POST

Quid vero alterum Crassum temporibus isdem
—num aut clarissimi viri Iulii aut summo ingenio
praeditus M. Antonius potuit imitari?

1–20 *Asconio abiudicavit Madvig*   2 ac neque illius] atque
illius *scr. Poggius, mox ipse delevit*   factum neque Σ, *corr. Poggius
in mg.* P   4 *M'. add. Manutius*   5 eam *Poggius*, M : enim
SP¹ (ṇọṇ P *mg.*)   6 simul Σ, *corr. Poggius*   7 ut semper Σ,
corr. Manutius   inferat S   8 et neque cum dicimus ut neque
hoc Σ, *corr. Lodoicus*   9–10 quave ... adiecerit *om.* S   10
ita usus *Poggius*, M : ṣ usus P¹   11 ut non KS : ut nomen Σ : et
nomen *Manutius*   17 ut sine Σ, *corr. Manutius*   uideamus Σ,
corr. Manutius   18 quasi *Bücheler* : quo sit Σ : post *Manutius*
23 nam Σ. *corr. ed. Ald*   ingenio Σ : imperio *Cic.*

Immediately following

*And neither was M'. Aquilius, who had enjoyed the same honours, able
despite extreme gallantry in warfare to copy the deed of that elder
Crassus.* This wording which Cicero now employs—'*and neither*'
(*neque*) seems to have the characteristic of not normally being used
on its own, since it is a disjunctive connective and always requires the
importation of a corresponding '*nor*' (*neque*), as when we say '*neither
this nor that*'. In what circumstances and for what reason it has
happened that Cicero in this passage has used this phrase in this
way (especially when he adds that extra word), without later using it
a second time, I have not been able to perceive, and I am perfectly
sure requires attention, since I cannot ignore the man's impeccable
authority. Nor am I unaware that this word (*neque*) is at times used
by itself, just as Cicero himself earlier in this same speech set down:
'*This, gentlemen of the jury, is the fact of the matter; nor (*neque*) is this
a new point of dispute raised by me, but it has been investigated by
others.*' But in this passage we see that it is used both without that
word in front, and there is something acting like the second element—for when he says '*nor is this a new point of dispute raised by me*',
he imports '*but it has been investigated by others*'.

A little further on

*So then? Could either the Iulii, men of the greatest distinction, or
M. Antonius, a man endowed with the highest talent, emulate the
other Crassus at that time?*

25C

   Hic alter Crassus idem est de quo supra diximus. Alterum autem eum appellat, quia ante mentionem fecit P.
Crassi qui fuit pontifex maximus et bello Aristonici in Asia
dedit operam ut occideretur. Iulios autem cum dicit, duos
5 Caesares fratres C. et L. significat: ex quibus Lucius et
consul et censor fuit, Gaius aedilicius quidem occisus est,
sed tantum in civitate potuit ut causa belli civilis contentio
eius cum Sulpicio tr. fuerit. Nam et sperabat et id
agebat Caesar ut omissa praetura consul fieret: cui cum
10 primis temporibus iure Sulpicius resisteret, postea nimia
contentione ad ferrum et ad arma processit. Idem inter
primos temporis sui oratores et tragicus poeta bonus admodum habitus est; huius sunt enim tragoediae quae inscribun-
tur Iuli. Et hi autem Iulii et Antonius a satellitibus Mari
15 sunt occisi, cum Crassus, ut supra diximus, eundem casum
sua manu praevenisset.

CIR. MEDIVM

   Neque   vero   haec   ipsa   cotidiana   res   Appium Claudium illa humanitate et sapientia praedi-
20 tum per se ipsa movisset, nisi hunc C. Claudi fratris
sui competitorem fore putasset. Qui sive patricius
sive plebeius esset—nondum enim certum constitutum erat—cum illo sibi contentionem fore putabat.
Fuerunt enim duae familiae Claudiae: earum quae Mar-

---

   3 pene max. *S*   Asiam Σ, *corr. Beraldus*   4 iulius *S*   6
censor *Madvig* : pretor Σ   Gaius] C. *PM* : cum *S*   7 causas *SP*[1],
corr. Poggius, M   8 P. Sulpicio *KS* (*in Addendis*)   tr. pl. *KS*
9 omissa (omm. *M*) *PM* : ob omissa *S*   10 resistat *SP*[1], *corr. Poggius, M*   postea *P* : et postea *SM*   11 idem ... bonus *om.*

S   12 sūī tēmporis *P*   20 C. *Cic.* : *om.* Σ   21 competitorem
P : compeditorem *S* : comperitorem *M*   22 nondum Σ : non *Cic.*
pal. A   constitutum erat Σ : constituerat *Cic.*   23 illo Σ : hoc *Cic.*

24 Claūdiae fāmiliae *P*   earumque Σ : *corr. Lodoicus*

This 'other Crassus' is the same man of whom we have spoken above.   25C
But he calls him 'the other' because earlier he has mentioned
P. Crassus who was *pontifex maximus* and in the war against Aristonicus in Asia took care to get himself killed. In referring to the Iulii,
he means the two brothers Lucius and Gaius Caesar, of whom Lucius
was consul and censor, and Gaius was killed while no more than ex-
aedile, for sure, but was so politically powerful that his quarrel with
P. Sulpicius the tribune was a cause of civil war. For Caesar both had
hopes of being made consul without holding the praetorship and was
working to that end, and although Sulpicius opposed him in the
earlier stages by legal means, later when the dispute grew excessively
fierce resorted to weapons and armed force. This same man was
reckoned among the leading orators of his time and a particularly
good tragic poet: there exist tragedies of his which carry the inscription 'By Iulius'. And anyhow, these Iulii and Antonius were slain by
the followers of Marius, while Crassus, as we said above, anticipated
the same fate by his own hand.

Around the half-way point
*Nor indeed would this everyday occurrence of itself alone have
influenced Appius Claudius, endowed as he is with that humanity and
wisdom of his, had he not thought that this man was going to be the
electoral rival of his brother C. Claudius. And he thought that whether
patrician or plebeian—and it had not yet been decided for certain—he
would be in contention with that man* (namely, Scaurus). There
were two families of Claudii. The one called that of the Marcelli

26C

cellorum appellata est plebeia, quae Pulchrorum patricia.
Sed hoc loco urbane Cicero lusit in *C.* Claudium, cum quo
in gratiam non redierat.   Nam quia is P. Clodi erat frater
qui ex patricia in plebeiam familiam transierat per summam
5 infamiam, eum quoque dubitare adhuc dixit.

POST DVAS PARTES ORATIONIS

dicit dein de Scauro quem defendit:
Nam cum ex multis unus ei restaret Dolabella paternus inimicus qui cum Q. Caepione pro-
10 pinquo suo contra Scaurum patrem suum subsigna-
verat: eas sibi inimicitias non susceptas sed
relictas et cetera.
Ne forte erretis et eundem hunc Cn. Dolabellam putetis
esse in quem C. Caesaris orationes legitis, scire vos oportet
15 duos eodem *eo* tempore fuisse et praenomine et nomine et
cognomine Dolabellas.   Horum igitur alterum Caesar accusavit nec damnavit; alterum M. Scaurus et accusavit
et damnavit.

POST TRES PARTES *A* PRIMO

20   quo loco defendit, quod tam magnificam domum Scaurus
habet:
Praesertim cum propinquitas et celebritas
loci suspicionem desidiae tollat aut cupiditatis.

1 plebeiaque (-que et *P*) Σ, *corr. Manutius*   2 C *add. Rau*   5
eum *scripsi* : se Σ : ipsum *Madvig* (*vel* C.)   7 dixit Σ, *corr. Man-*
utius   dein de *S* : deinde *P* : dein *M*   8 dolabella *M* : dolobella
SP (*ita semper*)   9 quicumque *S*   10 suum *del. Halm* obsi-
gnauerat Σ, *corr. Mommsen*   11 eas] ceteras *add. S* (*e v.* 12 *repetit.*) :
steteras *add. PM, del. Kreyssig* sibi *om. S*   12 relatas Σ, *corr.*
Beier   13 erretis *S²P* : erratis *S¹M*   esse putetis *S*   15
eodem eo tempore *scripsi* : eodem tempore Σ : eodem tempore eodem
Baiter   16 Dolabellam *post* alterum *add.* Σ, *del. Manutius*   19
POST TRES PARTES. Primo *P* : prioribus continuant *SM*   A *om.* Σ,
suppl. Baiter

was plebeian; that of the Pulchri patrician. But in this passage Cicero 26C
wittily mocks C. Claudius, with whom he had not been reconciled.
For since he was the brother of P. Clodius who had transferred from
his patrician family into a plebeian one amid outrageous scandal, he
says that he too was still in doubt.

After two-thirds of the speech
Then he speaks of the Scaurus whom he is defending: *From a long list
there remained for him just the one enemy of his fathers, Dolabella, who
along with his relative Q. Caepio had joined in prosecuting Scaurus his
father; that was an enmity which he had not begun himself, but
inherited ... (etc.).* Lest you mistakenly suppose that this Dolabella
is the same as the one who is attacked in the speeches of Caesar which
you are reading, you ought to know that there were two Dolabellae at
that same time with the same forename, name, and surname. One of
these, then, Caesar accused but did not secure his condemnation; the
other M. Scaurus both accused and got condemned.

After three-quarters from the beginning
The passage where he is offering defence for the fact that Scaurus
possesses such a fine house: *Especially when the vicinity and the busy
location eliminate any suspicion of sloth or greed ...*

27C

Demonstrasse vobis memini me hanc domum in ea parte
Palatii esse quae, cum ab Sacra via descenderis et per proxi-
mum vicum qui est a sinistra parte prodieris, posita est.
Possidet eam nunc Largus Caecina qui consul fuit cum
5 Claudio. In huius domus atrio fuerunt quattuor columnae
marmoreae insigni magnitudine quae nunc esse in regia
theatri Marcelli dicuntur. Vsus erat iis aedilis—ut ipse
quoque significat—in ornatu theatri quod ad tempus perquam amplae magnitudinis fecerat.

10   VER. A NOV.✳✳✳

Haec cum tu effugere non potuisses, con-
tendes tamen et postulabis ut M. Aemilius cum
sua dignitate omni, cum patris memoria, cum avi
gloria, sordidissimae, vanissimae, levissimae genti
15 ac prope dicam pellitis testibus condonetur?
Avum hunc Scauri maternum significat L. Metellum
pontificem maximum, quem postea nominat quoque. Nam
paternus avus proavusque Scauri humiles atque obscuri
fuerunt.

20   VER. A NOVIS. CLX

Vndique mihi suppeditat quod pro M. Scauro
dicam, quocumque non modo mens verum etiam
oculi inciderunt. Curia illa vos de gravissimo

---

3 est ab *P*   proderis Σ, *corr.* ς, *ed. Iunt.*   4 posset *SP*¹, *corr.*
Poggius, M   Largus *Lipsius* : longus (lognus *S*) Σ   cicina *S* :
PM, corr. Manutius   7 is (his *P*) Σ, *corr. Beraldus*   8
ut in Σ, *corr. Poggius*   9 ampla Σ, *corr. KS*   magnitudine
Poggius   magne *post* magnitudinis *add.* Σ, *del. Manutius*   11
effugere *P* : effigere *SM*   12 postulas *S*   13 cura
patris *S*   14 levissime *hoc loco hab. S, ante* vanis. *P, om.*
M   16 nunc Σ, *corr. KS*   scaurum *S*   17 quoque nominat
P   18 maternus *S*   scauri *P* : ....*S* : scaur..........
M : Scauri ut supra diximus *KS*   23 inciderint Σ, *corr. Halm*
grauissimo *PM* : clarissimo patri *S*

I recall that I made it clear to you that this house is on that part of the   27C
Palatine which is situated as you come down from the Sacred Way
and go on through the next street which is on the left. The present
occupant is Caecina Largus, who was consul with Claudius. In the
hall of this house were four pillars in marble of remarkable size,
which are now said to be in the portico of the Theatre of Marcellus.
He had made use of them as aedile—as Cicero himself also
indicates—to embellish the theatre of enormous size which he had
constructed for the occasion.

Line ... from the end

*Since you could not have evaded these matters, are you all the same
going to insist in demanding that M. Aemilius, with all his high
standing, with the remembrance of his father, with the renown of his
grandfather, should be handed over to the tender mercies of the most
unclean, most empty-headed, most irresponsible race imaginable, who
turn up, I might almost say, in their animal skins to bear their testimony?* In this case he means the maternal grandfather L. Metellus, the
pontifex maximus, whom he later also names. For Scaurus' paternal
grandfather and great-grandfather were of low standing and obscure.

Line 160 from the end

*On all sides, wherever my thoughts turn or indeed my eyes alight, I
find material for my defence of M. Scaurus. The senate hall*

28C

principatu patris fortissimoque testatur; L. ipse
Metellus, avus huius, sanctissimos deos illo consti-
tuisse templo videtur in vestro conspectu, iudices,
ut salutem a vobis nepotis sui deprecarentur.
5 Castoris et Pollucis templum Metellus quem nominat
refecerat.

Laudaverunt Scaurum consulares novem, L. Piso, L. Volcacius, Q. Metellus Nepos, M. Perpenna, L. Philippus, M.
Cicero, Q. Hortensius, P. Servilius Isauricus pater, Cn.
10 Pompeius Magnus. Horum magna pars per tabellas laudaverunt quia aberant: inter quos Pompeius quoque; nam
quod erat pro cos. extra urbem morabatur. Vnus praeterea
adulescens laudavit, frater eius, Faustus Cornelius Sullae
filius. Is in laudatione multa humiliter et cum lacrimis
15 locutus non minus audientes permovit quam Scaurus ipse
permoverat. Ad genua iudicum, cum sententiae ferrentur,
bifariam se diviserunt qui pro eo rogabant: ab uno latere
Scaurus ipse et M'. Glabrio, sororis filius, et *L.* Paulus et
P. Lentulus, Lentuli Nigri flaminis filius, et L. Aemilius
20 Buca filius et C. Memmius, Fausta natus, supplicaverunt;
ex altera parte Sulla Faustus, frater Scauri, et T. Annius
Milo, cui Fausta ante paucos menses nupserat dimissa a
Memmio, et C. Peducaeus et C. Cato et M. Laenas Curtianus.

25 Sententias tulerunt senatores duo et xx, equites tres et
xx, tribuni aerarii xxv: ex quibus damnaverunt senatores
iiii, equites ii, tribuni ii.

---

3 in templo *P*   4 deprecaretur *PM*   6 referat Σ, *corr.*
Beraldus   7 L. Volcacius, Q. *Manutius* : m. uol. quintus *S* : m. uol.
Q. *P* : m. uol. uolq̅ *M*   8 M. Perpenna] L. Murena *Manutius*
9 hisauricus pr. Σ, *corr. Manutius*   11 qui aberant Σ, *corr.*
Manutius   14 humiliter *P* : similiter *SM*   16 cum *om. S*
17 se diuiserunt *P* : sed iusserunt *M* : set uisserunt *S*   18
M. Σ, *corr. Manutius*   L. *add. KS* (*in Addendis*)   21
T. Annius Milo *Beier* : C (gn. *S*) aronius limo Σ   23 C. Peduc.
S : T. Peduc. *PM*   et Molena (M. olena *P*) scortianus Σ, *corr. Mad-*
vig   25 duo et] iv et *Manutius*   26 xxv] xxii *Manutius*

there bears witness to the supreme dignity and courage with which his   28C
father headed the house; L. Metellus in person, his grandfather, seemed
to have installed the most holy gods in their temple so that in your sight
they might win their plea for the salvation of his grandson. The
Metellus whom he names had repaired the Temple of Castor and
Pollux.

Laudatory testimonials for Scaurus were given by nine men of
consular rank—L. Piso, L. Volcacius, Q. Metellus Nepos, M. Perpenna, L. Philippus, M. Cicero, Q. Hortensius, the elder P. Servilius
Isauricus, Cn. Pompeius Magnus. Of these, the large part entered
their testimonials by letter, since they were absent, among them also
Pompeius, for since he was proconsul he was waiting outside the city.
In addition one young man gave a testimonial, his half-brother
Faustus Cornelius, son of Sulla. He, in saying a great deal in his
testimonial in humble vein and with tears, moved his hearers no less
than Scaurus himself had done. At the knees of the jury, when the
votes were being cast, those who were pleading for him divided into
two groups—to the one side Scaurus himself; and M'. Glabrio, his
sister's son; L. Paulus; P. Lentulus, son of Lentulus Niger the *flamen*;
and the younger L. Aemilius Buca and C. Memmius, son of Fausta,
made supplication; to the other side Sulla Faustus, half-brother to
Scaurus; T. Annius Milo, whom Fausta had married a few months
earlier on being divorced by Memmius; C. Peducaeus; C. Cato and
M. Laenas Curtianus.

Votes were cast by twenty-two senators, twenty-three knights,
twenty-five *tribuni aerarii*, out of which four senators, two
knights, and two *tribuni aerarii* were for condemnation.

Cato praetor, *Cicero* cum vellet de accusatoribus in consilium mittere multique e populo manus in accusatores intenderent, cessit imperitae multitudini ac postero die in consilium de calumnia accusatorum misit. P. Triarius nullam
5 gravem sententiam habuit; subscriptores eius M. et Q. Pacuvii fratres denas et L. Marius tres graves habuerunt. Cato praetor iudicium, quia aestate agebatur, sine tunica exercuit campestri sub toga cinctus. In forum quoque sic descendebat iusque dicebat, idque repetierat ex vetere con-
10 suetudine secundum quam et Romuli et Tati statuae in Capitolio et in rostris Camilli fuerunt togatae sine tunicis.

1 praetor *Sozomenus* : praeter *S* : praeterea *PM*   Cicero *supplevi* (*videtur* C. *ante* cum *excidisse, cf.* 48.14, 33.23)   4 P. *KS* : C. Σ (*cf.* 18.19)   5 Q. pacuvii *P* : que pacubii *SM*   7 aestate *P* : etate *S* : a frate *M*   8 campestre Σ, *corr.* Beraldus   9 descenderat Σ, *corr.* Orelli   reppererat Σ, *corr.* Patricius (*cf.* 55.10) et uetere Σ, *corr. ed. Iunt.*   10 et Tati *KS* : ac Tati *Gronovius* : etatis Σ   statuae π : capuae (-yae *S*) Σ

Cato the praetor, when [Cicero?] wanted the jury to consider its
verdict on the accusers, and many from the people shook their fists at
the accusers, yielded to the ignorant mob and next day had the jury
consider its verdict in the matter of false accusation on the part of the
prosecutors. P. Triarius had no votes of censure against him, but his
subsignatories M. and Q. Pacuvius had ten and L. Marius three.

Cato the praetor ran the trial, because it took place in summer,
without a tunic, wearing only a loincloth under his toga. He also used
to come down into the forum in these clothes and dispense jurisdiction, and had reintroduced this practice from ancient custom,
according to which the statues of both Romulus and Tatius on the
Capitol, and that of Camillus on the *rostra* were dressed in togas
without tunics.

Pro Milone

Orationem hanc dixit Cn. Pompeio III COS. a. d. VII
Id. April. Quod iudicium cum ageretur, exercitum in foro
et in omnibus templis quae circum forum sunt collocatum
a Cn. Pompeio fuisse *non* tantum ex oratione et annalibus,
5 sed etiam ex libro apparet qui Ciceronis nomine inscribitur
de optimo genere oratorum.

ARGVMENTVM HOC EST

T. Annius Milo et P. Plautius Hypsaeus et Q. Metellus
Scipio consulatum petierunt non solum largitione palam
10 profusa sed etiam factionibus armatorum succincti. Miloni
et Clodio summae erant inimicitiae, quod et Milo Ciceronis
erat amicissimus in reducendoque eo enixe operam tr. pl.
dederat, et P. Clodius restituto quoque Ciceroni erat
infestissimus ideoque summe studebat Hypsaeo et Scipioni
15 contra Milonem. Ac saepe inter se Milo et Clodius cum
suis factionibus Romae depugnaverant: et erant uterque
audacia pares, sed Milo pro melioribus partibus stabat.
Praeterea in eundem annum consulatum Milo, Clodius
praeturam petebat, quam debilem futuram consule Milone
20 intellegebat. Deinde cum diu tracta essent comitia
consularia perficique ob eas ipsas perditas candidatorum

Tit. PRO M. SCAVRO FINIS INCIPIT PRO MILONE *SP* : *om.* M   1 orationem *add. hoc loco Stangl, post* hanc *KS*   VII *scripsi* : VI Σ   3
omnibus in *P*   4 non *Poggius, Sozomenus* : *om.* Σ   ex ea
ratione Σ, *corr. Manutius*   5 describitur *S*   8 T. *add. Manutius*
hypseus *M* : hyphaeus *S* : hipseus *P*   11 quod] q. d. *S*   12
tr. pl. *Rinkes* : rei p. Σ   13 quoque *S* : que *P* : *om.* M   16 erat
Σ, *corr.* ς, *Baiter*   17 pares *P* (*teste Skutsch*)

He delivered this speech on 8 April in the third consulship of Cn. Pompeius [52 BC]. While the trial was in progress an armed force had been stationed by Pompeius in the Forum and in all the temples sited round it, as is clear not only from the speech and from annals, but also from the work attributed to Cicero entitled *On the Best Kind of Orators.*

This is the explanatory preface

T. Annius Milo, P. Plautius Hypsaeus, and Q. Metellus Scipio sought the consulship not only by openly lavished bribery but also surrounded by gangs of armed men. Milo and Clodius were deadly enemies, both because Milo was a close friend of Cicero and had as tribune of the plebs made great exertions to bring him back from exile, and because P. Clodius remained extremely hostile to Cicero even after his restitution, and for that reason was a very strong supporter of Hypsaeus and Scipio against Milo. And Milo and Clodius had often engaged in battle with each other in Rome with their partisans, and both were equally reckless, but Milo stood on the side of 'the better cause'. Moreover, Clodius was seeking the praetorship in the same year as Milo was the consulship and he knew perfectly well it would be hamstrung if Milo were consul. Eventually, after the consular elections had been long postponed and could not be completed just because of these reckless clashes of the candidates,

contentiones non possent, et ob id mense Ianuario
nulli dum neque consules neque praetores essent tra-
hereturque dies eodem quo antea modo—cum Milo
quam primum comitia confici vellet confideretque cum
5 bonorum studiis, quod obsistebat Clodio, tum etiam populo
propter effusas largitiones impensasque ludorum scaeni-
corum ac gladiatorii muneris maximas, in quas tria patrimonia effudisse eum Cicero significat; competitores eius
trahere vellent, ideoque Pompeius gener Scipionis et
10 T. Munatius tribunus plebis referri ad senatum de patriciis
convocandis qui interregem proderent non essent passi,
cum interregem prodere stata res esset—: a. d. xiii Kal.
Febr.—Acta etenim magis sequenda et ipsam orationem,
quae Actis congruit, puto quam Fenestellam qui a. d. xiiii
15 Kal. Febr. tradit—Milo Lanuvium, ex quo erat municipio et
ubi tum dictator, profectus est ad flaminem prodendum postera die.   Occurrit ei circa horam nonam Clodius paulo ultra
Bovillas, rediens ab Aricia, prope eum locum in quo Bonae
Deae sacellum est; erat autem allocutus decuriones Arici-
20 norum. Vehebatur Clodius equo; servi xxx fere expediti,
ut illo tempore mos erat iter facientibus, gladiis cincti
sequebantur. Erant cum Clodio praeterea tres comites
eius, ex quibus eques Romanus unus C. Causinius Schola,
duo de plebe noti homines P. Pomponius, *C. Clodius.*
25 Milo raeda vehebatur cum uxore Fausta, filia L. Sullae
dictatoris, et M. Fufio familiari suo. Sequebatur eos

3 cum *Baiter* : dum Σ   4 conficeretque Σ, *corr. Rinkes*   5
obsidebat *S*   6 impensas quoque Σ, *corr. Baiter*   7 gladiatorii
P : gladiatoru; *M* : gladiatorum *S*   patrimonia π, *M* : p̄lia
S : prelia *P¹*   9 genere *S*   10 l. numatius Σ, *corr. Manutius*
12 proderent *M¹*   stata res esset *Mommsen* : obstatores essent
S : ortatores esset *P* : ostatores esset *M* : *fort.* hortatus eos esset (*cf.* 33.
1)   xiii *Hotoman* : iii *SP* : tersa *M*   13 magis *om. M*
16 ibi *P*   prodendum. Postera *P*   21 iter facientibus *P* : inter-
ficientibus *SM*   23 eques r. *P* : eque (aeque *S*) sr̄. *SM* Cassinius
Σ, *corr. Halm*   24 noti *Madvig* : noui *P* : non *SM* C. Clodius
add. Manutius   26 fusio Σ, *corr. Manutius*   familiare Σ, *corr. ed.*
Ald.

and for this reason when January came there were not yet any consuls   31C
or praetors, and the date was being put back in the same way as
before: Milo wanted the elections over as soon as possible, and put
his trust in the support both of the *boni*, because he was opposed to
Clodius, and in the people on account of his general bribery and
huge expenditure on dramatic spectacles and a gladiatorial show, on
which Cicero indicates that he had spent three inheritances. On the
other hand his competitors wanted delay, and for that reason Pompeius, Scipio's son-in-law, and T. Munatius, tribune of the plebs, had
not allowed any initiative in the senate on the matter of convening
the Patricians in order to appoint an *interrex*, although it was a
constitutional requirement to appoint one.

On 18 January—for I think that the *Acta* and the speech, which
agrees with the *Acta*, should be followed, rather than Fenestella,
whose account has the 17th—Milo set out for Lanuvium, his native
town, where at the time he was dictator, in order to appoint a *flamen*
the next day. At about the ninth hour Clodius, who was returning
from Aricia, encountered him a little beyond Bovillae, near the site of
a shrine to the Bona Dea: he had been addressing the local councillors of Aricia. Clodius was on horseback, and had an escort of about
thirty slaves ready for action, as was the custom in those days for
those on a journey, and wearing swords. Also with Clodius were three
of his companions: one Roman knight, C. Causinius Schola, and two
well-known members of the plebs, P. Pomponius and C. Clodius.
Milo was riding in a carriage with his wife Fausta, daughter of the
dictator Sulla, and his friend M. Fufius. Their escort was a

32C magnum servorum agmen, inter quos gladiatores quoque
erant, ex quibus duo noti Eudamus et Birria. Ii in ultimo
agmine tardius euntes cum servis P. Clodi rixam commi-
serunt. Ad quem tumultum cum respexisset Clodius
5 minitabundus, umerum eius Birria rumpia traiecit. Inde
cum orta esset pugna, plures Miloniani accurrerunt.
Clodius vulneratus in tabernam proximan *in* Bovillano
delatus est. Milo ut cognovit vulneratum Clodium, cum
sibi periculosius illud etiam vivo eo futurum intellegeret,
10 occiso autem magnum solacium esset habiturus, etiam si
subeunda esset poena, exturbari taberna iussit. Fuit ante-
signanus servorum eius M. Saufeius. Atque ita Clodius
latens extractus est multisque vulneribus confectus. Cadaver
eius in via relictum, quia servi Clodi aut occisi erant aut
15 graviter saucii latebant, Sex. Teidius senator, qui forte ex
rure in urbem revertebatur, sustulit et lectica sua Romam
ferri iussit; ipse rursus eodem unde erat egressus *se* recepit.
Perlatum est corpus Clodi ante primam noctis horam,
infimaeque plebis et servorum maxima multitudo magno
20 luctu corpus in atrio domus positum circumstetit. Augebat
autem facti invidiam uxor Clodi Fulvia quae cum effusa
lamentatione vulnera eius ostendebat. Maior postera die
luce prima multitudo eiusdem generis confluxit, complures-
que noti homines visi sunt. Erat domus Clodi ante
25 paucos menses empta de M. Scauro in Palatio: eodem
T. Munatius Plancus, frater L. Planci oratoris, et Q.
Pompeius Rufus, Sullae dictatoris ex filia nepos, tribuni

---

2 eudamius *S*   ii] ·ıı· *S*   5 rumpia traiecit *P* : rumpit atraie-
cit *S* : rumpi atra traiecit *M*   7 in *add. Madvig*   bovillano
P : uobillano *S* : bobillano *M*   11 tabernam Σ, *corr. Madvig*   aut
signa unus Σ, *corr. ed. Ven.*   12 M. fustenus (*om. P¹*) Σ, *corr.*
Manutius   15 latebant] iacebant *Halm*   Tedius Σ (*at cf. C.I.R.*
i. 1090)   16 in *om. S*   17 egressus se *Madvig* : regressum Σ
19 infirmeque Σ, *corr. ed. Iunt.*   20 corpus *del. Halbertsma*   24
visi ς, *Rinkes* : elisi Σ   inter quos C. Vibienus senator *post* sunt
add. Σ *ex Cic.* § 37, *del. Rinkes*   26 T. *add. Manutius*

large train of slaves, also including gladiators, two of them well-known ones, Eudamus and Birria. These, making rather slow progress at the back of the column, started a scrap with Clodius' slaves. Clodius had turned to direct his menacing eye upon this brawl, when Birria pierced his shoulder with a hunting-spear. Then as a battle developed more of Milo's men arrived on the scene. The wounded Clodius was carried off to a nearby tavern in the territory of Bovillae. When Milo learnt that Clodius was wounded, he took the view that his survival would be something of a danger to himself, whereas his death would greatly relieve his own feelings, even if he had to pay the penalty for it, and so ordered him to be turned out of the tavern. His slaves' commander was M. Saufeius. And so Clodius was dragged out from hiding and killed with many wounds. Since Clodius' slaves had either been killed or had gone into hiding with severe injuries, the body was left in the road, and Sex. Teidius, a senator, who chanced to be on his way back to the city from the countryside, picked it up and gave orders for its conveyance to Rome in his litter, while he himself withdrew to his original point of departure.

Clodius' body arrived soon after nightfall, and a huge crowd of the lowest commoners and slaves stood round it in the hallway of his house in deep sorrow. Clodius' wife Fulvia was bent on inflaming anger at the deed by displaying his wounds with effusive lamentations. On the next day at dawn an even greater crowd of the same sort came flooding up, and several well-known figures were sighted. Clodius' house, which had been purchased a few months earlier from Scaurus, was on the Palatine, and that was where T. Munatius Plancus, brother of the orator Lucius Plancus, and Q. Pompeius Rufus, grandson of Sulla the dictator (by his daughter), tribunes

plebis accurrerunt: eisque hortantibus vulgus imperitum corpus nudum ac calcatum, sicut in lecto erat positum, ut vulnera videri possent in forum detulit et in rostris posuit. Ibi pro contione Plancus et Pompeius qui competitoribus
5 Milonis studebant invidiam Miloni fecerunt. Populus duce Sex. Clodio scriba corpus P. Clodi in curiam intulit cremavitque subselliis et tribunalibus et mensis et codicibus librariorum; quo igne et ipsa quoque curia flagravit, et item Porcia basilica quae erat ei iuncta ambusta est.
10 Domus quoque M. Lepidi interregis—is enim magistratus curulis erat creatus—et absentis Milonis eadem illa Clodiana multitudo oppugnavit, sed inde sagittis repulsa est. Tum fasces ex luco Libitinae raptos attulit ad domum Scipionis et Hypsaei, deinde ad hortos Cn. Pompeii,
15 clamitans eum modo consulem, modo dictatorem.

Incendium curiae maiorem aliquanto indignationem civitatis moverat quam interfectio Clodi. Itaque Milo, quem opinio fuerat ivisse in voluntarium exsilium, invidia adversariorum recreatus nocte ea redierat Romam qua incensa erat
20 curia. Petebatque nihil deterritus consulatum; aperte quoque tributim in singulos milia assium dederat. Contionem ei post aliquot dies dedit M. Caelius tribunus plebis ac Cicero ipse etiam causam egit ad populum. Dicebant uterque Miloni a Clodio factas esse insidias.
25 Fiebant interea alii ex aliis interreges, quia comitia consu-

1 accurrerunt *S* : accucurrerunt *PM*   obstantibus Σ, *corr.* π
2 ac calcatum *Daniel* : caldatum Σ : calciatum *Manutius*   3 possent
P : possint *SM*   5 duce Sex. *P* : duces et *SM*   7 menis *S* :
mens *PM, corr.* ς, *ed. Iunt.*   9 basilica *P* : ballica (bali- *M*) *SM*
12 sed inde *Halm* : deinde Σ   13 luco *Wagener* : lecto Σ   libi-
tineratos Σ, *corr. Manutius*   14 adortos Σ, *corr. ed. Iunt.*   17
interfectio *P* : interfecti *SM*   19 retractus *S*¹   romam *P* :
domum romam *S* : romam romam *M*   20 nihil deterritus *Madvig* :
milo deterius Σ : nihilo deterius *ed. Ald.*   21 singulos singula *KS*
23 ac Cicero ς : ac ci *P* : acci *S* : aci *M* : atque *Madvig*   egit
Madvig : etiam (et *M*) Σ : eius egit *Halm*   dicebat *Madvig*   25 qui
Σ, *corr. Beraldus*

of the plebs, came running. It was with their encouragement that the   33C
ignorant mob took the corpse, stripped and bruised, just as it had
been dumped on the bier, down into the Forum and placed it on the
rostra in order to exhibit the wounds. There before a *contio* Plancus
and Pompeius, who were partisans of Milo's electoral rivals, aroused
resentment against him. The populace, led by Sex. Cloelius the *scriba*,
took off the body of P. Clodius into the senate house and cremated it
on a pyre of benches, platforms, tables, and copyists' notebooks, and
in the conflagration the senate house itself caught fire and also the
adjoining Basilica Porcia was engulfed in flame. The houses also of
M. Lepidus the *interrex*—for he had been appointed a curule magistrate—and of Milo, who was not there, were attacked by the same
Clodian mob, but it was driven off with a barrage of arrows. Then the
mob seized bundles of *fasces* from the grove of Libitina and took
them to the homes of Scipio and Hypsaeus, then to the suburban
estate of Cn. Pompeius, yelling its acclamation of him by turns as
consul or dictator.

The destruction of the senate house by arson aroused somewhat
greater indignation in the community than the murder of Clodius.
And so Milo, who was thought to have gone off into voluntary exile,
was revived by the unpopularity of his opponents and had returned
to Rome on the night when the senate house was fired. And nothing
abashed he persisted in his candidature for the consulship: quite
openly he had made gifts around the tribes of 1000 *asses* per man.
Some days later M. Caelius, as tribune of the plebs, gave him the
opportunity to address a *contio*, and [Cicero?] himself pleaded his
case to the people. Both claimed that an ambush had been set for
Milo by Clodius.

Meantime there came a series of *interreges*, one after another,
because the consular elections,

34C

laria propter eosdem candidatorum tumultus et easdem
manus armatas haberi non poterant. Itaque primo factum
erat S. C. ut interrex et tribuni plebis et Cn. Pompeius,
qui pro cos. ad urbem erat, viderent ne quid detrimenti
5 res publica caperet, dilectus autem Pompeius tota Italia
haberet. Qui cum summa celeritate praesidium compa-
rasset, postulaverunt apud eum familiam Milonis; item
Faustae uxoris eius exhibendam duo adulescentuli qui
Appii Claudii ambo appellabantur; qui *filii* erant C.
10 Claudi, qui frater fuerat Clodi, et ob id illi patrui sui
mortem velut auctore patre persequebantur. Easdem
Faustae et Milonis familias postulaverunt duo Valerii,
Nepos et Leo. L. Herennius Balbus P. Clodi quoque
familiam et comitum eius postulavit; eodem tempore
15 Caelius familiam Hypsaei et Q. Pompeii postulavit. Adfuerunt Miloni Q. Hortensius, M. Cicero, M. Marcellus,
M. Calidius, M. Cato, Faustus Sulla. Verba pauca Q.
Hortensius dixit, liberos esse eos qui pro servis postu-
larentur; nam post recentem caedem manu miserat eos
20 Milo sub hoc titulo quod caput suum ulti essent. Haec
agebantur mense intercalari. Post diem tricesimum fere
quam erat Clodius occisus Q. Metellus Scipio in senatu
contra Q. Caepionem conquestus est de hac caede P. Clodi.
Falsum esse dixit, quod Milo sic se defenderet, sed
25 Clodium Aricinos decuriones alloquendi gratia abisse pro-
fectum cum sex ac xx servis; Milonem subito post horam

---

1 eosdem *Richter*: eorum Σ   eadem ... armata Σ, *corr.* ς, *ed. Iunt.*
2 habere *Poggius*   4 erant *SM*   9 filii *om.* Σ, *suppl. hoc loco*
KS, post Claudi *ed. Iunt.*   11 prosequebantur Σ, *corr. Beraldus*
12 ualerūtiae potes *S* : ualerii nepotes *PM, corr. Manutius*   13
L. *scripsi* : et L. Σ : *in sequentibus interpunctionem emendavi : vulgo*
semicolon post Caelius *ponitur (ita* Σ) *et lacuna ante* adfuerunt *sta-*
tuitur (contra Σ)   18 dixit *Beraldus* : dixitque Σ : fecit dixitque
KS   19 recentem *P* : tricentum *SM*   23 M. Caepionem Σ,
corr. Manutius cf. Phil. x. 26   de hac *SM* : hac de *P*   24 sed
scripsi : et Σ : *lac. statuit Halm*   25 uicinos Σ, *corr.* ς. *Manutius*
26 ex (et *M*) ac Σ. *corr. ed. Ven.*

due to these same bouts of violence on the part of the candidates and   34C
the same armed bands, could not be held. And so, for the first time, a
decree of the senate was passed that the *interrex*, the tribunes of the
plebs, and Cn. Pompeius, who as proconsul was close by the city,
should 'see to it that the state take no harm', and that Pompeius
should recruit troops all over Italy. He got together a protecting force
with the utmost speed, and then two young men both named Ap.
Claudius applied to him for the production of the slaves of Milo and
of his wife Fausta. These two were the sons of C. Claudius, who had
been Clodius' brother, and for that reason were bent on pressing the
matter of their uncle's death as if at the instigation of their father.
Production of the said households was also demanded by two Valerii,
Nepos and Leo. L. Herennius Balbus demanded the production of
Clodius' slaves also, and those of his companions; and at the same
time Caelius demanded that of the households of Hypsaeus and
Q. Pompeius. As advocates for Milo there presented themselves
Q. Hortensius, M. Cicero, M. Marcellus, M. Calidius, M. Cato, and
Faustus Sulla. Q. Hortensius said a few words to the effect that those
whose surrender was being demanded as slaves were in fact of free
status, for after the recent murder Milo had manumitted them on the
grounds that they had avenged an attempt on his life. All this was
going on in the intercalary month.

About thirty days after Clodius' killing, Q. Metellus Scipio in the
senate, speaking against Q. Caepio, entered a complaint about the
murder of P. Clodius. He said that Milo's defence on these lines was a
lie, but that Clodius had set out [from Rome] in order to address the
local councillors of Aricia with twenty-six slaves; whereas Milo,
suddenly, after

35C

quartam, senatu misso, cum servis amplius CCC armatis
obviam ei contendisse et supra Bovillas inopinantem *in*
itinere aggressum. Ibi P. Clodium tribus vulneribus
acceptis Bovillas perlatum; tabernam in quam perfugerat
5 expugnatam a Milone; semianimem Clodium extractum
. . . . in via Appia occisum esse anulumque eius ei
morienti extractum. Deinde Milonem, cum sciret in
Albano parvolum filium Clodi esse, venisse ad villam et,
cum puer ante subtractus esset, ex servo Halicore quaestio-
10 nem ita habuisse ut eum articulatim consecaret; vilicum
et duos praeterea servos iugulasse. Ex servis Clodi qui
dominum defenderant undecim esse interfectos, Milonis
duos solos saucios factos esse: ob quae Milonem postero
die XII servos qui maxime operam navassent manu misisse
15 populoque tributim singula milia aeris ad defendendos de
se rumores dedisse. Milo misisse ad Cn. Pompeium dicebatur qui Hypsaeo summe studebat, quod fuerat eius
quaestor, desistere se petitione consulatus, si ita ei videretur; Pompeius respondisse nemini se neque petendi neque
20 desistendi auctorem esse, neque populi Romani potestatem
aut consilio aut sententia interpellaturum. Deinde *per*
C. Lucilium, qui propter M. Ciceronis familiaritatem amicus
erat Miloni, egisse quoque dicebatur ne se de hac re consu-
lendo invidia oneraret.
25 Inter haec cum crebresceret rumor Cn. *Pompeium* creari
dictatorem oportere neque aliter mala civitatis sedari posse,

2 uobillas *SP* : bubillas *M* (*ita mox*)   in *add. Manutius*   3 ubi
S[1] 5 extractum . . . . (10 *litt. P*) Σ : *fort.* iussu Milonis *sup-*
plendum   6 eius] etiam *Eberhard*   8 paruulum *S*   esse,
uenisse *Baiter* : in uenisse *SM* : uenisse *P*   9 Halicore *SP* :
talicore *M* : Olipore *Mommsen* 10 consecarent Σ, *corr. Manu-*
tius 12 defenderint Σ, *corr. KS* milo (-os *M*[1]) Σ, *corr.*
π 14 nauassent *P* : nauantessent *S* : narrassent *M* (*in mg.* na-
nassent) 16 miloni (milo *M*) misse Σ, *corr. Poggins* 17 qui
Baiter : quod Σ fuerat eius] feraticus Σ 19 Pompeium Σ,
corr. KS 21 consilium aut sententiam Σ, *corr. Richter* 25 Pompeium *add. ed. Ven.*   26 neque oportere Σ, *corr. Madvig*

the fourth hour, after the senate had adjourned, had hastened to
confront him with more than three hundred slaves under arms, and
beyond Bovillae had attacked him unawares on his journey. There
Clodius, wounded three times, had been carried off to Bovillae, but
the tavern in which he had taken refuge had been stormed by Milo;
Clodius had been dragged out half-alive ... killed on the very Via
Appia, and his ring pulled off his finger as he expired. Then Milo,
when he found out that Clodius' little son was at his Alban estate, had
gone to the villa, and since the boy had been smuggled away before-
hand, had interrogated the slave Halicorus by torture, slicing him up
limb by limb, and had cut the throats of the estate-manager and two
slaves. Of Clodius' slaves who had defended their master, eleven had
been killed, but only two of Milo's had sustained wounds. On that
account Milo, next day, had manumitted the twelve slaves whose
services had been greatest, and had distributed 1000 *asses* a man to
the people by tribes, in order to allay rumours about himself. It was
being said that Milo sent word to Cn. Pompeius, who was a very
strong supporter of Hypsaeus (since he had been his quaestor), that
he was giving up his candidature for the consulship, if Pompeius
thought that he should; but that Pompeius had replied that he was
not the arbiter as to who should stand and who should desist from
electoral candidature, nor would he obstruct the prerogatives of the
Roman people by offering any advice or opinion. Then by agency of
C. Lucilius, who on account of his friendship with Cicero was on
good terms with Milo, he is said to have taken steps also to avoid
being burdened by the resentment that might accrue from his being
consulted on this issue.

Meantime amid ever more frequent suggestions that Cn.
Pompeius ought to be made dictator, and that there was no
other means of settling the ills of the state,

36C

visum est optimatibus tutius esse eum consulem sine collega
creari, et cum tractata ea res esset in senatu, facto in M.
Bibuli sententiam S. C. Pompeius ab interrege Servio
Sulpicio v Kal. Mart. mense intercalario consul creatus est
5 statimque consulatum iniit. Deinde post diem tertium de
legibus novis ferendis rettulit: duas ex S. C. promulgavit,
alteram de vi qua nominatim caedem in Appia via factam
et incendium curiae et domum M. Lepidi interregis oppu-
gnatam comprehendit, alteram de ambitu: poena graviore et
10 forma iudiciorum breviore. Vtraque enim lex prius testes
dari, deinde uno die atque eodem et ab accusatore et a
reo perorari iubebat, ita ut duae horae accusatori, tres reo
darentur. His legibus obsistere M. Caelius tr. pl. studio-
sissimus Milonis conatus est, quod et privilegium diceret
15 in Milonem ferri et iudicia praecipitari. Et cum pertinacius
leges Caelius vituperaret, eo processit irae Pompeius ut
diceret, si coactus esset, armis se rem publicam defensurum.
Timebat autem Pompeius Milonem seu timere se simula-
bat: plerumque non domi suae sed in hortis manebat,
20 idque ipsum in superioribus circa quos etiam magna
manus militum excubabat. Senatum quoque semel repente
dimiserat Pompeius, quod diceret timere se adventum
Milonis. Dein proximo senatu P. Cornificius ferrum Milonem intra tunicam habere ad femur alligatum dixerat;
25 postulaverat ut femur nudaret, et ille sine mora tunicam
levarat: tum M. Cicero exclamaverat omnia illi similia
crimina esse quae in Milonem dicerentur alia.

---

1 eum *P* : cum *S¹M* (*in mg. S* 'c^S eum') 2 tracta *S* 4 v] 11 *S*
7 appia uia *P* : appiam uiam *SM* 9 poenam grauiorem et formam
iudiciorum breuiorem Σ, *corr. Richter* 11 dare Σ, *corr. Manutius* ab
reo *P* 13 assistere *S* 14 privilegium] peruulgatum *S* 16 legem
Σ, *corr. KS* 17 armis se *PM* : se armis *S* 19 et plerumque
Baiter 20 idque ipse ipsum Σ, *corr.* ς, Lodoicus magnanimus
Σ, *corr. Manutius* 21 militum *M* : multum *SP* repetundus
erat Σ, *corr. Baiter* 23 deind *P* 25 uideret Σ, *corr. Manutius*
26 lauarat (-er- *M*) *S¹M* exclamarat *S* similia *P* : simili *SM* 27
quae in *P* : quē *SM* dicerentur (-etur *SM*). Alia Σ, *corr. Manutius*

the *optimates* thought it safest that he should be appointed consul   36C
without a colleague. When the matter was debated in the senate a
decree of the senate was passed on the motion of M.
Bibulus; and Pompeius during the intercalary month, on the fifth day before
1 March, was appointed consul by the *interrex* Ser. Sulpicius and
immediately entered that office. Next, after an interval of three days,
he consulted (the senate) on the passage of new laws. He promulgated two by senatorial decree, one concerning violence, which
explicitly took into account the murder committed on the Via
Appia, the destruction by fire of the senate house, and assault on
the home of M. Lepidus the *interrex*; the other concerning bribery,
both with a heavier penalty and a curtailed form of trial. For each law
prescribed first the production of witnesses, then on one and the
same day completion of the cases both for prosecution and defence,
with two hours granted for the accuser, three for the defendant.
M. Caelius attempted to block this legislation as tribune of the
plebs and a doughty supporter of Milo, in that he claimed that a
special law was being aimed against Milo specifically, and that judicial processes were being unduly rushed. And when Caelius became
too persistent in attacking the laws, Pompeius' fury reached the point
where he declared that, if compelled, he would defend the state by
force of arms.

Now Pompeius was afraid of Milo, or pretended to be: for the most
part he stayed not in his town house but on his suburban estate, and
on higher ground at that, round which was also stationed at night a
large detachment of soldiers. Pompeius also on one occasion had
suddenly dismissed the senate on the grounds (he said) that he feared
the arrival of Milo. Then at the next senate meeting P. Cornificius
alleged that Milo had a weapon strapped to his thigh under his tunic
and demanded that he bare his thigh—and he without hesitation
lifted his tunic: at which Cicero cried out that all the other charges
that were being alleged against Milo were no different from that one.

37C

Deinde *T.* Munatius Plancus tribunus plebis produxerat
in contionem M. Aemilium Philemonem, notum hominem,
libertum M. Lepidi. *Is* se dicebat pariterque secum
quattuor liberos homines iter facientes supervenisse cum
5 Clodius occideretur, et ob id cum proclamassent, abreptos
et perductos per duos menses in villa Milonis praeclusos
fuisse; eaque res seu vera seu falsa magnam invidiam
Miloni contraxerat. Idem quoque Munatius et Pompeius
tribuni plebis in rostra produxerant triumvirum capitalem,
10 eumque interrogaverant an Galatam Milonis servum caedes
facientem deprehendisset. Ille dormientem in taberna pro
fugitivo prehensum et ad se perductum esse responderat.
Denuntiaverant tamen triumviro, ne servum remitteret : sed
postera die Caelius tribunus plebis et Manilius Cumanus
15 collega eius ereptum e domo triumviri servum Miloni
reddiderant. Haec, etsi nullam de his criminibus mentionem
fecit Cicero, tamen, quia ita compereram, putavi exponenda.
Inter primos et Q. Pompeius et C. Sallustius et T. Munatius
Plancus tribuni plebis inimicissimas contiones de Milone
20 habebant, invidiosas etiam de Cicerone, quod Milonem
tanto studio defenderet. Eratque maxima pars multitudinis
infensa non solum Miloni sed etiam propter invisum patrocinium Ciceroni. Postea Pompeius et Sallustius in suspi-
cione fuerunt redisse in gratiam cum Milone ac Cicerone;
25 Plancus autem infestissime perstitit, atque in Ciceronem

---

1 *T. add. KS*   3 is *Manutius* : *om.* Σ : qui *Lodoicus*   secum]
secuta *S*   4 insperuenisse Σ, *corr. Manutius*   6 perductos
del. Manutius (*fort.* perductos in villam Milonis per *etc. sic fere Hoto-*
man)   uillam Σ, *corr. Halm*   perclusos *S*   8 conflaverat
Rinkes   idem quoque *scripsi* : idemque Σ : itemque *Halm*
numatius Σ, *corr. ed. Ven.*   9 perduxerant Σ, *corr. ed. Ven.*   com-
pitalem *P*   10 milonis *P* : miloni *SM*   14 caecilius Σ,
corr. Lodoicus   cumanus *S* : camanus *PM*   16 reddiderunt Σ, *corr. Sauppe*   etsi *Lodoicus* : et Σ   18 Salu-
stius Σ (*ita semper*)   20 inuidiam Σ, *corr. Manutius*   21
eratque *Manutius* : atque Σ   multitudinis *P*¹ : populi *add. SP*²*M*,
del. Manutius   22 inuisum *P* : irrisum *SM*   Ciceronis patrocinium Σ, *corr. Hotoman*

Then T. Munatius Plancus, tribune of the plebs, presented to a   37C
public meeting one M. Aemilius Philemon, a well-known person,
freedman of M. Lepidus. He claimed that he, and with him four free
men, while on a journey, had turned up when Clodius was being
killed, and on that account, when they had raised an outcry, they had
been kidnapped and taken off to two months' captivity in a villa of
Milo's—and this gambit, true or false, brought Milo a good deal of
hatred. The same Munatius and Pompeius, tribunes of the plebs, also
produced on the *rostra* one of the *tresviri capitales* and questioned
him as to whether he had arrested a Galatian slave of Milo's in the act
of committing murders. He replied that the man had been arrested as
a runaway while asleep in a tavern and brought before him. They put
the *triumvir* under injunction not to release the slave, but next day
Caelius, tribune of the plebs, and his colleague Manilius Cumanus
snatched the slave from the *triumvir*'s house and returned him to
Milo. Although Cicero made no mention of these charges, all the
same, since such were my findings, I thought I ought to set them out.

Q. Pompeius, C. Sallustius, and T. Munatius Plancus, tribunes of
the plebs, were among the first to hold *contiones* that were extremely
hostile towards Milo, and calculated also to arouse animosity against
Cicero for his strenuous efforts to defend Milo. And a large sector of
the mob felt strongly not only against Milo, but also, for the protection
of him that it so disliked, against Cicero too. Later there was some
suspicion that Pompeius and Sallustius had became reconciled with
Milo and Cicero, but Plancus persisted in his stance of extreme enmity,

quoque multitudinem instigavit. Pompeio autem suspectum
faciebat Milonem, ad perniciem eius comparari vim vocifera-
tus: Pompeiusque ob ea saepius querebatur sibi quoque
fieri insidias et id palam, ac maiore manu se armabat.
5 Dicturum quoque diem Ciceroni Plancus ostendebat postea,
ante Q. Pompeius idem meditatus erat. Tanta tamen constantia ac fides fuit Ciceronis ut non populi a se alienatione,
non Cn. Pompeii suspicionibus, non periculo futurum ut
sibi dies ad populum diceretur, non armis quae palam in
10 Milonem   sumpta   erant   deterreri   potuerit   a   defensione
eius: cum posset omne periculum suum et offensionem
inimicae multitudinis declinare, redimere autem Cn. Pompeii animum, si paulum ex studio defensionis remisisset.

Perlata deinde lege Pompei, in qua id quoque scriptum
15 erat ut quaesitor suffragio populi ex iis qui consules fuerant
crearetur, statim comitia habita, creatusque est L. Domitius
Ahenobarbus quaesitor. Album quoque iudicum qui de ea
re iudicarent Pompeius tale proposuit ut numquam neque
clariores viros neque sanctiores propositos esse constaret.
20 Post quod statim nova lege Milo postulatus *est* a duobus
Appiis Claudiis adulescentibus iisdem a quibus antea familia
eius fuerat postulata; itemque de ambitu ab iisdem Appiis,
et praeterea a C. Ateio et L. Cornificio; de sodaliciis etiam

---

1 Cn. Pompeio *Bücheler*   2 comparavit eum Σ, *corr. Manutius*
3 fieri sibi quoque *P*   5 dictorum *SP*¹, *corr. Poggius, M*   postea,
ante *scripsi* : postea autem Σ (*cf.* 7. 22, 59. 21): posteaquam *Mommsen*
6 minitatus *Manutius*   8 periculum Σ, *corr. Poggius*   ut sibi
ς : ut si Σ : si *ed. Ven.* : si sibi *Manutius*   9 diceret Σ, *corr.*
Beraldus   10–11 eius ... offensionem *om. M*   11 inimicae]
sibi *add. S*   14 Pompeia *KS*   15 quaestor Σ, *corr.* ς, *ed. Ald.*   16
crearetur *P* : creatur *SM*   habuit Σ, *corr. Cobet*   est *Rinkes* :
erat Σ   17 ahenobarbus (aen- *suprascr.* h) *P* : herobarbus (ero- *M*)
SM   album *Cobet* : aliorum Σ   18 tale *SP*¹, *Cobet* : tales *P²M*
20 est *add. Madvig*   21 clodiis Σ, *corr.* ς, *Halm*   idem *S*   22
itaque Σ, *corr. Manutius*   23 praeterea] de vi *add. Manutius*
a C. Ateio *scripsi* : a c. ceteio Σ (*ante* a c. *P habet* ab appio cei) : a
C. Cetego ς, *Jordan* : a Q. Patulcio *Hotoman* (*cf.* 54. 18)   etiam *KS* :
et Σ

and stirred up the mob against Cicero as well. Moreover, he   38C
roused Pompeius' suspicions of Milo, bawling out that a gang of
thugs was being recruited for his destruction, and Pompeius for these
reasons was all the more frequently complaining that he too was
being made a target for ambush—and that quite openly—and
equipped himself with larger escorts. Plancus was also declaring the
intention of prosecuting Cicero at a later date, a move contemplated
earlier by Q. Pompeius. Such, however, was the unshakeable loyalty
of Cicero that neither his alienation from the people, nor the suspicions of Cn. Pompeius, nor the danger that he would be prosecuted
before the people, nor the arms which had openly been taken up
against Milo, could deter him from undertaking Milo's defence—
although he could have evaded the threat to himself and provocation
of the people's hostility and averted Pompeius' anger, if he had
tempered his commitment to the defence just a little.

Next, a law of Pompeius was put through in which it was also laid
down that a *quaesitor* be appointed by vote of the people from those
of consular rank. An election was held on the spot and L. Domitius
Ahenobarbus was appointed *quaesitor*. Pompeius put forward a panel
of jurors to be judges in this affair and it was agreed that never had
persons of greater reputation or integrity been nominated. After that,
immediately under the new law Milo was indicted by the same two
young Appii Claudii who had earlier demanded the appearance of his
slaves; and another charge was laid *de ambitu* by the said Appii, and
besides them by C. Ateius and L. Cornificius; and there was another
de sodaliciis

39C

a P. Fulvio Nerato. Postulatus autem erat et de sodaliciis et de ambitu ea spe, *quod* primum iudicium de vi futurum apparebat, quo eum damnatum iri confidebant nec postea responsurum.

5   Divinatio de ambitu accusatorum facta est quaesitore A. Torquato, atque ambo quaesitores, Torquatus et Domitius, prid. Non. April. reum adesse iusserunt. Quo die Milo ad Domiti tribunal venit, ad Torquati amicos misit; ibi postulante pro eo M. Marcello obtinuit ne prius causam de am-

10 bitu diceret quam de vi iudicium esset perfectum. Apud Domitium autem quaesitorem maior Appius postulavit a Milone servos exhiberi numero IIII et L, et cum ille negaret eos qui nominabantur in sua potestate esse, Domitius ex sententia iudicum pronuntiavit ut ex servorum suorum

15 numero accusator quot vellet ederet. Citati deinde testes secundum legem quae, ut supra diximus, iubebat ut prius quam causa ageretur testes per triduum audirentur, dicta eorum iudices consignarent, quarta die adesse omnes iuberentur ac coram accusatore ac reo pilae in quibus nomina

20 iudicum inscripta essent aequarentur; dein rursus postera die sortitio iudicum fieret unius et LXXX: qui numerus cum sorte obtigisset, ipsi protinus sessum irent; tum ad dicendum accusator duas horas, reus tres haberet, resque eodem die illo iudicaretur; prius autem quam sententiae

20 ferrentur, quinos ex singulis ordinibus accusator, totidem reus reiceret, ita ut numerus iudicum relinqueretur qui sententias ferrent quinquaginta et unus.

   1   fuluione rato Σ, *corr. Poggius*   2   quod *add. Manutius*
3 quo] quod *Poggius*   iri *P* : in *SM*   5 quaestore Σ, *corr. ed.*
Ald. (*ita mox*)   8 tribunale Σ, *corr. ed. Ven.*   misi tibi *S*   10
erat Σ, *corr. Beraldus*   14 suorum *ς, Wagener* : eorum Σ   15
quot *P* : quod *SM*   tutati Σ, *corr. Poggins*   18 confirmarent Σ,
corr. Manutius   omnes] in diem posterum *add.* Σ. *del. Eberhard*   21
LXX Σ, *corr. ed. Iunt.*   22 attigisset Σ, *corr. Manutius*   ipsi
Poggius : is   ei Σ : ei *Beraldus*   23 resque *Richter* : reusque Σ
26 relinqueretur *P* : relinquerentur *SM*   27 quinquagesimus et Σ

laid by P. Fulvius Neratus. He was charged on *de sodaliciis* and *de* 39C
ambitu in the expectation that the trial *de vi* would take place first, in
which they were sure he would be found guilty, and so make no
answer to the later indictments.

A *divinatio* for the trial *de ambitu* took place under the *quaesitor*
A. Torquatus, and both *quaesitores*, Torquatus and Domitius, ordered
the defendant to attend on 4 April. On the day in question, Milo
turned up at Domitius' court and sent friends of his to that of
Torquatus; there on the plea presented for him by M. Marcellus, he
was granted leave not to plead his case *de ambitu* until the trial *de vi*
was over. Before the *quaesitor* Domitius, the elder Appius demanded
the appearance of slaves of Milo, fifty-four in number, and when he
declared that those named were no longer in his possession, Domitius on advice of the jurors gave a decision that the accuser should
cite as many from the list of the said slaves as he might wish.
Witnesses then were called in accordance with the law which, as I
said above, prescribed that witnesses should be heard over three days
before pleas were made, and the jury should put their seals on their
evidence; and that on the fourth day all parties should be ordered to
attend and in the presence of accuser and defendant tokens inscribed
with the names of the jury should be made of identical appearance,
and then as a next step on the following day the jurors should be
appointed by sortition to the number eighty-one, and when that
number had been reached by lot, they should at that point take their
seats. Then the accuser should have two hours to plead, the defendant three, and that the issue should be decided on that same day;
that before votes were cast, the accuser might reject five jurors from
each of the orders and the defendant the same number, so that the
number of jurors left to cast their votes should be fifty-one.

40C

Primo die datus erat in Milonem testis *C.* Causinius
Schola, qui se cum P. Clodio fuisse, cum is occisus esset,
dixit, atrocitatemque rei factae quam maxime potuit auxit.
Quem cum interrogare M. Marcellus coepisset, tanto
5 tumultu Clodianae multitudinis circumstantis exterritus est
ut vim ultimam timens in tribunal a Domitio reciperetur.
Quam ob causam Marcellus et ipse Milo a Domitio praesidium imploraverunt. Sedebat eo tempore Cn. Pompeius
ad aerarium, perturbatusque erat eodem illo clamore: itaque
10 Domitio promisit se postero die cum praesidio descensurum,
idque fecit. Qua re territi Clodiani silentio verba testium
per biduum audiri passi sunt. Interrogaverunt eos M. Cicero
et M. Marcellus *et* Milo ipse. Multi ex iis qui Bovillis
habitabant testimonium dixerunt de eis quae ibi facta erant:
15 coponem occisum, tabernam expugnatam, corpus Clodi in
publicum extractum esse. Virgines quoque Albanae dixerunt
mulierem ignotam venisse ad se quae Milonis mandato vo-
tum solveret, quod Clodius occisus esset. Vltimae testimonium dixerunt Sempronia, Tuditani filia, socrus P. Clodi, et
20 uxor Fulvia, et fletu suo magnopere eos qui assistebant
commoverunt. Dimisso circa horam decimam iudicio T.
Munatius pro contione populum adhortatus est ut postero
die frequens adesset et elabi Milonem non pateretur, iudi-
ciumque et dolorem suum ostenderet euntibus ad tabellam
25 ferendam. Postero die, qui fuit iudicii summus a. d. VII

1 *C. add. KS*   Casinius Σ, *corr. Halm*   4 M. *PM, om. S* :
sequitur in SM 10 *litt. lac.*   coepisset *S* : cepisset *PM*   6
tribunal *P* : tribunale *SM*   recipitur *S*   7 M. caelius (cecilius
M) Σ, *corr. ed. Ald.*   13 et *add. ed. Ald.*   ipse multis Σ, *corr.
ed. Iunt.*   bouillis *P* : bobillis *S* : uobillis *M*   14 iis quae ibi *P* :
eis ubi *S* : his ibi que *M*   15 eoponem Σ, *corr. Sozomenus*   16
Albanae *Orelli* : alie (-ae *P*) Σ   20 et *om. S*   assistebant *SM* :
astabant *P*   21 demisso Σ, *corr. ed. Iunt.*   iudicio T.] iudicia-
tutus *S*   23 adesse te te labi *S*   25 qui fuit iudicissimus *SP*
(iudicibus. iudici. primus *Poggius scripsit in mg. P*) : iudicibus iudicii
primus qui fuit *M* : *corr. Rau*   ad Σ, *corr. Graevius*   VII *scripsi* :
III *PM* : II *S* : VI *Manutius*

On the first day there was produced as witness against Milo C.   40C
Causinius Schola, who stated that he had been with Clodius when he
was killed and exaggerated the savagery of the deed as much as he
could. M. Marcellus, when he began to cross-examine him, was so
terrified by the enormous tumult of the Clodian mob which surrounded the proceedings that in fear of extreme violence he was
given refuge on the *tribunal* of Domitius. For this reason Marcellus
and Milo himself begged Domitius for armed protection. At that
juncture Cn. Pompeius was in session at the *aerarium*, and was
disturbed by that same uproar; and so he promised Domitius that
on the next day he would come down with an armed guard, and did
so. At this, the Clodians were intimidated and allowed the evidence
of the witnesses to be heard over the (next) two days. They were
cross-examined by M. Cicero, M. Marcellus, and by Milo himself.
Many of those who lived at Bovillae bore testimony on what happened there—the innkeeper killed, the inn taken by storm, Clodius'
body dragged into the open. The Virgins of Alba also alleged that an
anonymous woman had come to them to discharge a vow at Milo's
bidding, for the killing of Clodius. The last to give evidence were
Sempronia, daughter of Tuditanus and mother-in-law of P. Clodius,
and his wife Fulvia, who greatly moved those present with their
weeping.

When the court was adjourned around the tenth hour T. Munatius
in a *contio* urged the people to attend next day in large numbers and
not allow Milo to escape, but to make clear their own view of the
matter and their own feelings of outrage as the jurors went to cast
their votes. On the next day, which was the last of the trial,

41C

Idus Aprilis, clausae fuerunt tota urbe tabernae; praesidia
in foro et circa omnis fori *aditus* Pompeius disposuit; ipse
pro aerario, ut pridie, consedit saeptus delecta manu militum.
Sortitio deinde iudicum a prima die facta est : post tantum
5 silentium toto foro fuit quantum esse in aliquo foro posset.
Tum intra horam secundam accusatores coeperunt dicere
Appius maior et M. Antonius et P. Valerius Nepos. Vsi
sunt ex lege horis duabus.

Respondit his unus M. Cicero : et cum quibusdam pla-
10 cuisset ita defendi crimen, interfici Clodium pro re publica
fuisse—quam formam M. Brutus secutus est in ea oratione
quam pro Milone composuit et edidit quasi egisset—Ciceroni id non placuit *ut*, quisquis bono publico damnari, idem
etiam occidi indemnatus posset. Itaque cum insidias Milo-
15 nem Clodio fecisse posuissent accusatores, quia falsum
id erat—nam forte illa rixa commissa fuerat—Cicero ap-
prehendit et contra Clodium Miloni fecisse insidias dispu-
tavit, eoque tota oratio eius spectavit. Sed ita constitit ut
diximus, nec utrius consilio pugnatum esse eo die, verum
20 et forte occurrisse et ex rixa servorum ad eam denique
caedem perventum. Notum tamen erat utrumque mortem
alteri saepe minatum esse, et sicut suspectum Milonem
maior quam Clodi familia faciebat, ita expeditior et paratior
ad pugnam Clodianorum quam Milonis fuerat. Cicero
25 cum inciperet dicere, exceptus *est* acclamatione Clodianorum, qui se continere ne metu quidem circumstantium

---

2 aditus *om. SP¹, suppl. Poggius, M*   4 prima *SM* : primo *P*
6 cum *S*   ceperunt Σ, *corr. ed. Ven.*   9 hic Σ, *corr. ed. Ald.*
12 quasi *Baiter* : quamuis Σ : quamuis non ς   13 ut quisquis
scripsi : quisquis *SP¹* : quod quis *Poggius, M* : quod qui *Manutius* :
quasi qui *KS*   14 occidit indemnans *SP¹, corr. Poggius, M*   18
eaque *M*   constituit Σ, *corr. ed. Ald.*   19 uerum ei Σ,
corr. Lachmann   20 et ex *Lachmann* : ex ea Σ   ad eam denique
scripsi : ad eandem Σ : ad eam *ed. Ald.* : tandem ad *Baiter* : ad
Jacobs   22 minatum *P* : minutum *S* : inmutū *M*   25 est
add. ed. Ald.   acclamatione *P* : a clamatione *SM*

on 8 April, shops were closed all over the city; Pompeius   41C
deployed armed guards in the Forum and round all the approaches
to it; he himself took his seat, as on the previous day, before the
Treasury, fenced in by a picked unit of troops. Then the sortition of
jurymen named on the first day took place. After that there was as
great a silence in the Forum as there could possibly be in any forum.
Then, before the second hour was past, the prosecution began to
plead—the elder Appius, M. Antonius, and P. Valerius Nepos. They
took up, as the law allowed, their two hours.

Cicero alone made reply to them, and whereas certain persons had
wanted to defend the case on the grounds that Clodius' murder was
in the public interest—the line which M. Brutus took in the speech
which he composed for Milo and published as if he had pleaded the
case—Cicero decided against this, on the grounds that (this implied
that) any person whose condemnation could benefit the state could
also be killed without being convicted. And so, when the accusers
propounded the view that Milo had set an ambush for Clodius, since
this was a lie—for the brawl had broken out by chance—Cicero
seized on the point and entered the counter-plea that Clodius had
set an ambush for Milo, and his whole speech focused on that issue.
But in fact, as I said, on that day the battle was unpremeditated by
either party, but they met by chance and from a squabble among the
slaves it finally ended in murder. It was, however, well known that
both had often threatened the other with death, and while the
superior numbers of Milo's entourage over that of Clodius suggested
Milo's guilt, on the other hand the band of Clodians had been
stripped for action and better equipped for a battle. When Cicero
began to speak, he was greeted by barracking from the Clodians, who
could not contain themselves despite their fear of the surrounding

42C

militum potuerunt. Itaque non ea qua solitus erat constantia dixit. Manet autem illa quoque excepta eius oratio:
scripsit vero hanc quam legimus ita perfecte ut iure prima
haberi possit.

5   # ENARRATIO

VERS. A PRIMO L

(§ 3.) Vnum genus est adversum infestumque
nobis et cetera.
    Ita ut in causae expositione diximus, Munatius Plancus
10 pridie pro contione populum adhortatus erat ne pateretur
elabi Milonem.

VER. A PRIMO CC

(§ 12.) Declarant huius ambusti tribuni plebis
illae intermortuae contiones quibus cotidie meam
15 potentiam invidiose criminabatur.
    T. Munatius Plancus et Q. Pompeius Rufus tribuni pl.,
de quibus *in* argumento huius orationis diximus, cum contra
Milonem Scipioni et Hypsaeo studerent, contionati sunt eo
ipso tempore plebemque in Milonem accenderunt quo
20 propter Clodi corpus curia incensa est, nec prius destiterunt
quam flamma eius incendii fugati sunt e contione. Erant
enim tunc rostra non eo loco quo nunc sunt sed ad
comitium, prope iuncta curiae. Ob hoc T. Munatium
ambustum tribunum appellat; fuit autem paratus
25 ad dicendum.

PAVLO POST

(§ 13.) Cur igitur incendium curiae, oppugna-

9 causae *Madvig* : ea Σ   17 in *add. Manutius*   19 accen-
derent *S*   quod Σ, *corr. Manutius*   20 esset Σ, *corr. Manutius*
destiterunt *P* : desisterunt *SM*

soldiery. And so Cicero spoke with less than his usual steadiness. 42C
What he actually said was taken down and also survives, but the
speech that we are reading is what he composed in writing, and with
such consummate skill that it may rightly be reckoned his finest.

Commentary

Line 50 from the beginning
Mil. 3: *One sort is opposed and hostile to us (etc.).* As we have said in
explaining the facts of the case, Munatius Plancus on the previous
day in a *contio* had urged that Milo should not be allowed to escape.

Line 200 from the beginning
Mil. 12: *It is made quite clear by those half-dead public addresses of this
well-singed tribune of the plebs, in which daily he sought to whip up
resentment by inveighing against my undue political power.* T. Munatius Plancus and Q. Pompeius Rufus, tribunes of the plebs, of whom
we have spoken in the explanatory preface to this oration, as partisans of Scipio and Hypsaeus against Milo, addressed a *contio* and
incensed the plebs against Milo at that very time when in dealing
with Clodius' corpse the senate house was set on fire, and did not
desist until they were driven from the *contio* by flames of the conflagration. For the *rostra* were at that time not sited where they now
are, but by the *comitium*, all but conjoined with the senate house. For
this reason he calls T. Munatius a 'well-singed tribune'. Well, he was
not lost for words.

A little further on
Mil. 13: *Why then did the senate decide that the firing of the senate
house, the siege*

43C tionem aedium M. Lepidi, caedem hanc ipsam
contra rem publicam senatus factam esse decrevit?
    Post biduum medium quam Clodius occisus erat inter-
rex primus proditus est M. Aemilius Lepidus. Non fuit
5 autem moris ab eo qui primus interrex proditus erat comitia haberi. Sed Scipionis et Hypsaei factiones, quia
recens invidia Milonis erat, cum contra ius postularent ut
interrex ad comitia consulum creandorum descenderet,
idque ipse non faceret, domum eius per omnes interregni
10 dies—fuerunt autem ex more quinque—obsederunt. Deinde
omni vi ianua expugnata et imagines maiorum deiecerunt
et lectulum adversum uxoris eius Corneliae, cuius castitas
pro exemplo habita est, fregerunt, itemque telas quae ex
vetere more in atrio texebantur diruerunt. Post quae
15 supervenit Milonis manus et ipsa postulans comitia; cuius
adventus fuit saluti Lepido: in se enim ipsae conversae
sunt factiones inimicae, atque ita oppugnatio domus interregis omissa est.

PAVLO POST

20 (§ 14.) Quod si per furiosum illum tribunum pl.
senatui quod sentiebat perficere licuisset, novam
quaestionem   nullam   haberemus. Decernebat
enim ut veteribus legibus, tantum modo extra ordinem, quaereretur. Divisa sententia est postu-
25 lante nescio quo.—Sic reliqua auctoritas senatus
empta intercessione sublata est.
    Quid sit dividere sententiam ut enarrandum sit
vestra aetas, filii, facit.
    Cum aliquis in dicenda sententia duas pluresve res com-

---

1 aedem hanc *S*   6 factionis Σ, *corr. ς, Lodoicus*   9 et domum
Σ, *corr. ς, ed. Ald.*   10 fuerant *P* : fuerat *SM, corr. KS*   obside-
runt Σ, *corr. ed. Iunt.*   13 itemque *Manutius* : uterque Σ   14
texebantur *P* : textebantur *SM*   quae *Rinkes* : que *PM* : *om.   S*
15   superuenenum *S*[1] : supervenerunt *Sozomenus*   ipse *P*[1]   28

facit *Poggius* : faciat (i͡tP[1]) Σ

of M. Lepidus' house, and this very slaughter, were contrary to the   43C
public interest?

Two and a half days after Clodius was killed, M. Lepidus was
named as the first *interrex*. Now it was not customary for elections
to be held by the man who was first produced as *interrex*. But the
factions of Scipio and Hypsaeus, because hostility towards Milo was
still fresh, demanded contrary to law that the *interrex* should come
down to the *comitia* with a view to appointing consuls, and when he
would not do so, laid siege to his home on each and every day of his
interregnum—which numbered the customary five. Then they broke
through the gateway with all manner of violence and pulled down his
ancestral portraits, broke up the symbolic marital couch of his wife
Cornelia, a woman whose chastity was considered an example to all,
and also vandalized the weaving-operations which in accord with
ancient custom were in progress in the entrance-hall. After that,
Milo's gang, itself also demanding an election, came on the scene.
Its arrival was Lepidus' salvation, since the hostile factions turned on
each other, and in this way the assault on the house of the *interrex*
was abandoned.

A little further on

Mil. 14 : *But if the senate had been allowed by that power-crazed tribune
to put its opinions into effect, we should have no new form of inquisition. For it favoured a decree that the inquiry should proceed in
accordance with existing laws, albeit outside normal procedure. On
the demand of someone or other the proposal was divided up. Thus
the rest of the senate's draft decree was subverted by means of a
corruptly suborned veto.* You are young enough, my sons, to need
some comment on what it is to 'divide up a proposal'.

When a man in making a proposal encompasses two or more
points,

44C   plectitur, si non omnes eae probantur, postulatur ut di-
vidatur, id est de rebus singulis referatur. Forsitan nunc
hoc quoque velitis scire qui fuerit qui id postulaverit.
Quod non fere adicitur: non enim ei qui hoc postulat
5 oratione longa utendum ac ne consurgendum quidem utique est; multi enim sedentes hoc unum verbum pronun-
tiant Divide: quod cum auditum est, liberum *est* ei qui
facit relationem dividere. Sed ego, ut curiosius aetati
vestrae satisfaciam, Acta etiam totius illius temporis perse-
10 cutus sum; in quibus cognovi pridie Kal. Mart. S. C. esse
factum, P. Clodi caedem et incendium curiae et oppugna-
tionem aedium M. Lepidi contra rem p. factam; ultra
relatum *in* Actis illo die nihil; postero die, id est Kal.
Mart., *T.* Munatium in contione exposuisse populo quae
15 pridie acta erant in senatu: in qua contione haec dixit
ad verbum. Cum Hortensius dixisset ut extra ordinem quaereretur apud quaesitorem; existimaret
futurum ut, cum pusillum dedisset dulcedinis, largiter acerbitatis devorarent: adversus hominem
20 ingeniosum nostro ingenio usi sumus; invenimus
Fufium, qui diceret 'Divide'; reliquae parti sen-

---

1 si *scripsi* : et si Σ : si cui *KS*   eae (-ę) *SP* : ē̃e *M* (eae si non
omnes probantur *Manutius* : et si non omnes aeque probantur *Baiter*)
postulat Σ, *corr. Manutius*   diuidantur Σ, *corr. Baiter*   3 hoc
om. *P*[1]   qui id *KS* : quid *S* : qui *PM*   4 fere adicitur *scripsi* :
ferat adiutor Σ : fere traditur *Madvig* (*cf.* 58.6, 77.12) non eme (-e' *P*)
qui *SP* : noñe me qui *M, corr. Baiter*   5 consulendum quidem
Σ, *corr. Manutius*   7 divide *Manutius* : denique Σ   est *add.*
Orelli   8 rationem *SM* : orationem *P, corr. Becker*   curiositati
vestrae *Bücheler*   9 prosecutus *P*   10 S. C. *Manutius* : sic
Σ   13 in *om.* *SP*[1], *suppl. Poggius, M*   14 T. *add. KS*   16
cum *KS* : q̄ *S* : que *P*[1]*M* : Q. *Poggius* : quod Q. *Baiter*   Horten-
sium dixisse Σ, *corr. Baiter*   ut *om.* *P*[1]   17 quaestorem Σ, *corr.*
Manutius   existimaret *scripsi* : estimare (ext- *M*) Σ : aestimare *ed.*
Iunt.   18 utrum Σ, *corr. Poggius*   dedisset *PM* : dixisset *S* :
edissent *Mommsen*   largiter *S* : largitur *PM*   19 deuoraret Σ, *corr.*
Rinkes   20 nostro *Bücheler* : non   Σ : *del. Mommsen*   21
fusium Σ, *corr. Manutius* (*ita mox*)   diuideret Σ, *corr. Baiter*   partis
                                                                         ri
P : paries *S* : partes *M, corr. Manutius*   sententiam Σ, *corr. Baiter*

if they do not all meet with approval, the demand is made that it   44C
should be divided up—that is, that the vote should be taken one
point at a time. Perhaps at this juncture you would like to know who
it was who made this demand. This is not generally added to the
record, since the man who makes the demand does not need to
employ a long oration, nor even for that matter get to his feet.
Many indeed while seated utter this single word 'Divide!', and
when this is heard, it is open to the man putting the question to
divide it up. But to spend a little more trouble over meeting your
youthful needs, I have looked up the *Acta* for the whole of this
period. In them I have discovered that on the day preceding
1 March, a senatorial decree was passed that the murder of P. Clodius,
the firing of the senate house, and the siege of the home of
M. Lepidus had been acts contrary to the public interest. Nothing
else was entered that day in the *Acta*. On the next day—that is, 1
March—it is recorded that T. Munatius in a *contio* explained to the
people what had been transacted on the previous day in the senate. In
that *contio* he spoke as follows—his actual words: *When Hortensius
had spoken in favour of a special inquiry before a* quaesitor, *and was
calculating that in the outcome, after he had offered them a spoonful of
honey they would swallow any amount of bitter medicine, to combat
this crafty fellow we resorted to our own craftiness. We found a Fufius to
say 'Divide!', and*

45C tentiae ego et Sallustius intercessimus. Haec
contio, ut puto, explicat et quid senatus decernere volu-
erit, et quis divisionem postulaverit, et quis intercesserit
et cur. Illud vos meminisse non dubito per Q. Fufium
5 illo quoque tempore quo de incesto P. Clodi actum est
factum ne a senatu asperius decerneretur.

De L. Domitio dicit:

(§ 22.) Dederas enim quam contemneres populares insanias iam ab adulescentia documenta
10 maxima.

Constantiam L. Domiti quam in quaestura praestitit
significat. Nam eo tempore cum C. Manilius tribunus
plebis subnixus libertinorum et servorum manu perdi-
tissimam legem ferret ut libertinis in omnibus tribubus
15 suffragium esset, idque per tumultum ageret et clivum
Capitolinum obsideret, discusserat perruperatque coetum
Domitius ita ut multi Manilianorum occiderentur. Quo
facto et plebem infimam offenderat et senatus magnam
gratiam inierat.

20 (§ 32.) Itaque illud Cassianum indicium in his
personis valeat.

L. Cassius fuit, sicut iam saepe diximus, summae vir
severitatis. *Is* quotiens quaesitor iudicii alicuius esset in
quo quaerebatur de homine occiso suadebat atque etiam
25 praeibat iudicibus hoc quod Cicero nunc admonet, ut quaereretur cui bono fuisset perire eum de cuius morte quaeritur.
Ob quam severitatem, quo tempore Sex. Peducaeus tribunus
plebis criminatus est L. Metellum pontificem max. totum-

---

7 *om. M*   11 CN. (GN. *M*) domiti (-ii *M*) *PM* : GN. pompeii *S*,
corr. Manutius   praetura Σ, *corr. Manutius*   12 C. malius *S* :
CN. mallius *M* : CN. manlius (manilius *ς*) *P, corr. Manutius*   tribus
Σ, *corr. ed. Iunt.*   16 capitolinum *P* : capitolium *SM*   prŭper̄
atque *S*   17 manlianorum *P*   occiderentur *SM* : interfice-
rentur *P*   18 infirmam ostenderat Σ, *corr. Lodoicus*   19
ingerat *S*   20 indicium *Purser* : iudicium Σ : cui bono fuerit
Cic.   22 C. T. crassus *S*   23 is *add. KS*   quaesitor *P* :
quaestor *SM*   24 quaerereretur *P*   25 quaerebatur *Baiter*

Sallustius and I vetoed the remaining portion of the proposal. This   45C
contio, I imagine, explains both what the senate wanted to decree,
who demanded the division of the draft, who entered the veto and
why. I do not doubt that you remember that it was by agency of
Q. Fufius that it was contrived that no particularly harsh decree was
voted by the senate at that time also when business was transacted
over P. Clodius' sexual violation of religion. On L. Domitius he
says—*For you had given the most convincing proofs of how much you
despised populist lunacies.* He is referring to the steadfastness of
L. Domitius which he exhibited in his quaestorship. For at the time
when C. Manilius as tribune of the plebs, supported by a gang of
freedmen and slaves, was passing an utterly immoral law to allow
freedmen the vote in all of the tribes, and was pursuing this aim with
rioting and was blockading the climb to the Capitol, Domitius
scattered and broke through the gathering so violently that many of
Manilius' men were killed. By this act he both gave offence to the
lower ranks of the plebs and acquired great goodwill in the senate.

Mil. 32: *And so let the 'Cassian test' hold good in the case of these
persons*—L. Cassius was, as we have already often said, a man of the
utmost severity. He, whenever he was the *quaesitor* in any trial in
which the object of the inquiry was a murder, used to press
upon the jury, and also take them through the point which
Cicero now raises—that it should be asked 'To whose advantage?'
was it for the man to perish whose death was being investigated.
On account of this severity, at the time when Sex. Peducaeus,
tribune of the plebs, attacked L. Metellus, the *pontifex maximus,*

46C

que collegium pontificum male iudicasse de incesto vir-
ginum Vestalium, quod unam modo Aemiliam damnaverat,
absolverat autem duas Marciam et Liciniam, populus hunc
Cassium creavit qui de eisdem virginibus quaereret. Isque
5 et utrasque eas et praeterea complures alias nimia etiam, ut
existimatio est, asperitate usus damnavit.

(§ 33.) Et aspexit me illis quidem oculis quibus
tunc solebat cum omnibus omnia minabatur.
Movet me quippe lumen curiae!

10 Hic est Sex. Clodius quem in argumento huius orationis
diximus corpus Clodi in curiam intulisse et ibi cremasse
eoque incenso curiam conflagrasse; ideo lumen curiae dicit.

(§ 37.) Quando illius postea sica illa quam a
Catilina acceperat conquievit? Haec intenta
15 nobis est, huic ego obici vos pro me passus non
sum, haec insidiata Pompeio est.

Haec intenta nobis est et obici vos pro me non
sum passus, manifestum est pertinere ad id tempus quo
post rogationem a P. Clodio in eum promulgatam urbe
20 cessit. Qua re dicat insidiata Pompeio est fortassis
quaeratis. Pisone et Gabinio coss. pulso Cicerone in
exsilium, cum III Idus Sextiles Pompeius in senatum venit,
dicitur servo P. Clodi sica excidisse, eaque ad Gabinium
consulem delata dictum est servo imperatum a P. Clodio
25 ut Pompeius occideretur. Pompeius statim domum rediit
et ex eo domi *se* tenuit. Obsessus est etiam a liberto

---

3 martiam Σ, *corr. Manutius*   liciniam *P* : licinniam (luc- *S*) *SM*
4 isque et *P* : et isque et *SM*   6 extimatio *P*   10 hoc est Σ,
corr. ed. Iunt.   11 attulisse Σ, *corr. KS* (*in Addendis*)   13
sic (si *M*) ulla qua matilina *SM*   14 intenta Σ, *Cic. codd.* Σ*H* :
intentata *cett. codd. Cic., ed. Iunt.*   15 huic *P, Cic.* : huius *SM*
non sum passus *Cic.*   16 hec *S* : hcc *M* : heọc *P*   insidiata *P* :
insidiato *S* : insidia *M*   17 hace *PM* : quod dicit *S*   intenta
SM : intentata *P*   obici vos *P* : obicimus *SM*   19 apud clodium
*SP*¹ : P. clodio *M, corr.* π   20 est *ed. Ald.* : et Σ   23
sica *P* : ita *SM*   24 delata] . . . . *S*   25 rediit ex eodem
tenuis Σ : rediit ex eo domi tenus *Poggius, corr. Rinkes*

and the whole College of Pontiffs, for reaching a false verdict in the
case concerning the sexual violation of religion by the Vestal Virgins,
because he had convicted only one, Aemilia, but acquitted two,
Marcia and Licinia, the people appointed Cassius to conduct a
quaestio regarding the said Virgins. And he, resorting to excessive
harshness, as the general opinion has it, convicted both of them and
several others in addition.

Mil. 33: *And he has looked at me with that very expression in his eyes
with which he used to make all his threats to everyone. How stirred I am
by this luminary of the senate house!* This man is Sex. Cloelius, who, as
we said in the explanatory preface to this speech, took the corpse of
Clodius into the senate house, cremated it there, and on getting it
alight burned down the senate house. That is why he calls him
'luminary of the senate house'.

Mil. 37: *At what time since then has that dagger of his that he inherited
from Catilina ever been at rest? This was the one levelled at me, the one
which I did not let you face on my behalf, the one which lay in wait for
Pompeius.* The words *This was the one levelled at me, the one which I did
not let you face on my behalf* plainly refer to that time when, after a bill
was promulgated against him by P. Clodius, he left the city. Perhaps you
might ask why he says *lay in wait for Pompeius.* In the consulship of Piso
and Gabinius, with Cicero driven into exile, when Pompeius entered
the senate on 13 July, it is said that a dagger was let fall by a slave of
P. Clodius, and when it was taken to Gabinius the consul, it was alleged
that orders had been given to the slave by P. Clodius that Pompeius
should be killed. Pompeius instantly returned home and thereafter
kept himself indoors. He was laid under siege by Clodius' freedman

47C Clodi Damione, ut ex Actis eius *anni* cognovi, in quibus
xv Kal. Sept. L. Novius tribunus plebis, collega Clodi, cum
Damio adversum *L.* Flavium praetorem appellaret tribunos
et tribuni de appellatione cognoscerent, ita sententiam dixit:
5 Et *si ab* hoc apparitore P. Clodi vulneratus sum,
et hominibus armatis praesidiis dispositis a re
publica remotus Cn. Pompeius obsessus*que* est,
cum appeller, non utar eius exemplo quem vitupero
et iudicium tollam, et reliqua de intercessione.
10   Haec viam Appiam monumentum nominis sui
nece Papiri cruentavit.

Pompeius post triumphum Mithridaticum Tigranis filium
in catenis deposuerat apud Flavium senatorem: qui postea
cum esset praetor eodem anno quo tribunus plebis Clodius,
15 petiit ab eo Clodius super cenam ut Tigranem adduci iuberet ut eum videret. Adductum collocavit in convivio, dein
Flavio non reddidit Tigranem; domum misit et habuit
extra catenas nec repetenti Pompeio reddidit. Postea in
navem deposuit, et cum profugeret ille, tempestate delatus
20 est Antium. Inde ut deduceretur ad se, Clodius Sex.
Clodium, de quo supra diximus, *misit.* Qui cum reduceret,
Flavius quoque re cognita ad eripiendum Tigranem profectus
est. Ad quartum lapidem ab urbe pugna facta est in qua
multi ex utraque parte ceciderunt, plures tamen ex Flavi,
25 inter quos et M. Papirius eques Romanus, publicanus, familiaris Pompeio. Flavius sine comite Romam vix perfugit.

---

1 anni *add.* Baiter : temporis *add. Manutius*   3 L. *add.*
KS   appellarent (-lauerunt S¹) Σ, *corr. ed. Iunt.*   5 etsi ab
KS : et Σ : ab *Pighius*   clodii P¹ : clodio SP²M   7
remotus … obsessusque KS : remotus sum … obsessus Σ   12
mithridaticum cum Σ, *corr. Poggius*   13 disposuerat Σ, *corr. ed.*
Ald.   L. Flavium KS (*in Addendis*)   imperatorem S   15
petit Σ. *corr.* ς   canam (caña S) Σ, *corr. Poggius*   16 conuiuium
Σ, *corr. Madvig*   17 flauio P : flauium SM   reddidit P¹ : reddit
SP²M   domum misit et *scripsi*: dimisit et Σ : domi suae *Bücheler*   18
repetente (repente S) Σ, *corr. ed. Ald.*   20 Antium *Hotoman*: tantum
Σ   inde *Baiter*: ille Σ   21 misit *add. Hotoman*   cum *Bücheler*:
cum Σ   22 diripiendum Σ, *corr. Bücheler*   25 et] etiam *coni.* KS

Damio, as I have learned from the *Acta* of that year, in which on
17 August L. Novius, tribune of the plebs, colleague of Clodius, when
Damio appealed to the tribunes against the praetor L. Flavius and the
tribunes were taking cognizance of the Appeal, expressed his view
thus: *And if I was wounded by this footman of Clodius, and Cn.
Pompeius, by means of armed men and the deployment of guard-
posts, has been taken out of political life and laid under siege, when
appeal is made to me, I shall not resort to following the example of the
fellow whom I am reviling and wreck the court* . . . and the rest of his
speech on the veto.

*This (dagger) stained with blood the Appian Way, monument to his
own name, with the murder of Papirius.* Pompeius after his Mithridatic triumph had deposited the younger Tigranes in chains in the
custody of Flavius, a senator. Later, when Flavius was praetor in the
same year as Clodius was tribune of the plebs, Clodius asked him at
dinner to order Tigranes to be brought in, so that he might see him.
When he was brought in he gave him a place in the banquet, and then
failed to hand back Tigranes to Flavius. He sent him to his own home
and kept him there without chains, and failed to surrender him to
Pompeius when he asked for his return. Later he put him on board a
ship, and Tigranes while making his escape was carried by a storm to
Antium. To ensure that he would be escorted to himself, Clodius sent
there Sex. Cloelius, of whom we have spoken above. While he was
bringing him back, Flavius too, on getting wind of the affair, went
out with a view to snatching Tigranes from him. At the fourth
milestone from the city a fight took place in which many on either
side fell, but more on that of Flavius, among them M. Papirius, a
Roman knight, tax-contractor and associate of Pompeius. Flavius,
without escort, barely got away to Rome.

48C

Haec eadem longo intervallo conversa rursus
est in me : nuper quidem, ut scitis, *me* ad Regiam
paene confecit.

Quo die periculum hoc adierit, ut Clodius eum ad Re-
5 giam paene confecerit, nusquam inveni; non tamen adducor
ut putem Ciceronem mentitum, praesertim cum adiciat ut
scitis. Sed videtur mihi loqui de eo die quo consulibus
Domitio et Messala qui praecesserant eum annum cum
haec oratio dicta est inter candidatorum Hypsaei et Milonis
10 manus in via Sacra pugnatum est, multique ex Milonianis
ex improviso ceciderunt. De cuius diei periculo suo ut
putem loqui eum facit et locus pugnae—nam in Sacra via
traditur commissa, in qua est Regia—et quod adsidue simul
erant cum candidatis suffragatores, Milonis Cicero, Hypsaei
15 Clodius.

(§ 38.) Potuitne L. Caecili, iustissimi fortissimi-
que praetoris, obpugnata domo?

L. Caecilius Rufus de quo dicitur fuit *praetor* P. Lentulo
Spinthere Q. Metello Nepote coss., quo anno Cicero resti-
20 tutus est. Is cum faceret ludos Apollinares, ita infima
coacta multitudo annonae caritate tumultuata est ut omnes
qui in theatro spectandi causa consederant pellerentur. De
oppugnata domo nusquam adhuc legi; Pompeius tamen
cum defenderet Milonem apud populum, de vi accusante
25 Clodio, obiecit ei, ut legimus apud Tironem libertum
Ciceronis in libro IIII de vita eius, oppressum L. Caecilium
praetorem.

2 est ..... per quidem *S*   me *Cic.* : *om.* Σ   4 eum ad *P*:
.....*S*: ....ad *M*   5 nusquam paene conueni Σ, *corr.*
       //   //
Baiter 9 milonis et hypsaei *P*   10 milonis Σ, *corr.* ς, *Beraldus* 11
diei *M* : de ei *S* : cede et *P*   13 ad id ue (adidue *M*) timuerunt
Σ, *corr. Baiter*   14 Cicero π : clodius *SP¹*: c. *M*   16........
potuitne *S*   praetoris........obpugn. *S*   18 dicit *KS* (*in*
Addendis)   praetor *add. hoc loco Baiter, ante* fuit *ed. Ald.*   19
spinthere *P* : pinchere *SM*   20 cum quo *S*   21 tumultuata *P* :
tumultu *SM*   23 nunquam Σ, *corr. ed. Iunt.*   25 ei ut *scripsi* :
et ut Σ : ut *Baiter*   26 oppressum] clodio *add.* Σ, *ego delevi* (a
Clodio *Lodoicus*)

This same (dagger of Clodius) after a long interval was once again   48C
turned against me: recently for sure, as you know, he almost did for me
near the Regia. On what day he had such a close call—being close to
getting finished off near the Regia by Clodius—I have nowhere been
able to discover, but I am not led to suppose that Cicero is lying,
especially since he adds—'as you know'. But I think he is talking
about the day in the consulship of Cn. Domitius and Messalla [53 BC],
who preceded the year in which this speech was delivered, on which
there was a battle on the Via Sacra between the retinues of the
candidates Hypsaeus and Milo, and many of the Milonians were
surprised and killed. What makes me think that he is speaking of
the peril of that day is both the location of the fight—for it is
recorded as having taken place on the Via Sacra, on which the
Regia is situated—and also the fact that their backers were duly
in attendance with the candidates—Cicero for Milo, Clodius for
Hypsaeus.

Mil. 38: *Could he do it after besieging the house of L. Caecilius, that*
most just and gallant praetor? L. Caecilius Rufus, of whom this is
spoken, was praetor in the consulship of P. Lentulus Spinther and
Q. Metellus Nepos [57 BC], the year in which Cicero was recalled.
While he was holding the Games of Apollo a mob of social dregs
gathered and rioted so violently at the high price of corn that all who
had taken their seats in the theatre to watch were driven off. So far I
have read nothing about a house siege, but Pompeius, while defending Milo before the people on the accusation of Clodius *de vi*,
charged him, as we read in Tiro, Cicero's freedman, in book 4 of
his *Life*, with harrying L. Caecilius the praetor.

PAVLO POST

(§ 45.) At quo die? quo, ut ante dixi, fuit insanis-
sima contio ab ipsius mercennario tribuno plebis
concitata.

5   Hoc significat eo die quo Clodius occisus est contionatum
esse mercennarium eius tribunum plebis. Sunt autem contionati eo die, ut ex Actis apparet, C. Sallustius et Q. Pompeius, utrique et inimici Milonis et satis inquieti. Sed
videtur mihi Q. Pompeium significare; nam eius seditiosior
10 fuit contio.

(§ 46.) Dixit C. Causinius Schola Interamnanus,
familiarissimus et idem comes Clodi, P. Clodium
illo die in Albano mansurum fuisse.

   Hic fuit Causinius *apud* quem Clodius mansisse In-
15 teramnae videri volebat qua nocte deprehensus est in Caesaris domo, cum ibi in operto virgines pro populo Romano
sacra facerent.

PAVLO POST

(§ 47.) Scitis, iudices, fuisse qui in hac rogatione
20 suadenda diceret Milonis manu caedem esse factam, consilio vero maioris alicuius. Me videlicet
latronem et sicarium abiecti homines ac perditi
describebant.

   Q. Pompeius Rufus et C. Sallustius tribuni fuerunt quos
25 significat. Hi enim primi de ea lege ferenda populum hor-

2 at quo *Cic.* : at quod Σ   die quo ut *om. SP*[1] : *suppl.* π, M *ex*
Cic.   dixi *Cic.*   dixit Σ   11 Causinius *Cic.* : Cassinius Σ
Schola *Cic.*: ...... *SM* : *om. P*   Interamnanus *Cic.* : inter
amnanos *S* : inter ānos *M* : interamnis *P*   12 familiarissimus ......
(12 *litt. M*) *SM* : familiarissimus meus et *P*[1] : familiaris meus et idem
Poggius, corr. ed. Ald. ex Cic.   13 in *om. P*   Albano *Cic.* : alba
Σ   fuisse *Cic.* : fuit Σ   14 fuit *om. P*   causinius
S : cassinius *MP*   apud *ed. Iunt.*: ...... (9 *litt. PM*) Σ   16 pro
p. r. *P* : per praetorem *S* : per pr̄ *M*   20 diceret Σ, *Cic. codd.* Σ*H*,
Schol. Bob. : dicerent *cett. codd. Cic.*   22 et Σ : ac *Cic.*   abiecti
P : obiecti *M* : obiecit *S*   ac *Cic. codd.* Σ*H*, *om. SM* : et *P*,
cett. codd. Cic.   23 describebant *P*, *Cic.* : describant (di- *M*) *SM*
24 tribuni *Manutius* : tr. *P* : tribus *SM*

A little further on

Mil. 45: But on what day? The day, as I said before, when there was an utterly crazy contio *summoned by that very man's hired tribune.* By this he means that on the day when Clodius was killed, his hired tribune addressed a *contio.* Those who held *contiones* on that day, as is clear from the *Acta*, were C. Sallustius and Q. Pompeius, and both were enemies of Milo and somewhat turbulent. But I think he means Q. Pompeius, for his *contio* was the more seditious.

Mil. 46: C. Causinius Schola of Interamna, a very close associate and travelling companion to boot of Clodius, has said that Clodius on that day was going to stay on his Alban estate. This was the Causinius at whose house at Interamna Clodius wanted it to be thought he had stayed on the night when he was caught in Caesar's house, when the Virgins were performing sacred rites there in private for the good of the Roman people.

A little further on

Mil. 47: You are aware, gentlemen of the jury, that there has been a person who in urging this bill maintained that the murder was committed by the hand of Milo, but at the instigation of some more important figure. Obviously there were some wretched desperadoes who were ready to put me down as a brigand and assassin. Q. Pompeius Rufus and C. Sallustius were the tribunes whom he means. For these were the first to

50C   tati sunt et dixerunt a manu Milonis occisum esse Clodium
et cetera.

(§ 49.) Atqui ut illi nocturnus adventus vitandus
fuit, sic Miloni, cum insidiator esset, si illum ad
5 urbem noctu accessurum sciebat, subsidendum et
cetera.

Via Appia est prope urbem monumentum Basili qui locus
latrociniis fuit perquam infamis, quod ex aliis quoque multis
intellegi potest.

10 (§ 55.) Comites Graeculi quocumque ibat, etiam
cum in castra Etrusca properabat.

Saepe obiecit Clodio Cicero socium eum coniurationis
Catilinae fuisse; quam rem nunc quoque reticens ostendit.
Fuerat enim opinio, ut Catilina ex urbe profugerat in castra
15 Manli centurionis qui tum in Etruria ad Faesulas exercitum
ei comparabat, Clodium subsequi eum voluisse et coepisse,
tum dein mutato consilio in urbem redisse.

(§ 67.) Non iam hoc Clodianum crimen timemus,
sed tuas, Cn. Pompei—te enim appello, et ea voce
20 ut me exaudire possis—tuas, inquam, suspiciones
perhorrescimus.

Diximus in argumento orationis huius Cn. Pompeium
simulasse timorem, seu plane timuisse Milonem, et ideo ne
domi quidem suae sed in hortis superioribus ante iudicium
25 mansisse, ita ut villam quoque praesidio militum circum-
daret. Q. Pompeius Rufus tribunus plebis, qui fuerat
familiarissimus omnium P. Clodio et sectam illam sequi se

---

1 a *del. ed. Ald.*   2 et cetera *supplevi* : consilio uero maioris
alicuius *S ex Cic.*   3 uitandus *P* : ui tantus *S* : sinitantus *M*
5 noctu Σ, *Cic. codd.* Σ*H* : nocte *cett. codd. Cic.*   et cetera] et
......*M*   7 basilii Σ, *corr. Orelli*   8 perquam infamis *Manutius* :
per quam is Σ : perinfamis *Baiter*   15 manli *P* : mallii *S* : manili
M   16 eum] cum *S*   17 tum dein mutato *P* : cum (tum *M*) de
imutato *SM*   18 iam *Cic.* : tam *PM* : tamen *S*   quotidianum Σ,
corr. Manutius ex Cic.   19 et (ex *M*) Σ : *om. codd. Cic.*   20 tuas
Σ, *Cic. codd.* Σ*H* : tuas tuas *cett. codd. Cic.*   22 pompeium...
.......*S*   pompeii ....*M*   23 timorem *SM* : timere *P*
26 Rufus *5, Baiter* : fuit Σ   27 suam Σ. *corr. Stangl*   insequi *S*

encourage the people in the matter of passing this law, and they   50C
said that 'Clodius had been killed by the hand of Milo—etc.'

*Mil. 49: And just as he needed to avoid arrival by night, so too Milo, if
he knew that Clodius would be getting near the city in the dark, needed,
as one lying in ambush for him, to take up station etc.* On the Appian
Way near the city there is the monument of Basilus, a spot particularly notorious for robberies, a fact which can also be gathered from
many other sources.

*Mil. 55: He had Greekling fellow-travellers wherever he went, even
when he was hurrying off to his base in Etruria.* Cicero often charges
Clodius with having been associated with Catilina's conspiracy, a
point to which he implicitly alludes here too. For there had been a
belief that, when Catilina had fled the city to the base of the centurion Manlius, who at that time was recruiting an army for him in
Etruria at Faesulae, Clodius wished to follow on behind him, and
started out, but then changed his mind and returned to the city.

*Mil. 67: We no longer fear this charge regarding Clodius, but are
utterly horrified, Cn. Pompeius—and yes, I am addressing you, and
loud enough for you to be able to hear me—at the suspicions raised by
you—yes, you!* We said in the explanatory preface of this speech that
Cn. Pompeius pretended fear—or else really was afraid—of Milo,
and for that reason did not remain in his house but in the higher part
of his suburban estate before the trial, and he surrounded the villa
too with a guard of troops. Q. Pompeius Rufus, tribune of the plebs,
who had been closest of all to P. Clodius and had openly professed

51C palam profitebatur, dixerat in contione paucis post diebus
quam Clodius erat occisus: Milo dedit quem in curia
cremaretis: dabit quem in Capitolio sepeliatis. In
eadem contione idem dixerat—habuit enim eam a. d. VIII
5 Kal. Febr.—cum Milo pridie, id est VIIII Kal. Febr., venire
ad Pompeium in hortos eius voluisset, Pompeium ei per
hominem propinquum misisse nuntium ne ad se veniret.
Prius etiam quam Pompeius ter consul crearetur, tres
tribuni, Q. Pompeius Rufus, C. Sallustius Crispus, T.
10 Munatius Plancus, cum cotidianis contionibus suis magnam
invidiam Miloni propter occisum Clodium excitarent, produxerant ad populum Cn. Pompeium et ab eo quaesierant
num ad eum delatum esset illius quoque *rei* indicium, suae
vitae insidiari Milonem. Responderat Pompeius: Licinium
15 quendam de plebe sacrificulum qui solitus esset familias
purgare ad se detulisse servos quosdam Milonis itemque
libertos comparatos esse ad caedem suam, nomina quoque
servorum edidisse; *se* ad Milonem misisse utrum in potestate
sua haberet; a Milone responsum esse, ex iis servis quos
20 nominasset partim neminem se umquam habuisse, partim
manumisisse; dein, cum Licinium apud se haberet,......
Lucium quendam de plebe ad corrumpendum indicem
venisse; qua re cognita in vincla eum publica esse con-
iectum. Decreverat enim senatus ut cum interrege et
25 tribunis plebis Pompeius daret operam ne quid res publica
detrimenti caperet. Ob has suspiciones Pompeius in

1 paucis post *S* : post paucis *PM*   2 milonem dedi *S*   3 dabo
Σ, *corr. Rau*   5 id est ... Febr. *del. Manutius* (*sed cf.* 44. 13)
VIII *S* : VII *PM, corr. Schütz*   6 in ortis Σ, *corr. Manutius*   8
ter Σ : III *Manutius*   9 T. *Manutius* : L. Σ   10 clodianis *S*
11 occisum *S* : ọ *P* : *om. M*   13 illius] illud *ed. Ald.*   rei *add.*
Mommsen   14 licinium *PM*² : licinnium *SM* (*ita v.* 21 *S*)   15
sacrificorum Σ, *corr. Manutius*   17 liberos Σ, *corr. Graevius*   18
edisse Σ, *corr. ed. Iunt.*   se *add. Baiter*   utrum *scripsi* : ut eum
Σ : ut eos *Beraldus*   19 haberet.....(8 *litt. M*) Σ   22 cor-
rump.......*S*   23 in vincla *om. S*   24 decreuit *PM* : ..
.... *S, corr. Hotoman*   ut *PM* : *om. S*   25 tribuno *S*

that he was a devotee of his party, had declared in a *contio* a few   51C
days after Clodius' murder: 'Milo has given you someone to cremate
in the senate house: he will give you someone to bury on the Capitol.'
At the same meeting this man had averred—for he delivered it on 23
January—that when Milo had intended to visit Pompeius at his
suburban estate the previous day, that is on 22 January, Pompeius
had sent him a message by a kinsman not to approach him. Even
before Pompeius had been made consul for the third time, three
tribunes, Q. Pompeius Rufus, C. Sallustius Crispus, and T. Munatius
Plancus, after arousing great resentment against Milo for the murder
of Clodius at daily public meetings, produced Cn. Pompeius before
the people and asked of him whether any information had been laid
to him about that matter too—that Milo was plotting against his life.
Pompeius had replied that one Licinius, a certain petty priest from
the plebs who was accustomed to purify households, had brought
him information that certain slaves and for that matter freedmen of
Milo's had been suborned to see to his own murder, and had fur-
thermore revealed the names of the slaves; he had sent to Milo to ask
whether they were in his possession; the answer had been given by
Milo that of the slaves he had named, some he had never owned,
some he had manumitted; then, while he had Licinius with him ...
One Lucius, a man of the plebs, (he added) had come to corrupt
the informer, and when this was discovered he had been thrown
into public custody, in chains. The senate, I should explain, had
decreed that along with the *interrex* and the tribunes of the
plebs Pompeius should make it his concern 'that the State take no
harm'. On account of these suspect circumstances, Pompeius

superioribus hortis se continuerat; deinde ex S. C. dilectu
per Italiam habito cum redisset, venientem ad se Milonem
unum omnium non admiserat. Item cum senatus in porticu
Pompeii haberetur ut Pompeius posset interesse, unum
5 eum excuti prius quam in senatum intraret iusserat. Hae
sunt suspiciones quas se dicit pertimescere.

(§ 71.) Quid enim minus illo dignum quam cogere
ut vos eum condemnetis in quem animadvertere
ipse et more maiorum et suo iure posset? sed
10 praesidio esse et cetera.

Idem T. Munatius Plancus, ut saepe diximus, post audita
et obsignata testium verba dimissosque interim iudices
vocata contione cohortatus erat populum ut clausis tabernis
postero die ad iudicium adesset nec pateretur elabi
15 Milonem.

(§ 87.) Incidebantur iam domi leges quae nos
servis nostris addicerent.

Significasse iam puto nos fuisse inter leges P. Clodi quas
ferre proposuerat eam quoque qua libertini, qui non plus
20 quam in IIII tribubus suffragium ferebant, possent in rusticis
quoque tribubus, quae propriae ingenuorum sunt, ferre.

(§ 88.) Senatus, credo, praetorem eum circum-
scripsisset. Ne cum solebat quidem id facere, in
privato eodem hoc aliquid *profecerat*.
25 Significat id tempus quo P. Clodius, *cum* adhuc quaestor

1 dilectu *M* : delectu *SP*   4 unum] sinum *Poggius*   5 eum
Rinkes : tum Σ   intraret priusquam Σ : intraret Clodium π, *corr.*
ed. Iunt.   iusserant Σ, *corr. ed. Ven.* (*fort.* intraret, Clodiani iusserant)   6 se dicit *scripsi* : se Cicero dicit *S* : dicit se Cicero *P* :
dicit Cicero *M*   8 ut uos eum *Cic. codd.* ETδ : ut uuum *Cic.*
cod. Σ : ut uos *Cic. cod.* H : eum *PM* : eum ut vos eum *S*   9
et more *S, Poggius* (*cum Cic.*) : ex more *P¹M*   possit *Cic. cod.*
Σ   et praesidio esset Σ, *corr. Baiter ex Cic.*   13 clusis Σ, *corr.*
Lodoicus   14 nec] ne *SM*   labi Σ, *corr. ed. Ald.*   16 nos]
iam *add.* Σ, *del. Manutius ex Cic.*   18 lege s̃p. clodi *S*   20
IIII   tribubus *KS* : tribus Σ : tribubus urbanis quattuor *Mommsen*
22 circumscripsisse Σ, *corr. Manutius ex Cic.*   24 profecerat *Cic.* :
. . . . (6 *litt.* *P*) Σ   25 id *P* : ad *SM*   clodium . . . . . .
(6 *litt.* P, 9 S, 11 M) Σ, *corr. Manutius*

decided to keep to the gardens on the higher ground. Then, when he had returned from recruiting troops by senatorial decree all over Italy, and Milo came to visit, he refused admission to him alone. Again, when the senate was meeting in the Portico of Pompeius, so that Pompeius could attend, Milo was the only one whom he ordered to be searched before entering the senate. These are the 'suspicions' of which Cicero declares he is afraid.

Mil. 71: *For what is less worthy of him than to put pressure on you to convict a man against whom he could take action in his own person, both by established custom and by his own legal right? But (he says), it is a question of protection... (etc.).* The same T. Munatius Plancus, as we have often said, after the words of the witnesses had been heard and sealed, and the jurors had been for the present dismissed, called a *contio* and urged the people that the shops should be closed the next day, and that they should attend the court and not allow Milo to escape.

Mil. 87: *There were being engraved at his home laws which would have bound us over to our slaves.* I think that we have already indicated that there was among the laws of P. Clodius which he proposed to carry the one also whereby freedmen, who cast their votes in no more than four tribes, might also cast them in the rural tribes, which were exclusive to the freeborn.

Mil. 88: *The senate, I suppose, would have limited his scope as praetor. Not even when it was wont to do so, had this achieved anything in his case, even when he was without office.* He is referring to that time when P. Clodius, while still quaestor

53C designatus esset, *deprensus* est, cum intrasset eo ubi sacri-
ficium pro populo Romano fiebat. Quod factum notatum
erat..........S. C., decretumque *ut* extra ordinem *de ea
re* iudicium fieret.

⁵   VER. A NOVIS. CLX

quo loco inducit loquentem Milonem cum bonarum partium hominibus de meritis suis:
(§ 95.) Plebem et infimam multitudinem, quae P.
Clodio duce fortunis vestris imminebat, eam, quo
¹⁰ tutior esset vestra vita, se *fecisse commemorat ut
non modo virtute* flecteret, sed etiam tribus suis
patrimoniis deleniret.
    Puto iam supra esse dictum Milonem ex familia fuisse
Papia, deinde adoptatum esse ab T. Annio, avo suo materno
¹⁵ Tertium patrimonium videtur significare matris; *aliud* enim
quod fuerit non inveni.
    Peracta utrimque causa singuli quinos accusator et reus
senatores, totidem equites *et* tribunos aerarios reiecerunt,
ita ut unus et L sententias tulerint. Senatores condemna-
²⁰ verunt XII, absolverunt VI; equites condemnaverunt XIII,
absolverunt IIII; tribuni aerarii condemnaverunt XIII,
absolverunt III. Videbantur non ignorasse iudices inscio
Milone initio vulneratum esse Clodium, sed compererant,
post quam vulneratus esset, iussu Milonis occisum. Fuerunt
²⁵ qui crederent M. Catonis sententia eum esse absolutum;

---

1 esset ....(5 *litt.* *M*) Σ, *suppl. Madvig*   eo quo ubi *P*
3 erat ....(8 *litt.* *M*) *PM* : erat *S* : gravi *supplet Madvig*
ut add. Manutius   extra] ex *P*   ordinem (-e *P*) ....Σ,
suppl. Madvig   8 infirmam Σ, *corr. ed. Iunt.*   10 vita se
flecteret Σ, *med. omissis, suppl.* ς, *Manutius ex Cicerone* (se fecisse *Cic.
codd. plerique* : suam se fecisse *Cic. cod. H*)   14 T. *Manutius* : C. Σ
15 matrimonium *SP*¹, *corr. Poggius, M*   aliud *add. ed. Ald.*   16
inuenio Σ, *corr. KS* (*in Addendis*)   17 accusatores reus Σ, *corr.*
π, *M*²   18 et *add. Manutius*   19 unus *P* : uirum *SM*   20
XII absolverunt] di ab soluerunt *S*   VI *P* : ut *S* : VI ut *M*   21
IIII ... absolverunt *om. S*

designate, was caught after entering the place where a sacred rite   53C
for the good of the Roman people was in progress. This fact had been
remarked ... by senatorial decree, and it had been decreed that there
should be an extraordinary court-hearing on the matter.

Line 160 from the end

The passage where he brings on Milo in dialogue with men of the
party of the *boni,* on the subject of his services (to them): *Mil.* 95:
*Concerning the plebs and the basest mob, which under P. Clodius'
leadership menaced your fortunes, he gives a reminder that he took
action not only to show sterling worth in turning its attack aside, but
also in using his three inheritances to assuage its wrath.* I think it has
already been said above that Milo was from the family of Papii, and
then adopted by T. Annius, his maternal grandfather. By the third
inheritance he seems to mean that of his mother; for I have not
discovered any other that existed.

With the pleas completed on both sides, the accuser and the
defendant each rejected five senators and as many knights and *tribuni
aerarii,* with the result that fifty-one jurors cast votes. Of the senators,
twelve voted for conviction, six for acquittal; thirteen knights convicted, four acquitted; thirteen *tribuni aerarii* convicted, three acquitted. It appears that the jurymen were well aware that Clodius had
been wounded initially without Milo's knowledge, but found that
after he had been wounded he was killed on Milo's orders. There were
some who believed that the vote of M. Cato was for acquittal,

54C nam et bene cum re publica actum esse morte P. Clodi non dissimulaverat et studebat in petitione consulatus Miloni et reo adfuerat. Nominaverat quoque eum Cicero praesentem et testatus erat audisse eum a M. Favonio ante diem tertium 5 quam facta caedes erat, Clodium dixisse periturum esse eo triduo Milonem....... Sed Milonis quoque notam audaciam *remov*eri a re p*ublica* utile visum est. Scire t*amen* n*emo* umquam potuit utram sententiam *tulisset*. Damnatum autem opera maxime Appi Claudi pronuntiatum est. Milo 10 postero die factus reus ambitus apud Manlium Torquatum absens damnatus est. Illa quoque lege accusator fuit eius Appius Claudius, et cum ei praemium lege daretur, negavit se eo uti. Subscripserunt ei *in* ambitus iudicio P. Valerius Leo et Cn. Domitius Cn. f. Post paucos dies quoque Milo 15 apud M. Favonium quaesitorem de sodaliciis damnatus est accusante P. Fulvio Nerato, cui e lege praemium datum est. Deinde apud L. Fabium quaesitorem iterum absens damnatus est de vi: accusavit L. Cornificius et Q. Patulcius. Milo in exsilium Massiliam intra paucissimos dies profectus 20 est. Bona eius propter aeris alieni magnitudinem semuncia venierunt.

Post Milonem eadem lege Pompeia primus est accusatus

1 mortem Σ, *corr. Beraldus*   2 dissimulauerit Σ, *corr. ed. Iunt.* 3 eum *del. ed. Ven.*   4 fauonio *P* : fabonio *SM*   tertium *ed. Iunt.* : iii Σ   5 caedes facta *P*   6 milonem .... *SM* : milonem *P*   audaciam .... ueriar ep (c̄p *M*).....(8 litt. *M*) Σ : *suppl. Baiter*   7 sciret....(7 litt. *PM*) ne Σ, *suppl. Rau*   8 sententiam ....(4 litt. *P,* 9 *M*) Σ : *suppl. Lodoicus* 9 maxima Σ, *corr. ed. Ald.*   appius *SP¹, corr. Poggius, M*   claudii ....*P* : c. *M* : .... *S*   10 factus est *P* : factus ... *M* :......*S* : nova lege factus *Mommsen*   manlium *M* : mallium *SP*   13 eo se uti *Madvig* : reo ita Σ   ei *Richter* : et Σ   in *add. Manutius* iudicia Σ, *corr. Manutius*   14 C. f. (Of *S*) Σ, *corr. Manutius*   15 M. *S* : *om. PM*   fauonium *P* : fabonium *SM*   quaestorem Σ, *ita mox (bis), corr. KS*   16 P. clodio nerato reo *PM* : pdodione
                                                                    ‖   ‖
ratio reo *S. corr. Hotoman*   e *S* : *om. PM*   20 alieni aeris *P* semuncia (*ex* -iâ) *S* : semiuncia *PM*   22 pompeiia (-ii a *P,* -i a *M*) Σ. *corr. Manutius*

for he did not conceal his belief that the state had gained from the   54C
death of P. Clodius and he was a supporter of Milo in his candidature
for the consulship and had backed his defence. Cicero too had named
him as present and testified that he had heard from M. Favonius that
three days before the murder took place Clodius had declared that
within three days Milo would have perished. But it seemed beneficial
that Milo's notorious recklessness too should be taken out of public
life. However, no one has ever been able to find out for sure which
way he voted. It was announced that Milo was condemned, thanks
chiefly to Appius Claudius.

Next day Milo was indicted *de ambitu* before Manlius Torquatus
and convicted in his absence. Under that law too his accuser was
Appius Claudius, and although under the law a reward was granted
him, he declared that he would not take it up. The supporting
prosecutors in the case *de ambitu* also were P. Valerius Leo and Cn.
Domitius, son of Gnaeus. A few days later Milo was also convicted
before the *quaesitor* M. Favonius *de sodaliciis* on the accusation of P.
Fulvius Neratus, to whom under the law a reward was granted. Then
before the *quaesitor* L. Fabius he was again convicted on a charge *de
vi*: the accusers were L. Cornificius and Q. Patulcius. Milo within a
few days set off into exile at Massilia. His property, on account of his
enormous debts, sold for almost nothing.

After Milo, under the same Pompeian Law the first to be accused was

55C   M. Saufeius M. f. qui dux fuerat in expugnanda taberna
Bovillis et Clodio occidendo. Accusaverunt eum L. Cassius,
L. Fulcinius C. f., C. Valerius; defenderunt M. Cicero,
M. Caelius, obtinueruntque ut una sententia absolveretur.
5 Condemnaverunt senatores x, absolverunt viii; condemnaverunt equites Romani viiii, absolverunt viii; sed ex tribunis aerariis x absolverunt, vi damnaverunt: manifestum-
que odium Clodi saluti Saufeio fuit, cum eius vel peior
causa quam Milonis fuisset, quod aperte dux fuerat ex-
10 pugnandae tabernae. Repetitus deinde post paucos dies
apud C. Considium quaesitorem est lege Plautia de vi,
subscriptione ea quod loca *edita* occupasset et cum telo
fuisset; nam *dux fuerat* operarum Milonis. Accusaverunt
C. Fidius, Cn. Aponius Cn. f., M. Seius.........Sex. *f.*:
15 defenderunt M. Cicero, M. Terentius Varro Gibba. Absolutus est sententiis plenius quam prius: graves habuit xviiii,
absolutorias duas et xxx; sed e contrario hoc ac priore
iudicio accidit: equites enim ac senatores eum absolverunt,
tribuni aerarii damnaverunt.

20   Sex. autem Clodius quo auctore corpus Clodi in curiam
illatum fuit accusantibus C. Caesennio Philone, M. Alfidio,
defendente T. Flacconio, magno consensu damnatus est.

---

1 saufius Σ, *corr. ed. Iunt.*   expugnata *S*   2 bouillis *P*:
uobillis *S* : bullis (*suprascr.* -i) *M*   4 cecilius *SP*   5 vii Σ, *corr.*
Manutius   6 vii sed Σ, *corr. ed. Ald.*   8 salutis aufeio fuit *S*
9 expugnatione *S*   10 repetitus *S, Madvig* : repertus *PM*   11 C.
om. Σ : *suppl. Mommsen*   est *Madvig* : e *PM* : a *S*   12 loca...
....(11 *litt. M*) *PM* : loca *S, sed in mg. scr. Sozomenus* 'Spatium deficit
unius dictionis': *suppl. Mommsen*   13 nam .... (7 *litt.*
PM) Σ, *suppl. Mommsen*   14 apponius Σ, *corr. Hotoman*   seius
.... (7 *litt. P*) Σ   Sex. fil. *Manutius* : sex *PM* : set *S*
15   M. (*ante* Terentius) *P* : *om. S* : ....*M* galba *S*   16
est sententiis *Poggius* : autem est *P* : .... *S* : autem est sententiis *M*   17 ac *ed. Ald.* : a Σ   21 ciessennio *SP*:
cessennio *M, corr. Jordan*   filone Σ. *corr. Manutius*   alfidio *P*:
alphidio *SM* : Aufidio *Manutius*   22 defenderunt flaceonio Σ.
corr. Baiter   damnatusque est Σ. *corr. Manutius*

M. Saufeius, son of Marcus, who had taken the lead in storming
the tavern at Bovillae and in killing Clodius. His accusers were
L. Cassius; L. Fulcinius, son of Gaius; and C. Valerius; the defence
advocates were M. Cicero and M. Caelius, and they secured his
acquittal by a single vote. For conviction there voted ten senators,
with eight for acquittal; of the Roman knights nine were for conviction, eight for acquittal, but of the *tribuni aerarii* ten acquitted and
six convicted. The hatred of Clodius was obviously Saufeius' salvation, though his case was even weaker than Milo's, since he had
openly led the assault on the tavern. He was prosecuted again a few
days later before the *quaesitor* C. Considius under the Plautian Law
de vi with the additional charge that he had occupied high ground
and had been armed—for he had been a leader of Milo's gangs. The
accusers were C. Fidius, Cn. Aponius, son of Gnaeus, M. Seius ...
and ... son of Sextus; defending counsel were M. Cicero,
M. Terentius Varro Gibba. He was acquitted by a larger vote than
before—against, nineteen, for acquittal thirty-two, but the reverse
was the case of what happened with the previous trial, for the
senators and knights acquitted him, and the *tribuni aerarii* were for
conviction.

Sex. Cloelius, at whose instigation Clodius' corpse was taken into
the senate house, was condemned, to general approbation, on the
accusation of C. Caesennius Philo and M. Alfidius, with T. Flacconius
for the defence—

56C   sententiis   sex   et   xl;   absolutorias   quinque   omnino
habuit, duas senatorum, tres equitum.

Multi praeterea et praesentes et cum citati non respon-
dissent damnati sunt, ex quibus maxima pars fuit Clodia-
5 norum.

1 sex] vi *P*   quinque] v *P*

by forty-six votes. He had five for acquittal in all, two from senators,   56C
three from the knights.

Many others besides, both those who turned up and persons cited
but who made no answer, were condemned, of whom the majority
were Clodian partisans.

Q. Asconi Pediani Incipit
Pro Cornelio de Maiestate

HANC orationem dixit L. Cotta L. Torquato coss. post
annum quam superiores.

ARGVMENTVM

C. Cornelius homo non improbus vita habitus est.
5 Fuerat quaestor Cn. Pompeii, dein tribunus plebis C. Pisone
M'. Glabrione coss. biennio ante quam haec dicta sunt.
In eo magistratu ita se gessit ut iusto pertinacior videretur.
Alienatus autem a senatu *est* ex hac causa. Rettulerat ad
senatum ut, quoniam exterarum nationum legatis pecunia
10 magna daretur usura turpiaque et famosa ex eo lucra fierent,
ne quis legatis exterarum nationum pecuniam expensam
ferret. Cuius relationem repudiavit senatus et decrevit
satis cautum videri eo S. C. quod *aliquot* ante annos
L. Domitio C. Caelio coss. factum erat, cum senatus
15 ante pauculos annos *ex eodem* illo S. C. decrevisset ne quis
Cretensibus pecuniam mutuam daret. Cornelius ea re

Tit. Q. ASCONI ... . MAIESTATE *SP* : *om. M* 3 ARGVMENTVM
add. ed. Ald. 4 C. *add. Baiter* 6 M'. Glabrione *add. Baiter*
cos. (consule *SM*) Σ, *corr. Baiter* 7 iustior Σ, *corr. Manutius*
8 est ex *scripsi* : ex Σ (est *post* alienatus *suppl. Madvig*) 10
darentur *S* 12 ferat Σ, *corr. Manutius* rei lationem *Mommsen*
13 cautum *KS* : factum *PM* : .... *S* quod aliquot
scripsi : quod *S* : quo *PM* 14 L. *Manutius* : .... *S* : Cn. *P* :
Gneo .... *M* : septem et xx L. *Baiter* Coelio *KS* 15
paucos (*suprascr.* ul) *S* annos ...... (10 *litt. M*) *SM* : annos *P* :
suppl. KS 16 Cretensibus *PM* (*ante* 6 *litt. lac. M*) : Cretens ...
... *S* ea re *P* : ea ..... *M* : ea repulsa *KS*

Here begins the Commentary of Q. Asconius Pedianus on *On Behalf of Cornelius on the Charge* de maiestate

He delivered this oration in the consulship of L. Cotta and L. Torquatus [65 BC], a year later than the previous ones.

Explanatory preface

C. Cornelius was regarded as a man whose life was not disreputable. He had been a quaestor of Cn. Pompeius, then tribune of the plebs in the consulship of C. Piso and M'. Glabrio, two years before this speech was delivered. His conduct in that office gave the impression of being somewhat over-persistent. He was estranged from the senate for the following reason. He had made a motion before the senate 'that since sums of money were being passed to the envoys of foreign peoples at huge rates of interest, and scandalously immoral profits were accruing from this, there should be a regulation to prevent the dispensation of funds to the envoys of foreign peoples'. The senate rejected his motion and formally decided that sufficient safeguards appeared to have been established in the senatorial decree that had been passed some years before, in the consulship of L. Domitius and C. Coelius [94 BC], since the senate had decided just a few years earlier by reference to that very decree that no one should lend funds to the Cretans. Cornelius

offensus senatui questus est de ea *in contio*ne: exhauriri
provincias usuris; providendum ut haberent legati unde
praesenti *die* darent; promulgavitque legem qua auctoritatem
senatus minuebat, ne quis nisi per populum legibus solvere-
5 tur. Quod antiquo quoque iure erat cautum; itaque in
omnibus S. C. quibus aliquem legibus solvi placebat adici
erat solitum ut de ea re ad populum ferretur: sed paulatim
ferri erat desitum resque iam in eam consuetudinem venerat ut
postremo ne adiceretur quidem in senatus consultis de
10 rogatione ad populum ferenda; eaque ipsa S. C. per
pauculos admodum fiebant. Indigne eam Corneli rogationem tulerant potentissimi quique ex senatu quorum gratia
magnopere minuebatur; itaque P. Servilius Globulus tribunus plebis inventus erat qui C. Cornelio obsisteret. Is,
15 ubi legis ferundae dies venit et praeco subiciente scriba
verba legis recitare populo coepit, et scribam subicere et
praeconem pronuntiare passus non est. Tum Cornelius
ipse codicem recitavit. Quod cum improbe fieri C. Piso
consul vehementer quereretur *tollique* tribuniciam interces-
20 sionem diceret, gravi convicio a populo exceptus est; et
cum ille eos qui sibi intentabant manus prendi a lictore
iussisset, fracti eius fasces sunt lapidesque etiam ex ultima
contione in consulem iacti: quo tumultu Cornelius per-
turbatus concilium dimisit *actutum*. Actum deinde eadem
25 de re in senatu est magnis contentionibus. Tum Cornelius

---

1 ea.......ne Σ, *suppl. Sigonius*   2 prouidendum *PM* :
.... *S*   3 praesenti die darent *scripsi (cf. Dig.* xlv. 1. 41):
praesentia ...... (11 *litt. M*) darent Σ : praesentia munera darent
Mommsen auctoritatem (-te *M*) *PM* : ...... *S*   4 quis nisi *ed.
Ald.* : quiuis *S, Poggius* : quis *P*[1] : qui uisui *M*   6 adiecerat Σ,
corr. Lodoicus   7 ea *P* : *om. SM*   12 ex S. C. Σ, *corr. Sigonius*
13 inuentus erat tr. pl. *P*   14 C. *Manutius* : L. Σ   15 legis
ferundae *P* : legisfer un̄ *M* : legifer unde *S*   16 recitaret *M*
co..pit *S*[1] (*corr. in mg.*)   19 tollique *add. Hotoman*   21 cos
M : cos. (cons. *S*) *SP*   22 sunt *Gronovius* : cuncti Σ   24
actutum *Purser* : ...... *SM* : *om. P*   25 est magnis *om. S*

was annoyed over this matter, and protested against the senate   58C
in a *contio*. He claimed that the provinces were being bled white
with interest payments; that 'provision must be made for envoys to
have resources from which they might make payments of even their
current debts'. He promulgated a law by which he reduced the
authority of the senate, whereby 'no one should be exempted from
the laws except by vote of the people'. This safeguard had been
incorporated in ancient law too, and thus in all senatorial decrees
in which it was agreed to exempt a person from the laws the rider was
normally added that there should be referral to the people on the
point. But gradually the practice of referral had been abandoned, and
by now it had become habitual, in the end, that there should not even
be added to the senatorial decrees any rider requiring that the matter
be put to the people in a *rogatio*—and the senatorial decrees themselves were being passed by particularly small numbers present.

This bill of Cornelius was met with indignation from the most
powerful, and those senators whose influence was thus greatly to be
reduced, and so a tribune was found, one P. Servilius Globulus, to
obstruct C. Cornelius. This man, when the day came for passing the
law and the herald, as the *scriba* handed him the text, began to read
it to the people, refused to allow either the *scriba* to present the text,
or the herald to declare it. Then Cornelius himself recited the codex.
The consul C. Piso, on vehemently protesting that this was an
outrage, and asserting that the tribunician right of veto was being
subverted, was greeted with a torrent of abuse from the people. And
when he ordered the arrest by his lictors of those who were shaking
their fists at him, his *fasces* were broken and stones were hurled at
the consul even from the furthest fringes of the *contio*. Cornelius,
greatly concerned at this disorder, dismissed the *concilium*
forthwith. Then there were senatorial proceedings on this same
question, with a good deal of dissension. At this point Cornelius

59C   ita ferre rursus coepit ne quis in senatu legibus solveretur
nisi CC adfuissent, neve quis, cum solutus esset, interce-
deret, cum de ea re ad populum ferretur. Haec sine
tumultu res acta est. Nemo enim negare poterat pro
5 senatus auctoritate esse eam legem; sed tamen eam tulit
invitis optimatibus, qui per paucos *amicis* gratificari
solebant. Aliam deinde legem Cornelius, etsi nemo repu-
gnare ausus est, multis tamen invitis tulit, ut praetores ex
edictis suis perpetuis ius dicerent: quae res studium aut
10 gratiam ambitiosis praetoribus qui varie ius dicere assue-
verant sustulit. Alias quoque complures leges Cornelius
promulgavit, quibus plerisque collegae intercesserunt: per
quas contentiones totius tribunatus eius tempus peractum
est.

15   Sequenti deinde anno M'. Lepido L. Volcacio coss., quo
anno praetor Cicero fuit, reum Cornelium duo fratres Cominii
lege Cornelia de maiestate fecerunt. Detulit nomen Publius,
subscripsit Gaius. Et cum P. Cassius praetor decimo die,
ut mos est, adesse iussisset, eoque die ipse non adfuisset
20 seu avocatus propter publici frumenti curam seu gratificans
reo, circumventi sunt ante tribunal eius accusatores a notis
operarum ducibus ita ut mors intentaretur, si mox non

---

1   ferre rursus *P* : ferretur . . . . *S* : ferretur rursus . . . . *M*
1–2 in senatu . . . quis *om. S*   2 CC *P* : . . . CC *M* : CC non minus
Mommsen   solutus *PM* : . . . . *S* : quis ita solutus *Mommsen*
3   ad populum *PM* . . . . *S*   4   acta est *PM* : . . . . *S*
5   senatus auctoritate *M* : . . . . . . auctoritate *S* : auctoritate senatus
P   eam tulit *PM* : . . . . . . *S*   6   per *Mommsen* : vel Σ   paucos
. . . . (10 *litt. S*, 7 *P*, 5 *M*) Σ, *ego supplevi*   7   aliam *PM* : ali
. . . . . *S*   et sine more pugnare Σ, *correxit* π   9 studium
aut *scripsi* : eum aut Σ : summatim *Mommsen* : cunctam *Baiter*   10
assueverant] solebant *P*¹, *corr. Poggius*   11   sustulit *P* : substulit
SM   12   plerisque *SM* : plerique *P*   intercesserunt *P* : inter-
cesserū et *S* : intercessurum et̲ *M*   13   totius Σ : totus *Poggius*
eius tempus *KS* : tempore eius Σ : *fort.* tempus reliquum   15
M. Σ, *corr. Manutius*   16 reum Cornelium *om. M*   18 scripsit *S*
C. Σ : L. *Cic. Clu.* 99   20 auocatus *P* : aduocatus *SM*   21 ante
P : an *SM*

again initiated a measure, this time to prevent anyone being exempted from the laws in the senate unless there were present (at least) two hundred members; and to prevent anyone, when a person had been exempted, from exercising a veto when referral on the matter was made to the people. This business was transacted without uproar. For no one could deny that this law upheld senatorial authority. Yet even so he passed it against the wishes of the *optimates*, who had been wont to use minorities to do favours for their friends. Then Cornelius passed another law, although no one dared to oppose, but against the wishes of a great many, to require praetors to dispense justice in accord with their own standing edicts. This measure eliminated bias or undue influence from praetors looking for power who had acquired the habit of inconsistent jurisdiction. Cornelius promulgated several other laws too, against most of which his colleagues opposed their veto, and over these dissensions the whole period of his tribunate was spent.

Next year, in the consulship of M'. Lepidus and L. Volcacius [66 BC], the year in which Cicero was praetor, the two brothers Cominius indicted Cornelius under the Lex Cornelia *de maiestate*. Publius formally named him, and Gaius seconded. And when L. Cassius the praetor, on the tenth day, as is customary, required attendance in court, but on that day was himself absent—whether called away on account of his commissionership for the public corn supply, or to do the defendant a favour, the prosecutors were surrounded before his judgment-seat by known gangleaders, who even threatened them with death, if they

60C desisterent. Quam perniciem vix effugerunt interventu consulum qui advocati reo descenderant. Et cum in scalas quasdam Cominii fugissent, clausi in noctem ibi se occulta-verunt, deinde per tecta vicinarum aedium profugerunt ex 5 urbe. Postero die, cum P. Cassius adsedisset et citati accusatores non adessent, exemptum nomen est de reis Corneli; Cominii autem magna infamia flagraverunt vendi-disse silentium magna pecunia.

Sequente deinde anno L. Cotta L. Torquato coss., quo 10 haec oratio a Cicerone praetura *nuper* peracta dicta est, cum primum apparu*isset* Manilius qui iudicium per operarum duces turbaverat, deinde quod ex S. C. ambo consules........
.....praesidebant ei iudicio, non respondi*sset* a*t*que esset damnatus, recreavit se *Cominius, ut infam*iam acceptae 15 pecuniae tolleret, ac *repetiit* Cornelium lege maiestatis. Res acta est magna exspectatione. Paucos autem co*mites.* Cor-nelius perterritus Manili exitu......in iudicium adhi-buit, ut ne clamor quidem ullus ab advocatis eius oriretur.

Dixerunt in eum infesti testimonia principes civitatis qui 20 plurimum in senatu poterant Q. Hortensius, Q. Catulus, Q. Metellus Pius, M. Lucullus, M'. Lepidus. Dixerunt autem hoc : vidisse se cum Cornelius in tribunatu codicem

---

3 clauso Σ, *corr. Manutius*   4 aedium *P* : *om. SM*   5 P. *om.*
M   10 praetura nuper peracta *KS* : pretura pretore *P* : praetura
. . . . praetore *S* : . . . . pretore *M* : praetorio *Sigonius*
cum prima pars . . . . . . Manilius (pars M. Manilius *P*) Σ : *suppl.*
Sigonius   11 duces π : iudices *PM* : . . . *S*   12 turbauerat *πM* :
. . .bauerat *SP*   dein *P*   ambo *Popma* : anno Σ   cons. (cos. *P*)
. . . . (8 *litt. P*) praesidebant *SP* : consules praesidebant
M : *fort.* praesentes erant et *supplendum*   13 ei *KS* : et Σ
respondi (-is *P*) . . . . .que *SP* : respondi atque *M, corr.* π   14
recreavisset . . . . (*lac. om. S*) iam accepta pecunia tollere ait (et *S*)
. . . . .Cornelium Σ : *suppl. KS*   16 magna *om. S* autem comites
scripsi : ante (añ *S*) me go . . . . . . .Σ : autem homines *KS* : ante menses.
Ergo *Madvig*   17 exitu . . . . . . .Σ : recenti *suppl. KS*   18 illius
Σ, *corr. Manutius*   21 L. Lucullus *P* M'. *Manutius* : M. *P* : L. *SM*

did not desist forthwith. They escaped this peril with difficulty,   60C
on the intervention of the consuls, who had come down as advocates
for the defendant. The Cominii had taken refuge in some kind of
garret, locked themselves in and stayed there in hiding until nightfall;
and then fled from the city over the roofs of the adjoining buildings.
The next day, when L. Cassius took his seat and the accusers on being
called failed to present themselves, the name of Cornelius was struck
from the list of those awaiting trial—and the Cominii were engulfed
in blazing scandal for having sold their silence for a huge sum of
money.

Then in the next year, in the consulship of L. Cotta and L.
Torquatus (the one in which this speech was delivered by Cicero,
who had recently ended his praetorship), after Manilius, who had
broken up the trial by means of gangleaders, had first made a court
appearance and then, because in accord with a senatorial decree both
consuls ... were providing protection for that trial, he had made no
answer and had been condemned, Cominius recovered himself (and)
in order to allay the scandal of taking money, renewed his accusation
of Cornelius under the law *de maiestate*. The proceedings took place
amid widespread speculation over the outcome. Cornelius, greatly
alarmed at the political destruction of Manilius, brought few friends
into court, so that there should not be even any vocal demonstration
for him raised by his advocates.

In their hostility leading men of the state bore witness against
him—those who wielded most power in the senate, to wit,
Q. Hortensius, Q. Catulus, Q. Metellus Pius, M. Lucullus, Mam.
Lepidus. Their statements were as follows: that they had seen
(what happened) when Cornelius in his tribunate had read a codex

61C

pro rostris ipse recitaret, quod ante Cornelium nemo fecisse
existimaretur. Volebant videri se iudicare eam rem magnopere ad crimen imminutae maiestatis tribuniciae pertinere;
etenim prope tollebatur intercessio, si id tribunis permittere-
5 tur. Non poterat negare id factum esse *Cicero,* is eo confugit ut diceret non ideo quod lectus sit codex a tribuno
imminutam esse tribuniciam potestatem. Qua vero arte et
scientia orationis ita ut et dignitatem clarissimorum civium
contra quos dicebat non violaret, et tamen auctoritate eorum
10 laedi reum non pateretur, quantaque moderatione rem tam
difficilem aliis tractaverit lectio ipsa declarabit. Adiumen
tum autem habuit quod, sicut diximus, Cornelius praeter
destrictum propositum animi adversus principum voluntatem
cetera vita nihil fecerat quod magnopere improbaretur;
15 praeterea quod et ipse Globulus qui *interces*serat aderat
Cornelio, *et*—quod ipsum quoque diximus—quod Cornelius
Pompeii Magni quaestor fuerat, apud duas *decurias* profuit
equitum Romanorum et tribuno*rum aerariorum* et ex tertia
quoque parte *senatorum* apud plerosque exceptis eis *qui*
20 *erant* familiares principum civitatis. Res acta est magno
conventu, magnaque exspectatione quis eventus iudicii fu-
turus esset . . . . a summis viris dici testimo*n*ia et id
quod ei dicerent confiteri *reum* animadvertebant. Exstat
oratio Comini accusatoris quam sumere in manus est ali-

5 Cicero *add. Baiter*   4 etenim *Manutius* : et cum Σ   6 non
video qui Σ, *corr. Lodoicus*   11 aliis] Tullius *Rinkes*   13
animaduersus *S* : aduersus *PM, corr. KS*   14 improbaretur *P* :
improbabantur *S* : improbat˜ *M*   15 qui . . . . . . erat Σ, *suppl.
Manutius*   16 et *add. Hotoman*   17 Pompei *P* : . . . . . . *SM*
duas . . . . Σ, *suppl. Madvig*   profuit *scripsi* : praeferat *SM* :
praefecturas *P*   18 tribuno . . . . . . Σ, *suppl. Baiter*   19 parte
. . . . . . (*om. lac. M*) Σ : *suppl. KS*   exceptis iis (extepisus *S*)
. . . . Σ, *suppl. Madvig*   20 familiaris Σ, *corr. Madvig*   acta
est *PM* (*seq.* 8 *litt. lac. in M*) : . . . . . . *S*   magno . . . . testimonia *om. M*   21 exspectatione *P* : exspe . . . . *S*   22
esset . . . . *SP* : namque et *suppl. KS*   dicit extimo
. . . . . . *SP, corr. Manutius* (in Cornelium *add. KS*)   23 confiteri
. . . . . . (*om. lac. P*) Σ : *suppl. Manutius*   advertebant *S*   24
Comini *Gronovius* : hominis Σ   aliquot Σ, *corr. ed. Ven.*

before the *rostra* in person, which it was thought no one had   61C
ever done before Cornelius. They wished it to be seen that it was
their opinion that this conduct was highly relevant to the charge of
impairing the *maiestas* of the tribunate, for, if this were to be allowed
to individual tribunes, the veto was all but eliminated. Cicero was not
able to deny that this had been done, and so took refuge in saying
that the fact that the codex had been read out by a tribune did not
constitute violation of tribunes' powers. An actual reading of the
speech will reveal the skill and rhetorical expertise with which,
without impairing the standing of those most highly ranked citizens
against whom he was speaking, he avoided any damage being done to
the defendant by their authority; and with what tact he handled a
matter which others would have found so difficult. To help him he
did have the fact, as we have said, that Cornelius, besides his openly
declared singleness of purpose against the wishes of the leading men,
in the rest of his life had done nothing to deserve much censure; and
moreover Globulus himself, who had entered his veto, turned up to
back Cornelius; and the very fact—as we have also said—that Cornelius had been quaestor to Pompeius Magnus, told in his favour
with two *decuriae*, those of Roman knights and *tribuni aerarii*, and in
the case of the third with most of the senators except those who were
on close terms with the leading men of the state. Proceedings
took place in a huge gathering, and with much speculation as to
what the outcome of the trial would be ... They noted that
depositions were entered by the highest ranking men, and that the
defendant accepted the truth of what they said. There survives the
oration of Cominius the prosecutor, which it is worth getting into

62C

quod operae pretium, non solum propter Ciceronis orationes
quas pro Cornelio habemus sed etiam propter semet ipsam.
Cicero, *ut* ipse significat, quatriduo Cornelium defendit;
quas actiones contulisse eum in duas orationes apparet.
5 Iudicium id exercuit Q. Gallius praetor.

[In hac causa tres sunt quaestiones: prima, cum sit Cornelius reus maiestatis legis Corneliae, utrum certae aliquae
res sint ea lege comprehensae quibus solis reus maiestatis
teneatur, quod patronus defendit; an libera eius interpre-
10 tatio iudici relicta sit, quod accusator propoint. Secunda
est an quod Cornelius fecit †ne ca maiestatis teneatur.
Tertia an minuendae maiestatis animum habuerit.]

ENARRATIO

VER. A PRIMO CIRCI. CLX

15 Postulatur apud me praetorem primum de pecu-
niis repetundis. Prospectat videlicet Cominius
quid agatur: videt homines faeneos in medium ad
temptandum periculum proiectos.

Simulacra effigie hominum ex faeno fieri solebant quibus
20 obiectis ad spectaculum praebendum tauri irritarentur.

Quid? Metellus summa nobilitate ac virtute, cum
bis iurasset, semel privatim, *iterum lege*, privatim

---

1 opera etiam *S*   2 ipm̄ *P*   3 ut *add. KS*   4 quas
Lodoicus : duas Σ   cum in Σ, *corr. Beraldus*   appareat Σ, *corr. ς,*
Beraldus   5 Gallus Σ, *corr. Manutius*   6–12 *om. P,*
ed. V, alii   8 sunt *SM, corr. KS*   ex lege *SM, corr. Mommsen*
9 interpretatione iudicii *SM, corr. KS*   11 ne ca *S* : ne ea *M* :
ex eo *KS* : nomine *Purser*   13 *add. Baiter*   14 CLX *KS* : CLXI Σ
15 a me praetore Σ, *corr. Manutius*   primum *om. M*   18
proiectos *Poggius, M* : proiectus *SP¹*   19 effigies (-cies *M*) Σ,
corr. Baiter   22   priuatim *Poggius, M* : priua . . . . . . *S* : priuatus
P¹   iterum lege *suppl. KS*   priuatum patre Σ, *corr. KS*

your hands, not only because of Cicero's speeches which we possess   62C
in defence of Cornelius, but also for its own sake. Cicero's defence of
Cornelius, as he indicates himself, lasted four days; it is evident that
he compiled (material from) two processes into two orations.
Q. Gallius as praetor presided over this trial.

[In this case there are three points at issue. First, since Cornelius is
charged under the Lex Cornelia *de maiestate*, whether various quite
specific matters are covered by this law on which alone a defendant is
liable on a charge *de maiestate*—the basis of his advocate's defence:
or, as the prosecutor urges, the court enjoys freedom of interpretation. Second, whether what Cornelius did constitutes a liability
under the said Law *de maiestate*. Third, whether he had the intention
of impairing *maiestas*.]

Commentary

Around line 160 from the beginning
He is brought to court first before me as praetor in a suit de repetundis.
*Obviously Cominius is on the lookout for what is going on : he sees men
of straw cast into the open in order to assess the danger.* It was the
custom for representations in the likeness of men to be made which
for purposes of providing a spectacle were put up to confront bulls
and arouse their fury. *So then? Was Metellus, a man of the highest
birth and sterling quality, when he had sworn an oath, once in private,
again under the law—in private*

63C

patris, publice legis.....deiectus est? ratione an
vi? at utri*mque omnem* suspicionem animi tollit *et
C. Curionis* virtus ac dignitas et Q. Metelli s*pectata*
adulescentia ad summam laudem omnibus rebus
5 ornata.

Hoc exemplum affert hoc loco, quod vult probare desistere eum debere ab accusatione—quamvis neque accusatus
sit neque fecerit pactionem—nam Metellus et postulaverat
Curionem et destiterat. Confugit autem orator ad Metelli
10 nobilitatem et ad C. Curionis industriam ut tegeret id quod
illi utilius quam honestius fecerant. Res autem tota se sic
habet: in qua quidem illud primum explicandum est, de
quo Metello hoc dicit. Fuerunt enim tunc plures Quinti
Metelli, ex quibus duo consulares, Pius et Creticus, de
15 quibus apparet eum non dicere, duo autem adulescentes,
Nepos et Celer, ex quibus nunc Nepotem significat. Eius
enim patrem Q. Metellum Nepotem, Baliarici filium, Mace-
donici nepotem qui consul fuit cum T. Didio, Curio is de
quo loquitur accusavit: isque Metellus moriens petiit ab
20 hoc filio suo Metello ut Curionem accusatorem suum
accusaret, et id facturum esse iure iurando adegit. Metellus
fecit reum Curionem; cumque interim quendam civem
idem Metellus servum suum esse contendens vi arripuisset
ac verberibus affecisset, Curio assertorem ei comparavit.
25 Dein cum appareret eum exitum iudicii illius futurum ut

---

1   legis . . . . . . *SM* : *lac. om. P* : *fort.* religione *supplendum*   2   ad
utri . . . . (6 *litt. P*)   *SP* : ãia   aduerti . . . . *M* : *suppl.*
KS   tollit . . . . Σ, *suppl. Manutius*   3 spectata   *KS* :
s . . . . . . *SP* : . . . . *M*   4   omnibus   *P* : . . . . *S* :
om. M   5 ornatam Σ, *corr. Manutius*   6 adfert *PM* : . . . . *S*
hoc *om. SP*[1]   7 eum debere *PM* : . . . . *S* : Cominium debere
Madvig   quamquam *P*   accusatus sit *scripsi* : accusauerit *PM* :
. . . . . . *S* : reus factus sit *KS*   8 fecerint *S*   actionem Σ,
corr. Manutius   nam et *S*   9 desistere *SP*[1] : desiderat *M, corr.*
Poggius   10 legeret Σ, *corr. Orelli*   12 explicandum *P* :
explicare dum *SM*   13 dicat *KS*   15 cum non diceret *S*   17
balliarici *P* : balleari ei *M* : ualliarici *S*   Macedoni Σ, *corr. Beraldus*
19 accusabis *S*   20 accusare *S.*   21 esse] et se *S*   23 ui *P* : cui *SM*

at his father's behest, in public to satisfy the law ... robbed of his **63C**
objective? By reasoned argument, or by force? Yet on both sides all
suspicion of animosity is eliminated by the quality and ranking of
C. Curio and the proven early promise of Q. Metellus, adorned with
every promise of the highest distinction. He adduces this precedent at
this point because he wants to show that he (Cominius) ought to
desist from the prosecution—although he had neither been accused
nor had entered into any agreement—for Metellus had both indicted
Curio and desisted. But the orator takes refuge in the high birth of
Metellus and the persistent application of C. Curio in order to
conceal their actions, which were more expedient than honourable.
The whole affair is like this. The first point in it to be explained is the
identity of this Metellus of whom he speaks. For there were at the
time several persons named Q. Metellus, two of them ex-consuls,
Pius and Creticus, of whom it is clear that he is not speaking; and two
young men, Nepos and Celer, of whom at this point he is pointing to
Nepos. For the Curio of whom he is talking accused his father
Q. Metellus Nepos, son of Baliaricus [*sic*] and grandson of Macedonicus, who was consul with T. Didius; and this Metellus on his
deathbed begged this Metellus his son to accuse Curio, his own
accuser, and bound him by oath to do so. Metellus indicted Curio.
But when meantime the same Metellus seized a certain citizen,
claiming that he was his own slave, and gave him a beating, Curio
turned up to vindicate his free status. Then, when it became clear that
the outcome of that trial would

64C   liber is iudicaretur quem Metellus verberibus affectum esse
negare non poterat, inter Metellum et Curionem facta
concordia *est* pactione ut neque arbitrium de libertate pera-
geretur, esset tamen ille in libertate de quo *agebatur,* neque
5 Metellus perstaret in accusatione Curionis: eaque pactio ab
utroque servata est.   Huc ergo illud pertinet, cum iurasse
dixit semel privatim.......iterum lege, tum scilicet cum
in Curionem calumniam iuravit.   Cum hoc autem Metello
postea Cicero simultates gessit; evasit enim Metellus malus
10 atque improbus civis.
    Legem, inquit, de libertinorum suffragiis Cornelius C.
Manilio dedit.   Quid est hoc 'dedit'? Attulit? an rogavit?
an hortatus est?   Attulisse ridiculum est, quasi legem
aliquam aut ad scribendum difficilem aut ad excogitandum
15 reconditam: quae lex paucis his annis non modo scripta
sed etiam lata esset.
    P. Sulpicium in tribunatu hanc eandem legem tulisse iam
significavimus. Tulit autem L. Sulla qui postea Felix
appellatus *est* Q. Pompeio consulibus ante XXIII annos
20 quam haec dicta sunt, cum per vim rem p. possedisset *et*
ab initiis bonarum actionum ad perditas progressus esset:
quod et initium bellorum civilium fuit, et propter quod ipse
Sulpicius consulum armis iure oppressus esse visus est.

    2 inter *P*: . . . . . inter *M* : *lac.* 17 *litt. hab. S*   3 concordia est
pactione ut neque *Purser* : concordia ut neque *P*¹, pactione neque
P corr. m. 1: concordia *M*: . . . . *S*   arbitrium . . . de
quo *in. mg. hab. P*   peregeṝ. . . . .(9 *litt. M*) Σ, *corr. Mad-*
vig   4 esset *scripsi* : sed Σ : rediret *KS*   libertate *M* : libertatem
SP   agebatur *KS* : . . . . (8 *litt. M*) *SM* : *om. P*   5
in accusatione *P* : in ac (hac *M*) . . . . *SM*   6 servata
scripsi : firmata *PM* : . . . . . *S*   cum *P* : . . . . *SM* : quod bis
eum *KS*   7 priuatim . . . . *SM* : priuatim et *P* : apud patrem
suppl. KS   legatum Σ, *corr. Sigonius*   8 iurauit *P* : rogauit
curauit *S* : durarum *M*   11 cū Mallio (Manlio *M*) Σ, *corr. Manutius*
12 an tulit Σ, *corr. Madvig*   13 an tulisse Σ, *corr. Madvig*   15
recognitam Σ, *corr. ed. Iunt.*   17 iam *KS* : eam *SM* : *om. P*   18
significabimus Σ, *corr. ed. Ald.*   19 est *add. Madvig*   XVI Σ,
corr. Manutius   20 et ab *Beraldus* : ab Σ   23 consulum *Madvig*
coss. (cos. *P*) Σ   ire Σ, *corr. Sigonius*   esset uissus *S*

be a judgment of free status for the man whom Metellus could not
deny he had had beaten, harmony was established between Metellus
and Curio by an agreement whereby the case concerning free status
should not be pressed to a decision, but that the subject of it should
enjoy that status, but neither should Metellus persist in his accusation of Curio. And this agreement was honoured by both parties to
it. This then is the point, when he said that he had sworn one oath in
private ... and another under the law—that is, when he brought
false charges against Curio under oath. And Cicero later pursued
quarrels with this Metellus; for Metellus turned out to be an evil and
disreputable citizen.

*Cornelius, he says, 'gave' Manilius the law on suffrage for freedmen.
What does he mean—'gave' it? Presented him with a draft? Or passed it
for him? Or urged its passage? That he presented a draft is absurd, as if
it were some piece of legislation that was difficult to compose or an
obscure matter to think out: indeed this law for the last few years had
not only been on written record but actually passed.* We have already
indicated that P. Sulpicius in his tribunate passed this same law. He
passed it in the consulship of L. Sulla, who was later called Felix, and
Q. Pompeius twenty-three years before this speech was delivered, at a
time when he had taken control of the state by violence and after
starting with good measures had gone on to bad. This was the start of
the civil wars, and the reason why Sulpicius himself was regarded as
having been justifiably crushed by force of the consuls' arms.

65C
In quo cum multa reprehensa sint, tum imprimis celeritas actionis.

Celeritatem actionis significat, quod Manilius, sicut iam ostendimus, post pauculos statim dies quam inierat tribuna-
5 tum legem eandem Compitalibus pertulit.

Petivit tamen a me praetor maxima contentione ut causam Manili defenderem.

C. Attium Celsum significat, sicut iam ante dictum est.

VER. A PRI. DCCCL

10   dicit de eodem Manili tribunatu:

Nam cum is tr. pl. duas leges in eo magistratu tulisset, unam perniciosam, alteram egregiam: quod summae rei p. nocuisset ab illo ipso tr. abiectum est, bonum autem quod......summa resp. manet et †in vestri ordina...dis
15 fuit.

Dictum est iam supra de his legibus, quarum una de libertinorum suffragiis, quae cum S. C. damnata esset, ab ipso quoque Manilio *non* ultra defensa est: altera de bello Mithridatico Cn. Pompeio extra ordinem mandando, ex qua
20 lege tum Magnus Pompeius bellum gerebat.

---

1 sunt *Sigonius*   3 quod *Beraldus* : ut Σ : quia *Manutius*   6 praetor *ed. Iunt.* : p̃r. Σ : pater *ed. Ven.* : praetore *Manutius*   contentione *KS* : constitutione Σ : contestatione *ed. Ald.* : *fort.* in contione   8 Cattium (carti- *S*) Σ, *corr. Madvig*   9 DCCCL *P*   11 is tr. pl. *P*: T. ple *M*:..........*S*   tulisset in eo magistratu *P*   12 unam pernitiosam *PM* :.......ciosam *S*   summae rei p. *scripsi* :

_(ca)_

summa resp. (rep. *M*)   *PM* :....puS   nocuisset *scripsi* : non hesit sed Σ   13 ipso tr. *P* : ipso tribunum *M*: ipso *S*: ipso qui paraverat *KS*   14 quod.......*SM* : quod *P* : *fort.* poscebat supplendum   res p. Σ : in re p. *Mommsen*   in uestri ordina . . . . _(om. lac. M)_ dis fuit (dis...fuit *P*) Σ : imperi vestri ordinarios (!) hostes dispu-lit *Mommsen*   16   iam   *KS* : etiam   Σ   supra   dictis Σ, *corr. Manutius*   quarum una *Manutius* : quas nunc Σ : quas nunc tangit : altera fuit *Mommsen*   18 non *add. KS*   ultra] altera *Poggius*   20 cum Σ, *corr. ed. Ald.*

In this there are many matters that have occasioned reproach, but especially the swiftness of his action. By the swiftness of the action, he means the fact that Manilius, as we have already shown, just a few days after he entered his tribunate carried through this same law on the day of the Compitalia.

The praetor made every effort in begging me to undertake the defence of Manilius' case. He means C. Attius Celsus, as has already been said before.

Around line 850 from the beginning

He is speaking of the tribunate of Manilius: *For whereas he did, as tribune of the plebs, carry two laws in that office (one of them damaging, the other outstanding), the harm that he did to the vital interests of the state was set aside by that tribune himself; but the good that the state's vital interests †demanded† remains and …† [text awry] … was … to the gods.* Something has already been said above on these laws. One of them was on the voting rights of freedmen, which when it was condemned by senatorial decree, was not defended any further even by Manilius himself; the other concerned entrusting, outside normal practices, the Mithridatic War to Cn. Pompeius, and in accordance with this law Pompeius Magnus at that time was waging the war.

66C

Dicit de disturbato iudicio Maniliano:

Aliis ille in illum furorem magnis hominibus
auctoribus impulsus est qui aliquod institui exemplum disturbandorum iudiciorum *reip.* perniciosis-
5 simum, temporibus suis accommodatissimum, meis
alienissimum rationibus cupiverunt.

L. Catilinam et Cn. Pisonem videtur significare. Fuit
autem Catilina patricius et eodem illo tempore erat reus
repetundarum, cum provinciam Africam obtinuisset et
10 consulatus candidatum se ostendisset. Accusator erat eius
P. Clodius, adulescens ipse quoque perditus, qui postea
cum Cicerone inimicitias gessit. Cn. quoque Piso, adulescens potens et turbulentus, familiaris erat Catilinae omni-
umque consiliorum eius particeps et turbarum auctor.

15   VER. CIR. ∞X

Possum dicere hominem summa prudentia
spectatum, C. Cottam, de suis legibus abrogandis
ipsum ad senatum rettulisse.

Hic est Cotta de quo iam saepe diximus, magnus orator
20 habitus et compar in ea gloria P. Sulpicio et C. Caesari
...... Videntur autem in rebus parvis fuisse leges illae, quas
cum tulisset, rettulit de eis abrogandis ad senatum. Nam
neque apud Sallustium neque apud Livium neque apud
Fenestellam ullius alterius latae ab eo legis *est* mentio

---

3 aliquod *P* : aliquot *SM*   instituit Σ, *corr. Manutius*   4 rei
p. add. Patricius   5 eis Σ, *corr. Manutius* (*fort.* eius)   6 cupierunt
scripsi : cupierunt Σ   9 et consulatus . . . ostendisset *om. S*   10
erat *om. S*   12 inimicitias *P* : inimicitiam *SM*   Piso *Lodoicus* :
ipse Σ   15 ∞x *KS* : s xi Σ   17 spectatum *KS* : captum

(σ̲aptum *P*) Σ : clarum *Manutius* : praeditus *mg. Beraldi*   Cottam de *P* : cocta inde *S* : cottam in *M*   18 retulisset *S*   20
Caesari . . . . . . *SM* : *lac. om. P* : aequalibus *suppl. KS*   22   quas
cum *P* : . . . . . cum *SM*   iis *P* : his *SM*   24 legis *PM* : . . . . .
S   est *add. Bücheler*

He is speaking about the disruption of the trial of Manilius: *He was* **66C** *driven into that bout of madness on the instigation of other important individuals, who were eager to establish some precedent for disrupting trials—which was damaging in the extreme for the state, perfectly suited to their own circumstances, and completely contrary to my own political principles.* He seems to mean L. Catilina and Cn. Piso. Now Catilina was a patrician and at that same time had been arraigned *de repetundis*, after holding command in Africa and declaring himself a candidate for the consulship. His accuser was P. Clodius, a young man himself of rotten character, who later pursued enmity with Cicero. Cn. Piso too, a young man, powerful and a troublemaker, was on good terms with Catilina, party to all his counsels and instigator of riots.

Around line 1010
I can say that a man proven to be of the utmost wisdom, C. Cotta, himself raised the question in the senate of repealing his own laws. This is the Cotta of whom we have already often spoken, reckoned a great orator and on that score the equal in repute of P. Sulpicius and C. Caesar ... But those laws which he passed and then referred to the senate as to whether they should be repealed appear to have been concerned with small matters. For neither in Sallust nor Livy nor Fenestella is there mention of any second law passed by him

67C praeter eam quam in consulatu *tulit invita* nobilitate magno
populi studio, ut eis *qui tr. pl.* fuissent alios quoque magi
stratus *capere* liceret; quod lex *a* dictatore L. Sulla paucis
ante annis lata prohibebat: neque eam Cottae legem abroga-
5 tam esse significat.

SEQVITVR

Possum etiam eiusdem Cottae legem de iudiciis
privatis anno post quam lata sit a fratre eius *abro-*
gatam.
10 *M.* Cottam significat. Fuerunt autem *fratres* tres: duo
hi, C., M., tertius L. Cotta qui lege sua iudicia inter tres
ordines communicavit senatum, equites, tribunos aerarios:
adeptique sunt omnes consulatum.

STATIM

15 Legem Liciniam et Muciam de civibus redigendis video constare inter omnis, quamquam duo
consules omnium quos vidimus sapientissimi
tulissent, non modo inutilem sed perniciosam rei
publicae fuisse.
20 L. Licinium Crassum oratorem et Q. Mucium Scaevolam
pont. max. eundemque et oratorem et iuris consultum significat. Hi enim legem eam de qua loquitur de redigendis
in suas civitates sociis in consulatu tulerunt. Nam cum

---

1 consulatu *Madvig*: contione Σ .....(5 *litt.* S, 7 P, 12 M)
nobilitate Σ, *suppl. Manutius* 2 eis qui tr. pl. *Manutius*: his
...... SP, *om.* M   3 capere liceret *Manutius*: aliter et Σ
a *add. Manutius* dictatori S   paucis: ...... PM: *lac. om.* S.
suppl. Manutius 4 prohibebant SP (perhibebant *Poggins, M*), *corr.*
Manutius abrogatam ... legem (*v.* 7) *om.* S 7 eius Σ, *corr.*
Manutius 8 abrogatam *add. Manutius* 10 M. *add. Manutius*
fratres *add. Bücheler* 11 hic m Σ, *corr.* KS (hi C. et M.
Manutius) 15 redigendis *Schol. Bob. ad Sest.* § 30, *Pighius*:
regundis Σ 16 quam Σ, *corr. Halm* 17 quos PM: quos nos
S 20 L. *Manutius*: P. Σ 22 hic Σ, *corr. Poggius* regendis in
sua civitate Σ, *corr. Pighius* 23 in suo P nam cum KS: nam
SM: cum P: cum enim *Manutius*

other than the one which he carried in his consulship against the   67C
wishes of the nobility, but with great support from the people, that
those who had been tribunes of the plebs might be allowed to take
other offices also—which a law carried by Sulla the dictator a few
years earlier forbade. Nor does he mean that this law of Cotta was (in
fact) repealed.

There follows
I can (cite) also a law of the same Cotta on private jurisdiction, which a
year after its passage was repealed by his brother.
   He means M. Cotta. Now there were three brothers—these two,
Gaius and Marcus, and a third, Lucius Cotta, who in his law shared
the juries among the three orders: senate, *equites, tribuni aerarii.* And
all of them attained the consulship.

Immediately afterwards
I perceive that there is universal agreement that the Licinian and
Mucian Law on the restoration of proper citizen status, although the
two consuls were the wisest men of all we have seen, was not only of no
use to the state but actually damaging. He means L. Licinius Crassus
the orator and Q. Mucius Scaevola, *pontifex maximus,* who was also
himself an orator and legal expert. For these two in their consulship
passed the law of which he speaks on restoring the allies to their own
local citizenships. For at a time when

68C

summa cupiditate civitatis Romanae Italici populi tenerentur
et ob id magna pars eorum pro civibus Romanis se gereret,
necessaria lex visa est ut in suae quisque civitatis ius redi-
geretur. Verum ea lege ita alienati animi sunt principum
5 Italicorum populorum ut ea vel maxima causa belli Italici
quod post triennium exortum est fuerit.

Quattuor omnino genera sunt, iudices, in quibus
per senatum more maiorum statuatur aliquid de
legibus. Vnum est eius modi placere legem abro-
10 gari: ut Q. Caecilio M. Iunio coss. quae leges rem
militarem impedirent, ut abrogarentur.

Q. Caecilius Metellus Numidicus, M. Iunius Silanus, de
quibus facit mentionem, consules fuerunt bello Cimbrico
quod diu prave simul et infeliciter administratum est;
15 atque ipse quoque hic Iunius male rem adversus Cimbros
gessit... †ac plures leges quae per eos annos †quibus hec
significabantur populo latae erant, quibus militiae stipendia
minuebantur, abrogavit.

Alterum, quae lex lata esse dicatur, ea non videri
20 populum teneri: ut L. Marcio Sex. Iulio coss. de
legibus Liviis.

Puto vos reminisci has esse leges Livias quas illis consuli-

---

2 se gereret *P* : regeret *SM*   9 huius modi *S*   abrogare Σ,
corr. Beraldus   10 M. Iunio *Lodoicus* : m. emilio Σ   coss.
Lodoicus : cos. Σ (*cf.* 20)   12 Numidicus Metellus Σ, *corr.*
Lodoicus   siluius Σ, *corr. Manutius*   13 bellow cimbrico
PM (*post* bello *lac.* 7 *litt. in M*): -brico *S* *post* 20 *litt. lac.*   14
demonstratum *SM* : gestum *P*, *corr. KS*   15 Iunius *P* : unius
M :..........*S*   combros *S*[1]   16 gessit ac.. *P* :
gessit.....ac *M* : gessi...........*S* : gessit. Idem postea *Mad-*
vig   quibus hec significabantur *PM* :...........significabantur *S* :
quibus haec gerebantur *Manutius* : ab iis qui gratificabantur *Madvig*
18 abrogauit   *P* :   abroga.......*S*: abrogauit q......*M*   19
alterum   [i]*Manutius* : quartum (-u *M*) quae (q; *M*) *SM* : quantumque *P*
(*'Adnotatio cum sequenti locum mutasse videtur' KS*)   20 coss. *scripsi* : cos.
Σ   21 uiuis *S* : uiniis *M* : iuniis *P*, *corr. Manutius* (*ita*
mox)   22 illis *Poggius*, *M* : illi *SP*[1]

the Italic peoples were gripped by extreme eagerness for the Roman   **68C**
citizenship, and on that account a large portion of them was behaving as if they were Roman citizens, legislation appeared to be a
necessity so that each man should be restored to his proper legal
rights in his own community. However, by this law the loyalties of the
magnates of the Italic peoples were alienated, so that this was much
the most important cause of the Italian War which broke out three
years later.

*There are in all, gentlemen of the jury, four modes in which by
ancestral practice a decision on the laws may be made by the agency
of the senate. One is of the kind when it is resolved that a law should be
abrogated—for example, in the consulship of Q. Caecilius and M. Iunius*
[109 BC], *that the laws which were impairing military efficiency should
be abrogated.* Q. Caecilius Metellus and M. Iunius, of whom he makes
mention, were consuls in the Cimbric War, which for a long time was
conducted poorly and without success—and this Iunius himself also
failed against the Cimbri … and he abrogated several laws which
had been passed by the people during those years in which these
symptoms were evident, whereby the number of years required on
military service was being reduced.

*A second, [a resolution that] when law is said to have been passed, it
does not appear that the people is bound by it—as in the case of the
Livian Laws in the consulship of L. Marcius and Sex. Iulius* [91 BC]. I
think you remember that these are the Livian Laws which in that
consulship

69C bus M. Livius Drusus tribunus plebis tulerit. Qui cum senatus partes tuendas suscepisset et leges pro optimatibus tulisset, postea eo licentiae est progressus ut nullum in his morem servaret. Itaque Philippus cos. qui ei inimicus erat
5 obtinuit a senatu ut leges eius omnes uno S. C. tollerentur. Decretum est enim contra auspicia esse latas neque eis teneri populum.

Tertium est de legum derogationibus—: quo de genere persaepe S. C. fiunt, ut nuper de ipsa lege
10 Calpurnia cui derogaretur.

Lex haec Calpurnia de ambitu erat. Tulerat eam ante biennium C. Calpurnius Piso cos., in qua praeter alias poenas pecuniaria quoque poena erat adiecta.

P. Africanus ille superior, *ut* dicitur, non solum
15 a sapientissimis hominibus qui tum erant verum etiam a se ipso saepe accusatus est quod, cum consul esset cum Ti. Longo, passus esset tum primum a populari consessu senatoria subsellia separari.

Hoc factum est secundo consulatu Scipionis post septi-
20 mum annum quam Carthaginensibus bello secundo data est pax. Factum id esse autem Antias tradidit ludis Romanis quos fecerunt aediles curules C. Atilius Serranus, L. Scribonius Libo, et id eos fecisse iussu censorum Sex. Aeli Paeti, C. Corneli Cethegi. Et videtur in hac quidem
25 oratione hunc auctorem secutus Cicero dixisse passum esse

1 M. Iubilius Σ, *corr. Manutius*   3 ea licentia Σ, *corr. Lodoicus*
6 his Σ, *corr. Manutius*   8 abrogationibus Σ, *corr. Manutius*
quo in genere *Bücheler*   10 cui *Lambinus* : que (-ae S) Σ : quo
Bücheler   14 ut *add. ed. Ald.*   15 tunc S   16 est] esse *Baiter*
17 T. *SP* : ter *M, corr. Manutius*   primum a *Manutius* : plurima Σ
18 consensu Σ, *corr. Poggius*   21 tradidit *PM* : traduxit S : tradit
KS   22 C. *add. Manutius*   fecerint S   attilius *SM*   23
L. *Manutius* : T. Σ   et id eos *Baiter* : cideos Σ : id eos *Manutius*   ius Σ, *corr. Lodoicus*   24 leti Σ, *corr. Manutius*   Cetegi
Σ, *corr. Beraldus*   hac quidem oratione hunc *SM* : hac oratione
hunc quidem *P*   25 secutum *P*   passum *PM* : . . . . S

M. Livius Drusus passed as tribune of the plebs. He, after undertaking   69C
to defend the senate's interests and passing laws to the advantage
of the *optimates*, later went on to abandon inhibition to the point of
disregarding all established practice in these matters. And so Philippus the consul, who was his personal enemy, procured from the
senate a vote that all his laws should be disallowed by a single
senatorial decree. It was decided that they had been passed contrary
to the auspices, and that the people was not bound by them.

*The third concerns modification of laws. In this genre senatorial
decrees very often occur, like the one on the Calpurnian Law, that it
should be modified.*

This Calpurnian Law was about *ambitus*. C. Calpurnius Piso as
consul [67] had passed it two years before, and in it besides the other
penalties a financial one was added.

*The famous P. Africanus the Elder, it is said, was often criticized not
only by the wisest men of that age, but also by himself, for having
allowed, when consul with Ti. Longus* [194 BC], *the provision for the
first time of senatorial benches separate from the general seating available to the public.* This was done in the second consulship of Scipio,
seven years after peace was granted to the Carthaginians in the
Second Punic War. Antias relates that it was done for the Roman
Games which the curule aediles C. Atilius Serranus and L. Scribonius
Libo transacted, and that they did it on the orders of the censors Sex.
Aelius Paetus and C. Cornelius Cethegus. And in this speech,
anyhow, Cicero appears to have followed this author in saying that

70C Scipionem secerni a cetero consessu spectacula senatorum. In ea autem quam post aliquot annos habuit de haruspicum responso, non passum esse Scipionem, sed ipsum auctorem fuisse dandi eum locum senatoribus videtur significare.
5 Verba eius haec sunt: Nam quid ego de illis ludis loquar quos in Palatio nostri maiores ante templum Matris Magnae fieri celebrarique voluerunt?— quibus primum ludis ante populi consessum senatui locum P. Africanus II cos. *ille maior dedit* * * * *
10 et collega eius Sempronio Longo hoc tributum esse senatui scribit, sed sine mentione Megalesium—aediles enim eos ludos facere soliti erant—votivis ludis factum tradit quos Scipio et Longus coss. fecerint. Non praeterire autem vos volo esse oratoriae calliditatis ius ut, cum opus est, eisdem
15 rebus ab utraque parte vel a contrariis utantur. Nam cum secundum Ciceronis opinionem auctore Scipione consule aediles secretum ante omnis locum spectandi senatoribus dederint, *de* eodem illo facto Scipionis in hac quidem oratione, quia causa popularis erat premebaturque senatus
20 auctoritate atque ob id dignitatem eius ordinis quam posset maxime elevari causae expediebat, paenituisse ait Scipionem quod passus esset id fieri; in ea vero de haruspicum responso, quia in senatu habebatur cuius auribus erat blandiendum, et magnopere illum laudat et non auctorem fuisse dandi—
25 nam id erat levius—sed ipsum etiam dedisse dicit.

---

1 consessu (-sensu *M*) *PM*: .... *S*   2 post aliquot *P*: postulo quot *S*: postulo aliquot *M*   3 ipsum *om. S*   actorem *SM*
7 Matris Magnae Σ : in ipso Matris Magnae conspectu Megalesibus
Cic. (*Har. Resp.* 24)   8 ludis primum *Cic.*   consessum *P* :
consensum (-u *M*) *SM*   9 ille maior dedit *Cic.*, *om.* Σ : *post
hoc excidisse aliquid velut* Fenestella quoque a Scipione Africano II
cos. *monent post Madvigium KS*   10 colla *P*¹   13 nōs *P* 14 ius
del. Manutius : *fort.* istud   est *Baiter* : esset Σ   15 utatur *Beraldus*
18 de *add. KS*   20 possit Σ, *corr.* Orelli   21 elabari Σ, *corr.*
Beraldus   22 vero *Baiter* : oratione Σ : *del.* Manutius   de]
ad *S*   respondendo *S*   24 illum *P* : illam *SM* : *fort.* rem
illam

Scipio *allowed* the senators' viewing to be segregated from the rest 70C
of the general seating. But in the speech which he delivered some
years later *On the Answer of the Haruspices*, he appears to indicate
that Scipio did not *allow* it, but was himself the initiator in allocating
room for senators. These are his words: *For what am I to say about
those games which our ancestors decided should take place and be
celebrated before the Temple of the Great Mother? It was at these
games that the famous P. Africanus the Elder in his second consulship*
[194 BC] *first granted space for the senate in front of the general seating*
... ('X' also) writes that this was granted to the senate (by Scipio)
and his colleague Sempronius Longus, but without mention of the
Megalensian Games—for it had been customary for the aediles to
perform those games: he relates that it was done at votive games
which Scipio and Longus gave as consuls. However, I would not wish
you to fail to note the right allowed to the orator's craftiness, to make
use at need of the same facts on both sides of the argument, or even
in contradictory senses. For although in Cicero's view it was on
Scipio's authority as consul that the aediles granted senators a separate space for viewing in front of all (others), yet, concerning that
very action in this speech at least, since his argument was aimed at
the people and he was under pressure from the weight of senatorial
authority and therefore it was expedient for his plea that the standing
of the order should be as far as possible minimized, he claims
that Scipio regretted that he had allowed this to happen. But in the
speech *On the Answer of the Haruspices*, because it was being delivered in the senate, whose ears he had to flatter, he not only accords
the man high praise but also says, not that he was the instigator of the
grant—for that was not enough—but that he had made it himself.

71C

CIRCA MEDIVM

Quo loco enumerat, cum lex feratur, quot loca intercessionis sint, *ante quam qui legem fert populum* iubeat
discedere.

5   Est utique ius vetandi, cum ea feratur, quam diu
.......ferundi   transferuntur;   id   est........
lex, dum privati dicunt, dum........dum sitella
defertur, dum aequantur sortes, dum sortitio fit, et
si qua sunt alia huius generis.

10   †Alia populus confusus ut semper alias, ita et in contione.
†Id peractis, cum id solum superest ut populus sententiam
ferat, iubet eum is qui fert legem discedere: quod verbum
non hoc significat quod in communi consuetudine *est*, eant de
eo loco ubi lex feratur, sed in suam quisque tribum discedat
15 in qua est suffragium laturus.

PAVLO POST

Vnum tamen quod hoc ipso tr. pl. factum est
praetermittendum non videtur. Neque enim maius
est legere codicem, cum intercedatur, quam sitel-
20 lam ipsum coram ipso intercessore deferre, nec
gravius incipere ferre quam perferre, nec vehemen-
tius ostendere se laturum invito collega quam ipsi
collegae magistratum abrogare, nec criminosius
tribus ad legem accipiendam quam ad collegam

2 numerat Σ, *corr. KS* quot] quo *P*[1] 3 sunt Σ, *corr. Sigonius*
antequam ... populum *om.* Σ, *suppl. Sigonius* 4 dicere Σ, *corr.*
Sigonius 5 utique *P* : uti quod *SM* quamdiu .... Σ :
quibus ius est suffragii *suppl. Bücheler* 6 id est ....(11
litt. M) Σ : dum recitatur *suppl. KS* 7 dum ....(5
litt. M) Σ : summovetur populus *suppl. Mommsen* 8 aequantur
sortes *PM* : equo ... si fortes *S* 10 alia Σ : astat *Bücheler* : *fort.*
antea   alias *Beraldus* : alia Σ 11 id Σ : iis *ed. Ald.* : ideo
ceteris *KS* 12 eum *SM* : enim *P* dicere Σ, *corr. Rau* 13
est, eant *scripsi* : eant Σ : est *Manutius* : ut abeant *Mommsen* : erat
ed. Ven. 14 feratur *SM* : fertur *P* descendat Σ, *corr. Manutius*
15, *daturus S* 20 ipsam Σ, *corr. KS* coram *Rinkes* : cum Σ :
de *Madvig*

At about the half-way point   71C
The passage where he is listing the contexts, when a law is being
carried, in which a veto may be entered, before the one who is carrying
the law bids the people to take up its stations. *There exists the right of
veto, when the law is being carried, for so long as ... (?those ... who
have the right to cast a vote?) are being transferred; that is ... a law
(? while being carried may be vetoed?) while persons without office are
making speeches; while ... while the urn for lots is taken round; while
the lots are equalized; while the draw is being made—and any other
contexts of this nature.*

Some acts the people performs undifferentiated, as always in other
contexts, so too at the stage of the *contio*. When all else is done, and it
remains only for the people to express its view, the legislator bids it
'disperse', but this term does not bear the meaning that it does in
common usage—that they depart from the location in which the law
is being carried—but that each man should make his separate way
into his own tribal block in which he is to cast his vote.

A little further on
*However, it is clear that one thing which was done while this man was
himself tribune should not be passed over. For it is no greater matter to
read out a codex while a veto is being entered, than to take round the
urn for lots in person in the very presence of the person entering a veto;
nor a more serious matter to begin the passage of a law than to see it
through; nor more impetuous to show oneself ready to legislate against
the wishes of a colleague than to annul the office of the colleague himself;
nor any more a matter for criminal charges to summon the tribes to vote
for ratifying a law than*

72C reddendum privatum intro vocare: quae vir fortis, huius collega, A. Gabinius in re optima fecit omnia; neque, cum salutem populo Romano atque omnibus gentibus finem diuturnae turpitudinis et
5 servitutis afferret, passus est plus unius collegae sui quam universae civitatis vocem valere et voluntatem.

Manifestum est de ea lege *Gabini* Ciceronem nunc dicere qua Cn. Pompeio bellum adversus piratas datum est.
10 L. autem Trebellius *est* tribunus plebis quem *non* nominat: quo perseverante intercedere—nam senatui promiserat moriturum se ante quam illa lex perferretur—intro vocare tribus Gabinius coepit ut Trebellio magistratum abrogaret, sicut quondam Ti. Gracchus tribunus M. Octavio collegae
15 suo magistratum abrogavit. Et aliquam diu Trebellius ea re non perterritus aderat perstabatque in intercessione, quod id minari magis quam perseveraturum esse Gabinium arbitrabatur; sed post quam x et vii tribus rogationem acceperunt, ut una minus esset, et modo una supererat *ut* populi
20 iussum conficeret, remisit intercessionem Trebellius: atque ita legem Gabinius de piratis persequendis pertulit.

At enim de corrigenda lege rettulerunt.

Diximus iam in principio Cornelium primo legem promulgasse ne quis per senatum lege solveretur, *tum* tulisse ut
25 tum denique de ea re S. C. fieret, cum adessent in senatu non minus cc. Haec est illa quam appellat correctio.

1 qui *S*   2 A.] aut *SP*¹, *om. M* : Aulus *Poggius*   4 cupiditatis *ante* turpitudinis *add.* Σ, *del. Madvig* (captivitatis *Manutius*)
6 ualere *PM* : . . . . *S*   7 uoluntatem *P* : uoluntate *SM*   8 lege . . . . *SM* : lege *P* : *suppl. KS*   10 est *add. Baiter*
non *add. Manutius*   11 senatus Σ, *corr. Sozomenus*   13 abrogarent Σ, *corr. Manutius*   14 Ti. *Manutius* : C. Σ   tribus *S*
16 perterritus non Σ, *corr. Manutius*   in *P* : *om. SM*   qui quod *S*   id minari *KS* : damnari Σ : minari *Orelli*   19 ut una minus esset et modo una (una modo) *Madvig* : et una mens esset ut *P mg.* (*m.* 1) : et una modo *SP*¹ : et una quoque mens esset ut *M*   ut (*ante* populi) *add. ed. Iunt.*   24 tum *addidi* : *om.* Σ : deinde *add. Manutius*   26 cc *Manutius* : et Σ   est *Manutius* : et Σ

for rendering a colleague a private citizen. All these things a gallant   72C
person, this man's colleague A. Gabinius, did in an excellent cause, and
in bringing salvation for the Roman people and for all nations an end to
long-standing disgrace and servitude, did not permit the voice and
preference of one single colleague of his to prevail over those of the
state as a whole. It is obvious that Cicero is now speaking of the law of
Gabinius whereby the conduct of the war against the pirates was
given to Cn. Pompeius. Now L. Trebellius is the tribune of the plebs
whom he does not name. When this man persisted in his veto—for
he had promised the senate that he would die before that law was
carried through—Gabinius began to call the tribes to vote in order
to annul Trebellius' office, just as at one time Ti. Gracchus as tribune
annulled the office of his colleague M. Octavius. And for some time
Trebellius stood there unafraid and persisted in his veto, because he
considered that Gabinius was (merely) threatening it, rather than
intending to see it through. But after seventeen tribes accepted the
proposal so that there was (only) one too few, and only one remained
for confirmation of the people's command, Trebellius withdrew his
veto. And so Gabinius completed the passage of his law on hunting
down the pirates.

Yet they raised the question of amending the law. We have already
said at the start that Cornelius first of all promulgated a law that no
one should be exempted from law by the senate; then eventually
passed one that a senatorial decree on such a matter could be passed
provided that no fewer than two hundred were present in the senate.
This is what he calls an amendment.

Idem, *nisi* haec ipsa lex quam C. Cornelius tulit
obstitisset, decrevissent id quod palam iam isti
defensores iudiciorum propugnaverunt, senatui
non placere id iudicium de Sullae bonis fieri. Quam
5 ego causam longe aliter praetor in contione defendi, cum id dicerem quod idem iudices postea
statuerunt, iudicium aequiore tempore fieri oportere.

Quia defuerat superioribus temporibus in aerario pecunia
10 publica, multa et saepe eius rei remedia erant quaesita; in
quibus hoc quoque ut pecuniae publicae quae residuae apud
quemque essent exigerentur. Id autem maxime pertinebat
ad Cornelium Faustum dictatoris filium, quia Sulla per
multos annos quibus exercitibus praefuerat et rem publicam
15 tenuerat sumpserat pecunias ex vectigalibus et ex aerario
populi Romani; eaque res saepe erat agitata, saepe omissa
partim propter *gratiam* Sullanarum partium, partim ......
..... quod iniquum videbatur post tot annos *ut* quam
quis pecuniam acceperat resque .... redderet
20 rationem.

STATIM

Antea vero quam multarum rerum iudicia sublata sint, et quia scitis praetereo et ne quem in
iudicium oratio mea revocare videatur.

25 Bello Italico quod fuit adulescentibus illis qui tum in re
publica vigebant, cum multi Varia lege inique damnarentur,
quasi id bellum illis auctoribus conflatum esset, crebraeque

---

1 nisi *add. ed. Ald.*   2 decrevissem *Poggius*   3 pugnauerunt Σ,
corr. Bücheler   13 filium *PM* : .... *S*   14 et *P* : et quo
M : et quo tempore *S*   17 gratiam *S* : *om. PM*   syllanorum *Sozomenus* .... quod *S* : quod *PM* : etiam quod *KS* : *fort.*
propterea quod   18 tot annos ut *KS* : tot annos ∼∼∼ *P* : tota
ante 18 *litt. lac.* S : tota annos ..... *M* : *fort.* tot annorum spatium
quam quis *ed. Ald.* : quam qui Σ   19 resque .... (20
litt. S) : residuamque apud se habebat, eius *Mommsen*   22 iudicia
PM: .... *S*   23 scitis S^1P^1 : scistis S^2P^2M praeterea Σ,
corr. Manutius   et ne *S* : ut ne *PM*   25 illis *om.* S

The same persons, had not this very law which C. Cornelius carried   73C
been an obstacle, would have decreed what already these so-called
champions of the courts have fought for, namely that the senate did
not agree to the hearing concerning the property of Sulla taking place.
This cause I defended in a contio *as praetor, but in very different terms,*
when I said precisely what the jurymen themselves later decided, that
there ought to be a court judgment, but in more equitable circumstan-
ces. Because in earlier times there had been a dearth of public funds
in the treasury, many remedies had been sought for this problem,
and often—among them this one too, that any residual public funds
in any man's possession should be called in. But this was especially to
the point in the case of Cornelius Faustus, son of the dictator, since
Sulla over the many years when he had commanded and held the
state in his grip had taken funds from the taxes and the treasury of
the Roman people. Action on this matter had often been demanded,
often abandoned, partly on account of the influence enjoyed by the
Sullan party, partly ... since it seemed unjust after so many years
that anyone should render account for money and property that he
had received.

Immediately afterwards
However, how many hearings were annulled at an earlier time I forbear
to mention, both because you know (the facts) perfectly well, and to
avoid giving the impression that my speech is meant to summon anyone
back to court. In the Italian War which took place in the first youth of
those who were then the strong men in the state, at a time when
many were being unjustly condemned under the Varian Law on the
pretext that the war had been contrived at their instigation, and news

74C defectiones Italicorum nuntiarentur, nanctus iustitii occasionem senatus decrevit ne iudicia, dum tumultus Italicus
esset, exercerentur: quod decretum eorum in contionibus
populi saepe agitatum erat. Supererat autem ex eis qui
5 illa iudicia metuerant vigens tum maxime C. *Curio, pater*
Curionis adulescentis eius qui bello civili Caesaris fuit
partium.

PAVLO POST

Non Cn. Dolabella C. Volcacium, honestissimum
10 virum, communi et cotidiano iure privasset.

Duo fuerunt eo tempore *Cn.* Dolabellae, quorum alterum
C. Caesar accusavit, alterum M. Scaurus.

Non denique homo illorum et vita et prudentia
longe dissimilis, sed tamen nimis in gratificando
15 iure liber, L. Sisenna, bonorum Cn. Corneli pos-
sessionem ex edicto suo P. Scipioni, adulescenti
summa nobilitate, eximia virtute praedito, non
dedisset.

Hoc solum hic adnotandum est hunc esse L. Sisennam
20 qui res Romanas scripsit.

Qua re cum haec populus Romanus videret et
cum a tribunis plebis doceretur, nisi poena acces-
sisset in divisores, exstingui *ambitum* nullo modo
posse, legem hanc Corneli flagitabat, illam quae ex

---

1 nanctus *KS*: non tunc Σ : ob tunc *Poggius*   iustitii *Mommsen*:
eius tristitiae Σ   3 eorum] eo tempore *Mommsen* : *fort.* senatorum
4 erat *SP* : . . . . *M*   ṡupererant Σ, *corr. Madvig*   iis *P*:
his *SM*   5 metuerunt Σ, *corr. Beraldus*   uigentum Σ, *corr. Mad-*
vig   Curio pater *suppl. Manutius*   10 uirum *P* : *om. SM*   11
Cn. *suppl. Bücheler*   15 liberalis *Halm*   17 non *del. Manutius*
(*invita clausula. De* non *repetito cf. Mil.* 2)   21 haec *Rau* : hune
Σ : hoc *Mommsen*   22 doceretur *ed. Iunt.* : docere . . . *S* :
docere^tur . . . . . *P* : doceretur . . . . *M*   accessisse Σ, *corr. Poggius*
23 exstincti *S* : exstinct *P*¹ *M*¹, *corr. Poggius, M*²   ambitum
Halm: . . . . . (7 *litt. M*) Σ   ullo *SP*¹ : *corr. Poggius, M*

arrived again and again of rebellions among the Italians, on taking   74C
the opportunity to suspend public business the senate decreed that
the courts should not remain in use for the duration of the Italic
upheaval—a decree which had often been demanded in mass meetings of the people. Among those who had feared these trials there
survived as a powerful figure at that time especially C. Curio, father
of the younger Curio who belonged to the Caesarian party in the
Civil War.

A little further on
*Cn. Dolabella would not have debarred C. Volcacius, that most hon-
ourable man, from standard, everyday rights at law.* There were at the
time two persons named Cn. Dolabella. Caesar prosecuted one of
them, M. Scaurus the other.

*Nor—to conclude the list—would L. Sisenna, a man far different
from those persons in his lifestyle and wisdom, but even so excessively
generous in doing legal favours, have refused to grant possession of Cn.
Cornelius' property in accordance with his own edict to P. Scipio, a
young man of the highest birth and endowed with outstanding qualities.*
At this point only this needs to noted—that this man is the L. Sisenna
who wrote Roman history.

*For this reason, when the Roman people perceived this, and was
informed by the tribunes of the plebs that if some penalty were not to
be added against the distributors of bribes, it was impossible to eliminate
ambitus, it pressed for this law of Cornelius, and rejected the one which*

S. C. ferebatur repudiabat, idque iure, ut docti sumus duorum consulum designatorum calamitate—
et eadem de re paulo post:

Vt spectaculum illud re et tempore salubre ac
5 necessarium, genere *et* exemplo miserum ac fune-
stum videremus.

P. Sullam et *P.* Autronium significat, quorum alterum
L. Cotta, alterum L. Torquatus, qui cum haec Cicero dicebat
coss. erant, ambitus damnarant et in eorum locum creati erant.

10 Quid ego nunc tibi argumentis respondeam posse
fieri ut alius aliquis Cornelius sit qui habeat Phile-
rotem servum; volgare nomen esse Philerotis,
Cornelios vero ita multos ut iam etiam collegium
constitutum sit?

15 Frequenter tum etiam coetus factiosorum hominum sine
publica auctoritate malo publico fiebant: propter quod
postea collegia et S. C. et pluribus legibus sunt sublata
praeter pauca atque certa quae utilitas civitatis desiderasset,
sicut fabrorum fictorumque.

20 At enim extremi ac difficillimi temporis vocem
illam, C. Corneli, consulem mittere coegisti: qui
rem *p.* salvam esse vellent, ut ad legem accipiendam adessent.

C. Piso qui consul eodem anno fuit quo Cornelius tri-
25 bunus plebis erat, cum legem de ambitu ex S. C. graviorem
quam fuerat antea ferret et propter multitudinem divisorum
qui per vim adversabantur e foro eiectus esset, edixerat id

---

was being carried in accordance with the senatorial decree—and did so   75C
rightly, as we learned from the catastrophe which overtook the two
consuls designate— and on the same point a little later:

So that we might gaze upon a spectacle, which was in the fact of its
occurrence and timing salutary and unavoidable, yet in manner and in
the precedent it set depressingly mournful. He is referring to P. Sulla
and P. Autronius. L. Cotta and L. Torquatus, who at the time when
Cicero was delivering this speech were the consuls, had secured the
condemnation *de ambitu* of Sulla and Autronius respectively and had
been appointed in their place.

Why should I at this point need argumentation to give you an
answer—that it could be that there is some other Cornelius who owns
a slave called Phileros; that the name Phileros is common, and as for
Cornelii—there are so many that a collegium *of them has even been*
instituted? Very often at that time there came into being gatherings of
power-mongers without any public sanction, and to the public
detriment. For this reason later on *collegia* were suppressed, both
by senatorial decree and by several laws, with the exception of a few
whose legality was well established and which the public interest
required, such as those of the artificers and statue-makers.

Yet (it might be said) you forced the consul, C. Cornelius, to deliver
that utterance of extreme emergency, that those who wished for the
safety of the state... should present themselves for ratification of the
law. C. Piso, who was consul in the same year as Cornelius, was
tribune of the plebs, when in compliance with the resolution of the
senate he was in the process of carrying a law *de ambitu* weightier
than the one previously existing, and on account of the numbers of
bribe-distributors, who were resisting him by *vis*, had been thrown
out of the Forum, had issued the edict

quod Cicero significat, et maiore manu stipatus ad legem perferendam descenderat.

Plebem ex Maniliana offensione victam et domitam esse dicit:

5   Aiunt vestros animos propter illius tribuni plebis temeritatem posse adduci ut omnino *nomin*e illius potestatis abalienentur; qui restituerunt eam potestatem, alterum nihil unum posse contra multos, alterum longe abesse?

10   Manifestum puto esse vobis M. Crassum et Cn. Pompeium significari, e quibus Crassus iudex tum sedebat in Cornelium, Pompeius in Asia bellum Mithridaticum gerebat.

Tanta igitur in illis virtus fuit ut anno xvi post reges exacti propter nimiam dominationem po-
15 tentium secederent, leges sacratas ipsi sibi resti-tuerent, duo tribunos crearent, montem illum trans Anienem qui hodie Mons Sacer nominatur, in quo armati consederant, aeternae memoriae causa consecrarent. Itaque auspicato postero
20 anno tr. pl. comitiis curiatis creati sunt.

Inducor magis librariorum hoc loco esse mendam quam ut Ciceronem parum proprio verbo usum esse credam. Illo enim tempore de quo loquitur, quod fuit post xvi annos quam reges exacti sunt, plebs sibi leges sacratas non resti-
25 tuit—numquam enim tribunos plebis habuerat—sed tum primum eas constituit. Numerum quidem annorum post reges exactos cum id factum est diligenter posuit, isque fuit A. Verginio Tricosto L. Veturio Cicurino coss. Ceterum

5 aiunt *Madvig*: ante Σ : *fort.* putant   annos Σ, *corr. Patricius*
6 omnino . . . . . . ne Σ, *supplevi* : omnino a defensione *Mommsen*   7
potestate abalienemur Σ, *corr. Madvig*   10 nobis S   11 e quibus
P : equitibus *SM*   15 ipsis sibi *SP* : sibi ipsis *M, corr. Manutius*
                                ‖   ‖
16 duo *SP*[1] : duos *Poggius, M*   17 anienen trans *P*   20 anno *S* :
anno x *PM* : anno v *Rau*   23 de *S* : *om. PM*   26 eos Σ, *corr.*
Manutius   annorum Σ : anni *Mommsen*   27 cum *scripsi* : quam
Σ : quo *Manutius*   posuit isque *Madvig* : posuistis qui (q̄ *S*) *SP*[1] :
posuit is qui π, *M*   28 L. Vetrurio Σ, *corr. Baiter* (*cf. Liv.* ii. 28)
citurino *S* : cerurino *P* : crcurino *M, corr. Manutius*

to which Cicero refers, and come down with a larger band of men   76C
about him to secure the passage of the law.

He says that the plebs as a result of the discomfiture of Manilius
had been defeated and brought into subjection: *They claim that on
account of the rashness shown by that tribune of the plebs, your hearts
may be brought to detest even the very name of that power; that of those
who restored that power, the one can do nothing in the face of so many,
and the other is too far away.* I think it is obvious to you that M.
Crassus and Cn. Pompeius are meant, of whom Crassus at the time
was sitting on the jury in Cornelius' trial, Pompeius was waging the
Mithridatic War in Asia.

*So then such was their sterling quality that in the sixteenth year after
the expulsion of the kings, in view of the excessive despotism of the
powerful, they seceded, on their own behalf and in their own persons
restored religiously sanctioned laws, appointed two tribunes, and consecrated as an eternal monument the hill beyond the Anio on which they
had taken up their station under arms, which today is called the Sacred
Mount. And so in the next year, after the auspices were taken, tribunes
of the plebs were appointed by the curiate assembly.* I am inclined to
believe that this is an error of the copyists, rather than Cicero's use of
inappropriate terminology. For at the time of which he is speaking—
that is, sixteen years after the kings were driven out, the plebs did
not *restore* religiously sanctioned laws—for it had never had tribunes
of the plebs—but then for the first time *instituted* them. The
number of years after the expulsion of the kings when this was
done he enters with due care: this was the consulship of A. Verginius
Tricostus and L. Veturius Cicurinus [494 BC]. On the other hand,

77C   quidam non duo tr. pl., ut Cicero dicit, sed quinque tradunt
creatos tum esse singulos ex singulis classibus. Sunt tamen
qui eundem illum duorum numerum quem Cicero ponant:
inter quos Tuditanus et Pomponius Atticus, Livius quoque
5 noster. Idem hic et Tuditanus adiciunt tres praeterea ab
illis duobus qui collegae *essent lege* creatos esse. Nomina
duorum qui primi creati sunt haec traduntur: L. Sicinius L.
f. Velutus, L. Albinius C. f. Paterculus.

Reliqua pars huius loci quae pertinet ad secundam con-
10 stitutionem tribunorum et decemvirorum finitum imperium
et breviter et aperte ab ipso dicitur. Nomina sola non
adicit quis ille ex decemviris fuerit qui contra libertatem
vindicias dederit, et quis ille pater contra cuius filiam id
decrevit; scilicet quod notissimum est decemvirum illum
15 Appium Claudium fuisse, patrem autem virginis L. Vergi-
nium. Vnum hoc tantum modo explicandum, quo loco
primum de secunda secessione plebis, dehinc concordia
facta, sic dicit:

Tum interposita fide per tris legatos amplissimos
20 viros Romam armati revertuntur. In Aventino
consederunt; inde armati in Capitolium venerunt;
decem tr. pl. *per* pontificem, quod magistratus
nullus erat, creaverunt.

Legati tres quorum nomina non ponit hi fuerunt: Sp.
25 Tarpeius, C. Iulius, P. Sulpicius, omnes consulares; pontifex
max. fuit M. Papirius.

---

1 quidem Σ, *corr. Beraldus*   4 duos *S*   tudianus *SP* : tucli-
tanus *M, corr. Manutius (ita mox)*   Liuius quoque *SM* : Liuiusque
P   6 qui collegae essent *scripsi* : qui (que *M*) collegae *SM* :
collegas *P* : sibi collegas *KS*   lege *supplevit Purser*   7 sicinius *P* :
sicinus *SM* (Licinius *Liv.* ii. 33)   8 Bellutus *Manutius*   L. Albinius
(-nus) *Liv.* : labinius (lib- *S*) *SM* : lauinius *P*   patriculus Σ, *corr.* ς, *ed.*
Iunt.   12 qui *S* : *om. PM*   13 uindictae Σ, *corr. Beraldus*   quis
                                                                          e
illius ẹ pater *P* (*corr. m.* 1) filiam *P* : filium *SM*   15 patrem autem *P* :
autem patrem *SM*   uirginium Σ, *corr. KS*   16 explicanda *SP¹, corr.*
Poggius, M   21 capitolio Σ, *corr. Beraldus*   22 per *add. Manutius*
24 hi Σ : ii *Poggius*   Sp. *Manutius* (*e Liv.* iii. 50) : P. Σ

some relate that it was not two tribunes of the plebs, as Cicero says,   77C
who were appointed, but five, one from each of the classes. There are,
however, those who posit the same number as Cicero—that is, two—
among them Tuditanus and Pomponius Atticus and our friend Livy.
This same source and Tuditanus too add that three were appointed in
addition under a law by those two, to be their colleagues. The names
of the first two to be appointed are recorded as these: L. Sicinius
Velutus, son of Lucius; L. Albinius Paterculus, son of Gaius.

The remaining portion of this passage which concerns the second
institution of tribunes and the limitation on the power of the
decemviral commission is delivered with brevity and clarity. He
fails to add only names—who it was of the *decem viri* [Board of
Ten] who granted ownership contrary to claims of free status, and
who was the father against whose daughter he made this decision—
no doubt because it is common knowledge that the *decemvir* in
question was Appius Claudius and the father of the girl was L.
Verginius. Only the following point requires explanation, in the
passage where he speaks first of the second secession of the plebs,
and then of the resultant concord, as follows: *Then with mutual
trust established between the two sides by the agency of three envoys,
men of the highest standing, they returned to Rome under arms. They
took up their station on the Aventine; thence came on to the Capitol
under arms. Through the agency of the* pontifex, *since there were no
magistrates, they appointed ten tribunes of the plebs.* The envoys whose
names he does not enter were these: Sp. Tarpeius, C. Iulius,
P. Sulpicius, all of them ex-consuls. The *pontifex maximus* was
M. Papirius.

78C

Etiam haec recentiora praetereo: Porciam principium iustissimae libertatis; Cassiam qua lege
suffragiorum ius potestasque convaluit; alteram
Cassiam quae populi iudicia firmavit.

5 Quae sit illa lex Cassia qua suffragiorum potestas convaluit manifestum est; nam ipse quoque paulo ante dixit
legem Cassium tulisse ut populus per tabellam suffragium
ferret. Altera Cassia lex quae populi iudicia firmavit quae
sit potest quaeri. Est autem haec: L. Cassius L. f. Lon-
10 ginus tribunus plebis C. Mario C. Flavio coss. plures leges
ad minuendam nobilitatis potentiam tulit, in quibus hanc
etiam ut quem populus damnasset cuive imperium abrogasset
in senatu ne esset. Tulerat autem eam maxime propter
simultates cum Q. Servilio qui ante biennium consul fuerat
15 et cui populus, quia male adversus Cimbros rem gesserat,
imperium abrogavit.

Dicit de nobilibus:

Qui non modo cum Sulla verum etiam illo mortuo
semper hoc per se summis opibus retinendum puta-
20 verunt, inimicissimi C. Cottae fuerunt, quod is
consul paulum tribunis plebis non potestatis sed
dignitatis addidit.

Hic Cotta, ut puto *vos reminisci*, legem tulit ut tribunis
plebis liceret postea alios magistratus capere: quod lege
25 Sullae eis erat ademptum.

Quam diu quidem hoc animo erga vos illa plebs
erit quo se ostendit esse, cum legem Aureliam, cum
Rosciam non modo accepit sed etiam efflagitavit.

Aurelia lege communicata esse iudicia inter senatores et
30 equestrem ordinem et tribunos aerarios †quam L. Roscius

---

1 praeterea Σ, *corr. Manutius*   Porciam (-tiam) *SM* : ponam *P*
2–4 qua … Cassiam *om. S*   3 ius *P* : uis *M*   5 sit *Manutius* :
est Σ   10 C. Flavio *Sigonius* : C. (*om.* C. *S*) flacco Σ   14
Servilio *Sigonius* : cecilio Σ   16 imperium *hoc loco hab.* P, *post*
abrog. *M* : *om. S*   17 DICIT DE NOBILIBVS *P in mg.* : *om. M*   23
vos reminisci *suppl.* KS   25 iis *P* : his *SM*   30 aerarios quam
Σ : *fort.* aerarios diximus. Roscia est qua (*sic fere Sigonius*)

These more recent cases also I let pass—the Porcian Law, the funda-   78C
ment of liberty based on pure justice; the Cassian Law under which the
right and power inherent in the suffrage was restored to health and
strength; the second Cassian Law which consolidated the people's courts.
Which was the Cassian Law whereby the power inherent in the vote
was restored to health and strength is obvious, for he himself also a
little earlier has said that a Cassius passed a law that the people
should cast its votes by ballot. It can be asked which was the other
Cassian Law, which consolidated the people's courts. It is this:
L. Cassius Longinus, son of Lucius, tribune of the plebs in the
consulship of C. Marius and L. Flavius [104 BC], passed several laws
with a view to lessening the power of the nobility, among them this
one, to the effect that a man whom the people had condemned, or
whose power of command it had abrogated, should not be a member
of the senate. Now he had carried it chiefly on account of his personal
quarrels with Q. Servilius who had been consul two years before, and
whose power of command the people abrogated because of his failure
against the Cimbri.

He says of the nobility : *Those persons who not only along with Sulla*
but even after his death always believed that they should cling to this at
any cost, however great, were the deadly enemies of C. Cotta, for having
as consul made some small addition, not to the powers of tribunes of the
plebs, but to their standing. This Cotta, as I imagine you remember,
passed a law that it should be lawful for tribunes of the plebs to hold
other offices later—which had been taken away from them by a law of
Sulla.

For that long, certainly, the plebs so constituted will be of this
same mind towards you as it showed itself to be when it not merely
accepted but pressed demands for the Aurelian Law and the Roscian
Law. By the Aurelian Law the courts were shared among senators, the
equestrian order, and the *tribuni aerarii*—a law which L. Roscius

79C   Otho biennio ante confirmavit, in theatro ut equitibus Romanis xⅢⅠ ordines spectandi gratia darentur.

Memoria teneo, cum primum senatores cum equitibus Romanis lege Plotia iudicarent, hominem
5 dis ac nobilitati perinvisum Cn. Pompeium causam lege Varia de maiestate dixisse.

M. Plautius Silvanus tribunus plebis Cn. Pompeio Strabone L. Porcio Catone coss., secundo anno belli Italici cum equester ordo in iudiciis dominaretur, legem tulit adiuvanti-
10 bus nobilibus; quae lex vim eam habuit quam Cicero significat: nam ex ea lege tribus singulae ex suo numero quinos denos suffragio creabant qui eo anno iudicarent. Ex eo factum est ut senatores quoque in eo numero essent, et quidam etiam ex ipsa plebe.

15   *PRO CORNELIO*

Num in eo qui sint hi testes haesitatis? Ego vobis edam. Duo reliqui sunt de consularibus, inimici tribuniciae potestatis. Pauci praeterea adsentatores eorum atque adseculae subsequuntur.
20 M. Lucullum et M'. Lepidum significat. Quinque enim consulares, ut iam diximus, in Cornelium testimonium dixerunt: Q. Catulus, Q. Hortensius, Q. Metellus Pius pont. max., quos hac secunda oratione tractat, et duo qui non*dum* dixerant quos nunc significat Lucullus et Lepidus.
25 Quid? avunculus tuus clarissimus vir, clarissimo patre avo maioribus, credo, silentio, favente nobili-

---

1 cons. (cos. *P*) firmavit Σ, *corr. Sigonius*   4 hominem *PM*: homines *S*   5 perinusum *SM*   7 syllanus Σ, *corr. Manutius* Pompeio *P*: pompeius *SM*   9 ordo et in *M*   11 ex eo Σ, *corr. Patricius*   13 factum *S²P*: facto *S¹M*   15 PRO CORNELIO *SP*: *om. M*   Secunda Oratio *add. Poggius*   19 senatores (senta- *M*) Σ, *corr. Poggius*   20 M'. *Manutius*: M. Σ   23 non dixerunt Σ, *corr. Rau*

Otho consolidated two years before (this speech), in a measure   79C
whereby fourteen rows (of seats) should be granted to Roman
knights for watching public spectacles.

I have a clear recollection that as soon as senators served as jurors
with Roman knights under the Plotian Law, a person much hated by the
gods and the nobility, Cn. Pomponius, pleaded his defence on a charge
de maiestate *under the Varian Law.* M. Plautius Silvanus as tribune of
the plebs in the consulship of Cn. Pompeius Strabo and L. Porcius
Cato [89 BC], in the second year of the Italian War, when the
equestrian order held despotic power in the courts, passed a law
with the aid of the nobles. This law had the effect which Cicero
indicates. For in accordance with this law it was the practice for
each tribe to appoint from its own members by popular vote fifteen
persons to constitute juries for that year. It resulted in senators also
being included in that number, and some persons even from the very
plebs.

Defence of Cornelius

Surely you are not in difficulty over the identity of these witnesses? I
shall disclose them to you. There remain two from the ex-consuls, hostile
to the power of tribunes. There tag along behind them in addition their
flatterers and hangers-on. He is referring to M. Lucullus and Mam.
Lepidus. For there were five ex-consuls, as we have said, who made
depositions against Cornelius—Q. Catulus, Q. Hortensius, Q. Metellus Pius the *pontifex maximus*, whom he deals with in this second
speech, and two who had not yet spoken, whom he now indicates—
Lucullus and Lepidus.

Again—your uncle, a most illustrious man, with a most illustrious
father, grandfather and ancestry, I suppose,

80C tate, nullo intercessore comparato populo Romano
dedit et potentissimorum hominum conlegiis
eripuit cooptandorum sacerdotum potestatem.

Hoc egere enarratione, quia hoc loco nomen non ponit
5 quis fecerit, ei demum videri potest qui oblitus sit minus
ante xx versus haec *de* eo ipso Ciceronem dixisse:

Sed si familiariter ex Q. Catulo sapientissimo
viro atque humanissimo velim quaerere: utrius
tandem tibi tribunatus minus probari potest, C.
10 Corneli, an—non dicam P. Sulpici, non L. Saturnini,
non Gai Gracchi, non Tiberi, neminem quem isti
seditiosum existimant nominabo, sed avunculi tui,
Q. Catule, clarissimi patriaeque amantissimi viri?
quid mihi tandem responsurum putatis?

15   SEQVITVR

Quid? idem Domitius M. Silanum, consularem
hominem, quem ad modum tr. pl. vexavit?

M. Silanus quinquennio ante consul fuerat quam Domitius
tr. pl. esset, atque ipse quoque adversus Cimbros rem male
20 gesserat: quam ob causam Domitius eum apud populum
accusavit. Criminabatur rem cum Cimbris iniussu populi
gessisse, idque principium fuisse calamitatum quas eo bello
populus accepisset; ac de eo tabellam quoque edidit. Sed
plenissime Silanus absolutus est; nam duae solae tribus
25 eum, Sergia et Quirina, damnaverunt.

1 populo Romano dedit *Manutius*: proderit Σ   4 quia] qui *S*
5 ante minus *KS*   6 de *add. ed. Ald.*   Cicerone *S*   7 ex] et *P*[1]
Catulo *om. P*[1]   11 nominem *S*   13 Catuli Σ, *corr. Patricius*
patriaeque *Manutius*: atque Σ   14 quid *P*: qui *SM*   15 *continuant*
prioribus SM   16 quod Σ, *corr. ed. Ald.*   Domitium *S*   sylla-
num (syla- *P*) Σ, *corr. Manutius* (*ita mox*)   19 esset *S*: *om. PM*
21 accusauit *S*: accusabat *PM*   criminabat Σ, *corr. ed. Ven.*
rem cum *Stangl*: eum cum Σ: eum bellum *Manutius*: eum bellum
cum *Bücheler*   23 dedit *Manutius*

granted to the Roman people and snatched from the colleges of the chief   80C
potentates the power to co-opt priests—in complete silence, with the
support of the nobility, with no one enlisted to interpose his veto? That
this requires comment because in this context he does not enter the
name of the man who did this, may seem, I daresay, to be the case to
anyone who forgets that less than 20 lines earlier Cicero says about
that very person: *But if I wished to put a friendly question to*
Q. Catulus, that man so fully endowed with wisdom and humanity:
'Of the two, whose tribunate do you find yourself the less able to
endorse—that of C. Cornelius, or—I won't say that of P. Sulpicius,
nor that of L. Saturninus, nor Gaius Gracchus nor Tiberius: I shall
name no one whom those friends of yours regard as subversive—but,
Q. Catulus, that of your own uncle, that most illustrious and patriotic of
men?'—what do you think he would answer?

There follows

Again—by what methods did that same Domitius harry M. Silanus, a
man of consular rank? M. Silanus had been consul five years before
Domitius was tribune of the plebs, and himself also had failed against
the Cimbri. For this reason Domitius indicted him before the people.
The charges were that he had waged war on the Cimbri without
instructions from the people, and that this had been the start of the
catastrophes which the people had suffered in that war—and he also
issued a written memorandum about him. But Silanus was acquitted
by a very ample margin, for only two tribes voted his condemnation,
the Sergia and the Quirina.

81C   Haec est controversia eius modi ut mihi *probe-*
tur tr. pl. Cn. Domitius, Catulo M. Terpolius.
      Contemptissimum nomen electum esse ex eis qui tr. pl.
fuerant post infractam tribuniciam potestatem *a* Sulla, ante
5 restitutam a Cn. Pompeio apparet. Fuit autem is tr. pl.
ante XII annos D. Bruto et Mam. Lepido coss.; Cn. Domitius tribunus fuerat ante II de XL annos C. Mario II
C. Fimbria coss.

Magno numero sententiarum Cornelius absolutus est.

1 mihi (m *S*) . . . . . . Σ, *suppl. Madvig*   2 Turpilius *Pighius*
3–4   contemptissimum . . . fuerant *Asconio reddiderunt KS*   3
electum *Madvig* : eiectum (iect- *S*) Σ   iis *P* : his *SM*   4 fuerunt
Σ, *corr. KS*   a Sulla *Manutius* : Sylle Σ   6 et *del. KS*   Mam.
Sigonius : M. Σ.   7 an *S*   de XL *Manutius* : et XL Σ   8
C. *ed. Iunt.* : cons. *S* : coss. *P* : cos. *M*

This is the kind of dispute in which as tribunes of the plebs Cn.
Domitius gets my approval, M. Terpolius that of Catulus. It is evident
that the most despicable name has been picked out among those who
had been tribunes of the plebs after the tribunician power was
shattered by Sulla, and before its restoration by Cn. Pompeius.
Now this man was tribune of the plebs twelve years earlier, in the
consulship of D. Brutus and Mam. Lepidus [77 BC]; Cn. Domitius
had been tribune thirty-eight years earlier, in the consulship of
C. Marius and C. Fimbria [104 BC].

Cornelius was acquitted by a large number of votes.

In Senatu in Toga Candida
Contra C. Antonium
et L. Catilinam Competitores

Haec oratio dicta est L. Caesare C. Figulo coss. post
annum quam pro Cornelio dixerat.

ARGVMENTVM

Sex competitores in consulatus petitione Cicero habuit,
5 duos patricios, P. Sulpicium Galbam, L. Sergium Catilinam;
quattuor plebeios ex quibus duos nobiles, C. Antonium,
M. Antoni oratoris filium, L. Cassium Longinum, duos qui
tantum non primi ex familiis suis magistratum adepti erant,
Q. Cornificium et C. Licinium Sacerdotem. Solus Cicero
10 ex competitoribus equestri erat loco natus; atque in petitione patrem amisit. Ceteri eius competitores modeste se
gessere, visique sunt Q. Cornificius et Galba sobrii *ac* sancti
viri, Sacerdos nulla improbitate notus; Cassius quamvis
stolidus tum magis quam improbus videretur, post paucos
15 menses in coniuratione Catilinae esse eum apparuit ac
cruentissimarum sententiarum fuisse auctorem. Itaque hi
quattuor prope iacebant. Catilina autem et Antonius,

Tit. toga *ex* stola *P* (*Inscriptionem om. M*)   3 argvmentvm
add. hoc loco Baiter : *ante* Haec oratio *ed. Ald.*   6 duos *Sigonius* :
duo Σ   8 tantum *Manutius* : tamen Σ   12 suisique *P*   sobrii
π, *M* : sonii *SP*[1] ac *add. Beraldus*   13 sacerdotis *S*   quamvis
Bücheler : qui ineius *SP* : qui iners *Poggius*, *M* : qui iners ac *ed.*
Iunt., Baiter   14 magister *S*   post *Manutius* : sed (set *S*) Σ
15 eum esse *P*   16 itaque] atque *Bücheler*   17 prope *Rau* :
pro re Σ : *fort.* per se   tacebant *S*[1]

The Speech in the Senate as a Candidate against his Electoral Rivals C. Antonius and L. Catilina

This speech was delivered in the consulship of L. Caesar and C. Figulus, the year after he had spoken for Cornelius.

Explanatory preface

Cicero had six rivals in his bid for the consulship, two of them patricians, P. Sulpicius Galba and L. Sergius Catilina; four plebeians, of whom two were nobles, C. Antonius, son of M. Antonius the orator, and L. Cassius Longinus, and two who were merely not the first of their families to attain office, Q. Cornificius and C. Licinius Sacerdos. Cicero alone from this field of competitors was born of equestrian rank, and during the campaign he lost his father. The rest of his rivals behaved with decorum, and Q. Cornificius and Galba were of proven sobriety and integrity, Sacerdos with no mark of immoral conduct against him. Cassius, although at the time he seemed more stupid than immoral, a few months later was evidently included in Catilina's conspiracy and the origin of some extremely bloodthirsty expressions of opinion. So these four were all but beaten. But Catilina and Antonius,

quamquam omnium maxime infamis eorum vita esset,
tamen multum poterant. Coierant enim ambo ut Ciceronem
consulatu deicerent, adiutoribus usi firmissimis M. Crasso
et C. Caesare. Itaque haec oratio contra solos Catilinam
5 et Antonium est. Causa orationis huius modi in senatu
habendae Ciceroni fuit quod, cum in dies licentia ambitus
augeretur propter praecipuam Catilinae et Antoni audaciam,
censuerat senatus ut lex ambitus aucta etiam cum poena
ferretur; eique rei Q. Mucius Orestinus tr. pl. intercesserat.
10 Tum Cicero graviter senatu intercessionem ferente surrexit
atque in coitionem Catilinae et Antoni invectus est ante dies
comitiorum paucos.

ENARRATIO

Dico, P. C., superiore nocte cuiusdam hominis
15 nobilis et valde in hoc largitionis quaestu noti et
cogniti domum Catilinam et Antonium cum se-
questribus suis convenisse.

Aut C. Caesaris aut M. Crassi domum significat. Ei
enim acerrimi ac potentissimi fuerunt Ciceronis refraga-
20 tores cum petiit consulatum, quod eius in dies civilem
crescere dignitatem animadvertebant: et hoc ipse Cicero in
expositione consiliorum suorum significat; eius quoque
coniurationis quae Cotta et Torquato coss. ante annum
quam haec dicerentur facta est a Catilina et Pisone arguit
25 M. Crassum auctorem fuisse.

Quem enim aut amicum habere potest is qui tot

1 omnium *KS*: o̅m̅ *SM*: omnibus *P*   eorum *om. S*   2 plu
multum *P* : multum *M* : . . . . tum *S*   ambo ut *PM* : . . . . . .
. . . . *S*   5 in *P* : *om. SM*   6 habente *S*   7 propter *Pog-*
gius, *M* : praeter *SP¹*   et *om. S¹*   9 eique *Manutius* : et
(ei *P*) quoque Σ   11 contionem Σ, *corr. Manutius*   13 *add. Hoto-*
man   15 noti] docti *Halm*   18 ei *Bücheler* : et Σ   19 ac *SP* :
et *M*   20 petit Σ, *corr.* π   21 ạd animadvertebant *P*
22 suorum consiliorum *P*   eius *Poggius*, *M* : sexus *SP¹*   23
cocta Σ, *corr. ed.* V   24 pisonem *S*   26 habere potest *PM* :
potest habere *S*

despite having led the most disgraceful lives of all of them, even so   83C
had much power at their disposal. For both had entered an electoral
pact to keep Cicero out of the consulship, enjoying very strong
support from M. Crassus and C. Caesar. For this reason, the speech
is directed solely against Catilina and Antonius. The occasion for
Cicero to deliver an oration of this kind in the senate was that since
the scope for *ambitus* was increasing by the day through the blatant
effrontery of Catilina and Antonius, the senate had resolved that a
law should be carried *de ambitu* with increased penalties; and
Q. Mucius Orestinus, tribune of the plebs, had interposed his veto
against this initiative. At that point Cicero, with the senate much
displeased at the veto, rose and inveighed against the electoral pact of
Catilina and Antonius, a few days before the day of the elections.

Commentary

*It is my contention, Conscript Fathers, that last night Catilina and
Antonius met, with their followers, in the house of a certain person of
noble rank, a well-known and recognized figure in this business of
funding largesse.* He means the house of either C. Caesar or M.
Crassus. For they were the most determined and powerful of Cicero's
adversaries when he stood for the consulship, since they were be-
coming aware that his standing in the community was growing by
the day—and Cicero himself notes this in his *Explanation of his
Political Calculations.* And he charges Crassus with having also been
the instigator of the conspiracy which was formed by Catilina and
Piso in the consulship of Cotta and Torquatus [65 BC], the year before
this speech was delivered.

Whom can he count as a friend, he who

84C

civis trucidavit, aut *clientem* qui in sua civitate
cum peregrino negavit se iudicio aequo certare
posse?

Dicitur Catilina, cum in Sullanis partibus fuisset, crude-
5 liter fecisse. Nominatim etiam postea Cicero dicit quos
occiderit, Q. Caecilium, M. Volumnium, L. Tanusium.
M. etiam Mari Gratidiani summe popularis hominis, qui ob
id bis praetor fuit, caput abscisum per urbem sua manu
Catilina tulerat: quod crimen saepius ei tota oratione
10 obicit. Fuerat vero hic Gratidianus arta necessitudine
Ciceroni coniunctus.

Clientem autem negavit habere posse C. Antonium: nam
is multos in Achaia spoliaverat nactus de exercitu Sullano
equitum turmas. Deinde Graeci qui spoliati erant edu-
15 xerunt Antonium in ius ad M. Lucullum praetorem qui ius
inter peregrinos dicebat. Egit pro Graecis C. *Caesar* etiam
tum adulescentulus, de quo paulo ante mentionem fecimus;
et cum Lucullus id quod Graeci postulabant decrevisset,
appellavit tribunos Antonius iuravitque se ideo eiurare quod
20 aequo iure uti non posset. Hunc Antonium Gellius et
Lentulus censores sexennio quo haec dicerentur senatu
moverunt titulosque subscripserunt, quod socios diripuerit,
quod iudicium recusarit, quod propter aeris alieni magnitudinem praedia manciparit bonaque sua in potestate non
25 habeat.

1 trucidari Σ, *corr. Poggius*   clientem *add. Manutius*   4 dicitur
supplevi (*cf.* 91. 27) : significat *KS* Catilinam *M, Manutius*   5 fecisse
P : fecisset *SM*   6 Tantasium Σ, *corr. Manutius* (*e Cons. Pet.* 6)   7
popularis *P* : postularis *SM*   8 abscisum *S* : abscissum *PM*   12
negabat (-bit *M*) Σ, *corr. Baiter* : negat *Manutius*   14 qui Σ : quos
Poggius   spoliauerant (-unt *S*) Σ : spoliaverat *Poggius, corr. Madvig*

16 C. Caesar *add. Manutius*   18 quod (*ante* Luc.) Σ : 'c.̇ quom' π
19 ideo *SP, om. M* : id forum *Mommsen*   iurare Σ, *corr. Baiter*
20 equa in re Σ, *corr. Lodoicus*   hinc *Bücheler*   21 quo *PM* : quam
S : ante quam *KS*   22 titulosque *scripsi* : catulisque *S* : causasque
PM   23–24 recusavit...mancipavit Σ, *corr. Manutius*   24
non *om.* S¹   25 habeat *KS* : ht *SM* : habēt *P*

butchered so many fellow-citizens, or whom can he count as a client, he   84C
who claimed that in his own state he could not contend with an alien in
a fair trial? Catilina, when he had been one of Sulla's partisans, is said
to have acted with brutality. Cicero also later mentions by name
those whom he killed—Q. Caecilius, M. Volumnius, L. Tanusius.
Catilina had also cut off the head of M. Marius Gratidianus, a man in
great favour with the people, who on this account was twice praetor,
and had carried it through the city in his own hand—a charge which
he hurls at him several times throughout this speech. To be sure, this
Gratidianus had been linked by close family ties with Cicero.

He also declared it impossible for C. Antonius to have any clients.
For he had robbed many persons in Achaea on getting the use of
cavalry squadrons from Sulla's army. Then the Greeks who had been
robbed took Antonius to court before the praetor M. Lucullus, who
had jurisdiction in cases involving aliens. The action for the Greeks
was brought by C. Caesar, at the time only young, of whom we have
made mention a little earlier. When Lucullus decided the case in
accordance with what the Greeks were demanding, Antonius summoned the tribunes and swore an oath that he rejected the validity of
the court for the reason that he was unable to enjoy an equality of
rights. Six years before this speech was delivered, the censors Gellius
and Lentulus removed this Antonius from the senate and put their
signatures to a public listing of their reasons—that he had plundered
allies, rejected the judgment of a court, that on account of his vast
debts he had made over estates and held no property in his own name.

Nec senatum respexit cum gravissimis vestris
decretis absens notatus est.

Catilina ex praetura Africam provinciam obtinuit: quam
cum graviter vexasset, legati Afri in senatu iam tum
5 absente illo questi sunt, multaeque graves sententiae in
senatu de eo dictae sunt.

In iudiciis quanta vis esset didicit cum est
absolutus: si aut illud iudicium aut illa absolutio
nominanda est.

10 Ante annum quam haec dicerentur Catilina, cum redisset
ex Africa Torquato et Cotta coss., accusatus est repetundarum a P. Clodio adulescente, qui postea inimicus
Ciceronis fuit. Defensus est Catilina, ut Fenestella tradit,
a M. Cicerone. Quod ego ut addubitem haec ipsa
15 Ciceronis oratio facit, maxime quod is nullam mentionem
rei habet, cum potuerit invidiam facere competitori tam
turpiter adversus se coeunti: praesertim cum alterum
competitorem suum Antonium in eadem hac oratione sua
admoneat suo beneficio eum ex ultimo loco praeturae
20 candidatum ad tertium pervenisse.

Nescis me praetorem primum esse factum, te
concessione competitorum et collatione centuria-
rum et meo maxime beneficio ex postremo in
tertium locum esse subiectum?

25 Qui igitur Antonio suffragationem suam imputandam
putat, is *si* defendisset Catilinam, caput eius protectum
a se nonne imputaret? Quod ita esse manifestum est ex
eo quod statim dicit. Q. enim Mucius tr. pl. intercedebat

1 nec *Patricius* : ne Σ   se (si *S*, sc *P*¹) iam tum (tam *P*¹*M*)
Σ, *corr. Halm*   despexit Σ, *corr. Poggius*   3 prouinciam africam
S   4 iam] etiam *Halm*   5 in senatu de eo *PM* : de eo in
senatu *S*   13 Ciceroni *P*   14 *in mg. P. scr. π. 'Nota. Cicero
in quadam ad Atticum epistola scribit de Catilinae defensione quam
facere cogitabat.'*   21 te concessione *S* : tecum cessione *P* : tecum
concessione *M*   22 conlatine Σ, *corr. Poggius*   23 ex *KS* :
et *SP*¹ : te e *Poggius* : te et *M*   25 Antonio *om. P*¹   26
is si ς, *ed. Ald.* : is Σ   27 esset Σ, *corr. Manutius*

Nor did he respect the senate's will, when in his absence he was   85C
branded a criminal by your most weighty decrees. Catilina after his
praetorship held the command of Africa. After he had inflicted
serious harm on the province, African envoys while he was still absent
lodged formal complaints against him in the senate, and many highly
critical opinions were expressed about him in the senate.

He found out how effective the courts were on his acquittal—if that
(process) can be called a court or that (verdict) an acquittal. A year
before this speech was delivered Catilina on return from Africa in the
consulship of Torquatus and Cotta, was accused *de repetundis* by the
young P. Clodius, who was later Cicero's enemy. Catilina was
defended, according to Fenestella, by M. Cicero. This very speech
of Cicero makes me doubt this, especially since it contains no
mention of the fact at a time when he could have aroused ill-feeling
against his electoral rival for so shamefully entering into a pact against
him, and particularly since he reminds his other rival Antonius in
this same oration of his that it was thanks to his kindness that he
[Antonius] had, as a candidate for the praetorship, managed to win
third place instead of last.

Do you not realize that I was made praetor in first place, but you
(only) by compliance of our competitors, whipping in the votes of the
centuries, and in particular the good turn that I did you, were tacked on
in third place instead of last? Now a man who considers that his
electoral support for Antonius should count to his credit—surely if
he had defended Catilina, would he not claim credit for the protection of his citizen rights? It is obvious that this is so from what he says
in the immediate sequel. For Q. Mucius Orestinus was using his veto

86C ne lex ambitus ferretur; quod facere pro Catilina videbatur.
Hunc Mucium in hac oratione Cicero appellans sic ait:

Te tamen, Q. Muci, tam male de populo Romano
existimare moleste fero qui hesterno die me esse
5 dignum consulatu negabas. Quid? p. R. minus
diligenter sibi constitueret defensorem quam tu
tibi? Cum tecum furti L. Calenus ageret, me potis-
simum fortunarum tuarum patronum esse voluisti.
Cuius tute consilium in tua turpissima causa dele-
10 gisti, hunc honestissimarum rerum defensorem p.
R. auctore te repudiare potest? Nisi forte hoc
dicturus es, quo tempore cum L. Caleno furti
depectus sis, eo tempore in me tibi parum esse
auxili vidisse.

15   Vere cum egerit Muci causam Cicero sicut Catilinae
egisse eum videri vult Fenestella, cur iam, quamvis male
existimet de causa Muci, tamen ei exprobret patrocinium
suum, non idem in Catilina faciat, si modo pro eo dixit? et
cur ipsum illud iudicium saepius in infamiam vocat? quod
20 parcius videtur fuisse facturus, si in eo iudicio fuisset patronus.
Atque ut alia omittam, hoc certe vix videtur dicturus fuisse,
si illo patrono Catilina repetundarum absolutus esset:

Stupris se omnibus ac flagitiis contaminavit;
caede nefaria cruentavit; diripuit socios; leges
25 quaestiones iudicia violavit—et postea:

Quid ego ut violaveris provinciam praedicem?
Nam ut te illic gesseris non audeo dicere, quo-

2 appellans Cicero *P*   3 male de P. R. *Gronovius*: malecie (male

                                                                 s
cie *P*) tr. Σ : 'c. de re p.' π   4 hesterna (ext- *S*), *corr. ed. Ald.*   6
constituere Σ, *corr. Baiter*   7 tecum *Gronovius*: te Σ   9 tu et Σ, *corr.*
Orelli   consilium] auxilium *Halm*   in tua turpissima *om. M*   12
es *Manutius* : est Σ   13 detectus sit Σ, *corr. KS* (a L. Caleno

                                    ‖   ‖
furti delatus sis *Manutius*)   auxilii esse *P*   14 vidisse *ed. Ald.* :
uidisset Σ : vidisse te *Baiter*   15 uerum ut ageret Σ, *corr. Orelli*
16 egisset Σ, *corr. ed. Ald.*   iam *Lodoicus* : tam Σ : cum *Manutius*
quamuis *P* : quemuis *SM*   17 exprobet Σ, *corr. ed. V*   18
et *ed. Ald.* : ut Σ : aut *Baiter*   19 illum *SM*   20 uideretur Σ, *corr.*
Baitler   22 est Σ, *corr. Baiter*   25 ET POSTEA *P*   27 illis *S*

to prevent passage of a law *de ambitu*—a move evidently in Catilina's   86C
favour. In citing Mucius in this oration, Cicero speaks as follows: *As
for you, however, Q. Mucius, who yesterday alleged that I am not
worthy of the consulship, I am angered that you should have such a
low opinion of the Roman people. How so? Would the Roman people set
up a champion for itself with less circumspection than you did for
yourself? When L. Calenus sued you for theft, I was your first choice
as protector of your fortunes. Can the Roman people at your behest
reject as its champion in business of the highest honour the man whose
advice you preferred in your own most sordid little affair? Unless, I
suppose, you are going to say this—that at the time when you did your
deal with Calenus over theft, you saw that you could not get sufficient
assistance from me.* Since Cicero really did take Mucius' case, just as
Fenestella would have it that he apparently took Catilina's, why at this
point, when, although he has a low opinion of Mucius' case, he
nonetheless reproaches him with the fact that he gave him his services
as an advocate, would he not do likewise with Catilina, if he spoke for
him at all? And why does he invoke that very trial [*sc.* the trial of
Catilina] so often as a matter of scandal? He seems likely to have done
this far more sparingly, if he had been his advocate in that trial. And
leaving aside other examples, if Catilina had been acquitted *de
repetundis* with his advocacy, he certainly seems hardly likely to
have said: *He besmirched himself with all manner of sexual misconduct
and disgraceful acts, bloodied himself in criminal slaughter, despoiled
our allies; did violence to the laws, the courts, the judiciary*—and later:
*Why should I stress the violence you did to your province? For I hesitate
to tell of your conduct there,*

niam absolutus es. Mentitos esse equites Roma-
nos, falsas fuisse tabellas honestissimae civitatis
existimo, mentitum Q. Metellum Pium, mentitam
Africam : vidisse puto nescio quid illos iudices
5 qui te innocentem iudicarunt. O miser qui non
sentias illo iudicio te non absolutum verum ad
aliquod severius iudicium ac maius supplicium re-
servatum!

    Verine ergo simile est haec eum Catilinae obicere, si illo
10 defendente absolutus esset? Praeterea movet me quod,
cum sint commentarii Ciceronis causarum, eius tamen
defensionis nullum *est* commentarium aut principium.

    Ita quidem iudicio absolutus est Catilina ut Clodius
infamis fuerit praevaricatus esse : nam et reiectio iudicum
15 ad arbitrium rei videbatur esse facta.

    Populum vero cum inspectante populo collum
secuit hominis maxime popularis quanti faceret
ostendit.

    Diximus et paulo ante Mari caput Catilinam per urbem
20 tulisse.

    Me qua amentia inductus sit ut contemneret con-
stituere non possum. Vtrum aequo animo laturum
putavit? At in suo familiarissimo viderat me ne
aliorum *quidem* iniurias mediocriter posse ferre.
25   Manifestum est C. Verrem significari.

    Alter pecore omni vendito et saltibus prope
addictis pastores retinet, ex quibus ait se cum
velit subito fugitivorum bellum excitaturum.

    C. Antonium significat.

---

3 mentitum Σ, *corr. ed. Iunt.*   4 puto *Manutius* : apud Σ : aliud
Bücheler   illo Σ, *corr. Manutius*   9 verine] 'Vincis me.
Itaque puto non defendisse sed tantum de defendendo cogitasse quod
per epistolam negari non potest' π *in mg.*   10 est Σ. *corr. Baiter* 11
causarum *Baiter* : earum Σ   eius tamen defensionis nullum est
scripsi : etiam c̄ē *M*) defensionum Σ   13 ita quod Σ, *corr. KS*
absolutus est *PM* : est absolutus *S*   14 esset Σ, *corr. Madvig*
19 Mari] manu *S*   21 sit *Madvig* : est Σ   22 animo *om. P*
an in Σ, *corr. Madvig*   24 quidem *add. ed. Ald.*   25 significat Σ,
corr. ed. Iunt.   27 additis Σ, *corr. Beraldus*

since you were found not guilty. I must suppose that Roman knights told lies, the written depositions of a most honourable community were falsified, that Q. Metellus Pius told lies, that Africa told lies; that those jurymen who adjudged you innocent saw something or other (in your favour). What a wretch, that you should not perceive that by that judgment you were not so much acquitted as preserved for some sterner court-hearing and greater punishment! So is it probable that he would hurl these reproaches at Catilina, if he had been acquitted with Cicero defending him? Besides, I am also influenced by the fact that although there exist notes of Cicero's cases, even so there is no précis or preface extant for this one.

The manner of Catilina's judicial acquittal was such as to bring Clodius into ill-repute for collusion, for even the rejection of jurors seemed to have been performed to accord with the wishes of the accused.

How great is his regard for the people he demonstrated when in full sight of the people he severed the neck of a man who was a favourite of the people. We have said a little earlier that Catilina carried the head of Marius through the city.

By what fit of madness he was induced to show me contempt, I cannot establish. Did he suppose that I would accept it with indifference? Yet in the case of a very close associate of his he had seen that I could not take calmly even the wrongs done to others. It is obvious that C. Verres is meant.

The other, after selling all his livestock and more or less making over his grasslands, retains his shepherds, from whom, he says, he can whenever he wishes at a moment's notice whip up a runaway slave war. He means C. Antonius.

88C

Alter induxit eum quem potuit ut repente gladiatores populo non debitos polliceretur; eos ipse
consularis candidatus perspexit et legit et emit; *id
praesente populo Romano factum est.*

5   Q. Gallium, quem postea reum ambitus defendit, significare videtur. Hic enim cum esset praeturae candidatus,
quod in aedilitate quam ante annum gesserat bestias non
habuerat, dedit gladiatorium *munus* sub titulo patri se
id dare.

10   Quam ob rem augete etiam mercedem, si voltis,
Q. Muci ut perseveret legem impedire, ut coepit
senatus consultum; sed ego ea lege contentus
sum qua duos consules designatos uno tempore
damnari vidimus.

15   Legem Calpurniam significat quam C. Calpurnius Piso
ante triennium de ambitu tulerat. Quod dicit autem da-
mnatos esse designatos consules, P. Sullam et P. Autronium,
de quibus iam diximus, vult intellegi. Cognomen autem
Q. Mucio tribuno quem nominat fuit Orestinus.

20   Atque ut istum omittam in exercitu Sullano
praedonem, in introitu gladiatorem, in victoria
quadrigarium.

De Antonio dici manifestum est. Dicit eum in
exercitu Sullae praedonem propter equitum turmas
25 quibus Achaiam ab eo vexatam esse significavimus; in
introitu gladiatorem pertinet ad invidiam proscriptionis
quae tum facta est; in victoria quadrigarium, quod,
cum Sulla post victoriam circenses faceret ita ut honesti
homines quadrigas agitarent, fuit inter eos C. Antonius.

2 populo *S, Poggius* : poculo *P¹M*   eos] quos *Poggius*   3 consularis *S* : consularius *PM*   id *add. Orelli*   7 uertias *Σ, corr.
Manutius*   8 gladiatorium *P* : gladiatorum *SM* : gladiatores *Grono-
vius*   munus *supplevi* : *om.* Σ   patris Σ, *corr. Manutius*   10
augete *P* : augente *SM*   mercede *S* : mercedes *MP, corr. Madvig*
11 Q. mutium perreuerti Σ, *corr. Madvig*   12 senter $\widetilde{cos}$ Σ, *corr.
Madvig*   16 autem dicit *P*   17 Antronium (-tonium *M*) Σ, *corr.
Manutius*   20 ut *om. S*   23 dici *P* : dicit *SM*   est
Purser : est sed Σ : est. Et *KS*   25 Achaiam (-a *M*) πM : camiam
S : eamiam *P¹*   significamus Σ, *corr. Manutius*   28 pōt *S*

The other influenced a person (whom he was able so to influence)   **88C**
unexpectedly to promise the people gladiators that were not required of
him. These the consular candidate himself looked over, selected, and
bought. This was done in the presence of the Roman people. He appears
to mean Q. Gallius, whom he later defended on a charge *de ambitu.*
For this man, when he was candidate for the praetorship, since he
had had no beast to show in his aedileship which he had discharged
the year before, presented a gladiatorial event on the pretext that he
was giving it 'for his father'.

So then raise the price, if you wish, to be paid to Q. Mucius for
persisting in blocking the law, in the opening words of the senate's
decree. But I rest content with the law under which we have seen two
consuls designate condemned at one and the same time. He means the
Calpurnian Law which C. Calpurnius Piso had carried three years
earlier [67] *de ambitu.* In mentioning the condemnation of two
consuls designate, he wishes to be understood P. Sulla and P. Autronius, of whom we have already spoken. The *cognomen* of the tribune
whom he names, Q. Mucius, was Orestinus.

And to say nothing of this man as a brigand in Sulla's army, gladiator
at his entry (to Rome), charioteer in his Victory Games. It is clear that
Antonius is the subject of these remarks. He calls him *brigand in*
Sulla's army by reason of the cavalry squadrons by which we have
indicated that Achaea was harried by him; (the phrase) *gladiator at*
his entry applies to the hostility aroused by the proscription which
took place at that time; (he calls him) *charioteer in his Victory Games*
because when Sulla after his victory celebrated circus games which
involved respectable men driving four-horse chariots, C. Antonius
was among them.

89C

Te vero, Catilina, consulatum sperare aut cogi-
tare non prodigium atque portentum est? A
quibus enim petis? A principibus civitatis? qui
tibi, cum L. Volcacio cos. in consilio fuissent,
5 ne petendi quidem potestatem esse voluerunt.

Paulo ante diximus Catilinam, cum de provincia Africa
decederet petiturus consulatum et legati Afri questi de eo in
senatu graviter *essent*, supervenisse. Professus deinde est
Catilina petere se consulatum. L. Volcacius Tullus consul
10 consilium publicum habuit an rationem Catilinae habere
deberet, si peteret consulatum: nam quaerebatur repetundarum.   Catilina ob eam causam destitit a petitione.

A senatoribus? qui te auctoritate sua spoliatum
ornamentis omnibus vinctum paene Africanis
15 oratoribus tradiderunt?

Diximus modo de hoc.   Nam iudicium quoque secutum
est repetundarum, quo ipse per infamiam liberatus est Catilina, sed ita ut senatorum urna damnaret, equitum et
tribunorum absolveret.

20   Ab equestri ordine? quem trucidasti?

Equester ordo pro Cinnanis partibus contra Sullam
steterat, multique pecunias abstulerant: ex quo saccularii
erant appellati, atque ob eius rei invidiam post Sullanam
victoriam erant interfecti.

25   A plebe? cui spectaculum eius modi tua crudeli-
tas praebuit, ut *te* nemo sine gemitu ac recordatione luctus aspicere possit?

---

2 ex quibus Σ, *corr. Manutius*   4 Volcacius *Poggius*   fuisset
Σ, *corr. Madvig*   6 cum Catilinam *P*   8 essent *supplevi* (*hoc loco,*
post questi *Bücheler*) : *om.* Σ   supervenisse *scripsi* : pervenisset
(-ent *P*) Σ   (*cf.* 85. 4, 37. 4, 43. 15) : vituperatum esse *Bücheler*
est *P*: esse *SM*   9 uolcacios *P*   13 a *ed. Iunt.* : an Σ   15
aratoribus *Bardili* 17 est *add.*   KS quo *KS* : quod *SM* : a quo
P 18 sedit (sed id *S*) autem *SP*ᵗ, *corr. Poggius*, *M* : sed ita ut eum
    s
Hotoman   21 ei ūr Σ : 'c.   equester' π   22 multasque Σ,
corr. KS   contulerant *S*   25 cuius *S*   26–27 ut te...
possit *Madvig*: ut.... posset Σ

But come, Catilina, for you to hope for or even to think about a   89C
consulship—is that not a prodigy and a portent? Well, from whom are
you seeking to get it? From our leading statesmen? But when they acted
as advisers to the consul L. Volcacius, they were unwilling for you to
have even the right to stand. A little earlier we said that Catilina
turned up when he was retiring from his command in Africa with
the intention of seeking the consulship and African envoys had made
serious complaints about him in the senate. Then Catilina declared
his intention to seek the consulship. L. Volcacius Tullus the consul
held a meeting of his advisers on public affairs to consider whether he
ought to recognize the candidature of Catilina, if he were to seek the
consulship, since he was under investigation *de repetundis*. Catilina
for this reason gave up his candidature.

From the senators? Who on their own authority all but stripped you
of all honours and handed you over to spokesmen from Africa? We have
just said something on this. For a trial ensued *de repetundis*, in which
Catilina himself was scandalously acquitted, but by a verdict in which
the senatorial vote was for conviction, that of the knights and *tribuni*
aerarii for acquittal.

From the equestrian order? Which you butchered? The equestrian
order had stood for the Cinnan party against Sulla, and many had
stolen funds. On that score they were termed 'pickpockets', and on
account of the hostility that this aroused were killed after Sulla's
victory.

From the plebs? To whom your brutality presented a spectacle such
that no one can set eyes upon you without a groan and remembrance of
sorrow?

90C Eiusdem illius Mari Gratidiani quod caput gestarit obicit.
Quo loco dicit Catilinam caput M. Mari gestasse:
Quod caput etiam tum plenum animae et spiritus
ad Sullam usque ab Ianiculo ad aedem Apollinis
5 manibus ipse suis detulit.
Omnia sunt manifesta. Ne tamen erretis, quod his
temporibus aedes Apollinis in Palatio fuit nobilissima,
admonendi estis non hanc a Cicerone significari, utpote
quam post mortem etiam Ciceronis multis annis Imp.
10 Caesar, quem nunc Divum Augustum dicimus, post Actia-
cam victoriam fecerit: sed illam demonstrari quae est extra
portam Carmentalem inter forum holitorium et circum
Flaminium. Ea enim sola tum quidem Romae Apollinis
aedes.
15 Loquitur cum Catilina:
Quid tu potes in defensione tua dicere quod illi
non *dixerint? at illi multa* dixerunt quae tibi
dicere non licebit—
et paulo post:
20 Denique illi negare potuerunt et negaverunt: tu
tibi ne infitiandi quidem impudentiae locum reli-
quisti. Qua re praeclara dicentur iudicia tulisse
si, qui infitiantem Luscium condemnarunt, Catilinam absolverint confitentem.
25 Hic quem nominat L. Luscius, notus centurio Sullanus
divesque e victoria factus—nam amplius centies possederat—
damnatus erat non multo ante quam Cicero dixit. Obiectae

---

1 Mari *P* : mori *SM*   gestaret Σ, *corr. Manutius*   obit Σ,
corr. ς, *ed. Iunt.*   2 M. *om. P¹*   4 syllam usque *P* : syllanosque
SM   aedem *P* : aedilis *S* : eidem *M*   6 tamen *P* : tam *SM*
7 aedes *P* : aedilis *SM*   fuit] sit *Manutius* : est *Wesenberg*   8
ut puto Σ, *corr. Drakenborch*   9 post p *S*   10 Attiacam *P* : acticam
SM   13 quidem *Baiter* : demum Σ   Romae Apollinis aedes *P* :
romae ad aedilis *S* : adediles romae *M*   15 LOQVĪT cum Catilina *P*
in mg.   17 illi non dixerunt Σ, *suppl. Madvig*   22 dicuntur Σ,
corr. Manutius   23 condemnarint (-it *M*) Σ, *corr. Manutius*   25
Syllanus *Poggius*, *M* : syllanos *SP¹*   26 e *P* : ea *SM* : ex *KS*
27 dominatus Σ, *corr. Poggius*

He casts in his teeth the reproach of having brandished the head of   90C
that same Marius Gratidianus.

In the place where he says that Catilina brandished the head of M.
Marius: *That head, even then still showing every sign of life and breath,
he brought to Sulla in his own hands all the way from the Janiculum to
the Temple of Apollo.* Everything is obvious enough. However, to
avoid being misled by the fact that in our own day the Temple of
Apollo on the Palatine has been the best known, you should be
warned that it is not this one which is meant by Cicero—to wit,
the one which many years even after the death of Cicero the Imperator Caesar, whom we now call the Deified Augustus, constructed.
Rather, the one indicated is that which is outside the Gate of Carmentis, between the Vegetable Market and the Circus Flaminius. For
at that time this was the only Temple of Apollo in Rome.

He converses with Catilina: *What can you say in your defence which
they did not say (in theirs)? Yet they said a good deal which it will not be
open to you to say.* And a little further on: *In short, they were able to
make denial, and made it: you have left yourself no scope for the
impudence even of making a plea of Not Guilty. It follows that they
(the jurors) will be said to have brought in notable verdicts if, having
convicted Luscius on a plea of Not Guilty, they then acquit Catilina
despite his confession.* This man whom he names, L. Luscius, a
notorious centurion of Sulla's who made rich pickings from his
victory—for he had property worth more than HS 100,000—had
been convicted not long before Cicero's speech. He was charged

sunt ei tres caedes proscriptorum. Circa eosdem dies L.
quoque Bellienus damnatus est quem Cicero ait avunculum
esse Catilinae. Hic autem Lucretium Ofellam consulatum
contra voluntatem Sullae ad turbandum statum civitatis
5 petentem occiderat iussu Sullae tunc dictatoris. His ergo
negat ignotum esse, cum et imperitos se homines esse et,
si quem etiam interfecissent, imperatori ac dictatori paruisse
dicerent, ac negare quoque *possent*: Catilinam vero infitiari
non posse. Huius autem criminis periculum quod obicit
10 Cicero paucos post menses Catilina subiit. Post effecta
enim comitia consularia et Catilinae repulsam fecit eum
reum inter sicarios L. Lucceius paratus eruditusque, qui
postea consulatum quoque petiit.

Hanc tu habes dignitatem qua fretus me con-
15 temnis et despicis, an eam quam reliqua in vita es
consecutus? cum ita vixisti ut non esset locus tam
sanctus quo non adventus tuus, etiam cum culpa
nulla subesset, crimen afferret.

Fabia virgo Vestalis causam incesti dixerat, cum ei
20 Catilina obiceretur, eratque absoluta. Haec Fabia quia
soror erat Terentiae Ciceronis, ideo sic dixit: etiam si
culpa nulla subesset. Ita et suis pepercit et nihilo levius
inimico summi opprobrii turpitudinem objecit.

Cum deprehendebare in adulteriis, cum depre-
25 hendebas adulteros ipse, cum ex eodem stupro tibi
et uxorem et filiam invenisti.

Dicitur Catilina adulterium commisisse cum ea quae ei
postea socrus fuit, et ex eo natam stupro duxisse uxorem,

---

3 afellam *SP* : astalla *M, corr. Sigonius*   5 is Σ, *corr. Patricius*
6 ignarum Σ, *corr. Madvig*   cum...esse *om. S*   7 cum etiam *PM,*
corr. Madvig   8 possent *add. madvig* (ac negarent quoque *Baiter*)
12 lucullus Σ, *corr. Crevier*   peritus Beraldus   13 petiit *P*:
petit *SM*   15 qua Σ, *corr. Manutius*   reliqua in *scripsi* : reliquam
Σ : reliquum *Poggius* : reliqua *Manutius*   vita es *Manutius* : uite
Σ   17 quod non Σ, *corr. Beraldus*   23 obprobrii *S¹PM²*:
obprobii *S²M*   27 catilinam *S* (dicit Catilinam *Beraldus*)   28
natam ς, *Orelli* : nam Σ

with the murder of three of the proscribed. At about the same   91C
date, L. Bellienus too was convicted, who Cicero says was an uncle
of Catilina's. This man, on the order of Sulla, who was dictator at the
time, had killed Lucretius Afella, who was standing for the consulship
against the wishes of Sulla with a view to destabilizing the state. He
therefore declares that they were not excused, even though they
claimed that they were ignorant folk, and even if they had killed
anyone, had done it in obedience to their commander and dictator,
and could also offer denial; whereas Catilina could not plead Not
Guilty. A few months later Catilina did face the peril of trial on this
charge which Cicero levels at him. For after completion of the
consular elections and Catilina's electoral defeat, L. Lucceius, an
accomplished and learned man, who later also sought the consulship,
indicted him for murder.

*Do you possess the standing to justify your despising and insulting
me—or rather that which you have earned in the rest of your life? For
your life has been such that there has been no place so sacred that your
arrival there, even if there was no underlying guilt, did not occasion
criminal charges.* Fabia the Vestal Virgin had pleaded her defence on a
charge of fornication, when (misconduct with) Catilina was alleged
against her, and had been acquitted. It is because this Fabia was sister
to Cicero's wife Terentia that he said: *even if there was no underlying
guilt.* In this way he both spared his family embarrassment and lost
no weight at all from allegations against his enemy of sordid immor-
ality deserving of the deepest opprobrium.

*Whenever you were caught in adultery, whenever you caught adul-
terers yourself, when arising from the same act of gross indecency you
found yourself a woman to be both wife and daughter.* It is said that
Catilina committed adultery with the woman who was later his
mother-in-law, and took to wife the female offspring of that fornication,

92C   cum filia eius esset. Hoc Lucceius quoque Catilinae obicit
in orationibus quas in eum scripsit. Nomina harum mulie-
rum nondum inveni.

Quid ego ut violaveris provinciam praedicem,
5 cuncto populo Romano clamante ac resistente?
nam ut te illic gesseris non audeo dicere, quoniam
absolutus es.

Dictum est iam saepius Catilinam ex praetura Africam
obtinuisse et accusante eum repetundarum P. Clodio
10 absolutum esse.

Praetereo nefarium illum conatum tuum et paene
acerbum et luctuosum rei publicae diem, cum Cn.
Pisone socio, ne quem alium nominem, caedem
optimatum facere voluisti.

15   Quos *non* nominet intellegitis. Fuit enim opinio Catilinam et Cn. Pisonem, adulescentem perditum, coniurasse
ad caedem senatus faciendam ante annum quam haec
dicta sunt, Cotta et Torquato coss., eamque caedem
ideo non esse factam quod prius quam parati essent
20 coniuratis signum dedisset Catilina. Piso autem, cum
haec dicerentur, perierat, in Hispaniam missus a senatu
per honorem legationis ut †auus suus ablegaretur. Ibi
quidem dum iniurias provincialibus facit, occisus erat, ut
quidam credebant, a Cn. Pompeii clientibus Pompeio non
25 invito.

An oblitus es te ex me, cum praeturam peteremus,
mus, petisse ut tibi primum locum concederem?
Quod cum saepius ageres et impudentius a me

1   lucceius   *P* : lucteius   *S* : lucrerus   *M*   2   'nomen   uxori   fuit
Aurelia   Orestilla,   de   socru   ignoro'   π   4   violaveris   Σ : involaveris
in *Patricius*   5   Ro. clamante   Σ : reclamante   *Halm*   13   socium   Σ,
corr. *Poggius*   neque alio nemine   Σ, corr. *Gronovius*   15   non
add. *KS* (*cf.* 72. 10)   21   hispaniam   *M* : hispania   *SP*   22   auus
suus   Σ : ab suis   *Sigonius* : ab urbe   *Robortellus* : pravus civis   *Vonck* :
fort. a vitiis   ibi quidem *scripsi* : ibique   Σ : ibi   *Rau*   24   a Cn.
P : ac nō   *SM*   27   concederem   *P* : concederet   *SM*

although she was his daughter. This charge Lucceius also levels
against Catilina in the orations which he wrote attacking him. I
have not yet discovered the names of these women.

Why need I proclaim the damage you inflicted on your province,
amid the protests and opposition of the whole Roman people? For I
hesitate to say how you behaved there, in view of your acquittal. It has
been remarked often enough already that Catilina held the command
of Africa after his praetorship and was acquitted on the accusation *de*
repetundis brought by P. Clodius.

I let pass that criminal enterprise of yours, very nearly a day of
bitterness and grief for the State, when in collusion with Cn. Piso, not
to name any other, you wished to perpetrate a massacre of the best men
in the state (optimates). You are well aware of the identity of those
whom he forbears to name. For there was a belief that Catilina and
Cn. Piso, a young desperado, conspired to perpetrate a massacre of
the senate a year before this speech was delivered, in the consulship of
Cotta and Torquatus, and that this massacre did not take place
simply because Catilina gave the signal to the conspirators before
they were ready. Now Piso, when this speech was being delivered, had
perished in Spain on being sent there by the senate by way of an
honorific mission to get him out of harm's way. There, in fact, while
inflicting wrongs on the provincials, he was slain, as some believed,
by clients of Cn. Pompeius, not without Pompeius' approval.

Or have you forgotten that when we sought the praetorship you
besought me to yield first place to you? And when you kept on doing
this time after time, and pressed me

93C   contenderes, meministi me tibi respondere impudenter te facere qui id a me peteres quod a te Boculus numquam impetrasset?

Diximus iam supra Sullae ludis quos hic propter victo-
5 riam fecerit quadrigas C. Antonium et alios quosdam nobiles homines agitasse. Praeterea Antonius redemptas habebat ab aerario vectigales quadrigas, quam redemptionem senatori habere licet per legem. Fuit autem notissimus in circo quadrigarum agitator Boculus.

10   Dicit de malis civibus:

Qui postea quam illo *quo* conati erant Hispaniensi pugiunculo nervos incidere civium Romanorum non potuerunt, duas uno tempore conantur in rem publicam sicas destringere.

15   Hispaniensem pugiunculum Cn. Pisonem appellat, quem in Hispania occisum esse dixi. Duas sicas Catilinam et Antonium appellari manifestum est.

Hunc vos scitote Licinium gladiatorem iam immisisse capillum Catilinae †iudic. quā Q. ue Cu-
20 rium hominem quaestorium.

Curius hic notissimus fuit aleator, damnatusque postea est. In hunc est hendecasyllabus Calvi elegans:

Et talos Curius pereruditus.

Huic orationi Ciceronis et Catilina et Antonius contu-
25 meliose responderunt, quod solum poterant, invecti in

2 quod avunculus Σ, *corr. A. Augustinus*   3 impetrasses *SP*¹,
                                                                    ‖
corr. Poggius, M   4 ludos Σ, *corr. Beraldus*   8 in ς: id Σ (idcirco
‖
notissimus *P*)   11 illo quo *Mommsen*: illo *SP*¹ : *om. M* : illud *Poggius*   12 pugiuncula *SP*¹, *corr. Poggius, M*   14 rep. sicas
distringere Σ, *corr. Patricius*   16 dixit Σ, *corr. Manutius*   18 immisisse] *fort.* submisisse (*cf. Plin. Ep.* vii. 27. 14 reis moris est summittere capillum)   19 lapillum *S*¹   iudic. quā Q. ue Σ : *fort.*
iudicio, itemque   20 quaestorium] *fort.* quaestuosum   22 endesyllabus Σ, *corr. ed. Iunt.*   23 talos *L. Müller* : talus *P* : calus
SM : talis *Beraldus* curios Σ, *corr. ed. Ven.*   pererudiosius *S* : per
erudius *PM*, *corr. ed. Ven.*   25 responderant Σ, *corr. Manutius*

with excessive impudence, do you recall that I replied that it was   93C
impudent conduct on your part to request from me what Boculus
would never have obtained from you? We have already said above
that at Sulla's games which he celebrated to mark his victory
C. Antonius and certain other nobles drove four-horse chariots. In
addition Antonius had contracted with the treasury to supply four-
horse chariots for a fee—a contract which is legally available to
senators. And Boculus was the most notorious four-horse chariot
driver in the Circus.

He is speaking of bad citizens: *Those persons who, after they failed*
with the Spanish stiletto by which they made the attempt to slit the
sinews of Roman citizens, are now attempting to unsheathe two daggers
at once against the state. 'Spanish stiletto' is his term 'or Cn. Piso, who
as I said was killed in Spain. It is obvious that Catilina and Antonius
are termed the 'two daggers'.

You must note that this ruffian Licinius has already let his hair grow
on information being laid against Catilina, and so has Q. Curius, a
fellow of quaestorian rank. This Curius was a notorious gambler, and
was later convicted. Against him there is extant an elegant hendecasyllabic line of Calvus:

And Curius, of unmatched scholarship in dice.

To this speech of Cicero Catilina and Antonius made reply with
insults, which was all that they could manage, by way of attacking

94C novitatem eius. Feruntur quoque orationes nomine illorum
editae, non ab ipsis scriptae sed ab Ciceronis obtrecta-
toribus: quas nescio an satius sit ignorare. Ceterum Cicero consul omnium consensu factus est: Antonius pauculis
5 centuriis Catilinam superavit, cum ei propter patris nomen
paulo speciosior manus suffragata esset quam Catilinae.

3 Cicero solus *S*   6 esset *SP* : esse *M*

his standing as a *novus homo.* There are in circulation also orations   94C
published in their names, not written by them but by detractors of
Cicero, which I imagine it is better to disregard. Anyhow, Cicero was
made consul by general agreement. Antonius marginally beat Catilina by a handful of centuries, since on account of his father's name a
somewhat more reputable bunch canvassed for him than for Catilina.

COMMENTARY

The Commentary on Cicero's Speech *Against Piso*

Cicero delivered this invective against L. Calpurnius Piso Caesoninus in the senate in August 55 BC (see below). Piso had been consul in 58, and was involved in the tangled political process which led to the exile of Cicero in consequence of the tribunician laws, proposed by Cicero's arch-enemy, P. Clodius Pulcher, which were based on the allegedly illegal execution of the Catilinarian conspirators by Cicero at the end of his consulship in 63. Piso left Rome in 57 to command in the province of Macedonia. Cicero returned to Rome in September 57 and included attacks against the two consuls of 58 (Piso and A. Gabinius, who was governor in Syria) in a number of speeches including *On the Consular Provinces* (June 56). Piso returned to Rome in 55 and attacked Cicero in the senate. This speech was Cicero's response. In it he undertakes a prolonged comparison of Piso's consulship and his own (*In Pis.* 1–31), leading to a review of Piso's allegedly disgraceful tenure of the province of Macedonia, contrasted with his own period in exile (*In Pis.* 31–63). Cicero then derides Piso as an Epicurean *bon viveur* (*In Pis.* 63–72), and emphasizes his own good relations with Pompey and Caesar (who was Piso's son-in-law) (*In Pis.* 73–82). He then returns to the alleged horrors of Piso's governorship of Macedonia, and gives various reasons why he does not intend to prosecute Piso for these, at least yet (*In Pis.* 83–95), before recapitulating some of his earlier points at the end of the speech (*In Pis.* 96–9). The most useful and still accessible commentary on the speech of Cicero itself, which is almost fully preserved, is by R. G. M. Nisbet (1961).

1C. Asconius' introduction comes in his standard format: the consular dating (in the case of the *In Pisonem* argued at some length), followed by his exposition of the issues and circumstances of the oration and the persons involved; and finally the commentary. In this case, untypically, there is nothing on the outcome, since the occasion is not a trial.

second consulship of Cn. Pompeius Magnus and M. Crassus. See *MRR* 2. 214–15 for most of the evidence.

games ... are imminent. On Pompey's theatre and the associated Games of 55 BC, the evidence is vast: see *MRR* 2. 214–15, citing Drumann and Groebe

(1899–1929), 4. 526–30. For location and references, *LTUR* 5. 35–8 (P. Gros); Coarelli (1997), 539–80. These games are also termed 'most lavish' at *Fam.* 7.1.2. On their dating in the year 55, Marshall (1985*b*), 81–2, summarizing his article (Marshall (1975*b*), 88–93, citing the *Fasti* (Calendars) of Amiternum and Allifae (*CIL* 1². 244; 217 = Degrassi (1967), 191). They show the date of the opening of Pompey's theatre and the associated games as 12 Aug. 55, so that the speech was delivered some days earlier.

'X', certainly, identified. The scholar whom Asconius so acutely refutes here is not securely identifiable. Conjectures to fill the lacuna in the MSS have included Tiro (which is improbable, though it fits the size of the MSS lacuna rather well); Nepos (also about the right length and more plausible); Fenestella has been suggested by Renaissance editors, but, though he is often criticized by Asconius, is rather too long a name in this case.

Piso returned from his province. Macedonia, held 57–55 after his consulship of 58. See further *MRR* 2. 202–3, 210, 218; 3. 47, and esp. Cic. *In Pis.*, with Nisbet (1961), pp. xiv and 172–80.

return of Gabinius. From Syria, held 57–54 after his consulship as Piso's colleague in 58. Asconius is right that his recall accorded with Cicero's view (*sententia*) declared in the speech *On the Consular Provinces* (see below), but mistaken if he thought it was effected thereby. Perhaps here, however, we see merely Asconius' over-compression rather than outright error. See further *MRR* 2. 203, 210–11, 218. On Gabinius' subsequent trials for *maiestas* (autumn, 54—Cic. *QF* 3.1.15, 2.1–2, 3.3, 4.2–3, 5.5: acquitted through Pompey's influence) and then for extortion (53: condemned—Dio 39.63.2–5; Cic. *Rab. Post.* 19, 33; Val. Max. 4.2.4; on the date, Lintott (1974), 67–8; *CAH* IX², 401–2; Gruen (1974), 322–31; Tatum (1999), 233–4).

2C. views of Cicero ... speech *On the Consular Provinces*. This important speech of 56, after the Conference of Luca, on the senate's allocation (later superseded) under the Lex Sempronia (123 BC) of provinces to the consuls to be elected for 55, contributed to the removal of Piso from his Macedonian command and the continuation of Caesar's in Gaul. See (e.g.) *CAH* IX², 394–5; Gelzer (1968), 124–5; Rawson (1975), 129–30; Stockton (1971), 210–11; for edition and commentary in English, Butler and Cary (1924). Asconius' awareness of this speech is no proof that he wrote a commentary on it, but that he did is by no means unlikely.

son-in-law Caesar. Calpurnia (still Caesar's wife in 44) was this Piso's daughter. On Caesar's continuing influence in Rome even from Gaul—most notably from Cisalpine Gaul during the winters of his lengthy command, and especially in 56—still the best account is that of Gelzer (1968), 119–94.

Frugi. See Nisbet (1961), 53, esp. on Asconius' quotation of this fragment out of sequence. Not all Pisones, even among the known Calpurnii Pisones, have the extra *cognomen* Frugi ('The Virtuous') attested. This Piso, the consul of 58, for example, lacks it, but instead does bear the additional *cognomen* Caesoninus, borne by consuls in 148; 112 (presumed great-grandfather and grandfather of the consul of 58); probably also by a quaestor of 100 or 103, probably praetor in 90 (presumed father of the consul of 58), all of whom also apparently lack the name Frugi (Syme (1960); Syme (1986), 330). On the origins of the name Caesoninus, see Badian (1990), 400. There were also late Republican Calpurnii Bestiae and Bibuli, quite distinct from Pisones, either Frugi or Caesonini. It emerges that the relationship of the Calpurnii Pisones Frugi with the Calpurnii Pisones Caesonini is at best foggy and quite possibly spurious, whether or not Cicero was seriously attempting—in the senate—to mislead his audience here, or the jury in a somewhat similar allusion at *Sest.* 21, which was very likely also known to Asconius. If, as is perhaps just possible, Asconius in this comment is merely identifying Piso as a member of the *gens Calpurnia* which (sometimes) bore the name Frugi, he is of course correct. The suspicion persists, however, that he has been misled into thinking that this Piso (L. Caesoninus, cos. 58) could properly be reckoned one of the Pisones Frugi, at best only remote relatives.

I am in a great quandary as to what reason Cicero could possibly have for calling Placentia a *municipium*. If indeed Asconius hailed from Patavium (Transpadane Gaul), it is odd that he should be so confused over the status of Placentia, about which the facts are to us tolerably clear. Placentia (modern Piacenza), on the south bank of the Po, was indeed founded, as Asconius says, by a standard Triumviral Commission in 218, as a Latin colony (see Glossary) of the usual type at the same time as Cremona, officially on 1 June, and refounded some distance from the original site in 190 (Polybius. 3.40.9; Livy, *Per.* 20; 21.25.3, 37.57.1–8; Lintott (1999a), 12, with n. 10, citing for the formalities D. J. Gargola (1995), chs. 2–4). Cremona lay on the far bank and a little further downstream. They were both originally intended to pin down recently defeated Gallic peoples in the Cisalpina, not to face Hannibal, of whose intentions Rome knew nothing at the time. The key fact which Asconius ignores, or of which he was strangely ignorant, is that all Latin colonies in Italy south of the Po, including Placentia (and very probably Cremona too), became *municipia* (see Glossary) on acquiring full Roman citizenship (*civitas Romana optimo iure Quiritium*) under the Lex Iulia of late 90 BC during the Social War. His problem is therefore illusory.

The error may be due to Placentia being awarded 'colonial' status in the Triumviral or Augustan age.

3C. Cn. Pompeius Strabo... founded Transpadane colonies. The Lex Pompeia *de Transpadanis* passed in 89 by the consul Cn. Pompeius Strabo, father of Magnus, differentiated Gallia Transpadana from the rest of Italy, which had received full Roman citizenship in 90 under the Lex Iulia (see above) and granted its inhabitants the rights of Latins (see Glossary). In this sense, they could be said to have been 'founded' by Cn. Strabo, not with new settlers, but in their change of status. They were thus *not* in the true sense *coloniae*, but very probably tended to assume the title, much as later did the communities of Transalpine Gaul during or soon after the governorship of Caesar in the 50s and 40s. See further Sherwin-White (1973), 63, 159, 216; Salmon (1969), 162.

A Board of Three, P. Cornelius Asina, P. Papirius Maso, and Cn. Cornelius Scipio, founded it. And we have discovered that this colony was founded ... fifty-three ... Polybius 3.40.9–10 and Livy 21.25.3–5 record variant names and functions, and were therefore evidently not the annalistic sources cited anonymously by Asconius at this juncture. One view of the figure 'fifty-three' in the (apparently) damaged MSS is that Placentia was the fifty-third instance of colonization (of any status) sponsored by the Roman state, by whatever date, however calculated. Marshall (1985*b*), 89–90 reviews a range of modern suggestions, and offers (85–91) further detailed and extended commentary on the whole question of Asconius' account of Placentia, its foundation and its rights.

vied with all Italy when action was taken to secure his recall from exile. On Cicero's exile in 58 and his recall in 57 by a law passed in the centuriate assembly by the consul P. Lentulus Spinther (see below, on Ascon. 11C, *Pis.* 35), see *CAH* ix², 385–90; Rawson (1975), 118–23; Stockton (1971), 190–3. Cicero persistently claimed that his restoration enjoyed the full support not only of all respectable elements of the inhabitants of Rome but also of 'the whole of Italy' (*tota Italia*), a concept subsequently much used (and abused) in other contexts both by Cicero himself and others (e.g. *Comm. Pet.* 30; Cic. *Red. Sen.* 25, 26, 29, 39; *Red. Quir.* 1, 10, 16; *Dom.* 5, 75, 147; *Sest.* 35 (cf. 72); *Leg. Agr.* 2. 34; Augustus, *Res Gestae* 25.2). Placentia too, with a decree of its own, had subscribed to the (alleged) general enthusiasm for Cicero's return—cf. Capua at Cic. *Red. Sen.* 29, 31; *Mil.* 39.

4C. *this political community.* The phrase translates the Latin *civitas*, a general term applicable to any organized community, whether *colonia*, *municipium*, or other, urbanized or not.

originally reckoned a Gaul. It was a standard technique of Greek and Roman personal polemic (*vituperatio*) to cast aspersions on the target's parentage. The allegation of Transalpine, rather than Cisalpine, Gallic provenance is meant to make out Piso's maternal ancestry to be even more barbaric. See Nisbet (1961), 53; cf. Syme (1937), 130–1 on denizens of Spain. Nothing proves Asconius' belief in these slanders.

a father-in-law ... than did C. Piso? (*In Pis.* fr. 13) This C. Piso Frugi was married to Tullia, Cicero's own daughter, after betrothal in 67 (Cic. *Att.* 1.3.3), alive in 58 but dead before Cicero's recall from exile. See also below, pp. 197–8 (Ascon. 5C) on her later marriage(s).

that great sorrow of mine. Perhaps a reference to Cicero's exile (cf. Cic. *Planc.* 73), but Asconius' MSS (the only record for this fragment of Cicero) are too damaged for certainty.

5C. The identity of the elder Piso's father-in-law he himself declared above ... Asconius rightly indicates that his next quotation is a back-reference, and is here is out of place.

There was some Insubrian ... auctioneer. (*In Pis.* fr. 11) Therefore of disreputable origins and occupation. The Insubres were an old-established tribe centred near Mediolanum (modern Milan)—not 'Transalpine', but for a few years into the second century BC doughty enemies of Rome.

kleptomaniac individual Caesoninus. (*In Pis.* fr. 11) Almost certainly refers to L. Calpurnius L. f. C. n. Caesoninus, cos. 112, probably the Piso mentioned as defendant *de repetundis* in Cic. *De Or.* 2.265. See Syme (1955), 137.

Calventius. (*In Pis.* fr. 11) The name is well attested in Cisalpine Gaul, but with only three instances from Insubrian territory and one from Placentia (none from Transalpine Gaul). It is clearly of Italian, not Gallic origin, just possibly Etruscan. Piso's son appears in an inscription from Veleia (*ILS* 900).

Rutilius Nudus. This man apparently was quaestor in Macedonia, perhaps praetor by 74 and served under M. Cotta in 73 (or 74) (*MRR* 2. 105 [citing App. *Mith.* 71; Oros. 6.2.13], 3. 183; Marshall (1985b), 92). Fenestella's testimony (fr. 22P) cannot be tested. Cicero's, however, is clearly a distortion of some sort, if it contains any truth at all.

P. Lentulus ... childbirth. On Tullia's marriages, the last to P. Cornelius Dolabella (Lentulus after adoption) (51/50), and death (Jan. 45) see (e.g.) Rawson (1975), 47, 122, 144, 166, 180, 190–1, 197, 199, 205–7, 222–7. Shackleton Bailey (1965–70), 5. 324, believes that Lentulus' *praenomen* was in fact Cnaeus not Publius. The argument that Asconius errs in making this her second marriage, rather than her third, and omitting an intervening one to Furius

Crassipes (*c.*56–51—Cic. *QF.* 2.4.2; 6.1; *Fam.* 1.7.11; cf. 8.13.1; 2.15.2, mentioning only betrothal, but see also ibid. 1.9.20 referring to 'Crassipes my son-in-
law') is questioned by Clark (1991). Asconius agrees with Plut. *Cic.* 41, quite
possibly both deriving from Tiro's biography of Cicero, which on such a
matter is unlikely to have been wrong, but might perhaps have omitted the
insignificant and rather unsatisfactory second marriage. Asconius is, however, certainly mistaken, for whatever reason, in locating Tullia's death (Feb.
45 after childbirth in Jan.) at the house of Dolabella, from whom she had
been divorced a short time earlier (46/5). She died at Cicero's Tusculan villa
(Cic. *Fam.* 6.18.5).

In Pis. 4: *In the case of C. Rabirius, charged with* perduellio, *it was I who
despite resultant political hostility upheld the authority of the senate, which
had been asserted forty years before my consulship, and I who defended it.*
Asconius' comment is concerned solely with Cicero's approximate chronology. For a lucid and succinct narrative of the strange case of C. Rabirius in
63, and Cicero's defence of him on the charge of *perduellio* ('treason') for
allegedly having killed L. Saturninus in 100, see Gelzer (1968); *RE* 7A.1 (1939),
870–2. On the legal technicalities of *perduellio*, see Lintott (1999*a*), 150–2
(esp. 152 n. 18 for further bibliography of variant modern interpretations);
CAH IX^2, 501–2; for the political and jurisprudential issues, with a somewhat
different view of them from Gelzer's, Phillips (1974); Lintott (1999*b*), 159;
168–9, where the decree of the senate which authorized the use of armed
force against Saturninus and his supporters is regarded as the senate's (so-
called) Ultimate Decree (*senatus consultum (ultimum)*). Its normal wording, as used against Catilina in 63 and on other occasions, appears in
Asconius' next lemma (6C) below, but the decree of 100 is somewhat
differently formulated in Cic. *Rab. Perd.* 20—'that the consuls C. Marius
and L. Valerius should enlist those tribunes of the plebs and praetors whom
they thought fit and ensure the preservation of the rule (*imperium*) of the
Roman people and its overriding sovereignty (*maiestas*)'. In 63 the tribune
T. Labienus was chiefly instrumental in mounting a populist challenge to
senatorial authority by indicting by this antiquated process the aged senator
C. Rabirius for Saturninus' murder, seeking to discount the decree of 100 as
sufficient defence. Against, Cicero as consul and champion of the senate
pleaded its validity, whereby he 'upheld the authority of the senate'—that is,
its capacity and right to intervene in such a case. On the resulting call to
arms and some parallel instances, see below, p. 282 on Ascon. 75C.

**6C. senatorial decree that the consuls should see to it that the state take no
harm.** Supposedly the traditional formulation of the so-called last (ultimate)
decree of the senate (*senatus consultum ultimum*)—that is, last before leaving

it to the consuls to act to save the state. Discussion in Lintott (1999*a*), 89–93, and 228; (1999*b*), ch. 11; *CAH* IX², 494–6. In fact the first use of the term *senatus consultum ultimum* is Caesar's, of events in 49 (*Bell. Civ.* 1.5.3; 7.5). Earlier, with somewhat varied wording (e.g. above, on Ascon. 5C), in the internal crises of 123, 100, 83, 77, 67 (?), 63, and 52 the senate had passed resolutions enjoining the consuls (and on occasion other magistrates) to act to save the state. Such a decree did not give legal sanction for any magistrate to act beyond the law, and technically, like any other senatorial decree, amounted to no more than advice, recommendation, or request. Further, it was quite distinct from any decree, concomitant with it or not, that named persons or groups were to be treated no longer as Roman citizens but as *hostes* (enemies of the state).

In Pis. 6: ... *would allow no more than the oath.* An oath was normally required of magistrates on vacating office, as Cicero did on the last day of December 63. Having intended, no doubt, a lengthy address to the people, Cicero was thwarted by the intervention of the hostile tribune Q. Metellus Nepos. Even so, he evidently contrived a form of oath to suit his own purposes—that is, not that he had observed the laws, but that 'he had saved the state', thus evading the potentially embarrassing issue of legality. The following cross-reference in Asconius' comment must be to his exposition, now lost, of another speech. Likely candidates are the *Pro Sulla* (cf. 31), *Pro Sestio* (cf. 11, 72, 130), or possibly the lost *Contra Contionem Q. Metelli* (frs. 83–5 Puccioni).

7C. In Pis. 8: ... *the Crossroads Festival* ... *Sex. Cloelius..* This festival, the Compitalia (of the *compita*, the intersections of streets dividing the *vici* or 'wards' of Rome), which fell either in December or in early January at a few days' notice on a date nominated by the responsible officials, was chiefly for the benefit of slaves and freedmen, and part of the cult of the Lares. The associated games (Ludi Compitalicii) followed soon afterwards (A. K. Michels (1967), 205 and n.). Traditionally the *collegia* or Trade Guilds of artisans and *tabernarii* (shopkeepers, tradesmen) were the chief participants, the festival being organized by their *magistri*. While the celebrations of 1 January 58 were probably not of themselves illegal, despite many *collegia* having been outlawed in 64 (see below, on 8C), the prior promulgation of P. Clodius' tribunician rogations (see below, 8C), passed into law a few days later, together with the energetic pursuit of the rites and games would certainly have given his agent Sex. Cloelius every chance to muster mass support for the whole proposed legislative programme—see below. For his correct name—not 'Sex. Clodius'—see below, pp. 237–8, on Ascon. 33C. Lintott (1967), 163 suggests that Cloelius may have acted here as *magister* of the (or a) still legitimate *collegium* of *scribae*. For fuller exposition, Flambard (1977) and (1981).

collegia ... against the public interest were suppressed. In 64. See Lintott (1999*b*), 77–83. Some *collegia* held to be respectable for reasons of religion or antiquity survived—certainly those of the Builders (*fabri*) and Lictors (Ascon. 59C). Further, Lintott (1999*a*), 53 and n. 60, 177–8, 199. Gabba (1984), 85–6 suggests that the legend of foundation of the (or some) *collegia* by Numa may have originated in disputes of the late Republic over their roles and legitimacy.

magistri of the *collegia* ... dressed in the stripe-edged toga. This style of toga was mostly worn by higher magistrates, but also any person holding games, as well as freeborn boys (Mommsen (1887–8), 1³. 422). As Nisbet (1961), 66, observes, Cicero's gibe that Cloelius had never before worn the *praetexta* implies alleged servile origin.

despite his powers as consul, before the passage of the law ... Further, two years before ... Q. Metellus Celer, as consul designate. Clodius' law to restore the *collegia* banned in 64 was passed on 4 January 58, just after Piso assumed office. Cicero contrasts his failure in office with the success two years earlier on the part of Q. Metellus Celer in restraining *vicomagistri* from such (alleged) illegality, in virtue not of any legal powers, but of his mere prestige as consul designate, and still as such a private citizen.

the senate house was burnt down. See below on Ascon. 33C, etc.

L. Ninnius, tribune of the plebs. Vainly attempted to support Cicero throughout his year (58) and to secure his recall (*MRR* 2. 196).

whose name I have not yet been able to discover. Only two of the tribunes of 60 (who entered office on 10 Dec. 61) are known—L. Flavius and C. Herennius. The latter is a known friend of P. Clodius, but both clashed with Celer in 60 (*MRR* 2. 184).

8C. *In Pis.* 9: ... *three days later.* That is, on 4 January 58, quite possibly the first available day after promulgation at Clodius' entry into his Tribunate on 10 December 59, given the constitutional requirement under the Lex Caecilia Didia (98) of due notice for the minimum period of a *trinundinum*, and after it to wait for a subsequent *dies comitialis* (lawful day for a legislative assembly). For brevity, it must suffice here to state a preference for the thesis of Lintott (1965), (1968), and (1999*a*), 43 (*contra* Michels (1967), 36–60, esp. 46, 205), which accommodates satisfactorily the attested facts about the known dates in this period of *nundinae* (market days) and legislation. On this view, the *trinundinum* required for legislation after promulgation is of variable duration, being any period containing three *nundinae* in the sense of 'market days'—a minimum of seventeen days if promulgation was on a market day, a maximum of twenty-four if it was a day later. Further delay was then required after the last of the three at least until the next comitial day (see below), since no market day was such.

the Aelian and Fufian laws. These are now generally accepted as *two* laws, not one, not precisely datable, but from mid-second century and reaffirmed in the Lex Caecilia Didia of 98. The Lex Aelia provided for obstruction of political processes—chiefly or even exclusively, it would appear, legislation and elections—by the declaration (*obnuntiatio*) of bad omens. The Lex Fufia may have been concerned rather to define comitial days (*dies comitiales*)— that is those on which legislative (and probably other) assemblies of the people or plebs could be held—to exclude not only *dies nefasti*, which were not available for any public business, but also, among *dies fasti* certain others—e.g. the period between announcement and holding of elections (Schol. Bob. 148St); 'festival days' (*dies feriae*); market days (*nundinae*).

foul sexual vices ... the censorship. See below, on Asconius' comment.

We have said that ... P. Clodius ... passed four laws. So too Dio 38.13.1–6. Clearly the cross-reference is to a lost commentary on another speech— most probably Cic. *Sest.* 55–6, the only extant passage of Cicero which lists these same four laws together. The tally of Clodius' laws and rogations is far larger than this, but if Asconius is merely following Cicero in regarding these tribunician laws as (particularly) 'harmful' (*perniciosas*), that may call his judgment into question, but does not convict him of ignorance or careless omission. For the rest, which evidently came later, see *MRR* 2. 196; 3. 58.

corn law. For a concise account of the corn laws (*leges frumentariae*) since that of C. Gracchus in 123, see Marshall (1985*b*), 97; further, Rickman (1979), 158–73; Nicolet (1980), 186–205. Clodius' law was the most radical to date, and in the circumstances of 58 urgently needed by the urban plebs. It was intended to organize the whole system of supply (from Sicily, Sardinia, and Africa) and distribution through shippers and merchants at a rate of five *modii* per month at no charge for all citizens resident in Rome (Cic. *Dom.* 55; *Pis.* 9; Ascon 8C; Rickman (1979), 104–19; on problems of their numbers, definition, and provenance, *CAH* ix², 644–59). Clodius' henchman Sex. Cloelius, whatever his official status, if any, was to administer its provisions (Cic. *Dom.* 25–6), and even if he was well placed to organize distribution (see below, on *collegia*) proved unequal to the enormous task of procurement. The financial burden on the already over-stretched state treasury (*aerarium*) was no less enormous (Cic. *Sest.* 5; Plut. *Pomp.* 45; cf. *Caes.* 8; *Cat. Min.* 26), and ample explanation for Clodius' subsequent laws to confiscate the

Ptolemaic assets of Cyprus (cf. the treatment of Cyrene in 74) and to appoint M. Cato as *proquaestor pro praetore* for the purpose (Badian (1965); Fehrle (1983), 98–100). Similar exploitation of the empire for these purposes included Clodius' dealings with Brogitarus of Galatia and with magnates of Byzantium (*CAH* ix², 379), and there was a special issue of coinage by decree of the senate at this juncture (M. H. Crawford (1974), 1. 446–7; cf. 2. 636). For the sequel in 57 and later, below, p. 252, Ascon. 48C.

days on which it was legal to transact business with the people. That is, those allocated to such purposes, the *dies comitiales,* which excluded *dies nefasti, dies feriae,* and *nundinae.* Clodius seems to have tried to equate them with all *dies fasti* (Cic. *Sest.* 33; *Prov. Cons.* 46).

Aelian and Fufian laws. See above, p. 201 also below, p. 333, in Index of Laws and Rogations. In fact Clodius evidently did not totally repeal these laws, since there is at least one trial of the later 50s under the Lex Fufia (Cic. *Att.* 4.16.5), as well as some instances of *obnuntiatio* (see Glossary; Lintott (1999*a*), 62, 104; Weinrib (1970)). Clodius' reform came in the wake of L. Bibulus' attempts as consul in 59 to obstruct the legislative initiatives of his opponents—that is, chiefly his colleague C. Caesar and Caesar's ally the tribune P. Vatinius. See further (e.g.) Lintott (1999*a*), 62 and n. 95; Weinstock (1937), 215–16; Balsdon (1957), 15–16; Astin (1964), 421–45; Mitchell (1986), 172–6. For a determined attempt to sanitize the Ciceronian evidence (*Red. Sen.* 11; *Sest.* 33, 56; *Har. Resp.* 58; *Vat.* 18 ff.; *Prov. Cons.* 45–6; with Ascon. and Dio 38.13.6), see now Tatum (1999), 125–33, holding that Clodius aimed at no more than salutary revision and clarification.

restitution of *collegia*. That is, those dissolved by senatorial decree in 64.

and the institution of new ones. By implication, for Clodius' own nefarious purposes (Cic. *Red. Sen.* 33; *Dom.* 129; *Sest.* 34, 55; *Pis.* 9, 11; Dio 38.12.2)—but this is clearly a very biased view of the matter! Alongside provision of corn and perhaps, as attractively suggested by Tatum (1999), 124–5, intimately connected with its distribution through the *magistri* of the *collegia* (cf. Cic. *Dom.* 13, 89, 129), Sex. Cloelius also took entire charge of the restoration and reorganization of the *collegia,* based on the Temple of Castor and the Aurelian Tribunal, see below (Cic. *Sest.* 34; *Pis.* 11, 23; *Dom.* 110–11; *Har. Resp.* 28). For its location and history, *LTUR* 1. 247–55 (cf. esp. 242–5, I. Nielsen); Coarelli (1985), 190–200). Further, Lintott (1999*b*), 77–83; Flambard (1981), 143–66, Ascon. 6C, on *Pis.* 8.

to prevent the censors … Hardly major subversion of the censorship, still less its abolition, as Cicero may be taken to imply, here and elsewhere (*Pis.* 9; *Sest.* 55; cf. *Dom.* 130; *Har. Resp.* 58; *Prov. Cons.* 45)! Nisbet (1961), 68 infers from Cicero's juxtaposition here (in the lemma) of Clodius' vices and his attempt to curb the censorship that Clodius' move was for self-protection, against subsequent expulsion from the senate for the Bona Dea affair of 62. Marshall (1985*b*), 98 invokes the fate of Clodius' father at the hands of the censors of 86 (Cic. *Dom.* 84). Both considerations could be valid, but there is also much to be said for Tatum (1999), 133–5, arguing that his main purpose was to recruit widespread support from those of humbler ranking in a senate greatly overgrown since Sulla's provisions for its automatic recruitment from ex-quaestors: they had reason to fear that censors would soon be obliged to reduce numbers severely, as in 70 and as threatened in 64. Clodius' law converted the censors' revision of the senatorial list into a very public, open process in which both censors had to agree on candidates for expulsion, who in turn had the opportunity to present a case to both in judicial proceedings. There were many such hearings in 54, so that the census remained incomplete (Cic. *Att.* 4.9.1, 16.8; Mitchell (1986)) and, in fact so clearly unworkable on this basis that the Lex Clodia had to be abrogated in 52 by the consul P. Metellus Scipio (Dio 40.57.1–3).

9C. *In Pis.* 11: ... *the Aurelian* **tribunal.** A *tribunal* was normally a raised platform in the Forum from which a magistrate dispensed justice (for origins, Lintott (1999*a*), 45–6), but sometimes (perhaps as well as that) a monument to a person of special distinction. The exact site of the Aurelian Tribunal is unknown, but it should have been somewhere in the Forum, probably close to the Temple of Castor (see below; Coarelli (1985), 190–202, esp. 196–9; Patterson (1992), 192, with n. 67). It was apparently newly constructed in 74, most probably by M. Aurelius Cotta (cos. 75) or his brother Gaius (cos. 74) (less likely by the youngest brother of the three, Lucius (cos. 65)), with terraces like a theatre to accommodate those attending judicial proceedings, but evidently (or allegedly) might be used as a focal point for seditious activity (Cic. *Clu.* 93; cf. *Flacc.* 66; *Sest.* 34; and here at *In Pis.* 11).

Temple of Castor. An important site at the south-east end of the Forum (*LTUR* 2. 325–36 (Forum); 1. 247–52 (Temple of Castor)). Allegedly the rallying point, armoury, and pay-desk for Clodius' mobsters in 58 (Cic. *Dom.* 110; *Har. Resp.* 28; cf. above, on Ascon. 8C), but also where in the late Republic the vote of tribal assemblies meeting in the Forum was delivered (Lintott (1999*a*), 46 and n. 30; 55 and n. 69; Taylor (1966), 27–9, 41–3; Coarelli (1985), 190–202; Millar (1998), 41–3, 136–7; Tatum (1999), 142–3; 179 and nn.

In Pis. 23: ... *collusive prosecutor of Catilina.* That is, *de repetundis* in 65. See Ascon. 85C; Cic. *Har. Resp.* 42; cf. *Att.* 1.1.1; 1.2.1. As also at 87C (see below; cf. 92C), over Cicero's accusations, freely made in the 50s, but hardly supported by the letters of 65 to Atticus, Asconius seems cautious, doubtless rightly: see among moderns Gruen (1974), 271; Tatum (1999), 53–5; Alexander (1990), 106–7. There is no difficulty in assigning the cross-reference in Asconius' ensuing comment on Catilina's acquittal to his exposition of the speech 'As a Candidate' (cf. 85C, 87C, 89C, 92C).

latterly his avenger. Asconius offers no comment, but Cicero not only claims, almost certainly falsely, that Clodius had supported Catilina in 63 (Ascon. 50C, see below), but also apparently with more truth that Catilinarian survivors from 63/2 subsequently joined the following of Clodius. See further Lewis (1988), 31–2. It is no less interesting to trace the further drift after the murder of Clodius of these persons, and their connections, or those of them who survived, into the entourage of M. Antonius, Triumvir (Welch (1995)).

L. Lamia was banished from the city by the edict of the consul Gabinius. Apparently a lawful procedure, without trial, known as 'relegation' (*relegatio*)—in this case removal to a place 200 miles from Rome for a limited period (Cic. *Red. Sen.* 12; *Sest.* 29; *Pis.* 64; *Fam.* 9.16.2; Cassius Dio 38.16.4). Lamia in 58 was a leading Roman equestrian, later, in 43, with ambitions for a praetorship (Cic. *Fam.* 9.16.2). Asconius' cross-reference is most likely to his comment on Cic. *Sest.* 29, whence also Schol. Bob. 129St.

10C. *In Pis.* 24: *Even the Seplasia ... disowned you as Campanian Consul.* See next note for Asconius' comment, and further on the Seplasia in Capua, with its perfume market, a by-word for decadent luxury, the context in Cic. *Pis.* 24 with Nisbet (1961), ad loc.; Frederiksen (1984), 298–9.

It was noted in the speech against the agrarian law before the people ... The cross-reference to Cic. *Leg. Agr.* 2.94, reveals that Asconius wrote a Commentary, now lost, on this speech. Cicero's association of Piso with the supposed sensuous decadence of the Seplasia is of course deliberate. So too, of course, is his exercise of wit and historical awareness in terming him a Campanian consul, an allusion to Piso, while consul at Rome in 58, also assuming the patronage of Capua in serving as its chief magistrate (*Duumvir*—Cic. *Red. Sen.* 17; *Sest.* 19; *Dom.* 60; *Pis.* 24–5) in the first year after its 'founding' (i.e. resettling with large numbers from Rome) as a *colonia* by Caesar's consular legislation of the previous year; together with the historical point that back in 216, after Rome's defeat at Cannae by Hannibal, the Capuans had tried to extort from Rome, as the price of continued loyalty, the concession that one of the two consuls each year should be a Capuan (Campanian)—a demand which Rome rejected, later crushing the consequent Capuan revolt (216–211).

In Pis. 26: *Now what fire of any magnitude... in this city.* Dangerous conflagrations in Republican Rome were common among the high-rise timber-constructed slum dwellings of the pre-Augustan era—and not much less so later.

his house was first taken apart. The house was ransacked by Clodius' followers immediately upon Cicero's departure into exile in 58 (Cic. *Sest.* 55; *Red. Sen.* 18; *Dom.* 59, 62; *Pis.* 26; *Att.* 4.7.5, 7; *Fam.* 14.2.2; Plut. *Cic.* 23; Dio 38.17.6). On items allegedly transported to the home of Piso's mother-in-law, cf. Cic. *Dom.* 62. Asconius honestly admits ignorance (to date) of her identity. On the house itself, below, Ascon. 12C, *Pis.* 52.

the historians have not paid as much attention. Asconius clearly does not number himself among 'the historians' (*auctores rerum*). Jerome, recording Asconius' death in AD 76, calls him a 'famous historical writer' (*scriptor historicus clarus*), but what is known of his writings shows him to be literary commentator rather than a historian. It may be that Jerome does not call him a *grammaticus* because that would imply that he was a schoolteacher, a profession which no gentleman would pursue (Rawson (1986), 80).

11C. *In Pis.* 27: ... *Caesoninus, wallowing in your pig-dirt.* 'Caesoninus' is an editor's (Manutius') emendation. The MSS of both Cicero and Asconius in fact read *ceso, caeso,* or something very similar, of uncertain meaning, but very probably a term of abuse. Nisbet (1961), 90 suggests that it might be a synonym for *maialis*, used of Piso at Cic. *Pis.* 19, meaning a castrated pig, of which Cicero's clearly abusive *lutulente* ('mud-wallowing') would of course be entirely appropriate. The translation should perhaps be emended accordingly, although this ingenious conjecture is hardly proven.

Sterling Worth ... Cn. Pompeius is meant. That is, Asconius rightly interprets Cicero here to be presenting Pompeius as the personification of Sterling Worth ('Virtue' = *virtus*), taking steps to rescue Cicero from exile. Compare the somewhat similarly expressed sentiment of *Dom.* 25, most probably well known to Asconius.

In Pis. 35: ... *all the magistrates.* That is, those of 57.

with the exception of a single praetor, from whom it was not to be demanded ... two tribunes. Clodius' brother, Ap. Claudius, praetor in 57, was later reconciled with Cicero, at least in public life, through Pompey (Cic. *Mil.* 75; Quintil. 9.3.41). Asconius' identification of the two tribunes probably derives from *Sest.* 72, 87 (cf. 82, 85, 89, 94), and his cross-reference here will likewise most probably be to comment on that same speech (*Sest.* 77–8, 85, 87, 126). Otherwise on support for the rogation, *Red. Sen.* 19–23.

bought off the block. More abuse; a reference to the stone block on which slaves were displayed for sale.

passed in the centuriate assembly by P. Lentulus the consul. Moves for Cicero's recall from exile began as early as May 58, but successive speeches and decrees in the senate and initiatives in the tribal assembly, mostly by tribunes, had been thwarted both in that year and early in 57 by veto or violence. As that year progressed, however, led by the consul P. Lentulus Spinther and Pompey, who now exerted himself to raise support around the townships of Italy, Cicero's cause gathered momentum as the men from the *municipia* converged on Rome, first perhaps early in May, when Spinther secured a decree of the senate that all who valued the safety of the state should assemble there to vote for Cicero's recall; certainly in July when they massed there again to support the senate's demand for appropriate legislation and threatened to outlaw obstructionists. Clodius failed to halt the tide, which eventually on 4 August brought in the vote of the *comitia centuriata* for Cicero's return. Significantly, this law was passed not in the socially undifferentiated tribal assembly in the Forum, which at the time normally was dominated by Clodius' usual urban following, but in the timocratically stratified centuriate assembly, which was not. It was convened at some distance from the Forum in the Campus Martius, and on this occasion in particular was heavily packed with Cicero's supporters from 'all Italy', representing 'a closure not of the shops, but of the municipalities' (Cic. *Dom.* 90; cf. 47); for Cicero (e.g. *Red. Quir.* 4, 18; *Dom.* 75, 89–90; *Sest.* 107–9) the true Roman people, not just the *infima multitudo* of the metropolis. For fuller narrative and analysis, see *CAH* ix^2, 385, 387; Stockton (1971), 190–3; Rawson (1975), 118–23; Tatum (1999), 176–85; esp. Millar (1998), 16–18, 37–8, 148–55. Noticeably, the two hostile tribunes, neither of much weight or importance (*MRR* 2. 168, 184, 201–2, 219), did not venture to use their veto.

In Pis. 38–9: *This vulturine scavenger.* An established term of abuse. See Nisbet (1961), 100, citing Aemilius Scaurus (cos. 115) *ORF* fr. 89—*nefarius volturius* ('evil vulture'), fr. 10 *volturius rei publicae* ('vulture [gorged on the remains] of the Commonwealth'); Cic. *Sest.* 71 *duo volturii paludati* ('a pair of vultures in military cloaks', Piso and Gabinius, coss. 58).

was hailed … as Imperator! A victorious general, sometimes even for quite small exploits, might contrive to be hailed as *Imperator* ('Commander') by his troops as one prerequisite among others for claiming a triumph—as Cicero himself did in Cilicia in 51–50. More insults for Piso in this regard occur at *Har. Resp.* 35; *Prov. Cons.* 7, 15, 38; *Pis.* 44, 53–5, 61, 70, 91, 97.

Paulus. See Index of Personal Names, Aemilius Paulus, L. (cos. II 168). Asconius' comment explains the reference to Paulus, but perhaps trusts too readily Cicero's derisive assessment of Piso's military performance. For a fairer review of the evidence, Nisbet (1961), 176–80; Marshall (1985*b*), 100–1.

your accounts. In accordance with Caesar's recent Lex Iulia *de repetundis* of 59, which stipulated complex rules for this procedure: evidence in *MRR* 2. 188.

12C. which Marcellus. See Index of Personal Names, Claudius Marcellus, M. (cos. 222 etc.). Asconius' comment answers the question well enough in outline. For more on the grandson, pr. Spain 169–8; cos. 166; II 155; III 152 (procos. 151), *MRR* 1. 425, 428, 437, 449, 453, 455; Marshall (1985*b*), 101, the only man in the second century before C. Marius to hold three consulships, his third being the occasion for an attempt to forbid iteration altogether thereafter.

shipwreck off Africa itself shortly before the start of the Third Punic War. In fact in 148, shortly *after* that war began (Livy, *Per.* 50; *Oxyrh. Per.* 50; *MRR* 1. 462 n. 2). If he has not simply used a variant source, conceivably Asconius has confused the start of the war with the appointment of P. Scipio Aemilianus, cos. 147, to command in it. On the drowning of Marcellus, Cic. *Div.* 3.14; *Fat.* 33.

Temple of Honour and Virtue. Concisely expounded by Marshall (1985*b*), 102, with the evidence for the intimate Marcellan connection with the shrine, originally founded by Q. Fabius Maximus in 234 (Cic. *Nat. Deor.* 2.61; 2 *Verr.* 4.121; *Rep.* 1.21; Livy 25.40.1, 26.32.4, 27.25.7; Val. Max. 1.1.8, 29.11.13; Strabo 3.4.11). It was quite distinct from another such dedication by C. Marius after his victories of 102–101 over the Northmen, perhaps in emulation. See further *LTUR* 3. 3–4 (D. Palombi); Coarelli (1997), 461, 467, 567–9.

In Pis. **52:** *... from which you had expelled me and which you had set afire.* The man most obviously to blame was of course Clodius, whose law on Cicero's exile (*Lex de exsilio Ciceronis*) of 58 had included confiscation and demolition of Cicero's Palatine house, already pillaged by his followers (above, on Ascon. 10C; for the site, *LTUR* 2. 202–4 (E. Papi)). Unless, however, Cicero in rhetorical vein is turning aside from Piso to address him, 'you' should be Piso himself, deemed at this juncture in the speech to be the criminal in Cicero's eyes for having as consul allowed it to happen. Clodius proceeded to raze the property and on the site, together with those of two adjacent properties, to begin construction of a Temple of Liberty (*Aedes Libertatis*). That in turn was dismantled when Cicero, after a prolonged saga of debate (including his speeches *De Domo Sua* and *De Haruspicum Responso*) and some violence, was able at length to secure restoration of his property, for which there had been no provision in the law for his recall. For fully detailed narrative, Tatum (1999), 157–8, 186–92, 217–20.

13C. *a grant made previously to no one else.* Asconius' explanation is more satisfactory than his critique, at least as transmitted by the MSS. For concise exposition of the tangle, Marshall (1985*b*), 103–5. It appears that in the tradition there were three Valerii, sons of Volusus (or Volesus)—(1) the famous Publius Valerius Poplicola (Publicola), cos. 509; 508; 507; 504, awarded a *site* for a house at his own suggestion, according to Varro, as reported by Julius Hyginus in Asconius, but according to another version (Cic. *Rep.* 2. 3; Liv. 2.7.5–6, 10–12; Dion. Hal. 5.19.1–2; Val. Max. 4.1.1) also the house on it was to be built at public expense; (2) M. Valerius Volusus, cos. 505, *not* granted the *cognomen* Maximus, but awarded a house at public expense; (3) M'. Valerius Maximus, dict. 494 without having held any prior magistracy, *not* awarded a house at public expense. Both Marcus (cos. 505) and Manius (dict. 494) held triumphs over the Sabines. There is thus ample scope for confusion, more probably on the part of Antias than of Asconius (Wiseman (1979), 46, 120; cf. Varro (via Hyginus fr. 2P); Weinstock (1971), 278). On Antias' treatment of the early Valerii, see Wiseman (1998), 75–89.

Antias. The Annals of Valerius Antias (Valerius of Antium) are commonly dated (after Vell. 2.9.4) to the Sullan or immediately post-Sullan era, but to around 50–46 BC by Wiseman (1979), 113–21; Cloud (1977), 225–7: see, however, below, on 69–70C. He recycled the work of earlier annalists and was a major source of Livy. Antias himself wrote at least seventy-five books, more interested in entertainment than accuracy. See further *HRR* 1, cccv–cccxxxiii; 238–75; Wiseman (1979), esp. 22, 25, 32–3, 115–22, 127–8 (scathingly critical); Badian (1966), 1–38; Ogilvie (1965), 12–16. It is not quite clear that Asconius fully trusted his version, which appears in no other surviving source.

Iulius Hyginus. C. Iulius Hyginus, polymath, librarian of the Palatine library instituted by Augustus in 28. Asconius' reference to 'the earlier' (*priore*) book *On Famous Men* (*De Viris Claris*) would normally imply that there were only two books of that title, but Gellius (1.14.1), no mean scholar himself, cites a work which *may* be identical *De Vita Rebusque Illustrium Virorum* (*On the Lifestyle and Exploits of Distinguished Men*) and which extended to at least six books. His *Exempla* (*Illustrations*) might be identified with one (or both) of these works, if indeed they are not the same. Hyginus is a likely transmitter to Asconius of items from the autobiography of M. Aemilius Scaurus, see below, pp. 217, 221–4, with Lewis (2001*b*).

under the Velia, where the Temple of Victoria now stands. Properly speaking, this was the Temple of Vica Pota (see Platner and Ashby (1929), 196–7).

Atticus, in his *Book of Years*. Also cited at Ascon. 77C. The learned, careful, and scholarly friend of Cicero wrote a *Liber Annalis* (title at Cic. *Att.* 12.23.2; cf. *Brut.* 42; 72), which was, it seems, essentially a book of chronology, not extended narrative history, published in 47. Marshall (1985*b*), 106; Horsfall (1989), 39–40; Rawson (1985), 103.

son of King Antiochus, a hostage. That is, the son of Antiochus III, Seleucid King of Syria, defeated by Rome at Magnesia (Asia Minor) in 190/89. The son was kept in Rome as hostage for his good behaviour (App. *Syr.* 39) until the father died and then succeeded his elder brother Seleucus IV in 175 as Antiochus IV.

Varro. See Marshall (1985*b*), 106–7. For this cultural/antiquarian 'encyclopaedia', something of a novelty in Latin at the time, but probably after the manner of the Hellenistic writer Dicaearchus, much in vogue in Rome in the 50s and 40s, and for more on Varro as a writer of biographic sketches, Rawson (1985), 44, 164, 179, 198, 230, 242, 287. On the *Lifestyle of the Roman People* (*De Vita Populi Romani*), see the edition of Riposati (1939).

Mutina. Spelling of this Numidian tribal cavalry-commander's name varies in the sources. In Asconius he is 'Mutina'; in Livy, Muttines; in Polybius, Myttones; and in an inscription (*SIG*³ 585. 87) as M. Valerius 'Mottones', the Roman names taken from his patron, almost certainly M. Valerius Laevinus, cos. 210, to whom he deserted from the Carthaginians in Sicily and under whom he served against them and who secured for him by tribunician law his award of Roman citizenship (Livy 26.40, 27.5). Only Varro records award of a house at public expense. On Cicero's case, cf. Cic. *Har. Resp.* 16, more cautiously and correctly expressed than here in the speech against Piso.

14C. *In Pis.* 58: ...*Camillus...Marius*. A catalogue of Rome's military heroes from the semi-legendary Furius Camillus (early to middle fourth century) to C. Marius, cos. 107; 104–100; 86. See Index of Personal Names. For Camillus, see Furius; for Calatinus, see Atilius; for Scipio, see Cornelius; for Marcellus, see Claudius; for Maximus, see Fabius.

our present consuls. As Asconius now becomes aware, this evidence renders otiose the elaborations in his Introduction about the date of the speech *Against Piso*!

Pompeius' father ... Picentes. Cn. Pompeius Strabo triumphed later in his consulship on 25 December 89 (*Fasti Triumphales* in Degrassi (1947), 84–5 and 563), during a swift visit to Rome from Asculum, where he was commanding in the northern theatre of the Social War.

P. Crassus. Cos. 97, who commanded in Further Spain 96–93 and ended with a triumph over the Lusitanians on 12 June 93 (*Fasti Triumphales* in Degrassi (1947), 84–5 and 563).

In Pis. **62: ... C. Cotta ... P. Sulpicius.** Eldest of the three brothers Cotta, cos. 75. On this man and P. Sulpicius, tr. pl. 88, see further *MRR* 2. 96, 103, 111; 3. 31 (Cotta); 2. 41–2; 3. 202 (Sulpicius).

L. Crassus' colleague was Q. Scaevola the *pontifex*. This man is Q. Mucius P. f. P. n. Scaevola, cos. 95, also Crassus' colleague as aedile (between 105 and 100) and (by) 98 as praetor, as well as linked with him by a marriage tie. He is to be distinguished both from P. Mucius P. f. Q. n. Scaevola, cos. 133, *pontifex* from 131 to his death; and from Q. Mucius Q. f. Q. n. Scaevola, cos. 117, the Augur.

15C. vetoed the passage of the senatorial decree. This must have been in 95, exercising his power of veto as consul, since it was as consul that Crassus had conducted his campaign in Cisalpine Gaul and claimed a triumph on slender grounds (Cic. *Inv.* 2. 111; *Pis.* 62; cf. Val. Max. 3.7.6 (misleading, and not—*pace MRR* 2. 11 and 13—evidence that he was proconsul at the time)): observe also Asconius' note of Crassus' 'enormous power and ranking in the state', which despite his talent, could hardly apply earlier. On a consul's right of veto, see Lintott (1999*a*), 84 and n., 101.

This same man had set aside a province which had made many men—even men of sound principles—do wrong in their eagerness to hold it, lest his †officially sanctioned expense allowance† should occasion costs. This passage is highly contentious, and further bedevilled by a crux in Asconius' text. The phrase 'officially sanctioned expense allowance' translates not the normal expansion of the MSS compendium, which yields *oratio* ('speech, oration'), and as such makes no sense, but the commonly accepted modern reading *ornatio* (Reid (1909); Balsdon (1937), 8–10), which, however, is itself hardly satisfactory (see below).

Which was the province which most men were ready to transgress in order to obtain? Marshall (1985*b*), 110–11, suggests that the description fits almost any, and that Asconius intended no particular reference, but Asia is extremely likely. Since its regularization in 123 it had occasioned many difficulties, disputes, complaints, and trials *de repetundis*, and still in the 90s was a source of anxiety to the more responsible among Rome's governing class. Q. Scaevola certainly governed it, but for only nine months before leaving his consular legate P. Rutilius Rufus (cos. 105) in charge until a successor arrived, and himself returning to Rome, having won golden opinions and many honours among the provincials for his record in tackling their problems, aided and abetted by Rutilius (Cic. *Att.* 6.1.15, 5.17.5; Val. Max. 8.15.6; see further *MRR* 2. 4–6, with n. 2, 7 with n. 5, 11; 3. 145–6).

The date is still debated among moderns (notably Badian (1956*b*); Marshall (1976); Kallett-Marx (1989); *MRR*, ll.cc.). Some make Scaevola's attested command of Asia result from his consulship of 95. In that case, since it was certainly as consul in 95 that he used his power of veto against Crassus' claim to triumph, the governorship must almost certainly fall *after* his consular year, and therefore in 94. There is no room in 95 for a nine-month stay (Cic. *Att.* 5.17.5) between arrival there, which, even if not delayed by his consular legislation with Crassus, could not possibly have been much earlier than May, and his exercise of veto, still as consul, at the end of the year; neither is it at all plausible that Crassus' campaign and claim, and Scaevola's veto can be accommodated before the latter's departure for the East. Scaevola's attested title *proconsul* (Liv. *Per.* 70; *OGIS* 437, 439), however, is not finally decisive in favour of 94, since it could apply equally well to a command in Asia resulting from his praetorship of 98 (or earlier).

Crucially, however, although my translation 'had set aside a province' (*provinciam deposuerat*) is deliberately ambiguous, it is barely possible to interpret Asconius' Latin as a reference to Scaevola's premature departure from his actual command in Asia. Very much more probably, from what we know of this Latin usage (admittedly rather little: cf. Cic. *Phil.* 11.23), it means that, as Cicero later did in 63, he had declined to take any province at all, or else set aside or resigned the one allocated to him before taking command there (so Balsdon (1937)). It is, however, highly unlikely that as praetor in (at latest) 98 he would have taken such a step, which would have seriously damaged his prospects of a consulship, especially at a time when the Roman system (if it merits the term) was badly over-stressed. (See now Brennan (2000), 551.) To excuse himself from the consular command allocated under the Lex Sempronia before the elections of 96 (for 95) was a different matter, though the reasons for it can only be conjectured. It would almost certainly not have eliminated the need for *ornatio* (post-Augustan, but so too was Asconius) in its normal sense, due if not to Scaevola then to his substitute, unless his predecessor stayed on without supplement. The word just possibly might be taken as Asconius' extension of that meaning by transference to refer to Scaevola's expenses over and above any such grant, actually incurred during tenure—but in Asia he is said to have paid those from his own pocket (Diod. 37.5.1).

If, however, as seems very possible, his consular province was to be Asia (or anywhere else for that matter), he might have been somewhat reluctant to aggravate enmities in Rome which had fairly certainly accrued from an earlier term there *ex praetura*, and which in time (92) were so disastrous for his luckless deputy Rutilius. Or the circumstances which may have required Asia's designation as a consular province in 96 under the Lex Sempronia may have changed. Moreover, his exemplary governorship there resulted in countless honours, including a periodic religious festival (*OGIS* 437–9; Cic. *Verr.* 2.2.51; Ps.-Ascon. 202, 262 St.), and doubtless therefore large expense to the Asiatics, which he might not wish to see compounded by a second term among them. Nor would similar results elsewhere, with consequent *invidia* for Rome in addition, be welcome to anyone concerned. This notion might circumvent the objection that to plead the intention of mitigating or eliminating administrative costs—whether to the provincials or to the *aerarium*—was nugatory. (Compare from some two-and-a-half centuries later the excuse of the Emperor Antoninus Pius for avoiding tours round the empire in the manner of Hadrian—*SHA, Pius* 7.11.) It does seem marginally possible that the term *ornatio* might refer to honours paid to persons for distinguished services. That line of thought, however, suggests other possible readings, such as *adoratio*, of honours paid to the gods, such as were actually accorded Scaevola in Asia after his tenure there. The word is rare, but occurs in Pliny, *NH* 29.67, only some two decades later than Asconius, and is close to the MS reading. Alternatively, and perhaps more attractive, the MSS compendium may possibly conceal the reading <*c*>*oro*<*na*>(or, with *essen*<*t*>, <*c*>*oro*<*nae*>)—'honorific crowns)'.

In Pis. 62: ... **M. Piso.** Cos. 61 and earlier pr. 72 or 71, whence a Spanish triumph in 69: see *MRR* 2. 178; cf. 117, 124, 129, 133; 3. 177; on his familial connections, Marshall (1985*b*), 112; Syme (1960), 15. Information on his relations with Cicero perhaps reached Asconius from Tiro's biography of the orator, for which see further below, on 48C. Asconius' cross-reference here might be to commentary on 2 *Verr.* 1.37 or *Dom.* 55—or some other (e.g. the speech *Against Clodius and Curio* (62/1): see in J. W. Crawford (1994), 233–70.

16C. he was the first of all to put on show a battle of elephants in the Circus. More on Pompey's Games of 55—evidently not confined to his new theatre. For the elephant fight, cf. Cic. *Fam.* 7.1.3; Sen. *Brev. Vit.* 13.6; Pliny, *NH* 8.20–1; Plut. *Pomp.* 52; Dio 39.38.2–3. Pliny, *NH* 8.19 also has a variant from Fenestella (again silently rejected here by Asconius) making C. Claudius Pulcher the first to show elephants, not necessarily in combat, in his famous aedilician games of 99.

In Pis. 68: **Philodemus ... an Epicurean of the greatest repute.** One of the great names in Epicurean philosophy, born at Gadara, around 110 BC, a pupil in Athens of Zeno of Sidon, he moved to Rome in the later 70s to become a

protégé of Piso, certainly his chief but perhaps not sole patron. At that time
he was still writing poetry of considerable charm, elegance, wit, and skill, in
the 'neoteric' manner, of which some thirty specimens survive in the Greek
Anthology (*Anthologia Graeca Palatina*) on a wide variety of themes, some
of them recognizably Epicurean (friendship, moderate pleasures, finality of
death), including a dinner invitation to Piso, and a description of a dinner
given by him. Some of these epigrams, in a conventional manner, are 'erotic',
as here noted by Asconius. They are mischievously exploited by Cicero (*Pis.*
70–1), who surely exaggerates in using them to characterize life in Piso's
household, but Cicero's remarks could easily be Asconius' source, if, despite
awareness of their existence, he had not read the epigrams himself. See now
Sider (1997), esp. 5–11.

Later in life Philodemus turned to serious philosophical writing in prose,
and in a very different style, arid, meticulously detailed and technical, but no
more than acutely crafted elaborations on standard Epicurean themes, albeit
still over a remarkable range, including literary and aesthetic theory (poetry,
rhetoric, music); kingship in Homer (dedicated to Piso); logic; ethics (flat-
tery, malice); and the gods. For all his public criticism of Philodemus in
certain contexts for his own immediate purposes (as in this speech), Cicero
learned much about Epicureanism from him and later accorded him un-
equivocal respect (Cic. *Nat. Deor.* 1. 39–41 (see Pease (1955), ad loc.); *Fin.*
2.119), conceding some desirable qualities even in the *In Pisonem* and both
there and in the other polemic of 57–56 (*Red. Sen.* 14; *Sest.* 23) forbearing to
name him. The catastrophic eruption of Vesuvius in AD 79 destroyed at
Herculaneum a very large and sumptuously appointed villa, dating to the
first century BC. Excavation begun in 1750 recovered from the Library there
several hundred carbonized papyrus rolls, about 65 per cent of them the
work of Philodemus, for whose connection with Herculaneum and the area
round Naples a reasonable case can be constructed from one of the papyri,
one of his epigrams (*AP* 9.412), Cic. *Fin.* 2.119; Serv. *Ad Ecl.* 6.13; *Vit. Verg.* 6.
The villa can hardly have been owned by Philodemus, but there is also a
tolerably strong argument, albeit not quite conclusive, that it belonged to
Piso, and the poet-philosopher may have been resident there. For further
exposition and bibliography, see Nisbet (1961), appendices 3, 4; Rawson
(1985), 23–4, 59–60, 280–1; *CAH* IX², 695, 722–3.

In Pis. 89: ... *six hundred allies and tribute players.* Six hundred here stands
for an indefinitely large number (Nisbet (1961), 159).

17C. A law on the courts was passed ... The references are to (1) the Lex
Aurelia passed by L. Cotta as praetor in 70 (*MRR* 2. 127); (2) the Lex Pompeia

of 55 (*MRR* 2. 214, citing Cic. *Phil.* 1.20; *Pis.* 94; [Sall.] *Ad Caes.* 2.3.3; 7.11; Ascon. 17C), passed by Cn. Pompeius Magnus, cos. II. The first, apparently after some uncertainties, debate and, perhaps, dispute (Marshall (1975*a*)) abolished senatorial monopoly of juries for *quaestiones publicae*, and pre-scribed their appointment instead in equal proportions from the three orders of senators, *equites*, and the somewhat mysterious *tribuni aerarii*. These last were most probably of the same *property-rating* (*census*)—not slightly lower, as it has at times been argued—as the *equites*, but on criteria operated by the censors of 70 excluded from the higher *status* of the eighteen centuries of *equites* to whom they awarded (whether nominally or in reality) the Public Horse. It remains uncertain whether the *tribuni aerarii* of 70 were still the Roman tribes' military treasurers of remote antiquity (so Taylor (1960), 8, 16, 123, and esp. 293–4 and nn.; evidence for the office in Lintott (1999*a*), 53 n. 61; Mommsen (1887–8), 3. 189–91) or simply, with or without some specifically tribal associations, borrowed their designation from those officers of the distant past (so Henderson (1963), 63–4). Other than top (i.e. equestrian) census-rating (*contra*, Taylor (1964), 20; Nicolet (1966–74), 1. 598–600), however, their qualifications for it are unknown. That Pompey's law of 55 increased the census required for service on the juries of *quaestiones* is not impossible, but quite unattested—certainly not by this passage of Asconius, which shows no more than reinforcement of the Lex Aurelia by way of insistence upon the specified top property-rating for jury-service, implicit in the passage of Cicero (*Pis.* 94) on which he comments here. That passage also shows that the Lex Pompeia would insist upon service by those properly qualified, and not allow evasion which arguably since 70, in the absence of any duly completed census, had undermined enforcement of the property-qualification required by the Aurelian Law (so Henderson (1963), 63–4). Further discussion in Marshall (1985*b*), 115–17.

In Pis. 95: *L. Opimius … who both after his praetorship and as consul had freed the state from the gravest perils.* The phrase 'after his praetorship' is misquoted from Cicero, whose MSS have, correctly, '*in* his praetorship' (125), which is apparently what Asconius himself read, to judge from his comment.

The taint of criminal conduct and sense of guilt for it has remained attached, not to him on whom this outrage was perpetrated, but to those who perpet-rated it. Cicero's real sympathy for Opimius, a man of unsavoury repute in most sources, may be doubted, but Cicero needed to express approval of his actions, at least those of his consulship in 121, which provided Cicero as consul in 63 and later a target for Clodius and others, with a vital precedent for killing persons without trial under the provisions of the senatorial decree (later called the *senatus consultum ultimum*), which authorized executive action in an emergency.

Opimius in his praetorship. In 125. See *MRR* 1. 510.

captured Fregellae, and thereby appeared to have checked the rest of the allies of Latin status who were disaffected. Fregellae was a Latin *colonia* (see Glossary) founded in 328 at the strategically vital confluence of the Rivers Trerus and Liris near the fringes of (then) Samnite territory. (On recent excavations there, Coarelli (1981), (1986); M. H. Crawford *et al.* (1984–6).) The revolt of 125, which might well have spread if not promptly suppressed, was a culmination of smouldering discontent among non-Roman communities in Italy, including, it appears, several of Latin status. It is usually linked to the failure of the consul M. Fulvius Flaccus to carry a law in favour of Italian allies to allow them either full Roman citizenship or the right of *provocatio*; and also with the tribunician law passed by M. Iunius Pennus in the previous year to expel aliens from the city of Rome—which can hardly have been sustained in practice, but was nevertheless extremely unwelcome to the intended targets.

the same man in his consulship suppressed the consular Fulvius Flaccus and the ex-tribune C. Gracchus. Opimius as consul in 121 was notoriously brutal in suppressing what was presented as armed insurrection on the part of C. Gracchus, tr. pl. 123, 122, and his somewhat hot-headed and unreliable colleague of 122, M. Fulvius Flaccus, who had been consul in 125. These two were killed, and so were large numbers of their following. See *MRR* 1. 520–1 and standard accounts.

and on account of the resultant political hostility was the victim of judicial conspiracy and driven into exile. Opimius' brutality as consul in 121 provoked sharp reaction in 120 when a decidedly lively tribune, P. Decius Subolo, indicted him before the people for unlawful executions and imprisonments. See further Badian (1956*a*). This, however, was not the occasion of Opimius' exile, for he was acquitted. The 'judicial conspiracy' which exiled him doubtless did so all the more readily in view of his consular conduct, but in fact was the Quaestio Mamilia, an inquisition set up by the tribune C. Mamilius Limetanus in 109 to try persons accused of collusion and misconduct in dealings with Jugurtha of Numidia. Opimius was one of four ex-consuls to be convicted, in his case for corrupt handling of a mission to Numidia in 117 or 116 (Sall. *Jug.* 16.2–5; 20.1). He also gave his name to a particularly fine vintage of wine (Cic. *Brut.* 287; Pliny, *NH* 14.55)

The Commentary on Cicero's speech *On Behalf of Scaurus*

By no means all that we have of Cicero's defence of Scaurus appears in Asconius. Several other later commentators and scholars have preserved fragments and citations, and some fifty paragraphs in two sections (*Scaur.* 2–45; 46–50) variously survive in two rather battered MSS. The traditional arrangement of the whole collection appears in Latin at the end of the Oxford Classical Text of Cicero's Speeches, vol. 6. See further, Alexander (1990), no. 295.

As usual, Asconius gives the date of the case—in this instance extremely briefly, but followed by a much longer introduction, explaining the circumstances, than for the speech *Against Piso*. Then follow, again as usual, the Commentary by lemma and scholion, and finally details of the outcome.

18C. This speech too he delivered in the same consulship as the one for Vatinius. That is, in 54. The exact date will derive from the *Acta*. In 57 Cicero had attacked P. Vatinius, an ally of Caesar, but after the revival of the Caesar's alliance with Pompey and Crassus at Luca in 56 had been constrained to act against his own inclinations and in accord with their wishes: hence his defence of Vatinius *de sodaliciis* (Cic. *Fam.* 1.9.19, 5.9.1; *QF.* 2.16.3). On the wider context and circumstances of the speech for Scaurus, apart from standard works see also Gruen (1966*a*), 219–21, (1974), 331–7; Wiseman (1966), (1967); Alexander (1990), 143–4; for an overview of the case, Courtney (1961).

M. Scaurus, son of the M. Scaurus who was *princeps senatus* .... That is, the famous consul of 115. See Index of Personal Names, Aemilius, and for full career, *MRR* 2. 528; 3. 10–12. Modern accounts of Scaurus include Bloch (1908); Pais (1918); Fraccaro (1957); Flammini (1977), 37–56; Bates (1986); Lewis (2001*b*).

no gifts for himself, nor did he purchase anything at auction. Asconius evidently believes the defence on these matters (cf. 26C below), which refer to the distribution and sale of the assets belonging to the victims of Sulla's massacres and proscriptions of 82/1. Since Scaurus may have been very young at that time (quaestor *c.*66?—*MRR* 2. 153, 159, 163), perhaps even still not into his *toga virilis* and so not yet *sui iuris*, the denial may be true. His later conduct was almost certainly less innocent: see next note.

aedileship ... outstanding extravagance that he exhausted his own resources ... huge debt. On the aedileship of 58, which made an enormous impression (Cic. *Att.* 4.16), see *MRR* 2. 195; 3. 12. Vast debts resultant from such exhibitions were a commonplace (for example, compare Caesar's in 65), but Scaurus' games are elsewhere on record as exceptional, and indeed must have been, if he really did exhaust all his resources on them, for after his service under Pompey in the East (67(?)–61) his accumulated assets were apparently enormous. In particular, he seems to have 'acquired' a remarkable collection of jewels (*dactyliotheca*) (Pliny, *NH* 37.11; cf. for wealth in general, ibid. 36.113, his house (below, on 26–7C) and for his supervision and control as Pompey's (pro)quaestor of Mithridates' treasure Appian, *Mith.* 115; cf. Plut. *Pomp.* 36. For his corrupt practices in Syria as proquaestor in 64, Jos. *AJ* 14. 29–33; *BJ* 1.123–30; App. *Syr.* 51)

governor of Sardinia ... arrogance. In 55, after praetorship in charge of the *quaestio de vi* in 56.

This sort of behaviour ... from his father ... application to hard work. More on the parallels between the two Scauri below, on 19C. The father, in his three books of autobiography (Cic. *Brut.* 112) had almost certainly boasted of the *industria* which had revived the fortunes and senatorial rank of this decayed patrician family (Ascon. 23C; Val. Max. 4.4.11; Ps.-Vict. *Vir. Ill.* 72.1): Sallust almost certainly refers to his claims in characterizing him as 'ever-active' (*impiger*) in the famous thumbnail sketch of *Bell. Jug.* 15.4 (*nobilis impiger factiosus, avidus potentiae honoris divitiarum...*). See further Lewis (2001*b*).

act as an advocate. Not particularly well known, apart from successful prosecution of Cn. Dolabella, pr. 81 (see below, on 26C; 74C) and the defence of C. Cato in 54 mentioned here (see next note). Omitted from Cicero's canon of orators in the *Brutus*, but probably because still alive at the time of writing (46 BC).

defended C. Cato. Tr. pl. 56, a supporter of P. Clodius in 56, not to be confused with the far more famous M. Cato (Uticensis), pr. 54 (see Index of Personal Names, Porcius, and *MRR* 2. 209; 3. 169–70) and by 54 like his friend P. Clodius reconciled with Pompey. On the part played by criminal trials in the complex political convolutions of the mid-50s, especially among the lesser players, see further (e.g.) Gruen (1974), 287–357 (and on this trial esp. 314–15); Gruen (1966*a*), 222–5; Wiseman (1966). C. Cato was prosecuted twice in 54 for his part in disrupting elections of 56: the reference here is probably to the second trial. The main evidence is Cic. *Att.* 4.16.5; cf. 15.4; Sen. *Controv.* 7.4.7. For more on this trial, Tatum (1999), 228–30; and on C. Cato's previous activity for Clodius, ibid. 126, 197, 203–4, 214, 222–3.

On M. Cato, see especially *CAH* IX², index; Fehrle (1983); *MRR* 2. 606; 3. 170–1.

third day after. As always with Roman dates, by inclusive reckoning, so on 6 July.

19C. son of the man who had borne arms against M. Lepidus in Sardinia. That is, son of C. Valerius Triarius, who in 77 was propraetor there during the last stages of the civil war started by Lepidus as cos. 78. Hence some measure of patronage for the Triarii, father and son, in Sardinia (cf. Cic. *Scaur.* 29)—just as there appears to have been an earlier and probably more important *clientela* there for the Aemilii Scauri (see below, p. 219).

later ... legate to L. Lucullus in Asia and Pontus. See *MRR* 2. 113, 120, 125, 130, 134, 141, 148; 3. 214–15 for this service (73–67), terminated at Zela in his disastrous defeat and death at the hands of Mithridates (*CAH* IX², 243; Sherwin-White (1984), 184).

was assisted by L. Marius, son of Lucius, and the brothers M. and Q. Pacuvius. L. Marius is otherwise unknown. The *cognomen* of the Pacuvii is transmitted as 'Claudius' in the MSS, which is improbable. Humanist editors have opted for 'Claudus' ('lame') or 'Caldus' ('hot'), the latter being more plausible. (Caldus is an attested *cognomen* for the Coelii). On the 'seconding' (*subscriptio*) of a prosecution, Jones (1972), 63–4, 129 n. 121.

thirty days for investigations in the islands of Sardinia and also Corsica. Compare Cicero's well-known allowance of 110 days for gathering evidence against C. Verres on Sicily in 70. Sardinia and Corsica together had normally formed a single command since the mid-second century.

the consular elections were due to take place in the interim. In fact, political disruption and violence forced their repeated postponement until July 53, a year late. In July 54, however, Scaurus' accusers were ready to dispense with investigations in the province in order to get the trial started, not so much, as they said, to prevent further despoliations on his part, if elected consul, as to prevent him from standing altogether, if at all possible, or at the very least to damage his chances. For Scaurus' prospective candidature and competitors, intricacies of the politics of the day, Gruen (1974), 148–9, 159, 331–5, 451; Wiseman (1966); Lintott (1974); Tatum (1999), 231–3.

as his father had done, before a verdict ... would enter his magistracy, and once again despoil other provinces before giving due account for his previous administration. Marshall (1985*b*), 124–5 and (1977) identifies this episode in the career of the elder Scaurus with his known accusation *de* *repetundis* by one M. Brutus, and against the usual dating of that trial to 114, after Scaurus' consulship of 115, associates it with one of his consular candidatures of 117 (failed) and 116. This hypothesis lacks evidential support. The elder Scaurus' praetorship cannot have been later than 119, and was probably no earlier (Sumner (1973), 69), but it is possible that his allegedly criminal 'previous administration' was not as a magistrate or promagistrate, but a legateship—quite plausibly to Q. Mucius Scaevola, praetor commanding Asia in 120—an available if unproven interpretation of a fragment of Lucilius 2.55–95M; *MRR* 1. 523–4. On this view Scaurus proceeded directly to a praetorship himself for 119 and in that year and at least part of the next might plausibly be supposed to have held Sardinia, if Ps.-Vict. *Vir. Ill.* 72.4 is right in making him an opponent of Jugurtha 'as praetor' (cf. Sall. *Bell. Jug.* 15.4–5). He had in any case a connection with Sardinia from previous service there in the middle 120s, and it was very probably the commander of this province at that time who would manage Rome's very limited interests in Africa, where there was as yet no regular governor (if any at all, outside the Jugurthan war, before the 80s), and the neighbouring kingdoms. Compare the mission of C. Gracchus from Sardinia as proquaestor (125–4) to Micipsa of Numidia to negotiate corn-supplies (Plut. *CG* 2).

Scaurus reposed the utmost confidence in the standing of his father's name. The fragments of this speech show that like Scaurus himself (below, 20C) Cicero made much of it, and together with Asconius' comment do much to support the MSS reading of Cic. *Att.* 4.17.4—*Scaurus... absolutus, cum ego patrem eius ornatissime defendissem*—'Scaurus ... acquitted, after I had produced a wonderfully elaborated defence of his father'—to be read as a typical piece of irony on the part of Cicero, who privately was more or less convinced of his client's guilt (cf. ibid. 15.9). *Contra*, Shackleton Bailey (1965–70), ad loc., for no reason that I can understand: he accepts the humanist emendation *partem*, to mean 'part of him', a reference to the fact that Cicero had been one of six advocates—a joke even more frigid than one which Shackleton Bailey wishes to discount.

and a good deal in his connection with Cn. Pompeius Magnus. Sadly mistaken, as it turned out. See further below, pp. 220 and 229.

For he had a son who was half-brother to the children of Pompeius. That is, born of the same mother, Mucia Tertia (Dio 41.2.4), whom Pompey on his return from the East in 62 divorced for infidelity (Cic. *Att.* 1.12.3; Plut. *Pomp.* 42; Suet. *Div. Jul.* 50) and who fairly promptly married the younger Scaurus. The son was later a partisan of Sex. Pompeius and M. Antonius against Octavian and pardoned after Actium, but never reached the consulship (Dio

51.2.4). The grandson, who did (AD 21), had an evil reputation under Tiberius and was the last of the line (Sen. *Ben.* 4.31.3–5; Tac. *Ann.* 6.29).

Flaminia, Triarius' mother … Cato's half-sister Servilia … a mother's influence with Cato. Nothing more is known of Flaminia. For Servilia and the other kinsfolk of M. Cato, see the stemma (II) in the back of Syme (1986); see 23–4, 69, 116, etc. for her ambitions, authority, and standing.

But in that trial Pompeius failed to extend him any enthusiastic support. He did act as a 'character witness' in submitting a *laudatio* ('eulogy') (Ascon. 28C), but soon withdrew support for Scaurus' consular candidature (Cic. *Att.* 4.15.7). This may have much to do with Scaurus' subsequent indictment—again by P. Triarius—and conviction *de ambitu* towards the end of 54.

20C. Nor did Cato in any way deviate. The reputation of M. Cato (pr. 54 *de repetundis*) for rigid integrity was proverbial even in his own lifetime for almost all who knew him, friend and foe alike. Not quite unblemished, however, for C. Iulius Caesar, who in 45 issued detailed and virulent polemic in at least two books entitled *Anticato(nes)*, though they seem to have been more concerned with his private family affairs than his performance in public life. Several fragments survive (see Klotz (1927)).

Faustus Sulla, … son of Sulla Felix and maternal half-brother to Scaurus. Sulla the dictator had married the elder Scaurus' widow Caecilia Metella shortly after the old man had died in 89. She was mother to the younger Scaurus and Aemilia, second wife of Cn. Pompeius Magnus (Pompey). Faustus' sister Fausta had married C. Memmius, also a consular candidate in 54 and apparently a 'running mate' of Scaurus also enjoying—for a time—the support of Pompey and Caesar. His son appeared for Scaurus at this trial (28C).

protested that he had nearly been murdered by Scaurus' electoral rivals, and was proceeding on foot with an armed escort of three hundred. This looks very much like a political (or anyhow electoral) stratagem typical of these years, and little more than an excuse to resort to armed violence in political life. It should, however, be remembered that it would be a brave man among the magnates of Rome's political families who went abroad, especially at night, without an adequate escort—which would usually need to be armed in order to be effective. Cicero certainly employed one (evidence and comment in Lintott (1999*b*), 74–6, 90–1; add Cic. *Att.* 4.3.3 and Ascon. 48C, see below). Scaurus' electoral rivals were the pair eventually elected as consuls in July 53—for that year, after a very lengthy *interregnum*—that is, Cn. Domitius Calvinus and M. Messalla Rufus.

after the civil wars before the Lex Iulia. Which 'Julian Law' is meant is uncertain, for both Caesar in 46 and Augustus in 17 passed laws. Of Caesar's we know only that he reduced the three decuries of jurors to two, one senatorial, one equestrian (probably incorporating the *tribuni aerarii*); Augustus' were certainly wider ranging. Asconius probably means Augustus' Lex Iulia *iudiciorum publicorum*, since 'after the civil wars' can hardly refer to 46 BC and Asconius' sons would need to know about Augustus' legislation.

these were the six. Cicero and Hortensius, of course, dominate the rankings among advocates of their day, but Calidius (Quintil. 10.1.23; Cic. *QF* 3.2.1; *Brut.* 274–8; Ascon. 34C, 88C, etc.) and M. Marcellus, cos. 51 (Cic. *Brut.* 248) were also by no means insignificant. The oddity is the appearance of P. Clodius for Scaurus (with a long speech—Cic. *Scaur.* 37) alongside his two most irreconcilable enemies, Cicero and Milo (for the latter, 28C)—as well as L. Lentulus Niger (28C), who had worked against him in the Bona Dea affair of 61 (Cic. *Har. Resp.* 17). On Messalla Niger (cos. 61), see *MRR* 2. 482, 110, 162, 178, 229, 237; 3. 214 and Cic. *Brut.* 246.

spoke on his own behalf … dishevelled appearance and tears. The practices first adopted, we are told, by Ser. Sulpicius Galba at his trial (149) for gross misconduct in Spain (*MRR* 1. 459). As emerges later (28C) a further seven consulars also sent in 'testimonials' for Scaurus, and another ten persons joined in appealing to the jury for him—in all as many as twenty-three persons appeared for him, mostly of some rank and seniority.

his lavish aedileship … recollection of his father's position. Key factors in his defence, it seems. See above, on 18–19C.

When he lists the judicial indictments. A clear indicator of Cicero's methods at this point.

21C. *trial before the people.* That is, before a tribal assembly, not a jury court (*quaestio publica*, either *perpetua* or *extraordinaria*). Probably this case was tried in the *concilium plebis*, but just possibly the *comitia tributa?*—see Lintott (1999*a*), 53–4; also, on trials in assemblies, ibid. 126–7, 150–4; cf. Cloud in *CAH* IX², 501–3; Alexander (1990), no. 68.

consul with C. Cassius … tribune of the plebs. Cos. 96, tr. pl. 104 by the usual dating, which a few scholars have disputed and postponed to 103 (*MRR* 3. 82–3). Marshall (1985*b*), 129 offers some rather tenuous speculations on Domitius' possible links and earlier collaboration with this C. Cassius Longinus.

in anger against Scaurus for failing to co-opt him into the College of Augurs. It is often inferred from this passage that the elder Scaurus was an augur, against the apparent evidence of Suet. *Nero* 1.2, who says that Domitius was angered at the refusal of the pontiffs to co-opt him in place of his deceased father, and so legislated to transfer to popular election the right of appointing priests of the four major colleges—from which some moderns infer that Scaurus was not an augur, but a pontiff, it being impossible at that time for one man to hold both priesthoods. Debate is still unresolved. For more on this over-tortured question, Geer (1929), 292–4; Taylor (1942*a*), 388, 409; Taylor (1942*b*), 412–14; McDermott (1969), 242 n. 2; *MRR* 1. 562 n. 7; 2. 44 (see also 3. 11–12) for the pontificate; *contra* Badian (1968*a*), 29–31; Fears (1975), 597–8, for the augurate. See also Frier (1969), 190; Sumner (1973), 98–100; yet more in Marshall (1985*b*), 129–32.

Lavinium. A religious cult-centre of some importance in Latium for the Dioscuri, otherwise identifiable as the Penates. See Weinstock (1960), 112–18, with *ILLRP* 1271–1271a; *ILS* 5004–5 (with cross-references); Castagnoli *et al.* (1975); Castagnoli (1977); Coarelli (1987).

He was indicted by Q. Servilius Caepio under the Lex Servilia ... after the condemnation of P. Rutilius ... not to fear it. On the Lex Servilia of Glaucia, most probably of 101, see Laws and Rogations; *MRR* 1. 571, 3. 196; Marshall (1985*b*), 135; Cloud, *CAH* IX², 512–13. Besides changes concerning liability *de repetundis* and procedure (*comperendinatio*—below, on 62C), it passed membership of juries in the *quaestio de repetundis* and almost certainly all other *quaestiones publicae* entirely to the equestrian class, which in 92/1 scandalously condemned P. Rutilius Rufus (cos. 95) for his role as legate to Q. Scaevola in Asia (97/6 or 95/4), see *MRR* 2.8; above, pp. 210–12 on Asconius 15C. Further political outrages ensued on the part of the knights, or some of them, at least according to the optimate tradition, and in reaction the attempted reforms of the tribune M. Livius Drusus in 91, encouraged especially by Scaurus and the consular statesman L. Crassus (cos. 95). More in Badian (1964), 35–44; Gruen (1966*b*), 43–7. Q. Servilius Caepio was the son of the consul of 106, formerly of similar political persuasions to Scaurus, but by the middle or later 90s plainly his enemy.

his Asian posting. Both date and nature of this post are disputed. Unlikely to be earlier than 97, and possibly as late as 92; either as deputy to a governor, or as an envoy, most probably to Mithridates or to Nicomedes of Bithynia. For an alternative theory, making this a reference to the legateship of Rutilius Rufus and the unrest occasioned by his trial in 92/1, Alexander (1981). See also Badian (1956*b*), 120–1; Gruen (1966*b*), 55–9.

enter a counter-accusation against Caepio, and by obtaining an earlier date for the trial contrived that the latter should plead his case first. Caepio was apparently acquitted, probably *de repetundis*, since the hearing involved *comperendinatio* (*ORF* 167—a second *actio* or phase), but his case against Scaurus quite possibly never came to trial in the ensuing political turmoil.

he also urged M. Drusus, tribune of the plebs, to reform the courts. On Drusus' legislative programme of 91 and its failure, see further below, on 69C.

22C. ... *was summoned* ... *under the Lex Varia on a charge of high treason*: ... Q. Varius ... allies had taken up arms against the Roman people. The exact nature and content of the Lex Varia of 90 have been disputed. It is perhaps best seen as a seriously misguided attempt to curtail political disputes at Rome by rallying her politicians and people in patriotic fervour against the Italian rebels and any suspected of favouring them, by making persons convicted of the conduct specified in Asconius' summary liable under the Lex *de maiestate*. That is, it was in effect an extension of that law (presumably the law of Saturninus, 103 BC), not a replacement, although it seems to have instituted its own separate procedures for trials (Badian (1969), 460; Gruen (1965*a*), 59–60; Seager (1967), 37–40; see also *CAH* IX², 114–15, 518–19. The effects of the Varian *quaestio* were almost certainly seriously damaging to Rome's real interests—see, for example, Appian, *BC* 1.37165–38.169. On *maiestas* in general, Lintott (1999*a*), 159–60; Ferrary (1983).

he caused all present to change their minds. The story may be in essentials true, though it surely loses nothing in the telling and is strongly reminiscent of the manner in which P. Scipio Africanus is said to have dispelled the accusations of a vexatious tribune, M. Naevius, in 184 (*MRR* 1. 376). On Scaurus' reply, see further Val. Max. 3.7.8; Ps.-Vict. *Vir. Ill.* 72.11; Cic. *Sest.* 101; Quintil. 5.12.10. The suggestion that Varius was really of Iberian race is merely abusive polemic, though he may perhaps have been of 'colonial' (i.e. emigrant Roman or even Latin) stock, that is, *Hispaniensis*, not *Hispanus* (cf. Syme (1937), 130–1).

... *fond of him. He was, you see, the first to inspire me* .... For the elder Scaurus' patronage of the Tullii of Arpinum, Cic. *Leg.* 3.36; Nicolet (1967). Note also 'dedication' of his autobiography to the obscure L. Fufidius, perhaps also from Arpinum (*RE* no. 3; cf. nos. 1, 5, 7, with Cic. *Fam.* 13.11.1; 12.1—but *RE* no. 6 is from Puteoli). See also Wiseman (1971*b*), 232; Lewis (2001*b*). For another important influence on Cicero's formative years, Rawson (1971).

23C. And so Scaurus needed to work just as hard as any *novus homo*. By no means the only patrician whose family had been politically eclipsed by the middle of the second century BC. The prime example is L. Sergius Catilina, but compare also, of somewhat less long depressed stock, L. Cornelius Sulla; some at least of the Iulii Caesares; later, Ser. Sulpicius Rufus (cos. 51). In his autobiography Scaurus admitted the (comparative) poverty of his early years (fr. 1P = Val. Max. 4.4.11; Ps.-Vict. *Vir. Ill.* 72. 1 on his father's 'charcoal business'—probably implying ownership of hardwood-forests and equestrian status), and probably also contrasted his own *industria* in rising above this with the preceding generations' inertia. Marshall's note on this passage is confused in that (*a*) Asconius does not in fact say that patrician status brought advancement 'automatically' even for the lazy, but only that it had done so in some cases; (*b*) Cic. *Off.* 1.138 refers (chiefly) to the defendant of 54, and to the distinction of *his* father, the *princeps senatus*, cos. 115—not to the latter's father! Plut. *Mor.* 318c in calling the elder Scaurus a *novus homo* for whatever reason is simply wrong, though his ascription of 'lowly lifestyle and even more lowly family' suits his early years up to a point.

This L. Tubulus was of praetorian rank in the time of earlier generations of Cicero's family. When on account of his many outrages he was summoned from exile to be executed in prison he drank poison. L. Hostilius Tubulus (pr. 142) was notorious for taking bribes while presiding over murder trials (*MRR* 1. 475), and forced into exile the next year by the combined actions of P. Mucius Scaevola, then tr. pl., the senate, and the consul Cn. Servilius Caepio. See further Gruen (1965*b*). Tubulus' presidency of a court for murder is hardly evidence for the existence of a *quaestio perpetua inter sicarios* or *de veneficis* so early: see the sane appraisal of Cloud, *CAH* IX², 521–2. On the face of it his recall for execution, as Asconius has it, should have been legally impossible. Presumably the version of the story available to Asconius was deficient in vital information. His dating of Tubulus to the generation or age 'of Cicero's fathers' (in literal translation) is not very plausibly to be taken as a reference solely to Cicero's father, who would on this view, even if as much as ten years younger than Tubulus, have been some ten years older than Scaurus and around 64 at the birth of his elder son (106). It seems better therefore to understand Asconius' phrase as a reference to previous generations of the Tullii Cicerones, including at least the grandfather(s) as well as the father.

This Crassus was the father of the Crassus who was Cn. Pompeius' rival ... Cn. Octavius. That is, the consul of 97, who lost his life in the 'Marian terror' of 87/6. For this version (suicide) see also Cic. *Sest.* 48; *De Or.* 3.10; Liv. *Per.* 80; cf. Cic. *Tusc.* 5.55; Diod. 37.29.5. For a variant (assassination), Lucan 2.125; Plut. *Crass.* 4; Flor. 2.9.14; Aug. *CD* 3.27; a more sensationalist version in App. *BC* 1.72. On the Cinnan domination, Badian (1962); Bulst (1964). Other optimate casualties of 87/6 were numerous, including two Iulii and the famous orator M. Antonius, grandfather of the *triumvir*.

24C. *And neither was M². Aquilius, who had enjoyed the same honours, able despite extreme gallantry in warfare to copy the deed of that elder Crassus.* This will not be M². Aquilius the disreputable consul of 129, successor to P. Crassus Mucianus (see below) in the Asiatic war against Aristonicus. The far preferable identification is surely with his son, cos. 101, who had a tolerable military record until his fiasco against Mithridates in 89/8 which ended in his capture and execution (particularly brutal in some versions). See *MRR* for 101 and 88 (1.570–1; 2.43; 3.24). Madvig regarded the extended grammatical comment on Cicero's *neque* which follows as by an unknown scholar, not by Asconius. He did so for fair reasons: (i) comment on such matters appears nowhere else in Asconius; (ii) the writer is apparently unaware that a single *neque* of this kind is common in Cicero—and Asconius would certainly have known that; (iii) his third point, the lack of expected comment on M². Aquilius alongside the Crassi and M. Antonius, is less persuasive. One might add (iv), with Marshall (1985*b*), 142, that the writer misses the point—the oddity of Cicero's Latin (if it really is such) lies not in the failure to add a second 'disjunctive' (*neque … neque …*), but to precede the single, unanswered one with *ac* ('And'). Madvig did not include the *lemma* in his excision (despite what Clark says in his apparatus) and this, *pace* Marshall, leaves perfectly good sense. On this view Asconius quoted a *pair* of *lemmata* separated by a warning 'A little further on', indeed omitting comment on Aquillius, but concerned to distinguish the two Crassi, and both, in their manner of death, from the Iulii and M. Antonius.

So then? Could either the Iulii … or M. Antonius … emulate the other Crassus at that time? There is some temptation to emend the Latin (*quis* for *quid*) to yield 'Yet who at that time was able to emulate the other Crassus? For sure, not the Iulii … or M. Antonius … This is in any case a further reference to notable casualties in massacre of 87/6, as Asconius goes on to explain.

25C. This 'other Crassus' … of whom we have spoken above … P. Crassus who was *pontifex maximus* and … took care to get himself killed. The first Crassus referred to as mentioned earlier by Asconius (23C) is the consul of 97; the one mentioned earlier by Cicero (and Asconius at 24C) is P. Licinius Crassus Dives Mucianus, cos. 131, who contrived his own death after capture by the enemy—the forces of the insurgent Aristonicus—in Asia in 130. Evidence, with variant versions, *MRR* 1. 130—add Aelius Aristid. *Letter on Smyrna* 41.766 (Dind.).

the two brothers Lucius and Gaius Caesar … a cause of civil war. These persons are L. Iulius Caesar, cos. 90 and author of the vitally important law on enfranchisement of Italian Allies, whose censorship (89) with P. Crassus (cos. 97) was not completed (Cic. *Arch.* 11): see further *MRR* 2. 25, 32–3; 3. 109; C. Iulius Caesar Strabo Vopiscus, aed. cur. 90 (*MRR* 2. 26; 3. 109). The dating of his efforts to attain the consulship without first being praetor remains thoroughly contentious. There is a concise account of modern views in Marshall (1985*b*), 144–5. C. Caesar Strabo's clash with P. Sulpicius, tr. pl. 88, on this issue certainly led to violence, but that this was *the* cause of the civil war of 88 is surely an exaggeration, since the main reason for Sulla's march on Rome was unquestionably Sulpicius' attempt to deprive him of the command against Mithridates in favour of C. Marius—who was in turn a rival and enemy of C. Strabo, and whose followers killed C. Strabo in 87/6, as Asconius duly notes below. On this Caesar's rhetorical and literary abilities, see also Cic. *Brut.* 177; *De Orat.* 2.98; 3.30; Vell. 2.9.2; Ascon. 66C; Val. Max. 3.7.11.

these Iulii and Antonius were slain by the followers of Marius, while Crassus, as we said above, anticipated the same fate by his own hand. These are four prominent victims of the massacre of 87/6 blamed by some sources on L. Cinna, by others on C. Marius after their victory in the civil war of 87—data collected in *MRR* 2. 46. Asconius here opts for a version which incriminates Marius' uncontrolled hangers-on (*satellites*) (cf. Plut. *Mar.* 43–4 on the Bardyaei) rather than Marius himself, but at 23C blames Cinna for the death of his colleague Cn. Octavius (cos. 87) and apparently though not explicitly that of P. Crassus. M. Antonius (cos. 99, cens. 97), with L. Crassus leading orator and statesman of the 90s, is a leading interlocutor with him in Cicero's *De Oratore* and treated at some length in his *Brutus* (see with Sumner (1973) and Douglas (1966)). Among other casualties of the slaughter were Q. Lutatius Catulus, cos. 102; the praetorian Q. Ancharius; an Atilius Serranus; a P. Lentulus; L. Merula, *flamen Dialis* and cos. suff. 87. They are missing in Asconius, of course, because omitted by Cicero, who had no use for them at this point in his speech.

… *Appius Claudius, endowed as he is with that humanity and wisdom of his.* By 54 Cicero had been publicly reconciled with Ap. Claudius (Cic. *Fam.* 1.9.4, 19, 25; 2.13.2; *QF* 2.11.3; Quintil. 9.3.41), and this remark may be taken as an indication of that—but one cannot but suspect a measure of irony here too, for privately Cicero continued to view this powerful and haughty patrician with some caution: he was after all P. Clodius' brother.

had he not thought that this man was going to be the electoral rival of his brother C. Claudius. That is, in 54 for the consulship of 53. Since both he and Scaurus were patricians, both could not be elected. Evidence on the electoral ploys involved includes Cic. *Scaur.* 35–6; *Att.* 4.17.2; *QF* 2.12.3, 3.1.16, 3.2.3, 3.7.3.

There were two families of Claudii. In fact there were several others, mostly far less important than the Pulchri and Marcelli, but it is very odd indeed that Asconius omits the patrician Nerones, who produced the Claudian emperors. The Nerones, however, were not at all prominent in the Ciceronian age, and perhaps in any case Asconius is following Cic. *De Orat.* 1. 176.

26C. Cicero wittily mocks C. Claudius. Despite P. Clodius' appearance with Cicero for Scaurus, there had been no reconciliation between these two; nor, so Asconius here attests, with the second of the brothers Claudius Pulcher, Gaius. The 'witty mockery' (cf. another little stab at Clodius at *Scaur.* 37) is to say the least somewhat forced, since it was notoriously Publius who in 59 had contrived to change his status from patrician to plebeian in order to be eligible for the Tribunate of 58. He also adopted the 'common' spelling and pronunciation of his family name. Details in Gelzer (1968), 77; far more in Tatum (1999), ch. 4, 87–113.

From a long list there remained for him just the one enemy of his father's, Dolabella, who along with his relative Q. Caepio had joined in prosecuting Scaurus his father. Most of the elder Scaurus' numerous enemies were dead by the time his son became politically or forensically active. This Dolabella was the son of a man killed alongside L. Saturninus in rioting of 100, in which the elder Scaurus had proposed the fateful *senatus consultum* against the dissident tribune and his followers (Oros. 5.17.10). On Caepio's prosecution of Scaurus in 92/1, above, on 21C.

two Dolabellae at the at same time. See Index of Personal Names, Cornelius. They were not closely related. For depredations in Macedonia Caesar accused the consul of 81 (Cn. Cornelius P. f. L.n. Dolabella), who was defended by Q. Hortensius and Caesar's relative C. Cotta—perhaps more for publicity than with serious intent. Scaurus attacked the praetor of 81, Cn. Cornelius Cn. f. Cn. n. Dolabella *de repetundis* regarding Cilicia, and secured conviction allegedly on the evidence of his equally guilty legate C. Verres (Cic. *Verr.* 1.11; 2.41–102; 2.109; 3.177; Ascon. 74C).

Scaurus possesses such a fine house: ... *the vicinity and the busy location eliminate any suspicion of sloth or greed.* Thus, under the public gaze, the younger Scaurus would have to maintain his father's reputation for *industria*, and this consideration also serves to deny allegations against both of corruption. The location, just off the Via Sacra, would have abounded in the pulsating life of *tabernae* and *officinae* (shops and workshops of all kinds).

27C. I recall that I made it clear to you that this house is ... **the next street which is on the left.** This is perhaps most naturally taken as a cross-reference to Asconius' earlier remarks on the site from a lost commentary on another speech (which escapes identification). It remains possible, however, to take it much more literally and vividly, as does Marshall (1985*b*), ad loc., as his reminder to his sons that he had 'pointed out' the location to them on some past sightseeing tour round central Rome. For topography and a possible identification after excavations of the location, see *LTUR* 2. 26 (W. Eck); 5. 243 (E. Papi); A. Carandini (1986), 263–78; Coarelli (1989), 178–97; cf. Coarelli (1985), 234, 239; cautious appraisal and acceptance of the identification in Patterson (1992), 200–3. P. Clodius purchased it in 53: below, p. 237, on Ascon. 32C.

The present occupant is Caecina Largus, who was consul with Claudius. That is, in AD 42. This remark has implications for the dating of Asconius' Commentaries on Cicero's speeches: see Introd., p. xii.

four pillars in marble of remarkable size, which are now said to be in the portico of the Theatre of Marcellus. He had made use of them as aedile. For the Theatre of Marcellus, *LTUR* 5. 31–5 (P. Ciancio Rossetti); Coarelli (1997), 448–51, 453, 469–70, 486). The pillars in the house were, it seems, the biggest from a total of 360 used in the construction of Scaurus' temporary theatre for his aedilician games in 58 (Pliny, *NH* 36.5–7; cf. also ibid. 50, 113–16, 189).

he means the maternal grandfather L. Metellus, the *pontifex maximus*, whom he later also names. This is L. Metellus Delmaticus, cos. 119, *pont. max.* before December 114, died in 103, whose daughter married the elder Scaurus.

For Scaurus' paternal grandfather and great-grandfather were of low standing and obscure. Cf. Ascon. 23C, where Asconius notes the family's decrepitude for *three* generations before revival in the elder Scaurus, cos. 115. There is no real discrepancy: the variance is trivial.

28C. The Metellus whom he names had repaired the Temple of Castor and Pollux. From the booty of his Dalmatian campaign 119–117, which ended in a triumph (*Fast. Tr.* Degrassi (1947), 82–3, 560; Cic. 2 *Verr.* 1.154; Ps.-Ascon. 254St.). For more on this temple and its importance, above, p. 203.

Laudatory testimonials for Scaurus were given by nine men of consular rank. Support of this kind for the defence in criminal trials, generally in the form of appreciation of the subject's public services, but also on occasion of his private life and character, was normal, but in this case for it to come from so many ex-consuls, only one of whom (L. Volcacius) was a political lightweight, should probably be reckoned highly unusual. The nine consulars were: L. Calpurnius Piso Caesoninus cos. 58; L. Volcacius (Volcatius)

Tullus cos. 66; Q. Caecilius Metellus Nepos cos. 57; M. Perpenna cos. 92, censor 86; L. Marcius Philippus cos. 56; M. Tullius Cicero cos. 63; Q. Hortensius Hortalus cos. 69; P. Servilius Vatia Isauricus cos. 79; Cn. Pompeius Magnus cos. 70; see further, Index of Personal Names.

Of these, the large part entered their testimonials by letter, since they were absent, among them also Pompeius, for since he was proconsul he was waiting outside the city. Pompey of course by 54 had taken up his Spanish command, and could legally re-enter the *pomerium* only upon surrendering it. Whether Asconius should be read as indicating the absence of most of the others from Rome or simply from the trial, is quite unclear. Not many, if any, apart from Pompey, can have been 'away' on public service (*rei publicae causa*), as the detailed analysis of Marshall (1985*b*), 150–2 demonstrates.

In addition one young man gave a testimonial, his half-brother Faustus Cornelius, son of Sulla. Half-brother by the same mother, the elder Scaurus' widow Metella, whose second marriage was to L. Sulla Felix, *c.*89/8. As quaestor in 54 Faustus Sulla would have been at least thirty-one years old, but of course still technically 'a young man' (*adulescens*)—that is, of military age, under forty-six.

At the knees of the jury, when the votes were being cast, those who were pleading for him divided into two groups... For a fairly full prosopographic review of these persons, see Marshall (1985*b*), 150–5. The presence among them of relatives and family connections—M'. Acilius Glabrio, Sulla Faustus, and even both C. Memmius and Milo, despite their marital entanglements, is unsurprising, whatever other motivation each of these may have had (see below). Little or nothing more is known of P. Lentulus (if a real person at all, and not a MS or Asconius' error for L.), whose father seems to have been a comparatively minor figure of no strong political allegiance; L. Aemilius Buca, C. Peducaeus, and M. (Popillius) Laenas Curtianus, all thoroughly insignificant. More intriguing is the inclusion of L. Paulus, who is apparently L. Aemilius Lepidus Paulus, cos. 51, whom one would hardly expect to find among a support group for Scaurus which features—at this stage in 54, at least—so many adherents of Cn. Pompeius Magnus: Paulus' father was the rebel consul of 78 whom Pompeius had joined in suppressing. Paulus, however, was standing for the praetorship in 54 and possibly, like C. Memmius, the father of the above supplicant for Scaurus, and Scaurus himself as candidates for the consulship enjoying (thus far) or hoping for Pompey's electoral support. Or perhaps he was simply at odds with the incumbent consul Ap. Claudius, who was apparently the chief architect of the prosecution. On this we may only speculate.

This is in any case by no means the only or the least anomaly among Scaurus' supporters. P. Clodius, evidently at odds with his elder brother Appius (Cic. *Mil.* 75), was one of his six advocates, and so on the same side as his irreconcilable enemies Cicero and Milo. On this apparent anomaly, see also above, p. 221, on Ascon. 20C. It is most plausibly to be explained by Clodius' *rapprochement* with Pompey after the meeting at Luca in 56, and which in turn explains the participation of Clodius' henchman C. Cato. Again, the appearance of Q. Hortensius (cos. 69) for the defence perhaps appears a little odd, in view of his links with the Servilii Caepiones and those of Servilia with the prosecution—as well as his general lack of sympathy with Pompeius, clearly the pivotal figure behind the defence at this juncture in 54, though as Asconius notes (19–20C) his enthusiasm for Scaurus seems to have waned. Among Scaurus' *laudatores*, L. Piso may have cared little that his grandfather long ago had been defended *de repetundis* by the elder Scaurus, but in 54 he was presumably still Pompey's man, as he had been in 59/8. L. Volcacius, of all these consulars by far the least important, had tried to do Pompey a favour in 56 (Cic. *Fam.* 1.1.3; 2.1–2; 4.1). Cicero in 54, after Luca and its sequel, could almost certainly not have evaded, even had he wished, his part as *laudator* and advocate, whatever his true attitude to Pompeius Magnus. The other ex-consuls involved, however—Q. Metellus Nepos, who had a Pompeian past but had been estranged since 59; the aged M. Perperna, whose son had lost his life as an opponent of Pompey in the Sertorian War; L. Marcius Philippus; P. Servilius Vatia Isauricus—do not show any consistent political allegiance to Pompey, or indeed to anyone else. Nor is it possible to assert with confidence that they were motivated by enmity (or even temporary disagreement) with Pompey's opponents, such as Ap. Claudius. They are perhaps best seen as unattached, laying claim to the independence of judgment to which as consulars and (as such) *principes civitatis* (leading men in the state) and *auctores publici consilii* (initiators of public policy) they might feel entitled.

As Marshall (1985*b*), 150–6, sensibly concludes (despite some of his remarks on individuals), attempts to produce from analysis of the twenty-three known supporters of Scaurus in this case any very sophisticated or precisely focused, stable pattern of alignments in Roman politics even for the whole of 54 BC, let alone for any longer period, are almost certainly misguided, and derive from failure to appreciate the extreme complexity and fluidity of political and family relationships in the late Republic. It is also not inconceivable that Scaurus' supporters in this affair, ill-assorted bunch that they were on other matters, united in the face of a threat to the career of a patrician *nobilis*, which they regarded as a serious matter, but the apparent conundrum is notorious. For further sensible discussion, Gruen (1974), 333–6.

Votes were cast ... condemnation. The figures presumably derive from the *Acta*, recorded for each separate Order represented on the jury under the Lex Fufia (Caleni) of 59—see Dio 38.8.1. A total of seventy voted, which probably implies five abstentions, invalid votes, or rejection of jurors.

29C. Cato the praetor, when [Cicero?] wanted the jury to consider its verdict on the accusers ... That it was Cicero who raised the issue is little better than a guess by A. C. Clark in his OCT to remedy an error in the MSS. If nothing at all is supplied, the logic of the sentence is all but destroyed, and with it the view of Greenidge (1901), 468–9, who thought that here the initiative remained with Cato as president of the court. That does not seem to apply in the case of C. Sempronius and M. Tuccius in 51 (Caelius ap. Cic. *Fam.* 8.8.1–3), where apparently an acquitted defendant brings the accusation. It seems highly unlikely that the initiative ever lay with the presiding magistrate (Cavarzere (1982)). For more on *calumnia* and the converse but probably similarly managed charge of *praevaricatio* (see Ascon. 9C, 66C, 87C and commentary ad locc.), Zumpt (1865–9), 374–6; Greenidge (1901), 459, 468–70, 575; Jones (1972), 62–4, 73, 118 (n. 213); Ferhle (1983), 184.

Cato the praetor ran the trial, because it took place in summer, without a tunic, wearing only a loincloth under his toga. There is a good chance that this information derives ultimately from an account of the younger M. Cato by his friend Munatius Rufus, still available in Asconius' day and apparently the main source of another *Life of Cato* by P. Thrasea Paetus, opponent of the Neronian regime and executed under Nero in AD 66. Thence the data in Plutarch, *Cat. Min.* 6.3, 44.1, 50.1. Earlier there is the version of Valerius Maximus 3.6.7, cf. 4.3.2, which is certainly from Munatius (fr.1 Peter).

The Commentary on Cicero's speech *On Behalf of Milo*

On Cicero's speech itself there is an old but still handy basic edition with commentary by A. B. Poynton (1902), more accessible to those who have Latin than for those without. There is an even older but excellent account of Asconius' commentary by A. C. Clark in his edition of Cicero's speech (1895); and useful articles by Lintott (1974); Ruebel (1979); Wiseman (1966). More data in Alexander (1990), 151–2 to fit into the narratives of *CAH* ix², 407–11; Gruen (1974), 337–44.

Asconius (42C) regarded this speech—which is the published version and was never delivered in court—as Cicero's finest. This may be the reason why the introduction to his commentary on it is much longer and more detailed than any other of those extant. It supplies invaluable insights into the political intricacies and the state of Rome in the first half of that fateful year 52, and throws as much light on the speech and its circumstances as the commentary itself. Asconius' addendum or epilogue on the sequel—the trials that ensued upon Milo's condemnation and exile—is also an important supplement to the other sources for the year's developments.

30C. He delivered this speech on 8 April in the third consulship of Cn. Pompeius. The year (52) is quite clear, with Pompey sole consul until the appointment of a colleague, his father-in-law Q. Metellus Scipio, in July or August. For the day (the last of the trial), the MSS give 8 April, sometimes emended to the 7th, since although it is clear that the trial began on the 4th, Asconius accounts for only four days, not the five required by Pompeius' legislation for it. The MSS at 40–41C, where the date also appears, are corrupt and variously emended. Rather than emend the text here Marshall (1985*b*), 159–60 suggests that Asconius is simply inconsistent; see also Ruebel (1979), 239–49.

While the trial was in progress an armed force had been stationed by Pompeius in the Forum and in all the temples sited round it, as is clear not only from the speech and from annals, but also from the work attributed to Cicero entitled *On the Best Kind of Orators*. The 'annals' cannot be identified with any certainty, but Livy (whence probably Dio 40.53.2–3; cf. Liv. *Per.* 107) is likely enough. The references to Cicero are *Mil.* 1–3; *Opt. Gen. Orat.* 10. For the Forum, *LTUR* 2. 325–36 (F. Coarelli). On the Forum and its environs as the scene of trials and turmoil on this and similar occasions, see Millar (1998), 42–3, 136–7, 181–4.

T. Annius Milo, P. Plautius Hypsaeus, and Q. Metellus Scipio sought the consulship. That is, for 52. Pompey earlier, in 57, had encouraged Milo to hope for an eventual consulship, but by late 54 had abandoned this attitude in favour of neutrality or indifference, if not outright hostility—probably in consequence of his *rapprochement* with Clodius (Cic. *QF.* 3.8.6; App. *BC* 2.20). In 53 and early 52, having failed to influence the consular elections of 55 and 54, he was strongly backing the ever loyal Hypsaeus, formerly his quaestor (and doubtless proquaestor) in his eastern campaigns. His support for Q. Caecilius Metellus Pius Scipio Nasica (born a Scipio but adopted by Q. Metellus Pius, cos. 80) came later, after marrying his daughter—almost certainly somewhat later in 52, as part of his deal with the *optimates* which gave him the sole consulship (cf. p. 234 below, on Ascon. 31C; cf. Plut. *Pomp.* 55).

not only by openly lavished bribery but also surrounded by gangs of armed men. On levels of bribery, cf. Ascon. 31C, 33C, 35C. Note the context of recent trials and laws *de ambitu* and *de sodaliciis*. Electoral violence had been rife in recent years, notably 56, 54 (especially), and 53. For this background, *CAH* IX², 403–5; Gruen (1969*b*); more broadly and fully, Gruen (1974), 311–57; other evidence includes Cic. *Mil.* 25, 34, 41, 43; Ascon. 48C; Plut. *Caes.* 28; *Cat. Min.* 47; Livy, *Per.* 107; Dio 40.46.3, 48.2; Schol. Bob. 169, 172St. See further Alexander (1990), nos. 296–308 for collected evidence on known cases between Scaurus' acquittal *de repetundis* (54) and the main indictment of Milo (52).

Milo was a close friend of Cicero and had as tribune of the plebs made great exertions to bring him back from exile. Although Cicero acknowledged the debt in 57/6 (*Red. Sen.* 19, 30; *Rend. Pop.* 15, *Har. Resp.* 6–7, etc.), his active support for Milo may have developed somewhat later—quite possibly, it may be conjectured, from Cicero's prospects of helping Milo to the consulship of 52 and then using him to get his brother Quintus into that of 51, which would allow Cicero to claim (or reclaim) what he saw as his rightful place as a fully independent leading figure in Roman politics (one of the *principes civitatis, auctores publici consilii*—'leading statesmen', 'makers of public policy') and no longer at the service of Pompey and/or Caesar (after Crassus' death at Carrhae, 53). This might explain Cicero's enthusiasm for this somewhat unworthy protégé—in the outcome thwarted, of course. On Cicero's electoral support for Milo in 52, Cic. *Mil.* 34; more widely on their relationship, Lintott (1974); Wiseman (1966).

P. Clodius remained extremely hostile to Cicero even after his restoration, and for that reason was a very strong supporter of Hypsaeus and Scipio against Milo. Compare Cic. *Mil.* 25, 89. And in any case (1) Clodius wanted the support of Pompey, currently a supporter of Hypsaeus, as noted above, with whom he had been reconciled after a fashion, in his own candidature of

53 for the praetorship of 52; (2) as noted below by Asconius, his hopes of achieving much as praetor depended on Milo's failure to win the consulship for the same year (Cic. *Mil.* 25). Again, see Wiseman (1966), 108–15; Lintott (1974).

both were equally reckless, but Milo stood on the side of 'the better cause'. Or so Cicero, and after him Asconius (cf. 31; 53C), would have us believe. Certainly he opposed Clodius the *popularis*, and had friends among the *boni* ('Great and Good', 'Establishment'; *optimates*)—but then, so too did Clodius (Tatum (1999), *passim*).

31C. when January came there were not yet any consuls or praetors, and the date was being put back in the same way as before. That is, as in 55 and 54.

Milo wanted the elections over as soon as possible. Doubtless to limit expenditure and to get elected while his support was still enthusiastic and available.

and put … bribery and huge expenditure on dramatic spectacles and a gladiatorial show, on which Cicero indicates that he had spent three inheritances. That is, at *Mil.* 95, see below, p. 256 on Ascon. 53C; cf. *QF.* 3.8.6, 9.2–3; *Fam.* 2.6.3. This assertion may perhaps have been made because to give gladiatorial games within two years prior to standing for office was now illegal under Cicero's own law *de ambitu* of 63 'nisi ex testamento praestituta die'—'except under the terms of a will on a pre-ordained day' (Cic. *Vat.* 37; *Sest.* 133). On Milo's debts, Ascon. 54C; cf. Pliny, *NH* 36.104; Schol. Bob. 164, 169St., and for more on debt in political life, Frederiksen (1966).

Pompeius, Scipio's son-in-law, and T. Munatius, tribune of the plebs, had not allowed any initiative in the senate on the matter of convening the Patricians in order to appoint an *interrex*, although it was a constitutional requirement to appoint one. On the constitutional aspects of *interregnum*, Lintott (1999a), 31 (with n. 20), 67 (with n. 11), 164. Pompey was almost certainly not yet Metellus' son-in-law, nor perhaps even yet backing him for the consulship. In Plut. *Pomp.* 55, he marries Cornelia only after entering Rome on being appointed consul himself—which was *a. d. V Mart. mense intercalario* (Ascon. 36C): Asconius is anticipating. T. Munatius Plancus was a Clodian, rather than Pompeian, supporter (cf. Ascon 33C below), successfully prosecuted *de vi* by Cicero after his year of office (*MRR* 2. 235). The abuse of tribune's powers to thwart constitutional requirements was of course no novelty for these years.

After setting the political scene, Asconius proceeds with a narrative of the murder of Clodius. His is by far the fullest account of the episode (cf. Cic. *Mil.* 27 ff.; App. *BC* 2. 21.75–6; Dio 40.48.2; Schol. Bob. 111St.; Livy, *Per.* 107), and Cicero's speech itself is the only other significant source for it, differing somewhat in details and emphases.

On 18 January—for I think that the *Acta* and the speech, which agrees with the *Acta*, should be followed, rather than Fenestella, whose account has the 17th. Clearly Asconius has the correct date, from the *Acta*. Cf. Cic. *Mil.* 27, 98; *Att.* 5.13.1.

Milo set out for Lanuvium, his native town, where at the time he was dictator, in order to appoint a *flamen* the next day. Lanuvium was one of the many communities of Latium which in the settlement after the Great Latin War of 340–338 were absorbed into the Roman state with full Roman citizenship as *municipia* with their own governments of limited but effective powers for local administration. Several seem to have had, like Lanuvium, a single chief magistrate termed a *dictator*—e.g. Caere, Tusculum, Nomentum. Lanuvium had also produced another prominent client of Cicero's, L. Licinius Murena, cos. 62 (Cic. *Mur.* 90). The *flamen* to be appointed was most probably for the local deity of Juno Sospita (cf. Cic. *Nat. Deor.* 1.82; Livy 8.14.2; Coarelli (1987), 140–63; Marshall (1985*b*), 164). Asconius' notion that the appointment was to take place 'the next day' (19 Jan.) apparently conflicts with Cicero's explicit statement (*Mil.* 45–6) that it was to take place 'that self-same day' (18th)—unless, as Clark believed, he was being deliberately misleading (cf. *Mil.* 27–8).

At about the ninth hour Clodius ... Bovillae, near the site of a shrine to the Bona Dea. It seems that this time is likely to be correct, or anyhow nearer to the truth than Cic. *Mil.* 29, claiming that it was as late as the eleventh hour—improbable if Clodius' corpse was back in Rome (about twelve miles away) as early as the first hour of the night (32C); and if Milo was looking to appoint a *flamen* at Lanuvium, nearly eighteen miles from Rome, on 'the same day'. It was the ninth hour according to Milo's accusers (Quintil. 6.3.49). The proximity of a shrine to the Bona Dea was far too good a point for Cicero to miss (*Mil.* 86), and Asconius duly picks it up.

he had been addressing the local councillors of Aricia. Doubtless electioneering, to whip in the local tribal vote (Horatia) from that *municipium*. Before reaching Bovillae Clodius had called in at his own Alban villa and at Pompey's near by (Cic. *Mil.* 54).

Clodius was on horseback, and had an escort ... as was the custom in those days for those on a journey. Nothing significant can be read into Clodius' preference for a horse rather than a litter or carriage. The escort, as Asconius notes, was normal—and in the Italian countryside, still by no means free from brigandage, let alone similarly armed political rivals, every bit as necessary as was such an entourage on the violence-ridden streets of Rome. Compare that of M. Cato, en route for estates in Lucania, at Plut. *Cat. Min.* 20; see also Lintott (1999*b*), 28–9, 128; below on Ascon. 87C.

one Roman knight, C. Causinius Schola. From Interamna (Nahars) (Cic. *Mil.* 46), who tried to provide Clodius with an alibi—which Cicero demolished—for the Bona Dea affair of 62, on which see extended coverage in Tatum (1999), ch. 3, 62–86. For other municipal adherents of Clodius, Wiseman (1971*b*), 37 n. 5.

C. Clodius. This name was added to the text by Manutius in the sixteenth century to fill a lacuna. C. Clodius is mentioned by Cicero as present at Bovillae (*Mil.* 46), and may have been a freedman of P. Clodius (Gruen (1974), 339).

Milo was riding in a carriage with his wife Fausta ... M. Fufius. On Fausta, above, on 28C. Her presence tells against any premeditated ambush on Milo's part. 'Fufius' is the normally accepted emendation for MSS 'Fusius'.

32C. Their escort was a large train of slaves, also including gladiators. On Milo's use of gladiators (and beast-hunters), see Cic. *Vat.* 40; *Off.* 2.58. Their professional weapon-skills generally gave them the edge over Clodius' amateur gangsters. See also Lintott (1999*b*), 83–5.

Eudamus ... Clodius' slaves. Clodius had turned to direct his menacing eye upon this brawl, when Birria pierced his shoulder with a hunting-spear. From whatever source—the prosecution's speeches reported in the *Acta*, a historian (or more than one), or whatever—Asconius' account of the actual fight contains circumstantial detail and is in general more trustworthy than Cicero's, where it is missing or differently reported.

His slaves' commander was M. Saufeius. On whom see further 55C. Not himself a slave, as the name clearly shows, but possibly a Praenestine notable (*ILLRP* 167, 299, 652, 655, 654; Syme (1964*a*), 121). A C. Saufeius had been killed alongside Saturninus in 100; a Lex Saufeia *agraria* belongs to 91 (*MRR* 2. 21 on Degrassi (1937), 74) or perhaps a little earlier.

Clodius' wife Fulvia was bent on inflaming anger at the deed by displaying his wounds with effusive lamentations. This formidable woman was married to Clodius by 58, and possibly somewhat earlier, some time between 62 and 60. Like others of Clodius' set, she may have had a shadowy Catilinarian past, and she may have been closely related to the famous Sempronia of Sallust's *Bell. Cat.* 25. (See below, p. 246 on Ascon 40C.) Her father was a magnate of Tusculum, original home of the Fulvian *gens*. After Clodius' death she was married to the younger C. Scribonius Curio, and when he too perished in the early stages of Caesar's civil war, to M. Antonius. Thus Antonius may have been following the example she had set in displaying

Clodius' corpse to the mob when he did the same with the dead Caesar in 44. Interesting observations in Babcock (1965); Welch (1995).

several well-known figures were sighted. I have translated Clark's text, which with some justification radically emends the MSS *complures noti homines elisi sunt, inter quos C. Vibienus senator* ('several well-known men were ?crushed to death?, among them the senator C. Vibienus') to read *complures noti homines visi sunt*, with the reference to Vibienus, at Cic. *Mil.* 37 mentioned as killed in rioting in 58, deleted as an editor's erroneous gloss, rather than a gross blunder by Asconius himself.

Clodius' house, which had been purchased a few months earlier from Scaurus. Marshall conjectures that this would have been a consequence of Scaurus' heavy expenses, his conviction *de ambitu* and consequent exile. The sale realized HS 14,800,000 (Pliny, *NH* 36.103), from this passage of Asconius apparently in the second half of 53, but Scaurus was not convicted until 52, after Milo, unless Appian's dating (*BC* 2.24) is erroneous (Babcock (1965)). For the probable site, above, pp. 227–8, on Ascon. 27C, apparently adjacent to Clodius' own previous residence (*LTUR* 2. 85–6 (E. Papi); Coarelli (1985), 234, 239), which he seems to have used his new acquisition and other neighbouring property to extend, to make a veritable palace. Evidence on Clodius' dealings in property and building-projects includes Cic. *Har. Resp.* 53, 58; *Dom.* 51, 100, 103–4, 107–8, 110–12, 114–16, 122, 132; *Mil.* 74–5; App. *BC* 2.15.57–8; Plut. *Cic.* 33; Dio 38.17.6.

Ti. Munatius Plancus, brother of the orator Lucius Plancus, and Q. Pompeius Rufus, … tribunes of the plebs. Of the brothers Munatius, probably originally from Tibur, the tribune is otherwise known only for service with M. Antonius at Mutina in 43. His brother Lucius was far more distinguished, not only as an orator and writer, especially as a correspondent of Cicero's in 44/3, but also in politics, eventually consul in 42, founder of Lugdunum (Lyon) and censor under Augustus in 22; he is the addressee of Horace, *Odes* 1.7. Q. Pompeius Rufus, despite his pedigree, had an undistinguished career but a famous brother-in-law, C. Iulius Caesar—until Caesar divorced Pompeia in 62 in the wake of the Bona Dea affair as not above suspicion.

33C. partisans of Milo's electoral rivals. This leaves it unclear whether they were first and foremost enemies of Milo, Clodians, or (less likely at this stage) adherents of Pompeius Magnus or (also unlikely) simply friends of both Plautius Hypsaeus and Metellus Scipio with no other allegiance to motivate them.

Sex. Cloelius the *scriba*. This is the correct name (cf. Cic. *Dom.* 47, 83, 129; *Har. Resp.* 11; *Sest.* 133), to be substituted for the MSS *Clodius*. See Shackleton

Bailey (1960), confirmed in Shackleton Bailey (1973), 23–6 and (1986). Against, Flambard (1978). Further, Damon (1992); Badian (1989). See also above, p. 199; below, p. 259 on Ascon. 55C.

the senate house and cremated it ... in the conflagration the senate house itself caught fire and also the adjoining Basilica Porcia. For the buildings and their location, see *LTUR* 1. 187 (E. M. Steinby); 332–2 (F. Coarelli); Coarelli (1985), 22, 48, 50, 59–87 (esp. 59–67), 120, 131; and Marshall (1985*b*), 169, where also see more data on the damage done by the fire mentioned at Pliny, *NH* 34.21. On the role of the mob, Sumi (1977).

The houses also of M. Lepidus the *interrex* —for he had been elected a curule magistrate—and of Milo, who was not there, were attacked by the same Clodian mob. This Lepidus is the future triumvir, cos. 46, at this juncture probably having held the curule aedileship a year or two before, and so qualified to be appointed *interrex* (so e.g. Staveley (1954), 196–7; *contra* Sumner (1964), 43 n. 19, who argues for M'. Lepidus, cos. 66). On the date, Asconius' more detailed account at 43C (see note there) is to be preferred. Milo had two houses in Rome, on the Capitoline approaches and in the Cermalus quarter of the Palatine (*LTUR* 2. 32 (E. Papi)), both able to withstand attack (Cic. *Mil.* 64; *Att.* 4.3.3), but had not gone to either when he got back to Rome on the night of 19 January (Cic. *Mil.* 61; Ascon. 33C). For Lepidus' house (also below, p. 249), *LTUR* 2. 25–6 (W. Eck); Coarelli (1985), 153, 203, 206, 209. For the house of his father, M. Aemilius Lepidus, cos. 78, pre-eminently resplendent in 78 but greatly eclipsed by others over the next generation, see Pliny, *NH* 36.10, but this house of the *interrex*, cos. 46, is perhaps some other, since he was the younger son.

Then the mob seized bundles of *fasces* from the grove of Libitina and took them to the homes of Scipio and Hypsaeus, then to the suburban estate of Cn. Pompeius, yelling its acclamation of him by turns as consul or dictator. For the locations, see Introduction, pp. xx–xxii, with *LTUR* 3. 189 (Libitina (F. Coarelli)); 2. 158 (houses of Q. Metellus Scipio and P. Plautius Hypsaeus (E. Papi)). Pompey's suburban estate (*LTUR* 3. 78 (V. Jolivet)) on the Pincian Hill lay outside the *pomerium* (city-boundary—*LTUR* 4. 96–105 (M. Andreussi)), as did his theatre (*LTUR* 5. 35–8 (P. Gros); Coarelli (1997), 539–80), in the portico of which the senate held its meetings to allow him to participate even while proconsul and as such debarred from entering the *pomerium* (cf. Ascon. 28, 34, 52C). Libitina was a deity of corpses or death, and her grove the 'headquarters' of the *collegium* or trade-guild of Rome's undertakers, where their equipment was stored. Further, Bodel (1994), n. 55. For the grand funerals of aristocrats, especially those of long lineage, a supply of *fasces*, whether the real thing, or dummy sets, would have been required for the funeral ritual described by Polybius 6.53, esp. 7–8, which seems to have survived from his day (mid-second century) to Cicero's. The mob was apparently quite uncertain—or divided—as to whether to offer *imperium* to the anti-Milonian candidates as consuls, or to Pompey as consul or as dictator, earlier thought by some to be his ambition (see below, on Ascon. 35C).

he had made gifts around the tribes of 1000 *asses* **per man.** That is, HS 400 a head, more than the HS 300 that Caesar left in his will—a huge sum greatly increasing Milo's debts.

Some days later M. Caelius, as tribune of the plebs, gave him the opportunity to address a *contio***, and [Cicero?] himself pleaded his case to the people.** As an old enemy of Clodius (Cic. *Cael. passim*; *QF.* 2.12.2; cf. Caes. *BC* 3.21–2), Caelius was a natural ally of Milo and Cicero. The insertion of Cicero as a participant in this *contio* depends on a suspect MS reading accepted by Clark but absent from Cicero's own reference to the *contio* at *Mil.* 91. It is probably best excised, leaving Caelius himself and Milo as the only speakers. On the nature and working of a *contio*, Lintott (1999a), 41–2, 44, 45, 153; Millar (1998), 13, 59–60, 95–6, 126, 164, 216–18.

Both claimed that an ambush had been set for Milo by Clodius. The cornerstone of Milo's case—that Milo had acted in self-defence, apparently an adequate answer to the charge *de vi* under the law.

34C. And so, for the first time, a decree of the senate was passed that the *interrex***, the tribunes of the plebs, and Cn. Pompeius, who as proconsul was close by the city, should 'see to it that the state take no harm'.** Asconius' *primo* seems to mean not 'in the first instance', 'as a first measure', but rather 'for the first time', since in the traditional formula of this emergency *senatus consultum* it was the *consuls* who were enjoined 'to see that the state take no harm'. Since there were no consuls, only existing officers of state were available to receive and implement such advice—that is, the *interrex* and tribunes, and the proconsul Pompey, who was of course the only person near enough to Rome capable of taking effective action. Dio 40.49.5 dates this decree to 19 January, which must be too early (cf. Ascon. 33, 51C).

two young men both named Ap. Claudius applied to him for the production of the slaves of Milo and of his wife Fausta. C. Claudius' absence from Milo's trial(s) is explained by his exile following conviction, most probably for extortion from Asia, whence he returned from his post-praetorian command in 53 (Caelius ap. Cic. *Fam.* 8.8.2; *MRR* 2. 218, 229). Both these two sons bore the official *praenomen* Appius, an apparent anomaly. Their father was one of three brothers: Ap. Claudius Pulcher (cos. 54), C. Claudius

Pulcher (pr. 56), P. Clodius Pulcher (tr. pl. 58). C. Claudius had two sons. The younger was adopted by his uncle Appius and became Ap. Claudius Ap. f. The elder is Ap. Claudius C. f., cos. 38; the younger, far less reputable, turns up in the early years of Augustus' principate (*IGRR* 4. 332). For complete exposition see Wiseman (1970*a*). Their initiative here was apparently the start of a civil suit for damage inflicted by slaves on property (i.e. slaves) belonging to another person or persons. Although anyone bringing such a suit might properly apply to any holder of *imperium* for justice, the application in such a case and at such a time and place to Pompey as proconsul looks highly unorthodox. It should be remembered, however, that in the continued absence of the normal urban magistrates, only the current *interrex* (whoever he was) was available as an alternative, and the applicants may for some reason have preferred to avoid his jurisdiction in this matter.

L. Herennius Balbus demanded the production of Clodius' slaves also, and those of his companions; and at the same time Caelius demanded that of the households of Hypsaeus and Q. Pompeius. I have translated Clark's text, unconvinced by Marshall's argument (1985*b*), 173, for re-punctuation.

As advocates for Milo there presented themselves Q. Hortensius, M. Cicero, M. Marcellus, M. Calidius, M. Cato, and Faustus Sulla. As for Scaurus in 54, six persons, the first four also advocates for Scaurus, and Sulla, like his brother-in-law Milo, among his supporters. This is a very potent team indeed to appear in what would have been seen ordinarily as a relatively trivial civil action, which was in reality, in this case at least, nothing of the kind. In Milo's subsequent actual trial *de vi lege Pompeia*, apparently only Marcellus, Cicero, and Milo himself spoke for the defence: Cato was a juror (40–41C, 53C).

those whose surrender was being demanded as slaves were in fact of free status, for after the recent murder Milo had manumitted them on the grounds that they had avenged an attempt on his life. Hortensius seems to have argued successfully that slaves so manumitted could not be surrendered on demand for interrogation: at all events, this issue disappears in the sequel. Hortensius continued to support Milo, seeking his trial under existing laws, not Pompey's special legislation (Ascon. 44C).

All this was going on in the intercalary month. See below, on 36C.

Q. Metellus ... P. Clodius. This complaint came apparently several days before the start of the intercalary month, so that Asconius has somehow got events out of sequence. The name Q. Caepio is Clark's emendation, very plausible, of the MSS reading *M. Cepionem*, and as it happens, the adoptive and so official appellation, which would be entered in the senate's minutes (*acta senatus*), of M. Iunius Brutus, later Caesaricide: the identification here is possible but conjectural. The alternative reading, *M. Catonem* (see Marshall (1985*b*), 174–5) is less attractive. Metellus Scipio was evidently arguing among other things that Milo had sought to ambush Clodius, not vice versa. In view of its patently emotive and sensationalist content, it is not easy to credit his claim that Milo's armed escort, as against Clodius' entourage of only twenty-six, had numbered over three hundred, and of these he had manumitted only twelve. Milo's distribution of 1000 *asses* per head to the tribes, here allegedly to counter hostile rumours concerning the murder, is presented earlier by Ascon. 33C as simple electoral bribery.

35C. Milo sent word to Cn. Pompeius … Milo, of course, was trying to compromise Pompey and his protégé Hypsaeus, a move which Pompey coolly deflected with his answer of complete (and typically hypocritical) constitutional propriety, for only the magistrate presiding over an election had legal right to debar a candidature, and even then could be expected to give a legally convincing reason for doing so. Pompey was in very real anxiety, however, to avoid arousing political reaction against himself for abuse of *de facto* power. C. Lucilius Hirrus, tr. pl. 53, was a cousin of Pompey's who had already tried to float the idea of his being made dictator (*MRR* 2. 228). The acquaintance with Cicero, who had no very high opinion of him, hardly amounted to firm friendship (Cic. *QF.* 3.6.4; cf. *Att.* 7.1.8; *Fam.* 8.11.2), but apparently sufficed to assist his representation of Pompey's interests with Milo: Pompey refused to receive Milo (Ascon. 51C; Cic. *Mil.* 65, with a role in the incident also for Cicero himself).

ever more frequent suggestions that Cn. Pompeius ought to be made dictator. Pompey was thought to be deliberately manipulating the situation in order to be made dictator—see Cic. *Att.* 4.18.3; Plut. *Pomp.* 44; App. *BC* 2.20; Dio 40.45.5–46.1, 49.5–50.3. It is commonly held that the sole consulship, unlike the dictatorship, left him still liable to tribunician veto, but Livy records attempts (at least) to exercise it also against dictators' initiatives, at any rate within the *pomerium* (Lintott (1999*a*), 111 and n. 80). For the *optimates* even that was a last resort 'in the interests of the state' (*rei publicae causa*), not to do Pompey a favour (Plut. *Cat. Min.* 47–8; cf. *Pomp.* 54; Dio 40.50.3–4). For fuller discussion of the appointment, Gruen (1974), 153–5.

36C. a decree of the senate was passed on the motion of M. Bibulus. Bibulus, Caesar's rival as aedile 65 and enemy as cos. 59, was M. Cato's son-in-law. Among the intricacies of the Roman calendar, on the intercalary month the best guidance for the inquisitive is Michels (1967), 145–72, esp. 160–2. In brief, the better to realign the current calendar with the solar year, the Roman state found it necessary from time to time to shorten February to 23 or 24 days and add (intercalate) an intercalary month of 27 days. Pompey's appointment as sole consul was therefore on the 24th of the intercalary month (Ruebel (1979), 239–40).

Next, after an interval of three days, he consulted (the senate) on the passage of new laws. Asconius' Latin leaves it unclear whether this was on the fourth day after, or the third—that is, on the last day of the intercalary month of 52, or the day before. Moderns differ. For the last, or 27th, day of the extra month, Marshall (1985*b*), 177; Greenidge (1901), 391; for the day before (26th), Linderski (1972), 196–7; Lintott (1974), 72; Ruebel (1979), 240. The consultation was followed by the events of Ascon. 44C, which on the latter view took place on the 27th.

one concerning violence, which explicitly took into account the murder. Evidently for Pompey the existing Sullan Law on homicide (*de sicariis et veneficis*) and the Plautian Law on violence (*de vi*)—perhaps most particularly in the matters of procedures and penalties, but possibly also regarding definitions—did not suffice. See further Cloud in *CAH* IX², 520–4. If it was drafted specifically to deal with the disruptions of 52, presumably its currency ended once accusations and trials in respect of them were complete, and it had no prolonged validity beyond that point.

the other concerning bribery. Probably, unlike the Lex *de vi*, not to set up a special court for alleged electoral corruption in 53/2, but a general extension of existing law against electoral misdoing. See further Cloud in *CAH* IX², 516–17. Pompey's law operated against M. Messalla in 51, in a case quite divorced from the elections of 53 for 52, and the older Lex Licinia *de sodaliciis* was clearly still in force against Milo in 52 after the legislation of Pompey (Cic. *Fam.* 8.2.1; 4.1; 7.2.3, with Shackleton Bailey's commentary on all; Val. Max. 5.9.2; Ascon. 38–9C, 54C). Besides, Pompey's law was retroactive to cover cases earlier than 53/2 (App. *BC* 2.23; Plut. *Cat. Min.* 48) and still valid in Trajan's day (Plin. *Paneg.* 29.1; Tac. *Dial.* 38).

both with a heavier penalty. For the law *de vi*, Marshall (1985*b*), 179 suggests the addition of confiscation to exile, citing Cic. *Sull.* 89; *Sest.* 146; cf. Ascon. 54C for sale of Milo's goods, which, however, his debts would in any case have demanded: extension of interdiction to lifetime duration (Cloud, *CAH* IX², 516) is an alternative possibility. Similar doubts attach to Pompey's new penalties for *ambitus*, against which those existing were already severe (Ascon. 69C for the Lex Calpurnia of 67; Dio 37.29.1 for Cicero's Lex Tullia of 63, adding a ten-year exile to exclusion from public life and heavy fines).

and a curtailed form of trial. Additional data in Ascon. 38–39C, but his account is still incomplete: more in Dio 40.1 (limited number of advocates); Plut. *Pomp.* 55; *Cat. Min.* 48; Dio 40.2 (no written testimony from absentee advocates or witnesses); App. *BC* 2.24; Dio 40.3–4 (rewards and inducements for successful prosecution and 'turning state's evidence'); Cic. *Att.* 13.49.1 (predetermined dates for each trial). Some of the new procedure, if not all, was apparently meant to apply to all trials in any court (Marshall (1985*b*), 179–80).

Pompeius was afraid of Milo, or pretended to be: for the most part he stayed not in his town house but on his suburban estate. Compare items at Ascon. 33C, 46C, 50–52C; Dio 40.50.2. As proconsul Pompey could not attend meetings of the senate (or any other body) within the *pomerium*: once appointed consul he could and did (e.g. Cic. *Mil.* 66; cf. Plut. *Pomp.* 55). For the location of Pompey's town house, *LTUR* 2. 159–60 (V. Jolivet)—on the Fagutal in the area of the Carinae, near the Temple of Tellus (Plut. *Pomp.* 40; Suet. *Gram.* 15; Cic. *Har. Resp.* 49).

all the other charges that were being alleged against Milo were no different from that one. Namely, baseless. At the time in question it was not of itself illegal to carry a weapon, but only to do so 'with intent' to do various kinds of mischief. See Cic. *Mil.* 11; cf. Pliny, *NH* 34. 139; *Cael.* 1; Marshall (1985*b*), 181; Aigner (1976); Nippel (1995), 16–17. For an alleged incident (an armed slave of Clodius), Cic. *Dom.* 129; *Sest.* 69; *Har. Resp.* 49; *Pis.* 28; *Mil.* 18; cf. Plut. *Pomp.* 49.

37C. Then T. Munatius Plancus, tribune of the plebs, presented to a public meeting one M. Aemilius Philemon, a well-known personage, freedman of M. Lepidus. If he was a freedman of M. Lepidus, *interrex* of 52 (so Marshall (1985*b*), 181), since the house of the *interrex* had been attacked by a Clodian mob, for him to lay information against Milo as set out in the sequel by Asconius would be odd, though not inconceivable. On Philemon's status (and villa), cf. Cic. *Fam.* 7.18.3. Asconius here gives a clear instance of a private individual being enabled to address a *contio* duly convened by an officer of state (Lintott (1999*a*), 41–2, 44, 45; Pina Polo (1968), esp. 34.

a Galatian slave of Milo's in the act of committing murders. Probably another anti-Milonian item of false propaganda, though few at that time, of which it was typical, would have been deceived. Marshall (1985*b*), 182 takes 'Galata' as a personal name, not *per se* an ethnic, perhaps rightly since it is attested as a slave-name during the Principate (Solin (2003), 1. 654).

Although Cicero made no mention of these charges, all the same, since such were my findings, I thought I ought to set them out. Marshall's view

(1985*b*), 182–3 that Asconius' source here was the *Acta* is unconvincing: a historian of some kind, or even a speech, seems far more probable.

Q. Pompeius, C. Sallustius, and T. Munatius Plancus, tribunes of the plebs, were among the first to hold *contiones* that were extremely hostile towards Milo. Sallustius is the famous historian. For his involvement in this affair and acquaintance with other possible, probable, and certain connections of Clodius, and some possible inferences from them, Lewis (1988).

38C. the danger that he would be prosecuted before the people. Marshall (1985*b*), 183 is at a loss to see any possible charge, overlooking Ascon. 49C on Cic. *Mil.* 47 referring to a suggestion by one of his opponents that in the murder of Clodius Milo had been merely Cicero's agent. Whether such a charge would of necessity be brought before a popular assembly rather than the standing *quaestio de vi* is unclear to me. Possibly a tribune might prefer such a procedure, if available, as more likely to result in conviction. On trials of this kind, very rare after Sulla, see *CAH* ix², 501–3 (Cloud).

deter him from undertaking Milo's defence. Cicero's pertinacity may quite plausibly be explained by the realization that success might result in a consulship for Milo, and excellent chances of further political triumph for himself, not least liberation from thraldom to Pompey and Caesar, as well as major defeat for his more obvious enemies. Not to mention matters of honour, *fides*, and *dignitas*.

Next, a law of Pompeius was put through. The passage of Pompey's law was supported by the tribunes Q. Pompeius Rufus and C. Sallustius (Ascon. 49C). The exact date is disputed—16 or 23 March (A. C. Clark (1895), 103); 18 March (Lintott (1974), 73); perhaps earlier, possibly even 1 March (Linderski (1972), 197 n.). The appointment of Ahenobarbus, cos. 54, brother-in-law of M. Cato and hitherto an opponent of Pompey in 67, 58, 55, and 54, but now evidently Pompey's nominee (Cic. *Mil.* 22) signals the newly found readiness of Pompey and the *optimates* to collaborate. The simplest explanation for the appointment of special *quaesitores* ('investigators' or court presidents) is that so far in 52 no praetors, who might normally have done the job, had yet been elected. Pompey, however, specified a consular, presumably to ensure enhanced authority, to preside over the trial of Milo *de vi*. For his law *de ambitu* he seems to have been content with a praetorian, A. Manlius Torquatus (below, 39C), while the subsequent trials of Milo *de sodaliciis* and again *de vi*, were conducted by M. Favonius (aedile 53 or 52—see *MRR* 3. 90–1; Linderski (1972)) and L. Fabius (probably also an aedile or ex-aedile) (Ascon. 54C). In this period such employment for ex-aediles was nothing unusual.

Pompeius put forward a panel of jurors to be judges in this affair. Cf. Dio 40.52.1; Cic. *Mil.* 21—in total 360 (Cic. *Att.* 8.16.2; Vell. 2.76; Plut. *Pomp.* 55), presumably under the provisions of Pompey's own law *de vi*, and probably also of that *de ambitu*. This panel would supply the jury of fifty-one for any one trial by a process of reduction (39C).

and another charge was laid *de ambitu* by the said Appii, and besides them by C. Ateius and L. Cornificius; and there was another *de sodaliciis* laid by P. Fulvius Neratus. On the multiplicity of charges and accusers, Marshall (1985*b*), 185; also below, 53–54C. The name C. Ateius results from Clark's emendation of MSS *c. ceteio.* C. Ateius Capito was tr. pl. 55, then opposed to the consuls Pompey and Crassus, especially the latter; also a close friend of Cicero. Both circumstances make his appearance against Milo anomalous, but the identification is by no means impossible. The law *de sodaliciis* was that of Crassus, passed by him as cos. 55 (*MRR* 2. 215; Gruen (1974), 230–3, 316–18, 320, 342–3, 349; *CAH* ix^2, 517).

39C. A *divinatio* for the trial *de ambitu* took place. For this process, see Glossary. The best-known case is Cicero's successful plea of 70 to conduct the prosecution of C. Verres.

Domitius on advice of the jurors gave a decision that the accuser should cite as many from the list of the said slaves as he might wish. Here I have preferred the MSS reading *eorum* ('the said slaves') to the humanist emendation *suorum* ('slaves of his own'), which to my mind makes no sense in the context: nothing could emerge from interrogating the accuser's slaves! The point is surely that the accuser was permitted to insist on the production of the persons concerned, even if they no longer belonged to Milo, provided that they were still of slave-status. That should have enabled their examination under torture (Greenidge (1901), 47–80, 491–2; Brunt (1980), 256–65). How useful this may have been to the prosecution is beyond telling, but it would have met the (contemporary) requirements of equity and propriety. True, the reading *eorum* is somewhat feeble if this is the meaning, but there is no great difficulty in reading *illorum* or even *istorum* instead, which would remove that objection. Milo, of course, insisted that he had given these slaves of his their freedom.

the jurors should be appointed by sortition to the number eighty-one ... Asconius' account here seems incomplete. On the face of it, as is hardly plausible, all 360 members of the jury panel are to hear the evidence and approve a digest of it before lots are drawn to reduce their number to twenty-seven from each of the three orders—that is, to a total of eighty-one—on the last day of the trial. On the other hand there is an obscure hint at 41C that some selection from the 360 was to take place earlier—a mention of 'jurymen named on the first day'. As Gruen (1974), 238 n. 116, observes, the procedure overall meant that the final panel remained unknown until the day of the verdict, and reduced scope for bribery or intimidation. The three orders are the three categories of persons, senators, *equites* (knights), and *tribuni aerarii* from which juries were made up in equal proportions, following the passing of the Lex Aurelia of 70 (see *CAH* ix^2, 225–6, 509).

40C. Cn. Pompeius was in session at the *aerarium*, and was disturbed by that same uproar; and so he promised Domitius that on the next day he would come down with an armed guard, and did so. As consul Pompey could now operate within the *pomerium*. The introduction of troops into the city for purposes other than holding a triumph (or unavoidably in civil war, as e.g. in 88) was, however, an extremely dangerous precedent: Lintott (1999*b*), 200–1. For the site of the *aerarium* (Temple of Saturn), *LTUR* 1. 234–6 (F. Coarelli); Coarelli (1985), 174, 193.

The Virgins of Alba. Just possibly the Vestals, but rather more plausibly seen as priestesses of a cult originating in Alba and surviving at Bovillae— perhaps of the Bona Dea (Cic. *Mil.* 85–6; *ILS* 6188–9, 2988; Tac. *Ann.* 2.41).

The last to give evidence were Sempronia, daughter of Tuditanus and mother-in-law of P. Clodius, and his wife Fulvia. True to form—cf. 32C above. These were presumably the last witnesses for the prosecution: Asconius seems to ignore testimony for the defence, such as that of M. Favonius (Cic. *Mil.* 44; cf. 26—and confusion at 54C?). Syme (1964*b*), 134–5; (1986), 26 (citing also Cadoux (1980), 93–5) very plausibly conjectured that Fulvia's mother may have been sister to the famous Sempronia of Sallust's *Bell. Cat.* 25.

41C. M. Antonius. Clearly the future Triumvir, in the early 50s a friend of Clodius, more recently apparently estranged from him, if we believe Cic. *Mil.* 40–1, and perhaps here an accuser of Milo more from a desire to please Fulvia (his future wife) than from regard for the deceased Clodius—several of whose partisans, however, he appears later to have 'inherited'.

Clodius' murder was in the public interest—the line which M. Brutus took in the speech which he composed for Milo and published as if he had pleaded the case. On this relatively youthful rhetorical exercise, Quintil. 3.6.93, 10.1.20; Schol. Bob. 112 St. Brutus apparently had a penchant for pamphleteering with literary fictions of this kind—cf. his 'funeral speech' for his uncle M. Cato after the latter's suicide at Utica in 46, written when dissatisfied, it seems, with the one that he had commissioned from Cicero (Cic. *Att.* 12.21.1; *Orat.* 34); compare a similar piece on Ap. Claudius Pulcher of 48 BC quoted by Diomed. *GL* 1, p. 367. 26. For Brutus' literary skills, e.g. Cic. *Brut.* 331–2.

Cicero decided against this, on the grounds that (this implied that) any person whose condemnation could benefit the state could also be killed without being convicted. A dangerous line for Cicero himself to take, in view of his actions as consul in 63, so vigorously attacked by Clodius especially among others. On extra-legal votes of condemnation against alleged *hostes* (enemies of state), Lintott (1999*a*), 91–2.

entered the counter-plea that Clodius had set an ambush for Milo. Proven self-defence constituted an adequate rebuttal under the law of accusation for criminal homicide.

the battle was unpremeditated by either party. As Asconius perceives, plainly the truth of the matter.

both had often threatened the other with death. e.g. Cic. *Att.* 4.3.5; *Mil.* 25–6, 44, 52.

42C. And so Cicero spoke with less than his usual steadiness. An abject fiasco, according to Dio 40.54.2 (cf. 46.7.2–3); Quintil. 3.6.93; cf. Plut. *Cic.* 35, where, however, the troops of Pompey are the deterrent factor, not, as Asconius has it, the threatening Clodian mob, uncurbed by the said troops. Doubtless these are hostile exaggerations, though Cicero's later references to the episode (*Fam.* 3.10.10; *Att.* 9.7B.2; *Opt. Gen. Orat.* 10) hardly afford convincing apologia. He did, however, persist, despite Milo's conviction, in taking an effective part in the subsequent trials of the lesser dramatis personae.

What he actually said was taken down and also survives, but the speech that we are reading is what he composed in writing, and with such consummate skill that it may rightly be reckoned his finest. There is every reason to believe that the published versions of several of Cicero's other speeches—e.g. the Catilinarian orations—were not the same as those actually delivered. In this case, however, the differences may have been particularly striking. Milo is said to have remarked, on reading the published version, that had Cicero actually delivered it, he would never have enjoyed the fine mullet of Massilia, his place of exile (Dio 40.54.3–4). Cf. Settle (1963); Stone (1980); Marshall (1987); Berry (1993); Alexander (2002), 20–2.

For the *rostra* were at that time not sited where they now are, but by the *comitium*, all but conjoined with the senate house. For the changes by Asconius' day, *LTUR* 1. 309–13; 4. 212–14 (F. Coarelli); Coarelli (1985), 49, 56–7. For their vital importance, e.g. Millar (1998), 41, facing a somewhat conjectural map of the Forum area and markedly different from that offered in Patterson (1992), 191. Much remains open to dispute.

43C. Two and a half days after Clodius was killed, M. Lepidus was named as the first *interrex.* See above, on 33C, where Asconius' compression has given a false impression of the date, with the apparent implication that Lepidus was already *interrex* when the attack on his house occurred on 19 January. In fact, Asconius' chronology appears to agree with that of Dio 40. 48–9. According to Asconius 31–33C, on 18 January Clodius was killed and on 19 came the riot and Clodius' cremation in the senate house. This was, according to Dio, followed by a meeting of the senate where it was agreed to choose an *interrex.* According to Asconius 33C, Milo returned to Rome that night. The *interrex* was presumably chosen on 20 January. See Lintott (1974), 70 n. 94.

Now it was not customary for elections to be held by the man who was first produced as *interrex.* But the factions of Scipio and Hypsaeus, because hostility towards Milo was still fresh, demanded contrary to law that the *interrex* should come down to the *comitia* with a view to appointing consuls. Asconius' wording leaves it unclear whether for the first *interrex* of a series to hold elections contravened custom but not law, or both. Before the murder Milo had wanted an early election and his opponents delay (31C).

pulled down his ancestral portraits. The ancestral *imagines*, properly speaking and in the narrow sense, were lifelike wax masks from past generations of persons who had attained curule office (at least the aedileship), made during their lifetimes, and kept after their decease by their families in the *atria* (entrance-halls) of their houses, normally protected in closed *armaria* (cupboards). These were opened for display on special occasions, but even when the cupboards were closed, the collection was explicable to visitors with the aid of *tituli* (labels), which could be arranged in a *stemma* (family tree) on the wall or a board, with painted-in lines of descent, and perhaps with summaries of achievements (*res gestae*). Outside the home, the masks were paraded in public at family funerals, when they would be worn by actors impersonating the said ancestors and (probably) the recently deceased: the classic descriptions are Polybius 6.53–4; Pliny, *NH* 35.4–14. In a broader sense, the term *imagines* could include portrait busts, paintings, and other representations which might be displayed not only (in supplement) by aristocrats, but by householders of any class, but that is hardly what is meant here. For detailed and lucid exposition of the whole topic, see Flower (1996), esp. 5–6, 32–59, 185–222 (the *atrium*); also ch. 3 (uses for elections);

chs. 4–5 (funerals and funeral speeches); ch. 6 (comparison with *elogia* (public inscriptions) and *tituli*). For Lepidus' house, above, p. 238, on Ascon. 33C.

symbolic marital couch of his wife Cornelia, a woman whose chastity was considered an example to all. Asconius' accuracy over the identity of Lepidus' wife in 52 is not impaired by his marriage by February 50 to a Iunia (Cic. *Att.* 6.1.25), which is readily explained by death or divorce. The symbolic marriage-bed (*lectus* (or *lectulus*—diminutive) *adversus*) was another standard item for display in the traditional *atrium* for any household with claims to rank (Flower (1996), 201).

the weaving-operations which in accord with ancient custom were in progress in the entrance-hall. Probably still by no means especially unusual among aristocrats with pretensions to traditionalism. Compare the domestic activities of the empress Livia in Suet. *Div. Aug.* 73; cf. 64.2; others in *ILS* 8393; 8402; 8403. For ancient practice, Livy 1.57.9; see further Wallace-Hadrill (1996), 109.

what it is to 'divide up a proposal'. Asconius alone is reasonably clear, but for more, see (e.g.) Cic. *Fam.* 1.2.1; Sen. *Ep.* 21.9; *Vit. Beat.* 3.2; Plin. *Ep.* 8.14.6, 19, with Sherwin-White (1966), 462, 465; Lintott (1999a), 84. Compare Asconius' equally illuminating note on the operation of *discessio* in the procedures of the Comitia Tributa at 72C; Millar (1998), 81–2.

44C. on the day preceding 1 March, a senatorial decree was passed that the murder of P. Clodius, the firing of the senate house, and the siege of the home of M. Lepidus had been acts contrary to the public interest. Nothing else was entered that day in the *Acta*. The date is the last day of the intercalary month. From the sequel it is clear that the *Acta* recorded only what was decided, not the whole content of debates. Senatorial condemnation of acts as 'contrary to the public interest' was evidently used to facilitate prosecution and conviction *de vi*. Pompey's law *de vi* specifically included acts so condemned, according to Ascon. 36C.

When Hortensius had spoken in favour of a special inquiry before a quaesitor. On the most attractive interpretation (essentially that of Gruen (1974), 234–5), it appears that in the debate on Pompey's proposed laws, the senate had voted readily enough that the various recent acts of violence were contrary to the public interest (Cic. *Mil.* 12–13, 31; Ascon. 44C); Hortensius had then moved that any ensuing trials should be heard by a special court but under existing law—a move to give the appearance of reasonable appeasement of Milo's enemies and at the same time to improve the chances of acquittal and to thwart Pompey's initiative and keep his power within bounds. 'Division' of his motion had allowed the first part to be carried and the second to be vetoed by Plancus and Sallustius (below).

We found a Fufius to say 'Divide!' 'Fufius' is usually identified as Q. Fufius Calenus, tr. pl. 61; pr. 59; cos. 47 (see *MRR* 2. 180, 188–9, 286; 3.94), but see Marshall (1985*b*), 193–4 for uncertainty. On 'dividing' a proposal, see above on Ascon. 43C.

45C. I do not doubt that you remember that it was by agency of Q. Fufius. This is certainly Q. Fufius Calenus, as tr. pl. 61. See *MRR* 2. 180. It is not clear that Asconius is cross-referring to a previous commentary here, but if so it is more likely to have been on the lost *Against Clodius and Curio* (cf. Schol. Bob. 85–6 St.) than on *Flacc.* (13): see further J. W. Crawford (1994), 233–70.

L. Domitius ... in his quaestorship. For at the time when C. Manilius as tribune of the plebs .... The MSS read *in praetura*, but this must be an error, whether of a copyist or (less likely) a slip on Asconius' part. Manilius was tribune from 10 December 67 to 9 December 66, and on 29 December 67, designated by the praetor for the Compitalia, so a *dies feriae*, legislated therefore illegally with strong support from a mob—doubtless largely of freedmen, those most strongly interested in his proposal, to distribute their vote among all thirty-five tribes. Asconius narrates the violent sequel. The senate invalidated the law the next day. See further *CAH* ix², 338; Ascon. 65C below; Dio 36.42.4; Gell. *NA* 10.24.3; Varro, *LL* 6.20.

46C. the people appointed Cassius to conduct a *quaestio* regarding the said Virgins. This is the famous lawyer L. Cassius Longinus Ravilla, cos. 127, whose ever-recurrent cynical question *Cui bono?* has remained the motto of policemen, lawyers, politicians, and journalists ever since. For Cicero's awareness of it, see also *Rosc. Am.* 84; *Verr.* 1.30, 2.3.137; *Clu.* 107; also Val. Max. 3.7.9. The inquisition into erring Vestals belongs to 114–13 (*MRR* 1. 537 for full evidence; summary of the case in Marshall (1985*a*), 196–8; some observations in Lewis (2001*a*)). Asconius' multiple cross-reference ('often') could be to *Verr.* 1.30; 2.3.137; *Clu.* 107; *Sest.* 103, or *Rosc. Am.* 84—on which last it is all but certain that he did write a commentary (Gell. *NA* 15.28.4).

This man is Sex. Cloelius. Again, not Sex. Clodius, as Clark has it: see above, pp. 237–8 on Ascon. 33C.

Mil. 37: **At what time since then has that dagger of his that he inherited from Catilina ever been at rest?** 'He' is of course P. Clodius, and here the reference is to a literal if quite possibly mythical dagger. While Clodius had almost certainly not been involved in the Catilinarian insurrection (or any violence or revolts connected with it) in 63/2, there is probably more substance in

Cicero's declarations that Clodius' henchmen came to include several former adherents of Catilina and his associates (Lewis (1988)).

Pompeius instantly returned home and thereafter kept himself indoors. He was ever plagued with fears and threats of assassination, and ever cautious, perhaps since his youth—see Plut. *Pomp.* 3, 5; Cic. *Sest.* 69; *Mil.* 65–6; *QF.* 2.3.3–4; Ascon. 38C, 51C. On the 'plot' of 58, see further Cic. *Sest.* 69; *Dom.* 67; Plut. *Pomp.* 49.

47C. *This (dagger) stained with blood the Appian Way, monument to his own name, with the murder of Papirius.* Cicero's catalogue of Clodius' crimes continues. Other references offer minor supplement—little in Cic. *Dom.* 66; *Att.* 3.8.3; *Mil.* 18; Plut. *Pomp.* 48; somewhat more in Schol. Bob. 118–19 St. on the fight on the Via Appia; Dio 38.30.1–2 has a variant tale.

48C. *Mil.* 37: *This same (dagger of Clodius) after a long interval was once again turned against me.* Cicero's words 'after a long interval' and 'recently' tend to support Asconius' ensuing conjecture that the incident belongs to 53, and so does his awareness of a gang-fight quite certainly of that year which offered a plausible occasion for it and in which it was perfectly possible that Cicero was involved. It should probably be distinguished from a somewhat similar incident of 11 November 57 (Cic. *Att.* 4.3.3) in very much the same location (*LTUR* 4. 189–92 (R. T. Scott); Coarelli (1985), 57–9, 136–40, 172–6, 180, 192, 198, 209), though the parallelism is by no means exact in all detail. The alternative and less attractive view is that Cicero's lemma here in fact refers to a single incident, that of 57, and that Asconius was unaware of the true date because either he lacked access to Cicero's *Letters to Atticus* (or at any rate a correctly dated copy of the letter in question); or else failed to apply this evidence with due care (if at all).

The Regia was the official residence of the *pontifex maximus*, occupied since his election in 63 by C. Iulius Caesar until his departure for Gaul in 58, whether or not since then still by his household. It was a fittingly imposing building situated at the south-east corner of the Forum between the Temple of Castor and the foot of the Via Sacra, and therefore at no great distance from the Palatine houses of both Clodius and Cicero.

L. Caecilius, that most just and gallant praetor. L. Caecilius Rufus, uterine half-brother to P. Sulla (cos. des. 65) and therefore a connection of Milo's wife Fausta, with six of his colleagues and eight of the ten tribunes of 57 backed P. Lentulus Spinther's consular rogation to recall Cicero (Cic. *Red. Sen.* 22; *Mil.* 38) and as Asconius goes on to explain was subjected to violence by Clodius. A tombstone from Marinum, near Alba in Latium (*ILLRP* 391) gives his career, according to Degrassi (ad loc., citing ibid., nos. 342, 402) including the office of a praetor acting as proconsul (*praetor pro consule*), rather than a proconsulship to follow the praetorship (*praetor, pro consule*), the view preferred by Broughton (1946), 38; *MRR* 2. 200, 210 against Mommsen (1887–8), 2³ 650 n. 2. As tribune in 63 he had proposed restoration to the senate of his half-brother P. Sulla (with Autronius), but Sulla induced its withdrawal; then withdrew support from the agrarian proposals of P. Servilius Rullus and threatened to veto them instead (*MRR* 2. 167–8).

While he was holding the Games of Apollo a mob of social dregs gathered and rioted so violently at the high price of corn that all who had taken their seats in the theatre to watch were driven off. In 57 there was serious difficulty with the corn supply of Rome, no doubt largely because Clodius in 58 had provided for extensive free distributions but done far too little to ensure procurement. The crisis, already evident in serious rioting at the Games of Apollo (Ludi Apollinares) in the period 6–13 July (Ascon.; cf. Cic. *Dom.* 14–15.), after brief remission at about the time of Cicero's recall (4 August) peaked, it seems, in the first few days of September (Cic. *Dom.* 5–6, 12–13; Dio 39.9.2 for the rioting; Cic. *Att.* 4.1.6; *Dom.* 4–10 (esp. 6–7), 15–16; cf. Dio 39.9.3). Cicero's speech on 7 September proposing to appoint Pompey Commissioner for the Corn Supply with large powers, won the day against the motion of the tribune Messius to grant him even more. The result was a five-year command for Pompey (see *MRR* 2. 203–4, 211, 219, 225, 230; Balsdon (1957), 16–18; Stockton (1971), 195–6), in which the dearth of state funds prevented quick success: M. Cato did not bring back the treasures of Cyprus until 56, and meantime shortages in the metropolis persisted (Cic. *QF* 2.3.2–4, 6.1; *Dom.* 25–6), aggravated, if we are to believe the sources, by influx of population from the countryside (Sall. *Bell. Cat.* 37.4–7; Varro, *RR* 2.3; Appian, *BC* 2.120; Suet. *Div. Aug.* 42.3) and large-scale manumission of slaves by masters now looking at least in part to the state for their upkeep (Dio 39.24.1; Dion. Hal. *AR* 4.24.5; Suet. *Div. Aug.* 42.2). Importantly, this was the first time that the state had intervened to regulate the operation of corn-shipping (*CAH* ix², 629). On this crisis and others, see P. Garnsey (1988), 200, 206; Virlouvet (1985) and (1995).

as we read in Tiro, Cicero's freedman, in book 4 of his *Life*. Note the source and the author. See Index of Personal Names, under Tullius Tiro; more in McDermott (1972). Marshall's view (1985*b*), 72, 200, that Asconius is confused over the date is unjustified.

49C. turbulent. But I think he means Q. Pompeius, for his *contio* was the more seditious. That Asconius found this last item on the nature of

Pompeius' *contio* in the *Acta* seems unlikely, but to propose any other source is equally a matter of pure conjecture.

This was the Causinius at whose house at Interamna Clodius wanted it to be thought he had stayed on the night when he was caught in Caesar's house. Once more the Bona Dea scandal of 62, and the trial of 61 (see *MRR* 2. 173, 178, 180). Notoriously, it was Cicero's demolition (he claimed) of Clodius' alibi that engendered their undying mutual hatred. See (e.g.) Tatum (1990); Epstein (1986).

whom he means. For these were the first to encourage the people in the matter of passing this law, and said that 'Clodius had been killed by the hand of Milo—etc.' Hence, as suggested above on Ascon. 38C, the threat to indict Cicero after the trial and prospective conviction of Milo.

50C. On the Appian Way near the city there is the monument of Basilus, a spot particularly notorious for robberies. This is Asconius' gloss on Cicero's argument against the notion that Milo had sought to ambush Clodius: he would have lain in wait under cover of darkness in a spot well suited to the enterprise.

base in Etruria. **Cicero often charges Clodius with having been associated with Catilina's conspiracy, a point to which he implicitly alludes here too.** Arguably here Asconius is guilty not so much of error as of loose and elliptical expression. In fact (in extant writings, anyhow) Cicero nowhere accuses Clodius of participation in the insurrection of 63, but frequently does associate him with surviving Catilinarian followers ('conspirators') in the 50s (above, on 46C). Rightly or wrongly, Asconius believes that Cicero's use of the term *castra* ('base'), which primarily refers to Clodian armed depredations in Etruria frequently alleged in the *Pro Milone* (26, 50, 55, 74, 87, 98), is deliberately intended to evoke the Catilinarian connection and to suggest 'Catilinarian' behaviour. Clodius' 'Greekling fellow-travellers' were absent, as Cicero goes on to stress, from his entourage at Bovillae, though normally his constant companions as sources of recreation (*nugae*). These persons, as *comites* ('companions') were clearly not slaves, but none is readily identifiable. Elsewhere Clodius does seem to have some links with a Greek (?) architect, one Cyrus, with one Hermarchus of Chios (Cic. *Har. Resp.* 34—perhaps a financier), and perhaps two of the Latin grammarians of the age, L. Ateius Praetextatus and L. Plotius Gallus; and certainly his family had extensive *clientelae* in the eastern Mediterranean (Rawson (1973)). Cicero purveys in the *In Pisonem* a somewhat similar (and misleading) impression of the relationship between L. Piso and the Greek poet and philosopher Philodemus, on which see above, pp. 212–13 on Ascon. 16C.

It was nothing unusual for Roman notables with cultural interests or pretensions to include learned Greeks in their entourages: compare also, for a small sample, Lucullus and Antiochus; M. Piso and Staseas, Cicero himself and Diodotus (and many others); Cato the Younger and Athenodorus, Apollonides, and Demetrius. See further Rawson (1985), e.g. 80–1, 111–12.

For there had been a belief that, when Catilina had fled the city to the base of the centurion Manlius, who at that time was recruiting an army for him in Etruria at Faesulae, Clodius wished to follow on. Accepted by some moderns, but convincingly rejected by Tatum (1999), 59–61. No surviving evidence substantiates such a belief, fatally undermined by Plut. *Cic.* 29 and about which Asconius himself seems sceptical. He uses it, however, to explain the force, as he sees it, of Cicero's secondary allusion to the activities of Manlius in 63, on which see Sall. *BC* 24, 27–30, 33, 36; Plut. *Cic.* 14; Dio 38.30.4–5; Seager (1973); Phillips (1976).

51C. Licinius, a certain petty priest from the plebs who was accustomed to purify households. A 'petty priest' (*sacrificulus*) was a private-enterprise diviner, unrecognized by the state cults of Rome, and regarded as irresponsible and dangerous by the Roman authorities (see Livy 25.1.8; 35.48.13; 39.8.3; 39.16.8).

52C. Again, when the senate was meeting in the Portico of Pompeius, so that Pompeius could attend, Milo was the only one whom he ordered to be searched before entering the senate. For meetings outside the *pomerium* and Pompey's near-paranoia, see above, pp. 238 and 251 on Ascon. 33C and 46C.

The same T. Munatius Plancus, as we have often said, after the words of the witnesses had been heard and sealed, and the jurors had been for the present dismissed, called a *contio* and urged the people that the shops should be closed the next day, and that they should attend the court and not allow Milo to escape. Something untoward has happened here, since Asconius' remark bears no relation to the passage of Cicero on which on the face of it he is offering comment, and which clearly (see context in the speech) refers to Pompey. Perhaps the best solution is to suppose a sizeable lacuna in Asconius' MSS which should have contained comment on the *lemma* here cited and another *lemma* to which the present comment pertains. For Munatius' *contio*, cf. 40C. The closure of shops might be expected to increase the attendance of Clodius' partisans: such at any rate is the implication of Cic. *Dom.* 54, 89–90, of Clodius' legislative activity of 58 in the tribal assembly, held—like the courts—in the Forum, on the south side of which a great many shops (*tabernae*) were situated (*LTUR* 2. 325–36 (F. Coarelli); cf. Coarelli (1985), 138, 140–1, 145, 149–54, 172, 179, 201–2)—but of course elsewhere too at no great distance. See further (e.g.) Millar (1998), ch. 2; for collected evidence on closure of *tabernae*, P. J. J. Vanderbroeck (1987), 126–7. For their vital role, often with associated *officinae* (workshops) and dwellings, in the life of the urban plebs and particularly its freedman element and *collegia*, see the penetrating analysis of N. Purcell, *CAH* IX^2, 659–73 (esp. 663, 671–3), with further bibliography. For further important insights into the political aspects, ibid. 673–80.

I think that we have already indicated that there was among the laws of P. Clodius which he proposed to carry the one also whereby freedmen, who cast their votes in no more than four tribes, might also cast them in the rural tribes. It is reasonable conjecture to assign the cross-reference to comment on Cicero's lost speech *On Milo's Debts* (cf. fr. 17 Puccioni in Schol. Bob. 173 St.; J. W. Crawford (1994), 281–304), almost certainly the object of the cross-reference below (53C) to Milo's familial background and inheritances. Part of Clodius' programme as praetor, if elected, according to Cicero (*Mil.* 33, 89 (cf. 87); Quintil. 9.2.54) was redistribution of the freedman vote, often attempted in the past by various *populares* (e.g. C. Manilius, tr. pl. 66—see *MRR* 2. 153; 3. 134; below, pp. 271–2 on Ascon. 65–66C). For other cases, Treggiari (1969), 49–50, 164–6; Lintott (1999a), 51–2. The threat, real or imagined, was that this law would make it easier—perhaps far easier—for anyone who could control the votes of freedmen resident in or near Rome to influence the block votes of all thirty-five tribes, and not only those of the four urban tribes. Further, Clodius allegedly was seeking to count freed slaves as his own clients much as slaves liberated by Sulla in his proscriptions were termed *Cornelii*; or, according to Dio 39.23.2, Clodius himself had wanted slaves liberated by Cato on Cyprus under his legislation of 58 to be called *Clodii*.

53C. **P. Clodius, while still quaestor designate, was caught after entering the place where a sacred rite for the good of the Roman people was in progress. This fact had been remarked ... by senatorial decree, and it had been decreed that there should be an extraordinary court-hearing on the matter.** The Bona Dea affair of 62/1 again. Asconius' note of Clodius' status as quaestor designate explains Cicero's designation of him as 'a private citizen' at the time, which is, however, misleading if, as seems likely, he took up the office on the following day—before the senate's unavailing attempt to bring him to book. The lacuna must have contained a brief account of the sequel. The special *quaestio* established by senatorial decree and statute (Lex Fufia) of course failed to convict Clodius.

Concerning the plebs and the basest mob, which under P. Clodius' leadership menaced your fortunes, he gives a reminder that he took action not only to show sterling worth in turning its attack aside, but also in using his three inheritances to assuage its wrath. I think it has already been said above that Milo was from the family of Papii, and then adopted by T. Annius, his maternal grandfather. By the third inheritance he seems to mean that of his mother; for I have not discovered any other that existed. Asconius borrows Cicero's phrase *infima multitudo* ('basest mob') at 48C. Milo's family background is somewhat problematic. The Annii on his mother's side were quite likely descended from the consuls of 153 and 128 BC, though Cicero fails to mention this. Milo himself came from the *municipium* of Lanuvium in Latium (Ascon. 31C), possibly also the home town of the Papii (so tentatively Wiseman (1971b), 249, no. 305, on L. Papius, a Roman mint-official (*monetalis*) of c.78). Perhaps, however, alternatively, it was that of his mother Annia, and his natural father came from elsewhere—roundly claimed by Salmon (1967), 314; cf. 392, as a Samnite from Hirpinian Compsa. One C. Papius, of unknown origins and perhaps irrelevant here, was tribune of the plebs in 65 (*MRR* 2. 158). On the munificence of Roman magnates to the urban plebs by way of games (*ludi*), feasts (*epula*), handouts of cash, corn, or other benefits and other aspects of their metropolitan symbiosis, see again N. Purcell, *CAH* IX², 680–9, esp. 683–4, prime examples being the aedilician games of Scaurus in 58 and those for the opening of Pompey's theatre in 55 (above, pp. 193–4; 212; 216–17).

cast votes. Of the senators, twelve voted for conviction, six for acquittal; thirteen knights convicted, four acquitted; thirteen *tribuni aerarii* convicted, three acquitted. There seems to be a minor anomaly here, since the panel of eighty-one which was reduced to a final fifty-one, if these figures are correct, did not contain equal numbers of each order, but one extra senator and was short of one *tribunus aerarii*. The same was true of the ensuing case against Saufeius (55C).

It appears that the jurymen were well aware that Clodius had been wounded initially without Milo's knowledge, but found that after he had been wounded he was killed on Milo's orders. Indubitably the correct view, shared by Ascon. 41C.

There were some who believed that the vote of M. Cato was for acquittal, for he did not conceal ... He had also supported Pompey's appointment as sole consul to restore public order, but his stance was not necessarily self-contradictory—or so he might have argued. For more on Cato's role and attitudes in this affair, Fehrle (1983), 205–18, with the evidence.

54C. Cicero too had named him as present and testified that he had heard from M. Favonius that.... In fact at *Mil.* 44 (cf. 26) Cicero ascribes the allegation of Clodius' threat to Favonius' direct testimony. It appears that somehow a minor muddle has crept into Asconius.

It was announced that Milo was condemned, thanks chiefly to Appius Claudius. Necessary, so that he could claim the reward stipulated under the Lex Pompeia *de vi* for successful prosecution.

A few days later Milo was also convicted before the *quaesitor* M. Favonius *de sodaliciis* on the accusation of P. Fulvius Neratus, to whom under the law a reward was granted. On rewards for successful prosecution, Alexander (1985). The *quaesitor* M. Favonius was not praetor until 49, but perhaps delayed in his career and already in 52 a senator sufficiently senior for the task, probably aedile in 53, or even in this year: see above, p. 245 on Ascon. 38C.

he was again convicted on a charge *de vi*: the accusers were L. Cornificius and Q. Patulcius. Apparently under the Lex Plautia *de vi*, since a second trial under the Lex Pompeia would not be possible. Cornificius, after failing in the *divinatio* to secure the right to prosecute under the Lex Pompeia, seemingly found this consolation.

exile at Massilia. A favoured place of exile. Milo's attempted return to join M. Caelius against the Caesarians in 48 ended in disaster and death for both (Caes. *BC* 3.20–2).

His property, on account of his enormous debts, sold for almost nothing. This may be a severely telescoped and somewhat misleading way of saying that creditors claimed most of the proceeds, and little was left to the state by way of confiscated assets. There are perhaps complications to be considered. Milo complained to Cicero, who was involved in the transactions through his wife's freedman Philotimus, who may have embezzled some of the proceeds (Cic. *Att.* 5.8.2–3, 6.4.3, 5.2, 7.1; cf. *Fam.* 8.3.2). Cicero had formed a syndicate to purchase what it could, and, as Marshall (1985*b*), 208–9 suggests, if it was able to acquire assets in bulk at a low price and resell them piecemeal at a good profit, Milo could be allowed to benefit (rather than Cicero, as believed by Carcopino (1947), 1. 183–90; cf. Shackleton Bailey (1965–70), 3. 202–3, (1971), 98). Even so, Milo's creditors would take their share (*Att.* 6.5.2).

After Milo, under the same Pompeian Law the first to be accused was M. Saufeius, son of Marcus, who had taken the lead in storming the tavern at Bovillae and in killing Clodius. Cf above, p. 236 on Ascon. 32C. For Saufeii at Praeneste, Wiseman (1971*b*), 259; Syme (1964*a*), 121 on *CIL* 1^2.1,

p. 199; Plin. *NH* 7. 183; Cic. *Att.* 6.1.10; Nep. *Att.* 12.3; Shackleton Bailey (1965–70), 1. 287, 3. 245.

55C. His accusers were L. Cassius; L. Fulcinius, son of Gaius; and C. Valerius; the defence advocates were M. Cicero and M. Caelius, and they secured his acquittal by a single vote. Cicero and Caelius the tribune stand true to their recent alignment among Milo's friends. Of the accusers, L. Cassius is otherwise unknown, but just might be somehow connected with the Catilinarian condemned in 63, but not for certain killed (Sall. *Bell. Cat.* 17.3; 44.1–2; 50.4). It is tempting to connect L. Fulcinius with Fulcinii found in or near Amiternum, home town of C. Sallustius, pro-Clodian tribune of this year, whence comes also a late Republican gravestone to one L. Sergius L. l. whose wife was a freeborn woman, Rutila Fulcinia. See further, Lewis (1988), 31–42.

For conviction there voted ten senators, with eight for acquittal; of the Roman knights, nine were for conviction, eight for acquittal, but of the *tribuni aerarii* ten acquitted and six convicted. The same imbalance among the orders is apparent as in the trial of Milo, under the same Lex Pompeia *de vi*.

He was prosecuted again a few days later before the *quaesitor* C. Considius under the Plautian Law *de vi*. The Lex Plautia is first seen in operation in 63 (Sall. *Bell. Cat.* 31.4), and might have been passed by a tribune of 70 to extend the coverage of an apparently earlier Lex Lutatia (78) limited to sedition against the state. For outlines, see Marshall (1985*b*), 210; Gruen (1974), 225–7; Cloud, *CAH* IX², 524; more in Lintott (1999*b*), 107–24. The annotated charges should refer to clauses of the Lex Plautia, but that one of them was 'seizure of high ground' is quite uncertain and depends on filling a lacuna after MSS *loca* ('places') with Mommsen's conjecture *edita* ('elevated'), preferred by Clark and others (cf. Caes. *BC* 1.7.5) to (e.g.) *publica* ('public'), also offered by Mommsen, Kiessling–Schoell (cf. Paul. *Sent.* 5.26.3; *Dig.* 47.22.2).

The accusers were C. Fidius, Cn. Aponius, son of Gnaeus, M. Seius … and … son of Sextus; defending counsel were M. Cicero, M. Terentius Varro Gibba. Cicero laboured on, in this case assisted by a young protégé (*Fam.* 13.10.1), later quaest. 46, tr. pl. 43, not to be confused with the much older and more famous M. Terentius Varro, scholar, antiquarian, part-time politician and amateur soldier. The accusers are particularly obscure (and the damaged MSS unhelpful). M. Seius might be an equestrian businessman, *bon viveur* and acquaintance of Ap. Claudius (P. Clodius' brother and cos. 54 (Varro, *RR* 3.2.7–14, 6.33–6, 10.1; Plin. *NH* 10.52))—and of other Roman magnates (Cic. *Att.* 5.13.2, 12.11.1; *Fam.* 9.7.1, 11.7.1); alternatively, an aedile of 74 (Cic. *Off.* 2.58; *Planc.* 12) or, better, a homonymous son of his.

Sex. Cloelius, at whose instigation Clodius' corpse was taken into the senate house, was condemned, to general approbation, on the accusation of C. Caesennius Philo and M. Alfidius, with T. Flacconius for the defence—by forty-six votes. Once more note the defendant's true name—not Clodius, as in the MSS; cf. pp. 237–8 above, on Ascon. 33C. Among the advocates, the names Caesennius and Flacconius look possibly Etruscan by origin. From tangled evidence and modern debate (summary in Marshall (1985*b*), 212; fullest discussion in Linderski (1974)) it appears that Alfidius might be related to Alfidia, mother of the Empress Livia.

56C. Many others besides, both those who turned up and persons cited but who made no answer, were condemned, of whom the majority were Clodian partisans. Asconius omits them, even though some involved Cicero, presumably since none was directly connected with the speech for Milo—and he had to stop somewhere! Ten further known cases belong to the years 52/1: for evidence and details, see Marshall (1985*b*), 212. Among these, the two most actively daring and outspoken Clodian tribunes of 52, Q. Pompeius Rufus and T. Munatius Plancus Bursa, on demitting office were prosecuted under the Lex Pompeia *de vi* by M. Caelius Rufus (tr. pl. 52) and Cicero respectively, and were convicted. Pompey did nothing to help Pompeius Rufus and his attempt to assist Plancus by submitting a *laudatio* contrary to his own law was spotted by M. Cato and so thwarted (Val. Max. 4.2.7; Dio 40.55.3 (Pompeius); Cic. *Att.* 6.1.10; *Fam* 7.2.3; Plut. *Pomp.* 55; *Cat. Min.* 48). In addition, note that the third leading anti-Milonian tribune, the later historian C. Sallustius, was not prosecuted but in 51 removed from the senate by the censor Ap. Claudius Pulcher, despite his overt earlier Clodian allegiance (perhaps abandoned—Ascon. 37C).

Other defendants included connections of Cn. Pompeius Magnus himself. Q. Metellus Scipio, his new father-in-law, evaded prosecution by C. Memmius under Pompey's law *de ambitu* on being nominated by Pompey as his fellow-consul in August or September 52. C. Memmius himself, a former adherent of Pompey but by now abandoned, was under indictment on the same charge at the time—probably retrospectively, for electoral activities in 54. The case of M. Scaurus, first indicted *de ambitu* in late 54, but not tried until 52, Cicero again defending, is almost exactly parallel (Bucher (1995)). The most blatant of Pompey's betrayals, however, was that of P. Plautius Hypsaeus, his candidate in the consular elections of 52, but ditched on Pompey's own appointment as sole consul and subsequent choice of Metellus Scipio as colleague, leaving Hypsaeus to be convicted *de ambitu* under Pompey's law (Val. Max. 9.5.3; Plut. *Pomp.* 55).

The case *de ambitu* against M. Messala Rufus was apparently brought under the Lex Pompeia retroactively, concerning his blatant misdeeds (along with all three of his rivals) in the consular elections for 53: he was defended by Q. Hortensius and M. Caelius and acquitted, but later convicted *de sodaliciis* and exiled. Cicero secured the acquittal of his old ally P. Sestius, quaestor in 63 and tr. pl. 57, apparently *de ambitu*, but his personal aide in 63, the quaestor T. Fadius, was condemned by one vote (charge unknown) and undue influence—perhaps again Pompey's. Finally, one Servaeus, tr. pl. elect for 50, was convicted and condemned, presumably *de ambitu* or *de sodaliciis*—and replaced by the later Caesarian partisan the younger C. Scribonius Curio.

This catalogue does not feature 'a majority of Clodian partisans', but that does not imply error on the part of Asconius. There may have been several more cases, some of them against very minor figures, of which all trace has been lost. The most complete listing of known evidence is in Alexander (1990), 154–61.

The Commentary on Cicero's speech *On Behalf of Cornelius*

In his standard format—date, introduction, commentary by *lemma* and *scholion*—Asconius' account of Cicero's defence of C. Cornelius provides vital evidence for the 60s BC, a decade of Roman history for which, in metropolitan politics at least, the sources are disappointingly sparse before Cicero's consulship of 63. Asconius' own coverage is far from complete, and textual problems with his MSS abound, but what is offered cannot be ignored. The most useful readily accessible guide in English to this speech and its political context is Griffin (1973); for wider conspectus of the earlier 60s, Wiseman, *CAH* IX², 327–67, esp. 329–44; Seager (1969); Millar (1998), ch. 4, esp. 87–91. For a possible reconstruction of Cicero's twin speeches, now fragmentary, but not confined to the remnants in Asconius, Kumaniecki (1970); more recently, Alexander (1990), no. 209 (pp. 104–5); J. W. Crawford (1994), 67–148.

57C. He delivered this oration in the consulship of L. Cotta and L. Torquatus, a year later than the previous ones. That is, in 65. The known previous speeches of 66 are those *On the Command of Cn. Pompeius; For Cluentius* (both extant); *For Fundanius; For Manilius* (apparently in a *contio*); *For Mucius*. All the last three are lost, but again see J. W. Crawford (1994), 33–42; for the wider forensic context, Alexander (1990), nos. 194–210. That Asconius wrote a commentary on at least one of the speeches concerning Manilius (*On the Command of Cn. Pompeius; For Manilius*) is a likely inference from the cross-references at 64.17–18; 65.3–5; 65.8; 65.16C—see Ramsey (1980).

He had been a quaestor of Cn. Pompeius. *MRR* 2. 122 unaccountably cites this passage as evidence—which it is not—for his service in this capacity in Spain, and so in or before 71. That is of course possible, but so too is service as quaestor to Pompey in the latter's consulship of 70. There is little doubt of his Pompeian allegiance. He favoured better provincial government, defended the tribunes' rights restored by Pompey in 70, acted in collusion with another Pompeian tribune, C . Manilius (tr. pl. 66), and his prosecution was backed by five leading anti-Pompeian magnates, as well as C. Piso, cos. 67, all hostile to the tribunate as such. There is no reason, however, to deny Cornelius more than one motive. On this see, Griffin (1973), followed by Marshall (1985*b*), 214–15.

He was estranged from the senate for the following reason. Asconius presents a reasonably full and coherent explanation in what follows, but its chronology and logic differ considerably from the version of events found in

Dio 36.38–41. Griffin (1973) argues tenaciously and convincingly in favour of Asconius and against Dio. Asconius' order of events follows the likeliest reconstruction of Cicero's, and though Cicero's speech was by no means bound to follow the historical order of events in Cornelius' tribunate, it is likely enough that Asconius checked the order with his historical sources.

'that since sums of money were being passed to the envoys of foreign peoples at huge rates of interest, and scandalously immoral profits were accruing from this, there should be a regulation to prevent the dispensation of funds to the envoys of foreign peoples'. For instances and analysis, Badian (1968*b*), 66–73, 84–5 (cf. *SIG*³ 784.36, from 71 BC). Various attempts to check these practices had been made since the 90s, if not earlier (below, next note), none very successful, especially in view of the facility with which senators (and through them probably others) could secure exemptions from the laws (*privilegia*). The problem remained in 60 (Cic. *Att.* 1.19.9).

the senatorial decree that had been passed some years before, in the consulship of L. Domitius and C. Coelius. The (slightly obscure and scarcely valid) point is that the recent decree of either 70 or 69 (Dio fr.111; Diod. 40.1.1–3; Cic. 2 *Verr.* 2.76; Marshall (1985*b*), 218) in citing the earlier measure of 94 was held to demonstrate that it was still currently effective. My translation 'some years before' is of Clark's emendation of faulty MSS: perhaps better the earlier supplement to the lacuna first offered by Baiter, which yields 'twenty-seven years before'. The correction *L. Domitio* for MSS *Cn. Domitio* on which this depends is in any case unavoidable. 'Coelius' is a likewise necessary correction of MSS 'Caelius'.

58C. Cornelius was annoyed over this matter, and protested against the senate in a *contio*. But apparently let his proposal lapse, at any rate in this form. By the 50s there existed a Lex Gabinia which forbade lawsuits to recover loans at interest made to provincials (Cic. *Att.* 5.21.12, 6.2.7). So far as the Ciceronian evidence goes, however, this apparently applied only to such loans made *in Rome*. Perhaps Cornelius' tribunician colleague of 67, A. Gabinius, took up this issue successfully in that year, or legislated later as praetor, or even as cos. 58. Compare Cornelius' alleged collaboration with C. Manilius, tr. pl. 66 (Ascon. 64C). On the nature of a *contio*, Lintott (1999*a*), 41–5.

'provision must be made for envoys to have resources from which they might make payment of even their current debts'. That is, to avoid the need for further borrowing to make payments on what they already owed. Following Griffin (1973), 209 n. 123, I have abandoned Clark's faulty emendation of the lacunose MSS in favour of what appears to have been Cornelius' meaning, although various guesses might be made as to what was the original Latin.

He promulgated a law by which he reduced the authority of the senate, whereby 'no one should be exempted from the laws except by vote of the people'. That is, Cornelius dropped his more specific proposal on lending, on the face of it accepted the view of the senate that sufficient safeguards were already in place, and altered his angle of attack to place a severe general limit on exemptions from them or any other legal provision, at the same time reasserting the paramount authority (*maiestas*) of the people. Asconius goes on to explain the justification for this new move.

a tribune was found, one P. Servilius Globulus, to obstruct C. Cornelius. Who nevertheless turned up to support him in his trial of 65, for reasons quite unknown (Ascon. 61C).

the herald, as the *scriba* handed him the text, began to read it to the people. Note the procedure in the assembly—not in fact the *comitia* of the whole people but the *concilium plebis* (plebs only). The *scriba* would have been responsible for the technical drafting of the text of the law, the 'herald' or 'cryer' for reciting it in due form to the assembly. Further, Lintott (1999*a*), 46 with n. 28; Badian (1989).

The consul C. Piso, on vehemently protesting that this was an outrage, and asserting that the tribunician right of veto was being subverted. On this view, Cornelius, like C. Manilius next year, was following the precedent of Ti. Gracchus in 133 in seeking to override his colleague's right of veto (*ius intercessionis*). The constitutional propriety of this move was certainly open to question; its theoretical justification that the will of the people must be allowed to be paramount. This issue (on which see also Lintott (1999*a*), 124–5) had never been resolved since 133, except briefly under duress by Sulla, 81–70. Cornelius had also on the face of it committed another illegality in interrupting a (fellow-) tribune while he was addressing the people (Cic. *Sest.* 79; Val. Max. 9.5.2; Dion. Hal. *AR* 16.4–17.5; Lintott (1999*a*), 122). For more evidence on the ultra-conservative and singularly unattractive consul C. Piso, see *MRR* 2. 127, 142–3, 154, 159; 3. 46.

Cornelius, greatly concerned at this disorder, dismissed the *concilium* forthwith. Asconius presents Cornelius as a moderate, ready to respect law and order and to seek alternative methods—very probably the view promoted in Cicero's defence, on the face of it justifiably.

59C. Cornelius again initiated a measure. Here again Cornelius modified (and this time moderated) his previous proposal in order to preserve senatorial authority while at the same time seeking to check abuses. This time there were no valid grounds for opposition, and his law was carried, albeit apparently considerably less effective than Cornelius would have wished.

Cornelius passed another law, although no one dared to oppose, but against the wishes of a great many, to require praetors to dispense justice in accord with their own standing edicts. On the Praetorian Edict, see Kunkel (1973), 91–4, 211–12; Lintott (1999*a*), 109 (and n. 67), 200 (and n. 29) and for a reconstruction of the text, Lenel (1927). In effect, it was the declaration of a praetor designate of the principles by which he proposed to dispense justice during his term of office. It is a moot point whether, as Griffin (1973), 209 would have it, Cornelius intended this law to apply to ex-praetors who were provincial commanders, often termed *praetor* even when technically acting *pro consule* rather than *pro praetore*. By the 60s it is likely that many provincial governors followed the precedent set by Q. Mucius Scaevola in Asia in the mid-90s in issuing such an edict for provincial jurisdiction on the model of metropolitan custom. It seems difficult, however, to regard Cornelius' law as applicable to consular commanders, unless Asconius' report is somewhat inexact.

Cornelius promulgated several other laws too, against most of which his colleagues opposed their veto, and over these dissensions the whole period of his tribunate was spent. Only one more proposal is known, a measure against electoral bribery covered in Dio 36.38.4. Asconius was aware of it (74C) but gives no details. In the upshot it was not passed, but the initiative forced the passage of another by the agency of the consul C. Piso, the Lex Calpurnia *de ambitu* of 67, see below.

the year in which Cicero was praetor. *De repetundis*, in 66. See *MRR* 2. 152.

two brothers Cominius indicted Cornelius under the Lex Cornelia *de maiestate*. That is, under Sulla's law of 81 (for which see *MRR* 2. 75), still current, and apparently or allegedly applicable to the conduct of Cornelius tr. pl. 67. See further below, on 61C. The Cominius here given the *praenomen* Gaius, if as is probable identifiable with the brother of Publius mentioned in Cic. *Clu.* 100, might rather be a Lucius. Or the MSS of Cicero might be wrong and those of Asconius correct.

L. Cassius the praetor. Asconius' MSS record him as P. Cassius, but there is a case for identifying a Cassius who was praetor in 66 alongside Cicero with his consular competitor of 64, L. Cassius Longinus (Ascon. 82C; cf. *Comm. Pet.* 7), who turned Catilinarian and was condemned for it in absence in 63 (Sall. *Bell. Cat.* 17.3, 44.1–2, 50.4). *MRR* 2. 152; 3. 50–1 identifies him, after Shackleton Bailey (1976), 24, with a juror in the Oppianicus case of 74, also as juror in the case of Verres in 70 (Cic. *Clu.* 107; *Verr.* 1. 30).

on the tenth day, as is customary. On the procedures and the intervals required between the different stages, see Greenidge (1901), 466–8.

his commissionership for the public corn supply. Not noted by *MRR*, but by Mommsen (1887–8), 2. 238. See also Brennan (2000), 2. 419. The responsibility may have been under the Lex Terentia Cassia of 73, which restored some level of subsidized corn distribution after abolition by Sulla. It was an important and extremely difficult job: witness the problems of even Pompey in 57–6 (above, p. 252, on Ascon. 48C).

known gangleaders, who even threatened them with death, if they did not desist forthwith. Disruption of political and (at this stage more often) judicial processes was happening more frequently in the 60s than before, though it had perhaps not yet reached the levels seen in the next decade. Outlines and key instances in Millar (1998), chs. 2–7, esp. 4 and 5. The ringleaders were presumably motivated more by Cornelius' domestic political activity (e.g. support for C. Manilius' proposals on the freedman vote, or his general hostility to the *optimates*; for other instances, Ascon. 60C; Cic. *Sull.* 15, 68) than by his efforts on behalf of provincials.

60C. They escaped this peril with difficulty, on the intervention of the consuls, who had come down as advocates for the defendant. Their motives in appearing for Cornelius are undetectable. It was probably merely their arrival, presumably with lictors, that dispersed the gangleaders: they need not have intended to scatter Cornelius' support, especially if there were no actual gangs present. On the other hand, it was their duty to uphold law and order, if there were, and it does not seem likely that Cornelius would have welcomed violence in his favour.

The Cominii had taken refuge in some kind of garret. The Latin word translated 'garret' (*scalae*) literally means 'stairs' (Courtney (1980), 365).

when L. Cassius took his seat and the accusers on being called failed to present themselves, the name of Cornelius was struck from the list of those awaiting trial. The normal outcome of such an eventuality. See again Greenidge (1901), 466–8.

Manilius, who had broken up the trial by means of gangleaders, had first made a court appearance and then, because in accord with a senatorial decree both consuls ... were providing protection for that trial, he had made no answer and had been condemned. At this point the text is badly damaged, and I have simply adopted that of Clark: even so gaps remain unfilled. On demitting office as tribune on 9 December 66, Manilius was indicted before the praetor in charge of the court *de repetundis*—none other than Cicero (Cic. *Corn. ap.* Ascon. 62C; Plut. *Cic.* 9; Dio 36.44.1–2), who had spoken in support of his law on Pompey's command. The choice of accusation is not readily explicable: Bauman (1967), 27–30, 85–7 suggests that it might have been harder to pursue an indictment *de maiestate*, to which Manilius was more obviously open, than one *de repetundis*, but what as tribune in 66 he had done by way of unlawfully acquiring others' assets escapes detection. Cicero attempted to accelerate proceedings, probably intending to favour Manilius by his own friendly presidency over his trial, but under popular pressure agreed to postponement to a date in 65, when his own office would be ended and he would be free to defend him. When, early in 65, the trial came on, on one reconstruction Manilius' gangs broke up the hearing, and in response the consuls, backed by senatorial decree, turned up to give the court protection, which probably induced Cicero to abandon the defence. In any case Manilius himself did so: on failing to reappear he was condemned in absence and went off into exile. Other reconstructions are possible. Discussions include Ward (1970), 547–56; Phillips (1979), 597–9; Ramsey (1980) and (1985).

Cornelius, greatly alarmed at the political destruction of Manilius, brought few friends into court, so that there should not be even any vocal demonstration for him raised by his advocates. Apparently in a deliberate show of strictly constitutional behaviour, by contrast with Manilius' attempt to disrupt his own trial by violence. It is clear that Cicero's defence of Cornelius made much of the point (see below, p. 272 on 66C), and will be Asconius' source for this assertion, though that Cornelius was motivated by alarm rather than legal propriety is perhaps his own notion rather than Cicero's.

In their hostility leading men of the state bore witness against him—those who wielded most power in the senate, to wit, Q. Hortensius, Q. Catulus, Q. Metellus Pius, M. Lucullus, Mam. Lepidus. All ex-consuls: the first four unquestionably conservative ex-Sullans; the first two brothers-in-law; Q. Pius and M. Lucullus (the latter was brother to the more famous Lucius and son of a Caecilia Metella) equally conservative, ex-Sullan, and hostile to Pompey. As for the Lepidus in question, none of these attributes is demonstrable for M'. Lepidus, cos. 66 (preferred by Syme (1970), 31 n. 5, 141), who had turned up to *defend* Cornelius that year—and this identification, preferred by Clark, is itself an emendation of a single MS reading 'M.', the others plainly incorrect in reading 'L.' It is better to accept identification with the ex-consul of 77, Mam. Aemilius Lepidus Livianus (so Sumner (1964)), who had served earlier under Sulla, suffered an electoral defeat, most probably in 79 as Sulla's preferred candidate for the consulship against M. Lepidus, cos. 78 (Badian (1964), 217, 234 n. 17).

61C. Cornelius in his tribunate had read a codex before the *rostra* in person, which it was thought no one had ever done before Cornelius. They wished it to be seen that it was their opinion that this conduct was highly relevant

to the charge of impairing the *maiestas* of the tribunate. In this context the
term 'codex' refers simply to the sheaf or pack of tablets on which the
proposed law had been drafted. The next sentence is problematic. Clark
retained the MSS reading, which attributes to Asconius the notion (or
perhaps makes the five leading senators of the 60s allege) that the late
Republic recognized such a thing as the *maiestas*—that is, 'overriding
power' of tribunes. This is accepted by Millar (1998), 88–9, but neither
proposition is especially convincing (Livy 3.48.2 *pro maiestate imperii*, of a
decemvir, refers to one who *did* in 449—in the tradition—enjoy 'overriding
power'). One alternative approach is to substitute the reading *potestatis*
('constitutional power') for *maiestatis*, repetition of the phrase a line or
two later notwithstanding. 'Diminution of tribunician power', however, is
not in itself attested as an indictable criminal offence. Marshall (1985*b*), 227
preferred to delete *tribuniciae* ('tribunician') as an erroneous intrusion from
the later context, to yield the translation 'charge of impairing *maiestas*'—that
is, in this context and almost all others concerning late Republican politics,
'the overriding sovereignty (of the Roman people)'. This view derives some
support from Quintil. 4.4.8; 10.5.13. Against Marshall's suggestion is the
context. On the MS reading, Cornelius' opponents gloss *maiestas* (*populi
Romani*) to mean the *maiestas* of the tribunes collectively, as the popular
representatives (the *crimen maiestatis* was notoriously difficult to define).
Cicero's response, as reported by Asconius, picks up the contrast of the
allegedly delinquent individual with the collective, modifies the technically
non-existent accusation of diminishing the *maiestas* of the tribunate by
changing the word to *potestas*, and finally argues that the reading of a
codex by a tribune does not damage the *potestas* of the tribunate.

   For location of the *rostra*, *LTUR* 4. 212–14 (F. Coarelli); Coarelli (1985), 49,
56–7; their importance, Millar (1998), 41–2.

**for, if this were to be allowed to individual tribunes, the veto was all but
eliminated.** Their argument—surely hypocritical, since evidently none were
exactly enthusiasts for tribunes' rights and power and probably had supported Sulla's curtailment of them, finally removed in 70—was presumably
that for Cornelius to use his own tribunician power to persist with carrying
the *rogatio* even after a veto had debarred the herald from reading out the
text was to ignore his colleague's right of veto; that was in turn an infringement of tribunician rights (the negative power of the tribune being
paramount in Sulla's view), and as such an infringement ('diminution') of
the sovereign rights or overriding authority of the Roman people.

**Cicero was not able to deny that this had been done, and so took refuge in
saying that the fact that the codex had been read out by a tribune did not**

constitute violation of tribunes' powers. Cicero's defence appears to have contested each step in the argument against Cornelius. Cornelius had (1) read out the text not to contest Globulus' veto, but to remind all concerned (including himself) of the content of the proposal (cf. *Vat.* 5); (2) had no subversive intentions, as proven by his dismissal of the assembly on arrival of the consuls (*Vat.* 5; Ascon. 58C); (3) could in any case have been thwarted by repetition of the veto at any one of several later opportunities in the passage of the bill (71C); (4) was the target of grossly unfair and insincere attacks on the part of these magnates (78C, 79C). In any case, he seems to have argued (here, at any rate!), a tribune *did* have the right to override a colleague's veto, as Ti. Gracchus had done in 133 and much more recently C. Manilius in 66 (71–2C). On the legal question, see further chiefly Bauman (1967), 71–5; Meier (1968); Rilinger (1989); Lintott (1999*a*), 46 and n. 28, 125, cf. 207–9; summary of Republican legislation in *CAH* ix², 518–20.

without impairing the standing of those most highly ranked citizens against whom he was speaking, he avoided any damage being done to the defendant by their authority. Not quite true. A few months later Cicero was getting anxious about this with reference to his consular ambitions (*Att.* 1.2.2), having been critical of the said magnates in this speech (73C).

with two *decuriae*, those of Roman knights and *tribuni aerarii*, and in the case of the third with most of the senators. In this context and at this date, the term *decuria*, originally military parlance for a detachment of cavalry, means simply 'division' and the reference is to the three portions of the tripartite jury established under the Lex Aurelia *iudiciaria* of 70 BC. On its provisions and the three categories of those of the highest property-rating from which the juries were drawn, see above, pp. 213–14 on Ascon. 17C; Cloud in *CAH* ix², 509, 526.

There survives the oration of Cominius the prosecutor. Known also to Tacitus (*Dial.* 39.5) some fifty years later.

62C. Cicero's defence … lasted four days; it is evident that he compiled (material from) two processes into two orations. Rated highly by Quintil. 8.3.3. Here I translate the reading of all MSS, seeing no reason to follow Clark in accepting an emendation which yields 'compiled material from *these* processes into two orations'. Cicero's statement that his advocacy lasted four days reappears in Pliny (*Epp.* 1.8.20), who infers that he must have abridged and emended what he had said at greater length to appear as it did in a single large volume. On the other hand, Cornelius Nepos in his *Life of Cicero*, fr. 2P (= *HRR* 2. 34—from Hieron. *Ep.* 72) declared that he had himself heard Cicero's defence of Cornelius of which the published version was virtually a verbatim replica. The most plausible available synthesis would appear to be that Cicero, as otherwise attested, delivered a pair of *speeches*, almost certainly on two separate days, one in each of two separate processes or phases (*actiones*) of the whole four-day trial, but from the single large volume in which he published them—more or less as delivered, as Nepos attests—excised or abridged all or most of the other material from his role in the trial, such as procedural representations, interrogation of witnesses, and so forth. Thus, essentially, the interpretation of Stroh (1975), 38–9. *Pace* Stroh, however, this passage is at best dubious evidence that Cornelius' trial for *maiestas* was subject to *comperendinatio*—a day's intermission between first and second submissions (with witnesses) of both prosecution and defence, first introduced and made compulsory for cases *de repetundis* in the Lex Servilia of Glaucia in (probably) 101, but not elsewhere attested for any other Republican *quaestio*. In cases of extortion, which were of their very nature normally complex and lengthy, it eliminated *ampliatio*—a completely fresh hearing of both sides, previously required where more than one-third of the jury could not decide its verdict. There is no sign that this, either, applied to the trial of Cornelius. See further, Jones (1972), 53, 71; Greenidge (1901), 477–8, for whom a case of any other kind could also involve two *actiones*, before and after the production of witnesses, but without *comperendinatio*.

[In this case there are three points … the intention of impairing *maiestas*.] This analysis, though substantially correct and founded on the full text of Cicero, is missing in at least one important MS and several early editions of Asconius, and is generally regarded as an interpolation. The Cornelian Law on *maiestas* is of course that instituted by L. Sulla as dictator in 81, which on the rather meagre evidence that we have (*MRR* 2. 75) certainly did cover various quite specific actions. That, however, does not eliminate the possibility that it also included a blanket clause, perhaps tralatician from the *maiestas* law of L. Saturninus (103), to render indictable any conduct deemed to threaten the overriding sovereign power—for Saturninus, if not also for Sulla, that of the Roman people. Such a vague provision naturally left a very great deal open to interpretation. Secondly, given agreement as to what the tribune C. Cornelius had done, was it indictable under the (Sullan) *maiestas* law? And, thirdly, if it was (or even if it was not), did he intend to breach the law of *maiestas*, however interpreted? This analysis of issues is somewhat reminiscent of the jurisprudential models offered in theoretical handbooks of rhetoric current in this period—e.g. *Rhetorica ad Herennium* 1.19–25, esp. 20–1, 23–4. On *maiestas* in general, Lintott (1999*a*), 159–60; Ferrary (1983); above, p. 223.

He is brought to court first before me as praetor in a suit de repetundis. *Obviously Cominius is on the lookout for what is going on: he sees men of straw cast into the open in order to assess the danger.* Cicero's meaning is somewhat obscure, and Asconius offers little enlightenment. The reference is apparently to the initial charge against C. Manilius just after his tribunate, still in 66, at which Cominius turned up to observe the outcome. The use of the present tenses is simply to make the narrative more vivid.

Metellus, a man of the highest birth and sterling quality ... the quality and ranking of C. Curio and the proven early promise of Q. Metellus, adorned with every promise of the highest distinction. Highly complimentary to both parties, Q. Metellus Nepos, cos. 57, son of Q. Nepos, cos. 98; and C. Scribonius Curio, cos. 76.

63C. But the orator takes refuge in the high birth of Metellus and the persistent application of C. Curio in order to conceal their actions, which were more expedient than honourable. Their judicial collusion seems to be known to Asconius but to have been concealed by Cicero.

For there were at the time several persons named Q. Metellus, two of them ex-consuls, Pius and Creticus, of whom it is clear that he is not speaking; and two young men, Nepos and Celer, of whom at this point he is pointing to Nepos. Coss. 80, 69, 57, 60 respectively. Asconius is well informed and provides invaluable evidence on the stemma, here and below.

For the Curio of whom he is talking accused his father Q. Metellus Nepos, son of Baliaricus [*sic*] and grandson of Macedonicus, who was consul with T. Didius; and this Metellus on his deathbed begged this Metellus his son to accuse Curio, his own accuser. The father is Q. Nepos, cos. 98, son of Q. Balearicus, cos. 123 and grandson of the famous Q. Macedonicus, cos. 143. The consuls of 98 (the other being T. Didius) passed important constitutional legislation, see in *MRR* 2. 4.

the same Metellus seized a certain citizen, claiming that he was his own slave, and gave him a beating. To beat another man's slave was to violate his property; to beat a citizen, *ex hypothesi* a free man, violated the Porcian Laws (see on Ascon. 78C, p. 285 below).

64C. he brought false charges against Curio under oath. A more probable interpretation of the Latin, in my view, than an oath that Curio was guilty of *calumnia* (false accusation), which apparently would normally follow only a judicial verdict against Curio and in Metellus' favour—and it seems there was none. Compare events after the case *de repetundis* against Scaurus in 54 (29C).

And Cicero later pursued quarrels with this Metellus; for Metellus turned out to be an evil and disreputable citizen. Nepos entered office as tr. pl. for 62 and immediately attacked Cicero for his execution of Catilinarians (*MRR* 2. 174; also Cic. *Fam.* 5.1; 2).

he had taken control of the state by violence and after starting with good measures had gone on to bad. This was the start of the civil wars, and the reason why Sulpicius himself was regarded as having been justifiably crushed by force of the consuls' arms. That P. Sulpicius' tribunate of 88 started well and then went badly wrong seems to be the view of Cicero, whether entirely his own or a more balanced modification of the totally hostile view almost certainly presented in Sulla's memoirs and visible in nearly all of the rest of the tradition. The victors in Civil Wars, after all, are those who write their history. Hence the view that it was Sulpicius who was responsible for starting the civil wars (by which he seems to mean those of 88, 87, and 83–81 and perhaps the sequel down to 71/70); and that his killing was legally justified—as it could have been only on the view that he was a manifest enemy of state or would-be tyrant, a view ascribed to Sulla at App. *BC* 1.57.253 and by implication at 59.265 and 60.271; Cic. *Brut.* 168; Liv. *Per.* 77; Val. Max. 3.8.5; Flor. 2.9.8; Plut. *Sull.* 10; cf. Vell. 2.19.1. But on the early promise of P. Sulpicius, see Cic. *De Oratore* 1.30, 96–8; 2.89, 107–9, 202–3; and, on his fate, 3.11 'poena temeritatis'. Further, Meier (1980), 224.

65C. By the swiftness of the action, he means the fact that Manilius, as we have already shown, just a few days after he entered his tribunate carried through this same law on the day of the Compitalia. The tribunate began on 10 December 67, and the Compitalia apparently fell on 29 December, the last day of the year (Dio 36.42.2), so that Manilius' compliance with the legally required interval between promulgation and passage (*trinum nundinum*) must have been marginal, though we do not know the date of promulgation, and there is no certainty about the meaning and import of the *trinundinum* (see above, on Ascon. 8C). In any case, however, the day of the festival would be *dies non comitialis*, so that the legislation could readily be invalidated. In 67/6 the Compitalia would have gathered together large crowds of freedmen and slaves, as later on 1 January 58 (see above, on Ascon. 7C). This legislation of Manilius was in favour of freedmen, distributing their vote among all thirty-five tribes, and was violently opposed by the young L. Domitius Ahenobarbus (Schol. Bob. 119St.) and withdrawn almost as soon as passed. Dio 36.42.3–4 says that Manilius allayed the people's wrath at this by blaming Crassus and proposing his other law, notably supported by Cicero, to give Pompey his enormous eastern command against Mithridates.

The praetor made every effort in begging me to undertake the defence of Manilius' case. He means C. Attius Celsus, as has already been said before. It is quite uncertain whether this implies that Celsus' praetorship was in 66 or in 65, and no further conclusions can be drawn from it (Ward (1970), 549). The cross-reference, like those above to Sulpicius' and Manilius' laws on the freedman vote (64–65C) may indicate that Asconius wrote commentary on either or both of Cicero's orations *On Pompey's Command* and *For Manilius*.

One of them was on the voting rights of freedmen. This proposal revived a law of P. Sulpicius tr. pl. 88, rescinded on his death (cf. Livy, *Per.* 77; Cic. *Phil.* 8.7; App. *BC* 1.59.268), but the tribal distribution of the freedman vote had been a matter of contention long before that: for other cases, Treggiari (1969), 39–51, 163–5; Lintott (1999a), 51–2; and on further revival of the proposal by P. Clodius Pulcher in 53 (intended for 52), above, p. 255 on Ascon. 52C; Cic. *Mil.* 87; Tatum (1999), 236–8.

66C. He is speaking about the disruption of the trial of Manilius. As noted above, pp. 265–6, on 60C, apparently early in 65.

He was driven into that bout of madness on the instigation of other important individuals. Cicero doubtless found Manilius' conduct not only dangerous and unlikely to succeed, but also had a genuine aversion from flagrant breaches of law and order (at any rate at this time), and into the bargain saw this incident as a threat, by association, to his own consular ambitions—enough to explain his likely withdrawal from Manilius' defence, which he had originally been set to undertake (perhaps implied by *Comm. Pet.* 51 'in defending Cornelius, accepting the case of Manilius'). After Cicero's earlier denial of collusion between Cornelius and Manilius at the beginning of 66 (64C), the implicit effect of his remarks here is further to dissociate his client Cornelius, whom Cicero *is* perfectly willing to defend as champion of constitutional propriety, from Manilius, contrasting the latter's recklessness in attempting to disrupt his trial *de repetundis* early in 65. Further, after prominently supporting this tribune's law of 66 on Pompey's eastern command and initial readiness in 66/5 to plead for him in court, Cicero needed to distance himself also from the defendant's resort to violence, which he therefore here attributes to a 'bout of madness' incited by anonymous *éminences grises*. From the lemma it is quite unclear whether these 'important' persons are real or fictitious. Compare similar dark hints in his *Oratio in Toga Candida* ap. Ascon. 83C, see below.

He seems to mean L. Catilina and Cn. Piso. Misguidedly or not, Asconius attempts to identify the sinister hidden manipulators and offers his reasons: Catilina was a patrician, had recently held an ex-praetorian command in Africa, was a declared candidate for the consulship, so might perhaps be reckoned not unimportant—and moreover as one facing trial *de repetundis* might be thought to have an interest in subverting the courts. Cn. Piso was much more junior (*quaestor pro praetore* in Spain, 65–4)—a *nobilis*, here labelled 'powerful', 'an instigator of riots', a close associate of Catilina (cf. Sall. *Bell. Cat.* 18.4). That hardly amounts to much 'importance', despite the possible patronage (or not) of M. Crassus, alleged by Sallust (*Bell. Cat.* 19.1) but missing here in Asconius. His suggestions are lent a tinge of colour by Dio's garbled notion (36.44.3–5) that Manilius' trial was vitiated by the failed attempt of Cn. Piso and Catilina as agents of the deposed election-winners P. Sulla and P. Autronius to kill the replacement consuls (for 65) L. Aurelius Cotta and L. Manlius Torquatus—together with Cicero's (*Cat.* 1.15) claim that on 29 December 66 Catilina had appeared at the *comitium* with a weapon. The case, however, is not strong. This, the so-called 'First Catilinarian Conspiracy', most moderns now agree in dismissing as myth: for elegant, succinct, and sufficient summary, Wiseman, *CAH* ix^2, 342–3; Seager (1964). What Asconius says here is not necessarily a reference to this fabrication, still less evidence that he believed in it: he merely attempts comment on Cicero's allegation. See further below, on 83C and 92C.

and at that same time had been arraigned *de repetundis.* More literally 'was a defendant', which should imply that early in 65 his case had not yet come to trial (cf. 85C dating the accusation to 65). This is compatible with the evidence of Cic. *Att.* 1.1–2 of summer 65 that the trial was imminent, but is inconsistent with Sallust's evidence (*Bell. Cat.* 18.3) that Catilina had been indicted and was awaiting trial at the time of the supplementary consular elections of 66, shortly after the conviction for electoral malpractice of the consuls originally designated, P. Autronius and P. Sulla.

His accuser was P. Clodius, a young man himself of rotten character. Clodius' *praevaricatio* is hinted or asserted in several sources, notably Cic. *Att.* 1.2, on his idea of defending Catiline. See above, pp. 203–4; below p. 295 on Ascon. 9C and 87C.

Cn. Piso too, a young man, powerful and a troublemaker, was on good terms with Catilina, party to all his counsels and instigator of riots. This accords with Sallust, *Bell. Cat.* 18.4–5 (as does Ascon. 92C with Sall. *Bell. Cat.* 19.3–5 on his death), who further ascribes influence to M. Crassus (*Bell. Cat.* 19.1) in getting him sent to Spain. The original source might well be Cicero's posthumous political exposé *Expositio Consiliorum Suorum* ('Explanation of his Political Calculations'), see below on Ascon. 83C.

This is the Cotta of whom we have already often spoken, reckoned a great orator and on that score the equal in repute of P. Sulpicius and C. Caesar. This is C. Cotta, cos. 75. For Cicero's views on his skills and reputation as an orator, and those of his coevals, *Brut.* 182, 183, 206–7; *De Orat.* 2.98; 3.31; *Or.* 132. The multiple cross-reference should indicate that Asconius wrote a commentary on at least one earlier speech of Cicero that mentioned C. Cotta—most probably the Verrine dossier (cf. 2 *Verr.* 1.130; 3.18); perhaps *Pro Caecina* (97); *Pro Oppio* (Quintil. 5.13.20, 30, 6.5.10).

For neither in Sallust nor Livy nor Fenestella is there mention of any second law passed by him other than the one which he carried in his consulship against the wishes of the nobility. Asconius' reasoning appears to be that any law not mentioned by these historians cannot have been important. Yet from the immediate sequel (67C) is it clear that he knows of one on private lawsuits, and there may have been another to authorize consuls instead of censors to let state contracts (Cic. *Verr.* 2.3.18–19, 130; Ps.-Ascon. 251St.). That his law on ex-tribunes' rights was passed 'against the wishes of the nobility' does not necessarily make C. Cotta hostile to the aristocracy, for it may have been a matter of appeasing popular unrest already evident a year earlier, led by the tribune Cn. Sicinius. Sallust, *Hist.* 3.48.8 regards this Cotta as *ex factione media*, but it is still debated whether this phrase means 'from the heart of the power-group' or 'from a power-group holding the middle-ground' (i.e. between populists and extreme aristocrats). His known connections and recognizable Latin usage strongly favour the first interpretation, so that he was deemed to have passed this law despite them. For pertinent remarks on restoration of tribunes' rights after Sulla's severe restrictions, Lintott (1999*a*), 205, 210–11; on popular agitations of the 70s, *CAH* ix^2, 208–15; Millar (1998), ch. 3, 49–72. While it is clear that Asconius was familiar with Sallust's *Histories*, his use of the *Bellum Catilinae* is far less certain (see above, on the so-called 'First Catilinarian Conspiracy').

67C. And all of them attained the consulship. In 75, 74, 65. L. Cotta's judiciary law (above, pp. 213–14 on Ascon. 17C) belongs to his praetorship of 70.

He means L. Licinius Crassus the orator and Q. Mucius Scaevola, *pontifex maximus*, who was also himself an orator and legal expert. ... [68C]. For at a time when the Italic peoples were gripped by extreme eagerness for the Roman citizenship, and on that account a large portion of them was behaving as if they were Roman citizens, legislation appeared to be a necessity so that each man should be restored to his proper legal rights in his own community. This is the notorious consular law of 95, the Lex Licinia Mucia, legally impeccable, politically inept. Both these consuls, who despite a marriage link did not see eye to eye in all things (above, 14–15C), appear to have belonged to the reformist end of the aristocratic spectrum in Roman politics. In particular note L. Crassus' inspiration and support for the tribunician programme of M. Livius Drusus in 91; also his offer to defend T. Matrinius of Spoletium, enfranchised as a colonist under Saturninus' law of 100 but indicted under this very statute (Cic. *Balb.* 48–9). On their legal and rhetorical skills, Cic. *Brut.* 115 (with *De Orat.* 1.229), 145–8, 155, 163, 194; Pompon. *Dig.* 1.2.2.41. That both consuls undertook this legislation clearly indicates the importance attached to it. Their underlying intention arguably was to clarify matters (and possibly to appease reactionary opinion in Rome) in order to lay foundations for later progress towards broadening the Roman franchise, on the principle that it was proper 'not to permit a person who was not a citizen to be treated as if he were' (Cic. *Off.* 3.47). On the view that this law was a partisan move for 'the Metellan group' against C. Marius and his adherents, see Badian (1957); Gruen (1968), 202–3; Marshall (1985*b*), 243–4.

In Cicero's Latin here there is perhaps some surface ambiguity in the use of the verb *redigere*, which in its literal sense would mean 'lead back', and suggest bodily expulsion, but can equally well be used solely in a juridical sense to refer to re-registration in appropriate census-lists of the communities concerned. Despite the rhetoric of Cic. *Sest.* 30 and Schol. Bob. 129 St. ad loc., it is highly improbable, given the clear distinction made by Cicero in *Off.* 3.47 between this law and expulsion acts, that this law provided for actual physical expulsion of Latins and Italian allies visiting Rome or even resident there, which would have been virtually impracticable and unenforceable. Neither did it deprive of citizen's rights any ally who had been legally enfranchised, or bar the way to future legal enfranchisement (Cic. *Balb.* 54). It did, however, establish a *quaestio* ('inquisition') to investigate and try cases of alleged usurpation (Cic. *Balb.* 48; cf. Diod. 37.13), and most probably required inspection and revision of census lists, both at Rome and in allied communities.

However, by this law the loyalties of the magnates ... Note that it was the magnates of the Italian peoples who were of crucial importance in these developments, not the rank-and-file. It is evident that, legitimately or not, they had in recent years been exercising the rights of Roman citizens, and that they saw as threat to this practice the *quaestio* which this law established to investigate contested cases. Whether it was really the (or a) fundamental cause of the Marsic (or Social) War that broke out in 91/90 is still much debated. In giving the date Asconius' Latin formula means 'after three whole years but less than four' but is at best ambiguous and misleading, for even if the war might be said to have been 'set in train' (*exortum*) earlier, there were no hostilities at all before the late autumn or early winter of 91, and none on a serious scale until the spring of 90, although it is possible that the law belongs to the very end of their consulship rather than to its early months before Crassus (at least) went off to his province, Cisalpine Gaul.

One is of the kind when it is resolved that a law should be abrogated. On abrogation in general, Richardson (1998); see also Lintott (1999*a*), 62, 87; Carson (1988). Cic. *Rep.* 3.33 has four verbs— *obrogare; derogare; abrogare;* and *solvere*. Technically, the senate could pass a resolution expressing its advice, wishes, or preferences, but whatever it might achieve by interpretation could not (in this period) actually delete or even modify the letter of statute law. Hence Asconius' use of the standard rubric for a resolution decree of the senate (*senatus consultum*) 'it is the senate's pleasure that …', meaning 'the senate resolves that…'.

in the consulship of Q. Caecilius and M. Iunius, that the laws which were impairing military efficiency should be abrogated. In 109, when military resources were strained in confronting Jugurtha under Metellus (Numidicus) and the Cimbri and their allies under M. Iunius Silanus. Warfare against the Northmen had been going badly ever since their first appearance on Roman horizons, in 113. The law(s) that were deemed to be causing difficulty were probably those of C. Gracchus, passed in his tribunate of 123. Despite this measure of 109, problems with military efficiency and catastrophic defeats persisted down to (and indeed after) final victory over the Northmen in 101. (e.g. note the edict of P. Rutilius Rufus as cos. 105 after the disaster at Arausio to prevent men of military age leaving Italy.)

I think you remember that these are the Livian Laws. Not necessarily a cross-reference to an earlier commentary: just as easily taken as an item of elementary common historical knowledge.

69C. Philippus the consul … procured from the senate a vote that all his laws should be disallowed by a single senatorial decree. It was decided that they had been passed contrary to the auspices, and that the people was not bound by them. The laws remained unrepealed in a technical sense but it was the view of the senate and its advice to magistrates and people that they had no validity, because they were enacted improperly, that is, 'contrary to the auspices'—a matter on which Philippus as an augur (Cic. *Leg.* 2.14; 31) would have exerted considerable authority, especially if he also had the support of the augural college. Variant reasons are given elsewhere for the invalidation: (1) violation of the Lex Caecilia Didia of 98, possibly for ignoring omens rather than accumulation of disparate proposals under a single head; or lack of a *trinundinum* (see pp. 200–1 above, on Ascon. 8C) between promulgation and passage (Cic. *Dom.* 41, with Lintott (1999*b*), 140–1 and (1999*a*) 62, 87); (2) passage *per vim* ('by use of force'), as in Liv. *Per.* 71; Florus 2.5.9.

This Calpurnian Law was about ambitus. C. Calpurnius Piso as consul had passed it two years before, and in it besides the other penalties a financial one was added. The previous law of Sulla (81) had debarred anyone convicted for ten years from any further candidature (Schol. Bob. 78 St.). Piso's law of 67 barred them from senate and magistracies altogether and imposed fines (Dio 36.38.1), and also probably penalized recipients of bribes (Cic. *Mur.* 47). An increasing intensity of electoral competition in the conditions of the 60s and 50s is readily detectable. See further Cloud in *C\H* ix², 515–17.

the second consulship of Scipio, seven years after peace was granted to the Carthaginians in the Second Punic War. That is, in 194.

C. Atilius Serranus … The MSS offer no *praenomen*. Identification as 'C.' i.e. the praetor of 185—is humanist supplement (Manutius). Also available is 'A.', the praetor of 192, perhaps better, preferred by editors of Livy (34.54.3) and *MRR* 1. 343, 346 n. 2.

And in this speech, anyhow, Cicero appears to have followed this author. To be able to advance this idea Asconius must have believed that Antias wrote and published—at any rate on the early second century—before 65 BC, which accords tolerably well with the rather vague and unsatisfactory evidence of Vell. 2.9.4 that he was a contemporary of Claudius Quadrigarius, Rutilius Rufus (!) and L. Sisenna. On the other hand, it conflicts with the case argued but perhaps not quite proven from an impressive dossier of circumstantial evidence by Wiseman (1979), 113–21; Cloud (1977), 225–7, that Antias' work dates to the early 40s.

70C. **But in the speech which he delivered some years later** *On the Answer of the Haruspices,* **he appears to indicate that Scipio did not** *allow* **it, but was himself the initiator in allocating room for senators.** Moreover, at least in the later speech, quoted below by Asconius (not quite correctly—*Har. Resp.* 24), Cicero also differs from Antias (and Livy, 34.44.5; but cf. 54.4) in making the festival in question the Megalensian Games, for the Magna Mater, not the Roman Games.

('X' also) writes that this was granted to the senate (by Scipio) and his colleague Sempronius Longus. Apparently a third version, with the source's name lost. Quite probably Fenestella, from whom Asconius often differs.

71C. **The passage where he is listing the contexts, when a law is being carried, in which a veto may be entered, before the one who is carrying**

the law bids the people to take up its stations. There follows important evidence for legislative procedure in the tribal assemblies; unfortunately the lacunae of the MSS impede interpretation. More in Taylor (1966), esp. 39–54, 74–8; Hall (1964); Staveley (1972); Meier (1968); Rilinger (1989); Lintott (1999*a*), 40–64; Millar (1998), 81–2.

take up its stations. On the technical terminology (*discedere*), Lintott (1999*a*), 46 n. 29.

(?those ... who have the right to cast a vote?) are being transferred; that is ... a law (? while being carried may be vetoed?). I translate what seem to be the likeliest supplements where the MSS show lacunae, but the process of 'transference' remains obscure, not readily to be identified with that of 'dispersal' as explained by Asconius in what follows. It just might refer to the allocation of a tribe to any persons present of Latin status who wished to vote, but by 65 they can have been only very few. Even so, the technical possibility may still have existed for Cicero to cite in his speech.

However, it is clear that one thing which was done while this man was himself tribune should not be passed over. 'This man' is of course Cornelius the defendant, tr. pl. in 67. Cicero's point is simply that Gabinius in driving through his anti-pirate measure in that same year against conservative opposition (led by Q. Catulus, Q. Hortensius, and the consul C. Piso) had gone much further than Cornelius, and with impunity. The obvious parallel precedent is the measure of Ti. Gracchus to depose his tribunician colleague M. Octavius in 133. See Lintott (1999*a*), 207–8.

72C. after seventeen tribes accepted the proposal so that there was (only) one too few, and only one remained for confirmation of the people's command. Eighteen of the thirty-five tribes constituted the required simple majority. This passage appears to show, if not quite conclusively that they voted in succession, at least that their votes were declared one after another. More in Hall (1964), 284–6; Taylor (1966), 78; Staveley (1972), 181–2.

73C. *This cause I defended in a* contio *as praetor, but in very different terms.* Here we have the date (66) of the latest decision on Faustus Sulla and the contested assets, and evidence that Cicero's overall position on this issue was more moderate, in the *contio* which he mentions, than the language attributed to him, i.e. attacking a 'tyrannical minority' for malicious 'hatred' (Arusianus Messius = *Corn.* 2, frs. 11–13 P, but perhaps a fiction). The 'inequitable circumstances' alleged as grounds for Cicero's protestations on behalf of Faustus and the jury's decision consisted in the supposedly unfair degree of authority and influence enjoyed by the accuser as tribune (Cic. *Clu.* 94–5). The issue was still alive in 63 (Cic. *Leg. Agr.* 1, 12).

Because in earlier times there had been a dearth of public funds in the treasury, many remedies had been sought for this problem. There had certainly been such a crisis, albeit with somewhat different remedies, in 88 (Cic. *De Imp. Cn. Pomp.* 19; App. *Mith.* 22) and another in 75–4 (Sall. *Hist.* 2.47.6–7; 98.2; 98.7–10 M), and renewed fears of similar problems in 66 (*De Imp. Cn. Pomp.* 14–16). On defalcations by Sulla the dictator, App. *Mith.* 62; Plut. *Sull.* 25, with Plin. *NH* 33.16; cf. 14 for his death as 'the richest man in Rome'. For financial stringency in this period, Barlow (1980), 211.

the influence enjoyed by the Sullan party. Readily identified as the hard-core *optimates* featuring the five 'most powerful senators' of the day, named at 60C and 79C as bearing hostile testimony against Cornelius.

that anyone should render account for money and property that he had received. I translate by far the likeliest restoration of the MSS text, a formulation in legal language of the matter in hand, probably originating either in what was demanded of Faustus Sulla and others like him, or in the obstructive senatorial decree. On the technicalities of the case against Faustus Sulla, Shatzman (1972), 196. Later there was a Lex Iulia, mentioned in several passages of the *Digest*, to regulate 'residual public funds' and prevent their embezzlement—e.g. *Dig.* 13.13.4.3.

However, how many hearings were annulled at an earlier time I forbear to mention. According to Asconius (or his MSS), this follows the previous lemma *immediately*, which would show that Cicero is still referring, as in the previous quotation, to annulment or suspension of jurisdiction by the manipulation of interested parties, but here prefers to avoid explicit citation of cases and detail, on the pretext that they are familiar to the jury and that he wishes to deny any wish to revive old litigation, but quite possibly in fact because the precedents were much better justified than attempts to rescue Faustus Sulla.

In the Italian War ... at a time when many were being unjustly condemned under the Varian Law ... the senate decreed that the courts should not remain in use for the duration of the Italic upheaval. It would seem that this suspension of the courts was all that Asconius could call to mind as likely to be what Cicero meant by way of precedent for later interference discussed above. It is, however, uncomfortably distant in time, and if it was in fact what Cicero intended, his denial of any wish to revive cases under the Lex Varia must be regarded as one of his more ponderous jokes, for by 65 there was not the remotest chance that he (or anyone) would be willing or able to do anything of the kind. More likely, Cicero was referring to attempted litigation of the 70s or early 60s.

Nevertheless, Asconius provides valuable information on the scope and effects of the Lex Varia (debated by Gruen (1965a); Seager (1967); Badian

(1969)) and consequent attempts on the part of the senate to promote political concord in Rome in the crisis of the Italian War in suppressing the pursuit of political enmities by suspending the operation of the courts. From Cic. *Brut.* 304–5, it would seem that other courts were suspended while the Varian court continued for a time before itself (probably but not certainly) being suspended.

74C. a decree which had often been demanded in mass meetings of the people. Popular demand for this, amid widespread disquiet at the loss of able leaders who fell victims to the Varian witch-hunt, is attested by App. *BC* 1.37.165–38.169. On popular demand for various measures in which the people had vested interests, Lintott (1999*a*), 205. Those known to have been attacked under the Varian Law are M. Scaurus (evaded); C. Cotta (convicted, exiled); L. Calpurnius Bestia (did not face trial, exiled); Q. Pompeius Rufus (cos. 88, so not convicted); ?L. Memmius (Cic. *Brut.* 304) on whom see *MRR* 3. 142—outcome unknown, unless he is the same person as Asconius mentions below (see next lemma) or identical with the person whom Appian, *BC* 1.37 calls L. Mummius Achaicus (convicted though wrongly identified as the cos. of 146 in Appian); M. Antonius cos. 99, apparently acquitted; Q. Varius himself, under his own law, condemned and killed; Cn. Pomponius (below, p. 287, on Ascon. 79C)—outcome unknown.

Among those who had feared these trials there survived as a powerful figure at that time especially C. Curio, father of the younger Curio who belonged to the Caesarian party in the Civil War. The elder Curio held a consulship, probably delayed by the events of the past decade, in 76. Why Asconius should single him out for mention as especially influential at the time of the Social War is beyond guessing: in 90 he was a tribune, and on one occasion was deserted by a *contio* (Cic. *Brut.* 305). His name is, however, a restoration in the MSS, and sometimes disputed: perhaps the correct reading is L. (for MSS C., an easy alteration) Memmius, father-in-law to C. Curio the elder, not his son the Caesarian tribune of 50, on whom see Lacey (1961), with whom, on this view, Asconius confuses him.

Cn. Dolabella would not have debarred C. Volcacius, that most honourable man, from standard, everyday rights at law. Cicero here seeks to show the need for Cornelius' law on the Praetorian Edict by citing some bad decisions that could have been avoided had it been in force earlier. Cn. Dolabella is apparently Cn. f. Cn. n., praetor (probably urban) in 81.

There were at the time two persons named Cn. Dolabella. Caesar prosecuted one of them, M. Scaurus the other. They are the aforementioned praetor, probably *urbanus* 81, who is Cn. Cornelius Cn. f. Cn. n. Dolabella, prosecuted successfully by the young M. Scaurus *de repetundis* regarding his command in Cilicia; and Cn. Cornelius P. f. L. n. Dolabella, cos. 81, unsuccessfully but famously prosecuted by the young C. Caesar *de repetundis* regarding Macedonia. See above, on 26C.

Nor … would L. Sisenna, a man far different from those persons … have refused to grant possession of Cn. Cornelius' property in accordance with his own edict to P. Scipio. L. Cornelius Sisenna, respected as historian of the Social and Civil wars of the 80s down to at least 83 (Cic. *Brut.* 228; *Leg.* 1.7; Sall. *Bell. Jug.* 95.2; fragments in *HRR* 1. 276–95), who as praetor held both the urban and peregrine jurisdictions in 78, provides the last of Cicero's several instances of praetorian decision contrary to edict, cited to vindicate Cornelius' tribunician law on the subject. 'P. Scipio' is plausibly identified as the last of the line, adopted by Q. Metellus Pius to become Q. Metellus Scipio, cos. 52, anything but the worthy character here presented by Cicero. The identity of the Cn. Cornelius whose property was at issue is open to conjecture, as is the basis of the claim, but one possibility may be Cn. Cornelius Cn. f. Cn. n. Dolabella, pr. 81, convicted *de repetundis* most probably precisely in the year of L. Sisenna's praetorship—i.e. 78. For dealings with property after conviction, perhaps compare the aftermath of Milo's in 52–50, on which see above, p. 257 on Ascon. 54C. On the other hand, the case could have been concerned with any one of a much wider range of issues at Civil Law, reviewed by Lintott (1977), citing also Watson (1971), 71–2, 188–9; and (1965), 232–3.

when the Roman people perceived this, and was informed by the tribunes of the plebs that if some penalty were not to be added against the distributors of bribes, it was impossible to eliminate ambitus, it pressed for this law of Cornelius, and rejected the one which was being carried in accordance with the senatorial decree. Evidently Cornelius' proposals of 67 against *ambitus* were in this respect superior to those which were offered by the senate and were eventually passed instead as C. Piso's consular Lex Calpurnia *de ambitu.* See p. 277 above, on Ascon. 69C.

75C. He is referring to P. Sulla and P. Autronius. L. Cotta and L. Torquatus … appointed in their place. Prosecution *de ambitu* of magistrates designate by defeated rivals was common, success rare, especially regarding the consulship. In fact it was not L. Torquatus cos. suff. 65 who prosecuted in this case in person, but his son (Cic. *Sull.* 49–50; *Fin.* 2.62), but it is not clear that Asconius is guilty of worse error than over-compression.

it could be that there is some other Cornelius … a collegium *of them has even been instituted.* The plausible view is that Cicero here is bent on rebutting an allegation that a slave named Phileros, belonging to a Cornelius, had been involved in rioting—from the context in Cicero's speech, apparently to hinder the passage of Piso's law on *ambitus*. The mention of a *collegium* of Cornelii is best seen as a reference to the large numbers (allegedly as many as 10,000) of slaves manumitted by Sulla on the liquidation in 82/1 of their proscribed masters, and perhaps organized to dominate the streets of Rome—for a time (App. *BC* 1.100.469). Compare the alleged plans of Clodius in 58 (Dio 39.23.2, above, p. 255 on Ascon. 52C).

For this reason later on *collegia* were suppressed, both by senatorial decree and by several laws, with the exception of a few whose legality was well established and which the public interest required. Genuine old trade associations, often linked to a particular locality, for social and religious purposes were acceptable: gangs of thugs collected to disrupt public life were not. Hence various measures concerning the latter—a senatorial decree in 64 to suppress them (Ascon. 7C); their restoration by Clodius in 58; another senatorial decree to disband political clubs in 56 (Cic. *QF.* 2.3.5); a consular Lex Licinia of Crassus in 55 to curb (at least) the electoral activities of *sodalicia* (*MRR* 2. 215); later controls in a Lex Iulia *de vi publica* (*Dig.* 47.22.2).

that utterance of extreme emergency, that those who wished for the safety of the state. Appeals in these terms had been made in the past in times of crisis, as for instance (allegedly) by the young Scipio Africanus after the battle of Cannae in 215 (Livy 22.53.7), and by P. Scipio Nasica at the height of the disturbances involving Ti. Gracchus in 133 (Vell. Pat. 2.3.1; Val. Max. 3.2.17).

C. Piso ... in the process of carrying a law *de ambitu* ... thrown out of the Forum, had issued the edict to which Cicero refers, and come down with a larger band of men about him to secure the passage of the law. Piso's edict was in the standard form for a magistrate (or perhaps anyone) who invoked an emergency levy which—allegedly—threatened the safety of the state, and was the only legal basis on which he could seek reinforcements for his lictors by way of recruiting more manpower to secure the passage of his law against disruptives. Dio 36.39.1 appears to refer to this in saying that the senate voted the consuls a bodyguard for this purpose. Compare Cic. *Rab. Perd.* 20–1 (cf. 26); Val. Max. 3.2.18; Ps.-Vict. *Vir. Ill.* 72.9 on events of 100, when at the instigation of M. Scaurus, *princeps senatus*, and with the backing of a senatorial decree (apparently a version of the so-called 'ultimate decree'— see above, p. 198 on Ascon. 5C), a posse was raised by the consuls (and included other leading notables) against Saturninus; also the action in 133 of P. Popillius Laenas against Ti. Gracchus; Pompey's levy in Picenum as a *privatus* in 83. See further on such levies Lintott (1999*b*), 160; Linderski

(1984), 74–80, esp. 77 and n. 17, 79, who likens them to those of the *tumultus* in the strict sense—the emergency caused by sudden invaders from outside the city, typically Gauls or Italians (Cic. *Phil.* 8.3; but see also Livy 26.9–10 (211 BC); Sall. *Hist.* 1.69; 3.48.9 M; App. *BC* 1.107.503 (78 BC)). Asconius himself, however, uses the term at 45C of the riots in 66 allegedly incited by C. Manilius as tribune to secure passage of his law on the tribal distribution of freedmen's votes. Compare also his usage at 48C, where 'a mob of social dregs gathered and rioted (*tumultuata est*) at the high price of corn'; Florus 2.4 of the riot in 100 cited above.

76C. M. Crassus and Cn. Pompeius are meant, of whom Crassus at the time was sitting on the jury in Cornelius' trial, Pompeius was waging the Mithridatic War in Asia. Neither was likely to accept that their restoration as coss. 70 of full pre-Sullan powers to tribunes had turned out badly or to fail to defend them in 67. Pompey's enormous military powers had been granted him by Manilius' law, and Cornelius was plainly his supporter and perhaps 'agent'; Crassus was on the jury for Cornelius' trial and censor at the time and, whatever his views on Cornelius as an individual, would not readily allow his legislation of 70 to be undermined.

restored religiously sanctioned laws. An item perhaps open to dispute even in Asconius' day in what is in any case a hideously tangled tradition on the early development of the tribunate. Modern analyses are legion, among which see Ogilvie (1965), 309–11, 380–2, 489; *CAH* VII.2², 212–35; Cornell (1995), 258–65; summary in Lintott (1999*a*), 121 and n. 1. It is clear, however, that the setting up of the tribunate was a major item in the historical tradition of *populares* in the first century BC (see Sallust, *Bell. Jug.* 31, 41–2; *Hist.* 3.48 M). The principal sources for the 'first' institution of the tribunate are Livy 2.32–3, 58.1 (but 3.52.1, 54.9–10); Dion. Hal. 6.89; 9.41; Diod. 11.68, 12.24; Cic. *Brut.* 54; *Rep.* 2.5. Note that Asconius is at least as much interested in Cicero's wording as in the date and the original number of tribunes (see below), and thought his MS of Cicero corrupt in reading 'restored' (*restituerunt*) rather than 'instituted' (*constituerunt*), being convinced—probably rightly—that this occasion saw the creation of a new office, not any sort of revival.

consecrated as an eternal monument the hill beyond the Anio on which they had taken up their station under arms. It was clearly significant in the *popularis* tradition that the plebs had not merely seceded, but had done so under arms (Sall. *Bell. Cat.* 33.3; *Jug.* 31.6; 31.17; *Hist.* 1.11. M, 1.55.23 M, 3.48.1 M).

A. Verginius Tricostus and L. Veturius Cicurinus. In 494, otherwise recognized as the traditional date.

77C. On the other hand, some relate that it was not two tribunes of the plebs, as Cicero says, who were appointed, but five, one from each of the classes. And some said four (Diod. 11.68.8–9—in 471). That there were five was the version adopted by the second-century annalist C. Piso (frs. 22–3 P—an increase in 471 from two to five), apparently before C. Tuditanus and others (below). Livy (above) has two variants.

among them Tuditanus and Pomponius Atticus and our friend Livy. For the annalist C. Sempronius Tuditanus (cos. 129) and Cicero's equestrian friend T. Pomponius Atticus, see Index of Personal Names. Some take Asconius' wording *Livius noster* ('our Livy') as evidence that Asconius, like Livy, came from Patavium (Padua), but it may mean not 'our fellow-citizen', but 'our favourite'.

L. Sicinius Velutus, son of Lucius; L. Albinius Paterculus, son of Gaius. Needless to say, the extant tradition gives variants, which Asconius ignores, concentrating on Cicero's own preoccupation with number, date, and nature of the process. Likewise he shows no awareness of an increase to ten tribunes in 457 (Livy 3.30.7), but that is most probably simply because Cicero did not include it in this oration.

the second institution of tribunes. The main source is Livy 3.50–54 (preliminaries in 40–9); also Dion. Hal. *AR* 10.30.2. Discussion and more material in Ogilvie (1965), 446, 476–8, 494–5, 550–1; *CAH* VII.2², 227–35.

who it was of the *decem viri* [Board of Ten] who granted ownership contrary to claims of free status, and who was the father against whose daughter he made this decision. The story is presented as high melodrama and at some length in Livy 3.44–50 (see Ogilvie (1965), ad loc.); more briefly in Dion. Hal. *AR* 11.28–30; Diod. 12.24; Cic. *Rep.* 2.62. The legal issues involve fundamental concepts of Roman institutions and law, among them clientship; summons to law (*in ius vocatio*); claims to property, including slaves (*manus iniectio*); thereby asserting (*adserere, adsertio*) a claim to ownership (*dominium*) of an item of property (*mancipium*), made over by judicial assignment (*addictio*) on the part of the judge; a suit over status (*vindiciae*) resulting in confirmation of liberty or slavery (*vindicatio in* (or *secundum*) *libertatem* or *servitutem*). Many moderns regard the story of Verginia as myth: for variant opinions, e.g. Ogilvie (1965), on Livy 3.44–6; Watson (1975), 95–6, 100, 168–9, 171; Cornell (1995), 10–11, 13, 273, 275.

The envoys whose names … The *pontifex maximus* was M. Papirius. Livy agrees in specifying the same persons as envoys, but the somewhat suspect name of Q. Furius (whose *praenomen* is otherwise unknown among the Furii, but he also appears as cos. 441 (*MRR* 1. 54–5) as colleague of

M. Papirius!) as *pontifex maximus*. This is the first appearance of the office in Roman records. Further, Mommsen (1887–8), 2. 36. n. 2.

78C. *These more recent cases also I let pass.* That is, apparently, of important tribunician legislation.

the Porcian Law, the fundament of liberty based on pure justice. Since there appear to have been as many as three Leges Porciae, if it is the case that in this context Cicero is reviewing successful and famous *tribunician* legislation, this one (at least) should have been passed by a tribune, and the other two far more probably by persons holding other offices, one of them in that case M. Cato cos. 195, the famous censor, who did not hold the tribunate. All three, however, appear to have dealt with the Roman citizen's right of appeal against summary punishment (*coercitio*) by a magistrate outside Rome and in particular with corporal punishment (Cato, *ORF* 8. fr. 117; Cic. *Rep.* 2. 54; 2 *Verr.* 1.14, 5.151, 163, 173; *Rab. Post.* 8, 12; Sall. *Bell. Cat.* 51.21 and 40; Livy 10.9.4; Gell. 10.3.13). Since Cicero appears to be reviewing tribunes' laws in chronological order, the Porcian Law here in question should pre-date the Cassian Law of 137 (see below). The only Porcius *known* to have held the tribunate before that date is P. Porcius Laeca, tr. pl. 199. There are other Porcii whose careers are imperfectly known and *may* have done so. Of these, L. Porcius Licinus pr. 207 and P. Porcius Laeca cos.184 are unlikely, since any tribunate held by either, if it featured famous legislation, would hardly be missing in extant Livy, where there is no sign of it. This leaves M. Porcius Cato (Licinianus), pr. elect *c*.152; L. Porcius (Laeca?), senator *c*.165 (*MRR* 1. 495); L. Porcius Licinus, naval prefect 172.

a Cassius passed a law that the people should cast its votes by ballot. Perhaps because Cicero's own speech skipped the details, Asconius is incomplete here, giving neither date (137), identity of author (L. Cassius Longinus Ravilla, cos. 127), nor precise scope (the secret ballot applicable only to trials before the people, except those for *perduellio*—?treachery in warfare). More detail and evidence in *MRR* 1. 485; also Marshall (1985*b*), 269–70. Asconius does, however, have more to say of the less famous Cassius who follows. On the great importance of the *leges tabellariae* (Gabinia, 139; Cassia, 137; Papiria, 131 or 130; Coelia, 107), note Cic. *Leg.* 3.34–5; *CAH* IX², 45–6; 60–1; Millar (1998), 25–6.

L. Cassius Longinus, son of Lucius, tribune of the plebs in the consulship of C. Marius and L. Flavius, passed several laws. The known legislation of this tribune of 104 is confined to the law here outlined by Asconius. A colleague, Cn. Domitius Ahenobarbus, seems to have been at least as active, or more so, in attacking the *nobiles*—for example, by legislating for the election of the *pontifex maximus* by the people (*MRR* 1. 559–60).

Q. Servilius who had been consul two years before, and whose power of command the people abrogated because of his failure against the Cimbri. This is Q. Caepio, cos. 106, author of a judiciary law to split juries between senators and knights and disastrously defeated, with his successor Cn. Mallius, by the Cimbri at Arausio (Orange) in Gaul, in 105, causing panic and a declared state of emergency in Rome (*MRR* 1. 555, 557). On abrogation, with other instances, Lintott (1999*a*), 62 and n. 96.

Those persons who ... believed that they should cling to this at any cost, however great, were the deadly enemies of C. Cotta. Cicero alleges their utter determination to retain Sulla's bar on further office for ex-tribunes, removed by Cotta's consular legislation of 75. That they conceived 'deadly enmity' for Cotta as a result is highly implausible, especially if Sallust's description of him as *ex factione media* means 'from the heart of the dominant power-group', which as a Metellan connection he certainly was (see above, p. 274 on 66C).

the plebs so constituted. Literally 'that plebs' or perhaps 'that part of the plebs'—referring to its 'more respectable' components—e.g. the knights and others of greater rank and means than the proletariat.

the Aurelian Law ... which L. Roscius Otho consolidated two years before (this speech), in a measure whereby fourteen rows (of seats) should be granted to Roman knights for watching public spectacles. The Aurelian Law is (again) that of L. Cotta, pr. 70, so often cited by Cicero and Asconius, see above, pp. 213–14 on Ascon. 17C. How the Lex Roscia of 67 might be thought to have 'consolidated' it is difficult to see. It certainly did nothing to improve or confirm the legal rights and powers of the knights. It did, however, restore this recognition of the standing and function of *equites* alongside senators in public life, evidently lost at some earlier time—though perhaps as recently as the reforms of Sulla (81). It remains a thorny question what is meant in this context by the term *equites*. On one view (Wiseman (1970*b*)) they are defined here as those members of the eighteen equestrian centuries, awarded the 'public horse' by the censors (last operative in 70). Alternatively (Badian (1983)), they were those possessed of the equestrian property qualification, a census rating of HS 400,000 in land, a much wider category, especially after large-scale enfranchisement of Italian magnates after the Social War. These might include the somewhat obscurely named *tribuni aerarii*. The latter view, in my view, is preferable; the law may be said to have 'consolidated' the two categories, which in several cases Cicero saw reason to present undifferentiated as '*equites*', not least at *Mur.* 40, where, as Badian argues, he would otherwise have given considerable offence to a third of the jury—that is, the *tribuni aerarii*—in so praising the law's provisions. True, Roscius did support C. Trebellius against Gabinius (Dio 36.24.4; 30.3; Ascon 72C), which might suggest cautious conservatism, but that was hardly less characteristic of Italian magnates than of the senators' sons and the old *equites equo publico* who had formed the traditional eighteen equestrian centuries of the *comitia centuriata*. The 'equestrians' of the 60s were not in any case a social and political monolith, any more than were the senators. As membership of the senate was elective, not hereditary, most senators also started life as *equites*. See further, *MRR* 2. 145; Henderson (1963), 61–2, citing Cic. *Phil.* 2.44 (of 44) perhaps anachronistically for the situation in 63; Wiseman (1970*b*), esp. for collected evidence; Badian (1983), 84–5, and 144 nn. 9–14.

79C. *a person much hated by the gods and the nobility, Cn. Pomponius, pleaded his defence on a charge* de maiestate *under the Varian Law.* Although not all the components in the argument are equally cogent, there is a strong case for rejecting the MSS reading *Cn. Pompeius* and emending to refer instead to Cn. Pomponius, tr. pl. 90 (*MRR* 2. 26), ally of the infamous Q. Varius (Cic. *Brut.* 305; cf. 311) and on this evidence tried under Varius' own law. See Badian (1969), 467–74 and Marshall (1985*b*), 273–4.

Defence of Cornelius. This heading in the MSS evidently marks the beginning of Asconius' comments on the second of Cicero's speeches for Cornelius.

Surely you are not in difficulty over the identity of these witnesses? Cicero professes reluctance to believe that the jury would hesitate to acquit Cornelius just because of the rank and standing of the five consulars ranged against him, and offers reason why they should not take such a view.

Mam. Lepidus. On the case for emending MSS 'M. Lepidus' (there being no surviving ex-consul of that name in 65) to 'Mam. Lepidus' (cos. 77) rather than 'M'. Lepidus' (cos. 66), see above on Ascon. 60C.

80C. *Q. Catulus, that man so fully endowed with wisdom and humanity.* One might suspect a hint of irony. Lutatius Catulus, cos. 78, was perhaps not the most conspicuous example of these virtues—but he was a senior consular, with electoral influence, which, however, in 64, if not also in 63, he may have exerted against Cicero in favour of L. Catilina. He was also in some way influential in the escape of Catilina in 73 from a charge of violating the Vestal Fabia, half-sister to Cicero's wife Terentia: see below, p. 301 on Ascon. 91C; more in Lewis (2001*a*).

your own uncle, that most illustrious and patriotic of men. Cn. Domitius Ahenobarbus, tr. pl. 104, cos. 96.

M. Silanus had been consul five years before Domitius was tribune of the plebs, and himself also had failed against the Cimbri. For this reason Domitius indicted him before the people. M. Iunius Silanus was cos. 109 (above, 68C), his trial of 104, which ended in acquittal, parallel with that of another failed commander against the Northmen, Q. Servilius Caepio, cos. 106 (see above on Ascon. 78C), who was exiled. L. Cassius Longinus, cos. 107, was also badly defeated by them and killed in the battle. At this point in Roman history, before any law of *maiestas* existed, the indictment would have been for *perduellio*, treason, and the accused would have been brought to trial before the people in the tribal assembly.

issued a written memorandum about him. The Latin is highly obscure. This is by no means certainly the meaning, but circulation of such an item, somewhat like a modern 'handout leaflet', is likelier than the issue of rigged voting tablets or declaration from a written document, either of the verdict delivered or, before it, simply of how the accuser wished the people to vote. For review of these possibilities, Marshall (1985*b*), 279–80.

81C. *This is the kind of dispute in which as tribunes of the plebs Cn. Domitius gets my approval, M. Terpolius that of Catulus.* Of course Terpolius was by no means the only political featherweight to hold the tribunate after Sulla and before the part-restoration of status by C. Cotta in 75—or indeed after it. There were plenty of such persons in Sulla's senate too, easily dominated by such as Q. Catulus—which is Cicero's point. In his view (as presented in this speech, anyhow), tribunes should be able and assertive, but in sound causes.

Cornelius was acquitted by a large number of votes. This may be pertinent to an incident in late 63 or early 62, recorded by Plutarch, *Cat. Min.* 28. One of the new tribunes, Q. Metellus Nepos, proposed a law to recall Pompey in order to deal with the remnants of the Catilinarian insurrection. M. Cato, also tribune, interposed his veto to prevent its being read to the *concilium plebis*, whereat Metellus began to read it himself—as Cornelius in similar circumstances had done in 67. Cato's reaction was to snatch the document from him, and when Metellus began to recite the text by heart, another tribune, Minucius Thermus, intervened physically to prevent him and a riot ensued. Outlines in *CAH* ix^2, 359; Millar (1998), 112–14.

The Commentary on Cicero's speech *As a Candidate*

Asconius' standard format reappears—date, explanatory introduction, commentary by lemma and scholion, and outcome. This item is our only evidence for this speech, and of considerable interest not only for the political personalities and ambience of the time, but also for its evidently close relationship to the document known as the *Commentariolum Petitionis* ('The Election-Candidate's Handbook'). Whether or not that is really the work of M. Cicero's brother Quintus, is for some at least still an open question. For one view, and a useful account of the problem and its relation to this speech, see Richardson (1971); further, David *et al.* (1973), esp. 257–8; Henderson (1950); some acute observations in Tatum (1999), 19, 23–8. The transmitted title of the speech derives from the custom that those who stood for election to office in the Roman state for the duration of their canvass, whatever other badges of rank they may have been entitled to wear at other times, dressed in a plain white toga (*toga candida*)—that is, as a *candidatus*. In general, consult J. W. Crawford (1994), 163–203.

82C. This speech was delivered in the consulship of L. Caesar and C. Figulus, the year after he had spoken for Cornelius. The date is 64, but this note also perhaps reveals that in Asconius' listing the two speeches were consecutive. Whether they were so in historical reality is another question: *Comm. Pet.* 19 mentions a defence of one Q. Orchivius, listed after that of Cornelius, but perhaps it came after this electoral diatribe in the senate.

Cicero had six rivals in his bid for the consulship, ... Cicero alone from this field of competitors was born of equestrian rank. On the patriciate, see (e.g.) Cornell (1995), ch. 10, esp. 242–56. It is not to be confused with the somewhat different notion of *nobilitas*, nor is either of these the direct antonym of *novitas*, the status attributable to Cicero as a *novus homo*. For fuller exploration, see Brunt (1982). As patricians go, the Sulpicii Galbae had retained modest political success over the past century or more, though not without a villain or two, such as Ser. Galba, cos. 144. By contrast, the Sergii show no consul (or equivalent) since 397, after which we find before Catilina only a praetor 197, a legate 168, a quaestor *c.*94. C. Antonius, younger son of a famous orator and politician (cos. 99), should have had good prospects, but for his own thoroughly disreputable past for which he was expelled from the senate by the censors of 70. He had regained his place by holding a tribunate in ?68 and praetorship in 66. The Cassii Longini were a well-established family (coss. 171; 164; 127; 124; 107; 96; 73) but this individual had little distinction. No other record survives of earlier Cornificii and Licinii

Sacerdotes in office, but Asconius' information on this point can be trusted. Later, in 61, Cornificius was to play a leading part in denouncing P. Clodius over the Bona Dea scandal (Cic. *Att.* 1.13.3; cf. 12.17). In July 65 Cicero (*Att.* 1.1.1) lists as certain rivals only Galba, C. Antonius, Catilina, and Cornificius, and as possible competitors four more, none of whom in the event in fact stood—M. Caesoninus, C. Aquillius Gallus (because of ill health), T. Aufidius, and M. Lollius Palicanus.

during the campaign he lost his father. Asconius is mistaken: Cicero's father died in November 68. Perhaps (i) he lacked access to the corrective evidence (Cic. *Att.* 1.6.2), or (ii) if not, used an edition which misdated it, or else (iii) misdated it himself—conceivably by faulty memory of what may have been fact—that by then Cicero had begun to work towards candidature for his *praetorship* of 66. The commonly held view that this passage is evidence for the existence, if not also publication, of Cicero's Letters to Atticus by c. AD 55, is in my view extremely insecure. For (iv) Asconius could very easily have used, *faute de mieux*, an intermediate writer who did have access to those letters and, on the assumption that the order of letters was the same in the collection available to him as in the extant collection, made a careless inference from the fact that *Att.* 1.6 (perhaps Dec. 68) falls later in the collection than 1.1 and 1.2 (65) which, in a broad sense, concern Cicero's consular candidature. Of writers known to Asconius capable of such an error, the prime suspect is the far from meticulous Cornelius Nepos, who certainly knew of a collection of Ciceros' Letters to Atticus (Nep. *Att.* 16.2–4) in, according to the manuscripts, xi books (possibly a corruption of xvi, the extant number). These were still unpublished when he wrote the *Atticus*, and very likely furnished material for his full-length biography of Cicero. A similar work, also known to Asconius (48C), was a *Life of Cicero* by his learned freedman Tiro, who was, however, rather less likely to have been careless and inaccurate. For the view that it was Asconius himself who was misled by the order of letters as we have them see Stewart (1962), 469 n. 17. On the question of the survival and publication of the letters in general, see Nicholson (1998).

Cassius, although at the time he seemed more stupid than immoral, a few months later was evidently included in Catilina's conspiracy and the origin of some extremely bloodthirsty expressions of opinion. Cf. Sall. *Bell. Cat.* 17.3, 44.1–2, 50.4; Cic. *Cat.* 3.9, 14, 16, 25; 4.13; *Sull.* 36–9, 53 (also *Clu.* 107). Catilina seems to have moved towards illegality only after his third electoral mishap in 63—more than 'a few months' later than this speech of 64.

83C. Catilina and Antonius, despite having led the most disgraceful lives of all of them. The chief counts against C. Antonius were abusing a junior military post under Sulla in Greece to steal assets for himself and then evading conviction for it; bankruptcy resulting from recklessly incurred debts, and expulsion from the senate in 70. Catilina had allegedly taken a leading role among the killers in Sulla's proscriptions of 82/1, with personal responsibility for the death of Marius Gratidianus (see below); had been guilty of violating the Vestal Fabia but escaped penalty for it in 73 (Lewis (2001*a*)); had scandalously married Aurelia Orestilla; and been guilty of conspicuous misgovernment in Africa. There is a general sketch in Cic. *Cael.* 10–14, and a plethora of further allegations, mostly in general terms, in Sall. *Bell. Cat., passim.*

enjoying very strong support from M. Crassus and C. Caesar. This claim almost certainly derives ultimately from Cicero's own *Expositio Consiliorum Suorum* ('Explanation of his Political Calculations'), political memoirs which he began to write in the 50s, suppressing publication, however, until after his own death. See further below, on 83C; Rawson (1991), 408–13. Its veracity can be questioned (Brunt (1957)). In 64, despite a stunningly spectacular aedileship the year before, C. Iulius Caesar was still a relatively junior figure, but probably enjoying at least financial if not also political support from Crassus, who perhaps at this stage was similarly prepared to exchange favours with Catilina, but hardly to the extent indicated by sources hostile to them both for events in the years 66–64. It is unlikely that allegations and innuendo against Crassus for collusion with Catilina in the insurrection of 63 had any truth in them.

the senate had resolved that a law should be carried *de ambitu* **with increased penalties.** Recent efforts to curb *ambitus*, which had been aggravated by 64 expulsions from the senate in 70 and hence intensified competition for office in order to regain membership, were Sulla's law of 81, C. Cornelius' initiative as tribune, and C. Piso's consequent consular Lex Calpurnia of 67; and a senatorial decree of 65 calling for its amendment (Ascon. 69C). This move in 64 failed (see below), but was followed by Cicero's Lex Tullia *de ambitu* of 63, and more legislation later.

Q. Mucius Orestinus, tribune of the plebs, had interposed his veto against this initiative. This tribune, not known to have held any other office, was almost certainly related, though perhaps only by adoption, to Catilina's wife Aurelia Orestilla (Sall. *Bell. Cat.* 15.2) through the Aurelii Orestae. See further below, 85–6C; 88C.

last night Catilina and Antonius met, with their followers, in the house of a certain person of noble rank, a well-known and recognized figure in this business of funding largesse. The language is well chosen to convey an

atmosphere of secret intrigue and electoral malpractice, carefully declining
to name the Master Mind.

**He means the house of either C. Caesar or M. Crassus. For they were the
most determined and powerful of Cicero's adversaries … and Cicero
himself notes this in his *Explanation of his Political Calculations.*** Where
clearly he was no more specific about the venue of the alleged nocturnal
meeting of 64 than he was in this speech. It might very well have been a
fiction. The *Expositio Consiliorum Suorum* is to be identified with the work
mentioned by Dio 39.10.3; Cic. *Att.* 2.6.2, 8.1, 12.3, 14.17.6, 16.11.3; Plut. *Crass.*
13, suppressed by Cicero during his lifetime but evidently published after his
death (see Rawson (1982)). Cicero's 'growing standing in the community' at
this time is well enough otherwise attested. The site of Crassus' house is
obscure; Caesar after his election as *pontifex maximus* in 63 had his official
residence in the Regia, at the south-east end of the Forum, before that
somewhere in the Subura (Suet. *Div. Iul.* 46.1). See further *LTUR* 2. 128–9
(E. Papi); 73 (D. Palombi); Coarelli (1985), 173–6.

**And he charges Crassus with having also been the instigator of the con-
spiracy which was formed by Catilina and Piso in the consulship of Cotta
and Torquatus.** This, the so-called 'First Catilinarian Conspiracy' is now
generally regarded as fictitious, a myth originating in rumours of violence
alluded to by Cicero here and in *Cat.* 1.15; *Mur.* 81; *Sull.* 11–13, 67–8, 81, and
later developed by Cicero and other writers including Sallust, *Bell. Cat.*
18–19. The genesis and elaboration of the confection can fairly readily be
traced. See further Syme (1964*b*), 89–91; Henderson (1950); Brunt (1957);
Seager (1964); Gruen (1969*a*); Marshall (1974) and (1985*b*), 287–8; *CAH* ix²,
342–3. Whatever he found incorporated into the 'secret history' from
later development of the story, Asconius cannot have found Cicero's
'denunciation' in the speech of 64, which could at most have dropped
some murky hints of plans for mass murder (Ascon. 92C *caedes
optimatium*—'massacre of the Great and Good'; 93C *mali cives*—'wicked
citizens'). It is not clear from the Latinity of this passage whether Asconius
believed in the story of the 'First Catilinarian Conspiracy' or not, but see
below, on 92C.

**84C. Cicero also later mentions by name those whom he killed—
Q. Caecilius, M. Volumnius, L. Tanusius. … M. Marius Gratidianus.** The
cross-reference is to the context of Sulla's victory in the Civil Wars of the late
80s covered by Ascon. 90C. Note that the list of names differs from the one
found in *Comm. Pet.* 9–10, which omits M. Volumnius, but includes Titinii
and Nannii (probably to be reduced to singulars, like its reference to Tanusii

for Tanusius). Of these four alleged victims of Catilina, only M. Marius Gratidianus can be identified with any otherwise known individual.

Catilina had also cut off the head of M. Marius Gratidianus, ... linked by close family ties with Cicero. On this man's murder by Catilina and the later references to it in the speech, compare Plut. *Sull.* 32; Sall. *Hist.* 1.44 M; Livy, *Per.* 88; Val. Max. 9.2.1; Lucan 2.160–73; Flor. 2.9.26 and further below, Ascon. 87C, 90C. Variants in the story—at least two early versions—suggest that here too there was a considerable measure of fiction (Marshall (1985*a*) and (1985*b*), 291. See also Damon (1993) on a later conflation; cf. Sen. *De Ira* 3.18.1–2; Oros. 5.21.7–8). On Gratidianus' success as praetor (probably 85) in stealing the credit for much-needed monetary reform, *MRR* 2. 57; 3. 140–1; (Cic. *Off.* 3.80; Pliny, *NH* 34.27); M. H. Crawford (1968); and on his links with the Tullii Cicerones, that other leading family in his home town of Arpinum, see Carney (1961), 8–9, 77—mostly on Cic. *Leg.* 3.36; cf. also Nicolet (1967). Cicero's grandfather had married a sister of the local notable M. Gratidius, who had himself married a sister of C. Marius (cos. 107, 104–100, 86), and the son of this second marriage had been adopted by the great general's brother to become the M. Marius Gratidianus in question. See also Cic. *QF.* 1.1.10; *Flacc.* 49 for later developments in these relationships.

He also declared it impossible for C. Antonius to have any clients. For he had robbed many persons in Achaea. The clients meant are those in his province.

Then the Greeks who had been robbed took Antonius to court before the praetor M. Lucullus, who had jurisdiction in cases involving aliens. That is, in 76. Plut. *Caes.* 4 (whose MSS wrongly name Antonius 'Publius') is astray in making Lucullus governor of Macedonia (with supervision of Achaea), the province which he later held after his consulship of 73. Inference from M. Lucullus' function as *praetor peregrinus* that the case must have been a civil one is insecure, as praetors also presided over the public criminal courts.

he was unable to enjoy an equality of rights. Cf. Cicero's lemma above (84C), *he could not contend with an alien in a fair trial* (with *Comm. Pet.* 8 for virtually the same wording). Plutarch (loc. cit.) compounds his errors by inferring that the case took place in Greece.

85C. Catilina after his praetorship held the command of Africa. For the praetorship 68 is the latest possible date (*MRR* 2. 138).

He found out how effective the courts were on his acquittal. Irony, of course, whether taken to mean how great was the power of the courts to acquit even the flagrantly guilty, or how little in being unable to convict.

This very speech of Cicero makes me doubt this. From this it has been inferred that Asconius lacked access to Cicero's correspondence with Atticus, perhaps not published until *c.* AD 60, since Cic. *Att.* 1.2 where Cicero announces his intention to defend Catilina (although it does not prove that he did) is clearly relevant to the statement of Fenestella and might be expected to be mentioned by Asconius. See note on 82C above.

his electoral support for Antonius. What Cicero (or anyone else) could have done by way of furnishing electoral support for Antonius after having been declared top of the poll himself in the praetorian elections of 66 can only be guessed. Cicero does not claim credit for ensuring that Antonius did not fail to be elected at all. And was there any advantage, other than enhanced reputation and perhaps with that enhanced prospects for a consulship to follow, in high placing in the praetorian elections?

86C. *Q. Mucius, who yesterday alleged that I am not worthy of the consulship.* Somewhat reminiscent of Catilina's later sneer at Cicero for being an *inquilinus civis*—'a citizen of foreign extraction' (Sall. *Bell. Cat.* 31.7; cf. 23.5–6, 35.3; App. *BC* 2.2; Cic. *Sull.* 22). Catilina and Antonius riposted with an attack on Cicero's 'newness' (*novitas*—Ascon. 93C). Similar slurs on the 'unworthy' M. Lollius Palicanus were made by C. Piso in 67 (Val. Max. 3.8.3).

you did your deal with Calenus. That is, this private suit was settled by agreement between the parties.

all manner of sexual misconduct and disgraceful acts, bloodied himself in criminal slaughter. Lurid allegations against Catilina in Sall. *Bell. Cat.* 14–16; *Comm. Pet.* 9–10. On the scandal and trial of 73 BC, Lewis (2001a).

despoiled our allies. In Africa, 67, at least.

did violence to the laws, the courts, the hearings. Despite Ascon. 66C, perhaps not disturbances connected with the case against Manilius, 66/5. Plausibly Catilina's own trial *de repetundis*, 65—and others.

87C. *I must suppose that Roman knights told lies, the written depositions of a most honourable community were falsified, that Q. Metellus Pius told lies, that Africa told lies.* That is, on the view that Catilina really was innocent of wrongdoing in Africa. The 'Roman knights' here are not the non-senatorial section of the jury (see 89C on the way it voted), but contributors to the overwhelming evidence of Catilina's guilt—presumably as highly ranked citizens having dealings in Africa, just as various equestrians had suffered under Verres on Sicily. The 'most honourable community' is likeliest to be Utica. Q. Metellus Pius of course would have African *clientelae* inherited from his father Numidicus and his own stay in Africa after fleeing Rome and Italy in 87/6.

there exist notes of Cicero's cases. The Latin term *commentarii* can refer either to notes prepared by the speaker in advance of delivery, or an outline of a speech taken during or after delivery. Either might result in publication of the whole speech, or of the notes/outline alone (Quintil. 3.8.48 and 67, 4.1.69). Tiro had collected, edited, and published Cicero's *commentarii*, according to Quintil. 10.7.30–1, which, to be worth the effort, should have been fairly full. Letters of the Cicerones to Tiro, mostly those of Marcus the orator, his patron, a few from Quintus and the younger Marcus (cos. 32), are preserved as Cic. *Fam.* 16.

The manner of Catilina's judicial acquittal was such as to bring Clodius into ill-repute for collusion, for even the rejection of jurors seemed to have been performed to accord with the wishes of the accused. On Clodius' alleged collusion (*praevaricatio*), above, pp. 203–4, on Ascon. 9C. In any trial before a *quaestio* each side had the right to reject a certain number of jurors (see e.g. Jones (1972), 69). In July 65 Cicero wrote to Atticus (with his own consular candidature for 63 already in prospect): *Hoc tempore Catilinam competitorem nostrum defendere cogitamus. Iudices habemus quos voluimus, summa accusatoris voluntate.* The first sentence translates readily, if also somewhat ambiguously, as 'At the moment I am contemplating the defence of Catilina, my electoral competitor.' (He explains a little later that he was hoping that Catilina might work more closely with him in the election if acquitted.) From even this it is unclear whether Cicero is merely *considering* the prospect and its advantages, or already actively *planning* how to execute it. The second sentence, however, is also to my mind problematic. 'We have the jury we want, with the accuser's full consent.' This is sometimes taken (e.g. by Marshall (1985*b*), 299 and Shackleton Bailey (1965–70), 1. 67) to imply that Cicero must have withdrawn from the defence after proceedings had started, since (it is supposed) the formal rejection of jurors must already have taken place. The inference, however, is far from necessary. There could very easily have been an informal agreement between the two sides about juror rejections before any formal proceedings began, and on the likeliest interpretation of Cicero's Latin even before he finally made up his mind whether or not to act for the defence at all. None of this, it should be stressed, is proof of Clodius' actual connivance at the acquittal of Catilina, although after it, of course, it was the easiest of allegations to make against him, and after his irreconcilable rift with Clodius in 61 and its sequel Cicero duly made it, loud and often. How this view of the juror rejections reached Asconius is beyond telling, but it is worth noting that Asconius himself is by no means convinced of the veracity of the allegations.

It is obvious that C. Verres is meant. If so much were clear from the context of this speech the comment would be otiose, but Asconius' interpretation of Cicero's innuendo is almost certainly correct, and the implied association of Catilina with Verres, in view of their common Sullan past, is entirely plausible, whether or not actually true.

The other, after selling all his livestock and more or less making over his grasslands, retains his shepherds, from whom, he says, he can whenever he wishes at a moment's notice whip up a runaway slave war. **He means C. Antonius.** The point is that Antonius' bankruptcy had forced the sales of pastoral lands and stock, so that the shepherds, who would typically be slaves, were redundant, and their retention could only have been for nefarious purposes, given that they carried arms to protect their flocks. Violence in rural Italy, greatly aggravated by the availability of such personnel to pursue it, long remained a serious problem even after the slave revolt and suppression of Spartacus (73–71), as it clear from (e.g.) Cicero's defence of Cluentius (66); Cic. *Att.* 1.14.4 (Catilinarian troubles still smouldering 61 BC); Sall. *Bell. Cat.* 28.4 (63); Suet. *Div. Aug.* 3.1; 7.1 (activity near Thurii of Augustus' father C. Octavius (60)); Caes. *BC* 1.24.2; 3.21.4 (Milo, 48, again near Thurii). Further, Lintott (1999*b*), 29; 128–30.

88C. He appears to mean Q. Gallius, whom he later defended on a charge *de ambitu*. *Comm. Pet.* 19 lists this defence before that of Cornelius, which is consistent with the view that 'later' refers, not to a time after this speech in the senate, but to a date in 66 between Gallius' election as praetor of 65 (Ascon. 60C) and his taking up office, which would render him immune from prosecution until 64, too late for it to fall before the defence of Cornelius.

presented a gladiatorial event on the pretext that he was giving it 'for his father'. The best-known parallel instance of these years for such a pretext is the show presented by C. Caesar as aedile in 65 (Plin. *NH* 33.53; Dio 37.8; cf. for its spectacular displays further evidence in *MRR* 2. 158, esp. Vell. 2.43.4; Plut. *Caes.* 5–6; Suet. *Div. Jul.* 10–11).

He means the Calpurnian Law which C. Calpurnius Piso had carried three years earlier *de ambitu.* See above, Ascon. 75–76C.

P. Sulla and P. Autronius, of whom we have already spoken. The cross-reference is to the comment on *Corn.* at 75C.

The *cognomen* of the tribune whom he names, Q. Mucius, was Orestinus. As at 83C; cf. 85–86C.

when Sulla after his victory celebrated circus games which involved respectable men driving four-horse chariots, C. Antonius was among them. Sulla's celebrations of his decisive victory at the Colline Gate (Nov. 82) are authentic (Vell. 2.27.6; Cic. *Verr.* 1.31; Ps.-Ascon. 217 St.; *CIL* 1².1, p. 333; Plut. *Sull.* 35); this role for C. Antonius, probably Cicero's invention or exaggeration, is somewhat credulously accepted by Asconius. See Rawson (1982).

89C. L. Volcacius Tullus the consul held a meeting of his advisers on public affairs … Catilina for this reason gave up his candidature. That is, this consul (66) had charge of the elections that year and consulted his *consilium* on this issue. The reasons for the withdrawal (or on another view rejection) of Catilina's candidature are problematic. The main evidence apart from Asconius here is that of Sall. *Bell. Cat.* 18.2–3, who says that 'a little later [*sc.* after the conviction and consequent deposition of the consuls first designate, P. Sulla and P. Autronius] Catilina, defendant in a suit for recovery of funds [i.e. *de repetundis*] was debarred from seeking the consulship because he had been unable to declare his candidature by the legally stipulated date.' Among various possible interpretations of these severely compressed data, perhaps the best is that the imminent trial *de repetundis* had discouraged Catilina from standing in the original election; and that he was debarred from the second (supplementary) election by the very fact of non-participation in the first, expressed in Sallust, and very likely in the ruling given after due consultation by Volcacius (that the consul was not going to be able to accept Catilina's late entry into the field), as 'failure to declare candidature by the due date', this being constituted or implied, that is, by absence from the field in the first election. That absence would have raised the question of legitimacy of a new candidature in the second, on which Volcacius would have felt the need to sound senatorial opinion. The reason for the decision might have been published as non-timeous declaration of candidature, rather than the imminent trial, to avoid any suspicion of attempting to prejudice the said trial. Catilina's reason for final withdrawal will most probably, on this view, have been not so much the (still) imminent trial, as the doubtless all too clearly expressed hostility of leading senators, which was likely to ruin his chances in any case, even if Volcacius were to reject their view, or even if he did accept it and Catilina still stood for office in defiance of it. Besides, to persist might also provoke an adverse outcome in the forthcoming trial.

For a trial ensued *de repetundis*, **in which Catilina himself was scandalously acquitted, but by a verdict in which the senatorial vote was for conviction, that of the knights and** *tribuni aerarii* **for acquittal.** This shows clearly that the trial came later than Catilina's withdrawal from consular candidature. There was perhaps no *requirement* to place on public record the voting pattern of the three orders on a jury until the Lex Fufia of 59, but the evidence for that (Dio 38.8.1) also implies that earlier on occasion it might be revealed or rumoured. There is no need, then (*pace* Marshall (1985*b*), 305), to ascribe Asconius' awareness of it in this case of 65 to his own inference from the known hostility of senators to Catiline evinced in his recall from Africa. Nor is it likely that he would be guilty of the circularity involved in seeking to confirm that hostility by citing a mere inference based upon his other evidence for it. There is no difficulty in attributing his information to some historian or orator, and no point in attempting identification.

From the equestrian order? Which you butchered? Equestrian losses in the Sullan proscriptions were doubtless significant (as many as 1600 in App. *BC* 1.95.442; cf. Flor. 2.9.25; Val. Max. 9.2.1), but certainly did not engulf the whole order, from which Sulla must have recruited a majority of his new senators—see further Gabba (1976), 142–50. Nor in any case could Catilina have been solely responsible for the killings.

The equestrian order had stood for the Cinnan party against Sulla, and many had stolen funds. ... killed after Sulla's victory. One of the reasons alleged—perhaps in some cases, in those lawless years, with truth—to justify the executions and associated confiscations. Of course nothing like the whole of the equestrian order had supported Cinna and his followers against the Sullans. See Gabba (1976), 34 and 142–3.

90C. *all the way from the Janiculum.* Marius Gratidiaus was killed at the tomb of the Lutatii Catuli (*Comm. Pet.* 10; Val. Max. 9.2.1; Flor. 2.9.26), which was sited on the far side of the Tiber, where the Janiculum hill stood.

Rather, the one indicated is that which is outside the Gate of Carmentis ... Temple of Apollo in Rome. On the topography and its history, *LTUR* 1. 49–51 (Temple of Apollo—A. Viscogliosi); Coarelli (1997), 389; *LTUR* 1. 240 (Porta Carmentalis—G. Pisani Sarturio; cf. Coarelli (1997), 126 and (1985), 81–3); *LTUR* 2. 229 (Forum Holitorium—F. Coarelli); *LTUR* 1. 269–72 (Circus Flaminius—A. Viscogliosi). For the Porta Carmentalis as 'infamous' (*scelerata*), Fest. p. 450 L, for its association with the Fabii and their disaster at the river Cremera; location at *LTUR* 1. 240 (G. Pisoni Sarturio). The Circus Flaminius, in the Campus Martius and so outside the *pomerium* (*LTUR* 2 s.v.; Coarelli (1997), ch. 3, esp. 363–74), served on occasion as a venue for *contiones* (Cic. *Att.* 1.14.1–2; *Red. Sen.* 13; Millar (1998), 116, 139).

This man whom he names, L. Luscius, a notorious centurion of Sulla's who made rich pickings from his victory—for he had property worth more than HS 100,000—had been convicted not long before Cicero's speech. In the passages here expounded by Asconius Cicero has moved on to Catilina's exposure to accusation for murders during the Sullan proscriptions in a court evidently specially established in 64 to investigate such cases. The claim that Sulla's victory had greatly enriched the centurion Luscius accords well enough with Sallust's notion (*Bell. Cat.* 37.6; cf. *Hist.* 1.55.22 M; Oros. 5.21.3 on L. Fufidius or Fursidius, a 'chief centurion' in the latter; Wiseman (1971*b*), 232) that Sulla had admitted 'common soldiers' to the senate in his reforms of 81. Asconius' source attributes three murders to him: perhaps he is the anonymous killer of 'many' proscribed persons in Dio 37.10.2. There was an aged senator in 76 by the name of C. Luscius Ocrea (Cic. *Rosc. Com.* 43)—just conceivably related.

91C. **L. Bellienus too was convicted, who Cicero says was an uncle of Catilina's. This man, on the order of Sulla, who was dictator at the time, had killed Lucretius Afella, who was standing for the consulship against the wishes of Sulla with a view to destabilizing the state.** Bellienus, like Luscius, is again anonymous in Dio 36.10.2 (cf. also Plut. *Sull.* 33, who terms him a centurion, perhaps by confusion with Luscius; Liv. *Per.* 89; App. *BC* 1.101.471–3). The victim, a renegade Marian and Sulla's commander for the siege of Praeneste in 82 (*MRR* 2. 72), stood for the consulship with no prior magistracy to his credit. His *cognomen* was rather more probably Afella than Ofella, which is Clark's reading here (*MRR* 3. 130).

A few months later Catilina did face the peril of trial on this charge which Cicero levels at him. … indicted him for murder. From this and the preceding lemmata, if Asconius' evidence is taken to be reliable and at face value, it would appear that although there was some prospect of it at the time of this speech—namely, before the elections of 64—he was not formally indicted by Lucceius until they were over. The alternative and, I think, less plausible view (Marshall (1985*b*), 308) is to infer from the lemmata, somewhat contrary to Asconius' comment, that Catilina's case was already listed for trial before this speech, but not begun until after the elections, in which he was not legally debarred but much hampered by a move against him very similar to that which had (on one view) kept him out of the supplementary elections of 66. See above, on 89C. The later prosecutor of Catilina, L. Lucceius, must surely be the historian to whom Cicero in spring 55 addressed his famous plea (*Fam.* 5.12) for favourable treatment in his forthcoming history—that is, L. Lucceius Q. f. There was another contemporary L. Lucceius, also featured in Cicero's correspondence, son of a M. Lucceius, but it is almost certainly not he but, as Asconius clearly says, the historian who not only accused Catilina, but also stood for the consulship of 59 and contemplated collaboration with C. Caesar in the canvass for it (Suet. *Div. Jul.* 19.1; cf. Cic. *Att.* 1.17.11).

Fabia the Vestal Virgin had pleaded her defence on a charge of fornication, when (misconduct with) Catilina was alleged against her, and had been acquitted. The case dates to 73 (Cic. *Cat.* 3.9; Oros. 6.3.1). The notion that Clodius was the prosecutor on this occasion and was forced to withdraw by the intervention of M. Cato the Younger, based on Plut. *Cat. Min.* 19, is unlikely. At that date Clodius, born in 91, was only eighteen years old, not too young, perhaps, to try to initiate a prosecution (the prosecutor of Caelius Rufus in 56 was seventeen), but it would have been premature of him to be entertaining the 'major revolutionary designs' attributed to him by Plutarch, nor would such means be well suited to such a purpose. Cato, born in 95, was only twenty-two, and unlikely to have replied in the terms reported by Plutarch to the thanks of Cicero, already a senator, 'that all his policies were for the good of the state'. More probably Clodius' calumnies belong to a later date, and in fact the Bona Dea scandal of 62/1 offers an appropriate context (Moreau (1982), 234–6; for a rather less plausible alternative, Tatum (1999), 44). For the defence (apparently), the otherwise worthy but rather dull M. Pupius Piso made a name for himself, and Fabia was acquitted (Cic. *Brut.* 326; Ascon. 90C). That would have entailed not the *acquittal* but the *discharge* (note Orosius' *evasit*—'he got off', not *absolutus est*—'he won a verdict of acquittal') of any alleged paramour—in this case Catilina, who had, Orosius seems to say, actually been indicted (*accusatus*; cf. Cic. *ap.* Ascon. above—'*criminal charges*'). That is, with Fabia acquitted, the chances of securing his conviction, even for rape, were too slender for any prosecutor to find it worth while to pursue the case against him to a formal judicial verdict. There is no difficulty in attributing this result to the intervention of Q. Catulus (Oros. 6.3.1.; Sall. *Bell. Cat.* 15.1, 35.1), who is quite likely to have been president of the court, rather than a member of the panel of judges or an advocate. That is not to say that there would have been no case to answer, had Fabia been convicted—as Orosius (again) says, *arguebatur* ('there was evidence against him'). Since Fabia was not the only Vestal on trial at the time (Cic. *Brut.* 326; *Cat.* 3.9), to associate with hers the trial of her colleague Licinia for fornication with M. Crassus (Plut. *Crass.* 1) is highly plausible. The case against Crassus (and Licinia) turned on his having paid suspiciously over-attentive court to her in seeking to buy property from her. From Cicero's lemma (above—'*your arrival there*') in this passage of Asconius, it is tempting to infer that at least some of the evidence

against Catilina may have been similar, and no more substantial. Nevertheless, in this speech of 64, especially since there had been no final verdict in
the case, Cicero, as in this passage, could still revive dark hints to his
detriment. For fuller exposition, Lewis (2001*a*).

**It is because this Fabia was sister to Cicero's wife Terentia that he said: 'even
if there was no underlying guilt'.** Asconius' comment may well be valid,
though Fabia's relationship to Terentia (they must be half-sisters) might be
more pertinent to the circumstances of 62/1, if that is when Clodius tried to
re-open the question of Fabia's guilt (Plut. *Cat. Min.* 19—see above). In 64 it
would be very much in Cicero's own interests not to appear to challenge the
actual verdict of the court (a *res iudicata*) of 73, especially if Q. Catulus, still
in 64 a leading optimate, had been prominent in securing it, and such a
challenge could be represented as gratuitous slander (*calumnia*) by his
opponents.

**It is said that Catilina committed adultery with the woman who was later
his mother-in-law, and took to wife the female offspring of that fornication,
although she was his daughter.** Typical of several incredible tales of adultery,
incest, and murder about Catilina's family life. This one is partly echoed in
Plut. *Cic.* 10, and is no different in character from stories (1) that he killed his
own brother (Plut. loc. cit.); (2) that he had to murder his own son to win
the hand of Aurelia Orestilla (Sall. *Bell. Cat.* 15.2; App. *BC* 2.2; Val. Max.
9.1.9); (3) that he killed a former wife in order to take a new one—probably
again Orestilla (Cic. *Cat.* 1.14); (4) that he killed his sister's husband
Q. Caecilius (*Comm. Pet.* 9; cf. Plut. *Sull.* 32; *Cic.* 10); (5) that he had been
married to Gratidia, sister of his murder-victim M. Marius Gratidianus
(Berne Scholia to Lucan, 2.173). All that can be accepted from this with
any confidence is that Aurelia Orestilla, according to Sallust a woman of
some wealth and beauty but no morals (*Bell. Cat.* 15.2, 35.3), was not his first
wife. Any of the deaths of brother or adult son of Catilina, of a wife prior to
Orestilla, or of Q. Caecilius are likely to be no less historical than that of
Marius Gratidianus, but that Catilina was responsible for any of them is
quite beyond proof. Cf. the charges of unnatural lust and family murder
levelled against Oppianicus the elder in Cicero, *Pro Cluentio* 14–41 in 66.

**92C. This charge Lucceius also levels against Catilina in the orations which
he wrote attacking him. I have not yet discovered the names of these
women.** The occasion of the orations will have been, it seems, Lucceius'
prosecution of Catilina, after the elections of 64, for murder(s) committed
in the Sullan terror of 82/1. The identity of the mother is irrecoverable, but
Orestilla is probably meant as her daughter—and, allegedly, Catilina's.

You are well aware of the identity of those whom he forbears to name. For there was a belief that Catilina and Cn. Piso ... In the first sentence I translate Clark's text, emended from the MSS which yield, to my mind, poorer sense in the context: 'You know (all about?) those whom he names' (i.e. Cn. Piso and Catilina), preferred by Marshall (1985*b*), ad loc., following Brunt (1957), 193–4, on the ground that Asconius does not in fact manage to explain here the obscure reference to persons whom Cicero forbears to name. In fact, however, he does not need to do so, since this trust in his readers' awareness of their identity is based on his earlier remark at 83C, to which this is a cross-reference—namely, that Cicero had in his *Explanation of his Political Calculations* named Crassus as the off-stage manipulator behind the so-called 'First Catilinarian Conspiracy' here outlined in the following comment. Objection based on the view that Asconius' continuation '*For* ... Catilina and Cn. Piso ...' appears to identify these persons as those meant to be readily recognized by the readers is seen to be invalid on realization that the cross-reference (as I take it) is parenthetic, and the continuation '*For* ... (etc.)' is meant to explain not that, but Cicero's allusion to the alleged Conspiracy, related by Asconius in what follows in the version developed since 64 (cf. Cic. *Cat.* 1.15; *Mur.*1; *Expositio Consiliorum Suorum* ap. Ascon. 83C; Sall. *Bell. Cat.* 18; Liv. *Per.* 101; Suet. *Div. Jul.* 9). The description of the report as a mere 'belief' (*opinio*) seems to evince scepticism on Asconius' part.

that Catilina and Cn. Piso, a young desperado, conspired to perpetrate a massacre of the senate ... before they were ready. This version in essentials tallies with the fuller account of Sallust, *Bell. Cat.* 18, whether that is Asconius' source here, or, no less likely (as for Sallust too), Cicero's *Explanation of his Political Calculations*. This myth, the so-called 'First Catilinarian Conspiracy', was developed from almost nothing over the decade or so after the minor incidents in 65 which spawned it. See bibliography cited on 83C above.

Now Piso, when this speech was being delivered, had perished in Spain ... not without Pompeius' approval. Also in essentials parallel with the more detailed version of Sallust (*Bell. Cat.* 19). My translation is based on emending the corrupt MSS *ut* † *avus suus ablegaretur* to read, after Sallust, *ut avius ablegaretur*—lit. 'for him to be sent off to be remote', with MSS *suus* excised, but this can be at best tentative conjecture, not least because although Sallust may well be Asconius' source here, equally so too, again, may some source common to both, such as Cicero's *Explanation of his Political Calculations*. The 'honorific mission' (*legatio*) was not officially a legateship, but quaestorship with praetorian powers (as *quaestor pro praetore*—Sall. *Bell. Cat.* 19; *MRR* 2. 159).

93C. C. Antonius and certain other nobles drove. Cf. 88C, where these drivers are not 'nobles' but merely 'respectable'.

Antonius had contracted with the treasury to supply four-horse chariots for a fee—a contract which is legally available to senators. Compare Dio 55.10.5 for Augustus' extension of the privilege. On the difficulties, of interpreting the passage and, in particular, *vectigales* ('subject to tax' or 'bringing in profit'—here translated ambiguously as 'for a fee'), see Rawson (1981), 9–14 = (1991), 399–405.

He is speaking of bad citizens: *Those persons who, after they failed with the Spanish stiletto by which they made the attempt to slit the sinews of Roman citizens, are now attempting to unsheathe two daggers at once against the State.* Another of those Ciceronian dark hints with no specific reference, and perhaps in 64 with no basis in reality. Later, e.g. in the *Explanation of his Political Calculations* (*Expositio Consiliorum Suorum*), Cicero might have identified '*those persons*' as Crassus and Caesar. The '*Spanish stiletto*' is of course Cn. Piso, the Latin for it *pugiunculum*, a diminutive doubtless meant to express his puny ineffectuality.

You must note that this ruffian Licinius has already let his hair grow on information being laid against Catilina, and so has Q. Curius, a fellow of quaestorian rank. At this point the MSS text is severely damaged, and what is translated here is conjectural, chiefly based on an interpretation of Pliny, *Ep.* 7.27.14, a reference to accused persons letting their hair grow long as a sign of sorrow, to arouse sympathy; and on reading *indicio Q. quoque Curium...* for MSS †*iudic. Quā. ue Curium.* That is, on this view, Cicero is saying that one Licinius (unidentifiable to us) expects to be involved in some way in a forthcoming trial of Catilina, against whom information has been or soon will be laid. Q. Curius is likely to be the Catilinarian partisan of Sall. *Bell. Cat.* 17.3, probably the Q. Curius expelled from the senate in 70 (ibid. 23.1; App. *BC* 2.3; cf. *Comm. Pet.* 10), restored to the senate before 64 by holding a magistracy, to be distinguished from a Curius (or perhaps better Turius) found at Cic. *Att.* 1.1.2; *Brut.* 237, pr. by 67.

This Curius was a notorious gambler, and was later convicted. The date of the trial and the charges are unknown, except that it must fall after this speech, and if he had immunity for having laid information against Catilina (Sall. *Bell. Cat.* 26.3, 28.2; but cf. Suet. *Div. Jul.* 17), the charges will not have been for involvement in the insurrection of 63/2.

Against him there is extant an elegant hendecasyllabic line of Calvus:

And Curius, of unmatched scholarship in dice.

Calvus is C. Licinius Macer Calvus, son of the populist tribune and annalist C. Licinius Macer. He was famed as a neoteric poet and austerely Attic orator, living 82–47, so roughly coeval with Catullus, who addresses to him his poems nos. 14, 50, 96. Cicero respected his abilities but disliked his style. Fragments and Testimonia of orations in *ORF* (no. 165), 492–500; see further Gruen (1966*a*); Wiseman (1968); *CAH* IX², 393, 717. For the poetry, Hor. *Sat.* 1.10.19; Propert. 2.25.4, 2.34.89–90.

94C. There are in circulation also orations published in their names, not written by them but by detractors of Cicero. Cf. Ascon. 86C for polemic against Cicero as a 'new man'. For purported replies of Antonius and Catilina, Quintil. 9.3.94; App. *BC* 2.2; Schol. Bob. 80 St., the latter incorrectly including Clodius among the detractors of 64.

Anyhow, Cicero was made consul ... more reputable bunch canvassed for him than for Catilina. On the eventual ease of Cicero's election, Sall. *Bell. Cat.* 24.1; Plut. *Cic.* 11. C. Antonius' connections included a somewhat more reputable brother and a much more reputable father (cos. 99, deceased), as well as L. Caesar, consul in the year of the election, over which he may have presided.

Glossary

Acta   Archived records of transactions of the senate, assemblies of the Roman people, and its courts, often cited by Asconius and others as a reliable historical source.

aerarium   Lit. a place for depositing *aes* = bronze, money. Hence usually refers to the Treasury of the Roman state, properly the *Aerarium Saturni*, as it was kept in the Temple of Saturn. Also used as a repository of important documents, especially public documents.

as/asses   Basic unit of Roman (bronze) currency.

assembly, centuriate (*comitia centuriata*)   The assembly of the whole Roman people (*populus*), both patricians and plebeians, organized into block-voting units termed 'centuries' (*centuriae*), unequally allocated to the five *classes*, defined by property-rating and/or military function, and after *c.*241 BC also cross-divided by the thirty-five tribes.

assembly, curiate (*comitia curiata*)   The oldest of the Roman assemblies, of the whole Roman people organized by *curiae*, the oldest divisions of the populace. Used in historical times for ratification of certain matters of religious import—e.g. conferring the auspices on senior magistrates.

assembly, tribal (*comitia tributa*)   Assembly of the whole Roman people organized and voting by the thirty-five tribes alone, without reference to property-qualification. Compare the *concilium plebis* (see below).

boni   See below under **optimates.**

codex   In one of its earlier meanings, refers to a sheaf of waxed wooden writing-tables on which (e.g.) the text of a rogation (draft law) might be written, to be read out to an assembly prior to its ratification.

collegium (**pl.** *collegia*)   An association of persons in a common office (magistracy or priesthood) or purpose, in the latter case most frequently of trade-guilds in Rome (or elsewhere). Some of these latter were of great antiquity and respectable, but in the late Republic other so-called *collegia* claimed similar status but in fact were little more than gangs of thugs recruited for mass violence to disrupt or manipulate political and judicial processes. Hence legislation to control them—or to reinstitute them after dissolution—mentioned in Asconius.

colonia (pl. *coloniae*)   A new settlement instituted by Rome with an urban focal point generally of strategic importance, whether or not a previously inhabited site, and land (its *territorium*) distributed to the settlers, the *coloni* (lit. 'tillers'). Before all Italy south of the Po acquired full Roman citizenship in and after the Social War, there were in juridical terms two types of *colonia*—(i) those with full citizen status (*coloniae civium Romanorum*), until the middle third of the second century BC generally small (typically perhaps some 300 families), maritime, and on land contiguous with existing citizen-held territory (*ager Romanus*) fairly near Rome, with only basic organs of local administration and run largely from the metropolis; (ii) those with Latin status (*coloniae Latinae*), usually but not always inland, much larger (typically 3000–5000 settlers with families) with strong fortress sites for their urban centres, independent but privileged status as Latin allies, full apparatus for self-government. None of this status were founded after the 170s BC, when instead further settlements of this size and function were accorded full citizenship, but it may be that the urbanized communities of Transpadane Gaul, which under the Lex Pompeia of 89 BC were left with Latin status until the 40s BC, began to claim (fictitious, nominal, or titular) colonial status, whether or not it was officially recognized. The *coloniae Latinae* proper as a result of the Social War acquired full Roman citizenship and became *municipia* (see below).

Compitalia   A Festival in honour of the Lares, celebrated at the crossroads of the city of Rome in midwinter on a day appointed by the praetor (presumably *urbanus*).

concilium plebis   The assembly of the plebeians alone, excluding patricians, normally convened by tribunes of the plebs (but also on occasion by aediles, if plebeian?), in its legislative, elective, or judicial capacity, organized in its thirty-five tribes as block-voting units.

contio (pl. *contiones*)   In Roman public life, any magistrate or priest of sufficient standing, or tribune of the plebs, might summon a *contio*—lit. 'a coming together' or 'gathering', so a mass meeting in Rome, undifferentiated by tribes, centuries, etc. (although as Asconius explains a *contio* could be marshalled at a given juncture into one of the various forms of assembly). The term *contio* may also refer to speech or harangue delivered at such a meeting either by the official who convened it, or by any person whom he permitted to address it.

de ambitu (*lex/ quaestio/ iudicium*)   Statute, jury-court, or trial concerned with electoral malpractices defined under the statute, most commonly bribery, but there is no reason to exclude other kinds of electoral corruption.

decem viri   A board of ten persons, in extant Asconius the Decemviral Commission appointed in (trad.) 451 BC to publish the Laws of the Roman State. In due course and traditionally after some difficulty and dispute, they eventually produced and had ratified the famous Twelve Tables, the original systematized publication of Roman Civil Law.

decuria (pl. *decuriae*)   A division of a larger body, originally either one tenth of it, or else consisting of ten persons, but by the late Republic probably even in its technical or semi-technical usage simply referring to an officially recognized part of an officially recognized whole—most commonly of the *equites (Romani) equo publico* functioning as a component of a jury in a *quaestio publica*.

de maiestate (*lex/ quaestio/ iudicium*) (sc. *populi Romani imminuta*)   Statute, jury-court, or trial concerned not especially with charges of 'treason', as often maintained, but of disregarding or subverting the sovereignty (i.e. 'paramount superiority') of the Roman people.

de repetundis (*lex/ quaestio/ iudicium*)   Statute, jury-court, or trial originally concerned with actions for recovery of assets, financial or other, unlawfully taken in abuse of powers on the part of a Roman state official or senator. Later revisions of the law increase the severity of penalties by adding punitive damages, loss of rights; and very likely extended the range of criminal maladministration for which compensation/retribution might be sought by this process.

de sodaliciis (*lex/ quaestio/ iudicium*)   Statute, jury-court, or trial concerning the abuse (perhaps even the formation) of *sodalicia* or clubs or societies, especially 'Secret Societies' (= *collegia* under another name?) for electoral purposes. Attempts were made to outlaw these practices in the 50s BC.

de vi (*lex/ quaestio/ iudicium*)   Statute, court, or trial concerning charges of using 'violence' as defined by the series of statutes as it developed (from Sulla's dictatorship onwards, if not earlier), especially public violence— that is mass violence for the disruption or manipulation of legislative, electoral, and judicial processes in Roman public life.

dictator (Lanuvii)   In 52 BC Milo was evidently *dictator* at the *municipium* (see below) of Lanuvium, in Latium—that is, holder of the chief magistracy (most probably) of this local township. It would appear that Roman notables might at times accept such appointments as a matter of patronage, to extend or exercise *clientelae*, always valuable for marshalling the vote in the assemblies, especially for elections, and the more valuable if near Rome.

divinatio   A legal process preliminary to a trial under public law to decide which among competing would-be prosecutors is to present the case for the accusers.

edictum   Published declaration by a magistrate of anything which in his official capacity he wished to be made generally known. Often used of the Praetor's Edict—from *c.* mid-second century BC a declaration by the urban praetor of the principles by which he intended to interpret the civil law (*ius civile*) during his tenure. Often taken over by successive praetors, with whatever amendments (usually supplements) they thought fit. Similar practice was later adopted by (some) provincial governors— e.g. Q. Scaevola, apparently the first, in the 90s.

eques (pl. *equites*)   Lit. 'horseman' and often translated 'knight'. A member of a group which originally provided the cavalry in the Roman army, who was awarded a 'public horse' (*equus publicus*). By Cicero's time, the term seems to be used for all those with sufficient property to qualify for this group, and this social and economic class provided members of the juries in *quaestio* trials, along with senators and *tribuni aerarii* (see below).

flamen   Priest charged with cult practices of a single nominated deity.

haruspex (pl. *haruspices*)   Religious official(s) charged with the practice, almost certainly imported from Etruria and anyhow of great antiquity, of divining the outcome of some proposed action by examining the entrails of animals sacrificed prior to the enterprise.

imperator   In the Republic, an honorific appellation, rather than a title proper, conferred upon a successful military commander by his troops.

incestum   Offence against religious laws (syn. *sacrilegium*), esp. sexual outrage against same—e.g. the conduct alleged against P. Clodius in the Bona Dea scandal of 62; misconduct of/with Vestals, 114/13; 73.

intercalary month   In effect, an extension of February by twenty-two or twenty-three days starting on 24th or 25th, apparently always to make a total, including the 'lost' days of February, of twenty-seven days before 1 March. This insertion into the pre-Julian Roman Calendar was made from time to time as and when the need was perceived, in order to bring the civic year more closely into line with the solar year. Further analysis in Michels (1967), 145–72; Lintott (1968).

interrex (pl. *interreges*); *interregnum*   If, as happened in 52 BC, the official year at Rome began without any consuls having been elected, an *interrex* ('between-king', 'temporary ruler') would be appointed (by the patrician senators) to discharge the basic consular functions of state and to nominate a second *interrex* who would preside over consular elections in an effort to normalize the situation. If he failed, he would nominate a third *interrex* for the same purpose, and so the series would go on, until consuls were duly elected. An *interrex* could not hold his office (*interregnum*) for more than five days, and was always a senior (preferably, of course, consular) patrician.

iustitium Suspension of public business by senate and magistrates, usually on grounds of persistent public disorder, but sometimes for other reasons—e.g. religious, as in the case of the Latin Festival.

knight See *eques* above.

Latin (status) In brief, after 338 BC (if not earlier) Latin status comprised the private rights of Roman citizenship—namely, those of *conubium* (legally recognized marriage with Roman citizens, the children of which would enjoy the status of the father); *commercium* (the right to make contracts with Roman citizens that were enforceable under Roman civil law); *migratio* (modified 187; 177 BC) (the right to assume full Roman citizenship on moving domicile to Rome). Latins present in Rome at the time of a tribal assembly might on at least some occasions be allocated by lot a tribe in which they could cast a vote—surely never of any real significance—but otherwise lacked all Roman political rights, most notably not only any normal voting rights, but also the right to stand for office in the Roman state. From the Gracchan period, however, the magistrates of Latin communities could be and presumably normally were enrolled as full Roman citizens.

legatus (**pl.** *legati*) An appointee, deputy, or delegate. The term is most commonly used of (*a*) envoys, ambassadors; (*b*) deputies of provincial commanders, chosen or at least accepted by them and officially approved by the senate.

lictor (**pl.** *lictores*) Attendant(s) upon a curule magistrate, in varying numbers according to seniority, who bore before him bundles of rods and axe, the symbols of the right to inflict capital punishment.

magister (**pl.** *magistri*) Lit. 'a superior, master'—hence typically used of the chairman or president of a limited corporate community—most commonly a *collegium* ('guild'); a *vicus* ('village' in the countryside, or 'ward', 'quarter' of Rome—hence *vicomagister*); or of a schoolmaster, teacher.

manumit, manumission Liberation of a slave into legally free but still dependent status by his/her owner.

modius   A Roman measure of volume, generally of corn, for which it is the standard unit.

municipium (pl. *municipia*)   In the Republic, a community originally not of Roman status, but incorporated into the Roman state and liable to all imposts and duties to which Roman citizens were subject, whether or not, in addition to the private rights of citizens, the inhabitants also (as after the Social War was always the case) held the *ius suffragii*—the right to vote in the Roman assemblies and stand for Roman offices. *Municipia* were often, though not always, at some considerable distance from Rome and of considerable size—and therefore of necessity tended to enjoy a large measure of independence under local laws and local magistrates operating under an overall umbrella of Roman law operated from time to time by *praefecti* (prefects, deputies of the praetor). It would appear that the large-scale enfranchisement of Italian communities after the Social War necessitated and greatly accelerated the process of systematizing, by granting suitably devised 'charters', the previously often unsatisfactorily defined relationship between local and Roman institutions.

nobilis   'Noble'. In Roman political parlance this is a technical, or anyhow semi-technical term, *not* to be taken simply as a synonym for 'aristocrat', and most certainly not as a synonym for 'patrician'. The traditional definition, most clearly propounded by M. Gelzer (1969*b*), makes the term apply solely to persons of consular descent, and for most purposes this suffices. For revision and refinement, however, see Brunt (1982); comment by Badian (1990), 371–2; Burckhardt (1990), 89–98; Shackleton Bailey (1986); Vanderbroeck (1986).

novus homo   Lit. 'new man'. Again modern definitions have been somewhat variable. As a general rule the term most readily applies to persons entering the senate from non-senatorial families. It was rare (but perhaps not so rare as Cicero and Sallust sometimes maintain) for such persons to attain the consulship. For further inquiry and refinement, again see Brunt (1982) and other bibliography, as for *nobilis* above.

obnuntiatio   Obstruction of legislative assemblies in Rome by a curule magistrate's declaration of intention to watch the skies for unfavourable omens, typically under the Leges Aelia et Fufia, abrogated or modified by P. Clodius as tribune of the plebs in 58 BC.

optimates   The word is very rarely found in Latin before Cicero, who uses it to designate conservatively minded supporters of Senatorial dominance in Roman political life, often as an equivalent of his ironic term *boni*, roughly translatable as 'the great and good'. Such persons, contrary to some textbooks, never constituted anything that may reasonably be considered a political 'party' in any modern sense, but only a category of persons of certain persuasions and attitudes.

perduellio Hostile conduct against one's own state, treason, by the late Republic no longer necessarily exclusively an act of war, but in any case by then an almost unheard-of accusation in the courts, revived by Caesar and others in 63 BC against Cicero's client C. Rabirius for his (alleged) role against Saturninus and his followers in 100 BC, and threatened against Cicero by P. Clodius in 58 BC.

pontifex (maximus) The pontifices or pontiffs constituted the senior college (*collegium*) among Rome's major priesthoods, headed unlike other such colleges (e.g. the augurs) by an official presidential figure, the *pontifex maximus* (lit. 'Greatest Pontifex'), who was thus the High Priest of the Roman state. Access to the pontificate was from 300 BC under the Lex Ogulnia open to plebeians as well as patricians, and originally by co-optation, but after various earlier vicissitudes by popular election by 63 BC, when C. Iulius Caesar, already appointed a *pontifex* ten years earlier, was elected *pontifex maximus* (*MRR* 2. 171).

princeps senatus 'Leader of the senate', the first-named by the censors on the senatorial roll which it was one of their duties to revise, and generally the senior surviving patrician ex-consul.

provincia Often translated 'province', not always misleadingly. More accurately the sphere within which a magistrate exercises his powers—so not always to be defined in geographic terms, and often better translated 'remit', 'command', or 'command-area'.

quaesitor 'Investigator'—any magistrate or other duly appointed official presiding over an investigation, most commonly a trial. Notably for Asconius, *quaesitores* presided in 52 BC when no other suitable person (e.g. a praetor or consul) was available or appropriate, before the year's praetors could be appointed.

quaestio 'Inquiry', mostly commonly a court or trial, whether a standing jury-court (*quaestio perpetua*) under a statute regulating trials on defined charges and by a defined procedure; or *quaestio extraordinaria* set up by ad hoc provisions for a single case or set of cases.

regia Most commonly refers to the official residence of the *pontifex maximus*, but can also refer to the portico of any (large) public building—e.g. of Pompey's Theatre, built 55 BC.

rogatio   Legislative draft as presented to an assembly for ratification, after which it becomes statute law, whether in the form of a *lex* (a law in the proper statutory sense) or a *plebis scitum* ('ordinance of the plebs') which after the Lex Hortensia of 287 BC also had the binding force of law over the whole people (*populus*).

rostra   The main platform for speakers in the Forum Romanum, adorned with the ships' 'beaks' or prows, in the Roman tradition taken from the fleet of Antium captured in the Latin War in 338 BC.

scriba (pl. *scribae*)   Employee of the Roman state concerned with notarizing, drafting, recording, and archiving documents and producing them on demand, working under the direction of magistrates. Apparently of relatively high social ranking and census-rating.

tresviri capitales (single member *triumvir capitalis*)   An annually elected Board of Three very junior (pre-quaestorian) officers in charge of what limited (nocturnal?) policing was provided in the city of Rome; running prisons and possibly executions and basic judicial administration.

tres viri coloniae deducendae causa   Board of Three appointed ad hoc for the settling of a *colonia* or *coloniae*. (Exceptionally, such boards might exceed three in number.)

tribunal   Lit. a platform. Commonly in the Forum, to elevate the seat of a magistrate or officer presiding over a court hearing or making some other pronouncement.

tribuni aerarii   Patently numerous enough to provide one-third of a jury in the 'criminal courts' after 70 BC: perhaps the title is honorific, or applied to a class (however defined), rather than to appointed officials. Apparently by census-rating the equals, or very nearly so, of *equites* (knights), who in the late Republic had to be worth at least HS 400,000.

trinundinum (or *trinum nundinum*)   The statutory minimum interval between the promulgation of proposed legislation and putting it (*rogatio*) to an assembly for its ratification; or between announcing and holding elections; or between indictment and trial before an assembly (rather than in a *quaestio*). See further Lintott (1965), (1968), and (1999*a*), 44, 62; Michels (1967), 36–60 (esp. 46), 206; above, on Ascon. 8C.

Index of Personal Names

Acilius Glabrio, M'. (cos. 67) See *MRR* 2. 142, 154; 3. 2–3. Unremarkable, of established plebeian consular family. Granted command of Bithynia and Pontus by a tribunician law of A. Gabinius, supplanting L. Lucullus in those areas.

Acilius Glabrio, M'. Joined in dramatic pleas to the jury for M. Scaurus at his trial in 54, as son of Scaurus' sister.

Aelius Lamia, L. Equestrian allegedly (Cic. *Sest.* 12) banished 200 miles from Rome by A. Gabinius, as cos. 58.

Aelius Paetus, Sex. (censor 194) According to Antias, with his colleague C. Cornelius Cethegus ordered provision of separate seating for senators at the Roman Games given by the aediles of that year.

Aemilia Vestal condemned *de incesto* 114 by L. Metellus, *pontifex maximus*, cos. 119.

Aemilius Buca, L. (younger) Totally obscure, joined in dramatic pleading to jury for M. Scaurus, 54.

Aemilius Lepidus, M. (cos. 78) Attempted revolution against provisions of Sulla, 78/7, based in Etruria and Cisalpine Gaul. Failed against his fellow cos. Q. Lutatius Catulus (see below) and the young Cn. Pompeius. Died shortly afterwards on Sardinia.

Aemilius Lepidus, M. *Interrex* 52, later cos. 46, Caesarian, later IIIvir with M. Antonius and C. Caesar Octavianus. See standard accounts, esp. Syme (1939).

Aemilius Lepidus, M'. (cos. 66) Completely unremarkable, except for his Aemilian blood.

Aemilius Lepidus, Mam. (cos. 77) Unremarkable, but a kinsman of the rebel M. Lepidus. Survived long after this year as a senior consular.

Aemilius Paulus, L. (cos. II 168) The famous Paulus, son of the one beaten and killed by Hannibal at Cannae (216), himself victor of King Perseus of Macedon 168, winner of enormous booty, holder of most spectacular triumph to date, 167. Settled Greek East 167 (for a time); father of P. Scipio Aemilianus.

Aemilius Paulus, L. (cos. 50) Low profile. Probably bought by Caesar in political machinations before Civil War of 49.

Aemilius Philemon, M. Freedman of a M. Lepidus—perhaps *not* the *interrex* of 52.

issue by 131, held out until at least 129 when he inflicted a major defeat on Roman forces under P. Licinius Crassus, cos. 131 (see below).

Ateius, C. An accuser of Milo, 52, *de ambitu*, with the two Appi Claudii and L. Cornificius (see below). Perhaps the tr. pl. of 55, though at that time opposed to Pompeius and Crassus.

Atilius Calatinus, A. (cos. 258; 254) Relatively successful commander in the earlier stages of the First Punic War.

Atilius Serranus, C. (aed. cur. 194) Provided special seating for senators at the Roman Games given by himself and his colleague L. Scribonius Libo (see below).

Atilius Serranus, Sex. (tr. pl. 57) Only he and Q. Numerius (see below) of the year's tribunes opposed the consular rogation of P. Cornelius Lentulus Spinther to recall Cicero—or so Cicero avers.

Attius Celsus, C. (pr. 65) Urged Cicero to defend C. Cornelius.

Aurelius Cotta, C. (cos. 75) Eldest of three brothers. As consul, amid minor measures, proposed removal of Sulla's ban on tribunes taking further office.

Aurelius Cotta, L. (pr. 70; cos. 65) Youngest of the three brothers, as pr. 70 passed law to settle the problem of jury-composition for all *quaestiones publicae* by empanelling them from equal numbers of senators, *equites*, and *tribuni aerarii*. Elected consul with L. Manlius Torquatus, following the deposition for *ambitus* of those initially designated, P. Sulla and P. Autronius (see Glossary, *de ambitu*).

Aurelius Cotta, M. (cos. 74) The middle brother of the three Cottae. Commanded a fleet in the opening phases of the Third Mithridatic War, with no success, besieged at Chalcedon until relieved by his colleague L. Licinius Lucullus (see below).

Autronius Paetus, P. (cos. des. 65) Deposed after designation as cos., after being convicted *de ambitu* under the recent (67) Lex Calpurnia. Allegedly involved in the so-called First Catilinarian Conspiracy (largely or wholly fiction).

Basilus Obscure. Asconius offers a little information at 50C.

Bellienus, L. Allegedly killer of Q. Lucretius Afella (rather than Ofella) in 81 on Sulla's orders, for insisting on standing for the consulship in defiance of the dictator's wishes. According to Cicero, uncle to Catilina. Condemned *de sicariis*, in court probably presided over that year by C. Iulius Caesar as *iudex quaestionis*.

Birria Slave, gladiator, retainer of Milo, alleged first to strike Clodius in the brawl at Bovillae, 52, which ended in Clodius' death.

Boculus Famous or infamous charioteer *c.*67–64 (so Ascon. 93C).

Caecilius Metellus Balearicus, Q. (cos. 123) Eldest son of Q. Macedonicus (cos. 143). Minor anti-pirate campaign in Balearic Islands, 123. No distinction whatever except aristocratic blood. (Also true of his three brothers, L. Metellus Diadematus (cos. 117), M. Metellus (cos. 115), and C. Metellus Caprarius (cos. 113).)

Caecilius Metellus Celer, Q. (cos. 60) Should also be a son of Q. Metellus Nepos, cos. 98, but see Wiseman (1971a). As pr. 63 refused to accept custody of Catilina, but assisted in suppression of insurgents in Italy, holding Picenum and Ager Gallicus—presumably to preserve Pompeius' fiefdom there, having been his legate in the East 66. Married (at some stage) to his own cousin, eldest of the three Clodiae.

Caecilius Metellus Creticus, Q. (cos. 69) Attempted campaign as procos. 68–65 against pirates on Crete. No great success, overshadowed by Pompeius' giant command and rapid success of 67. Resultantly chilly attitude to Pompeius—and most others. Eventual triumph, hardly earned, in 62, after a supporting role in suppressing the Catilinarian rebels in Italy 63/2. His daughter, Metella, married the elder son of M. Licinius Crassus (cos. 70; 55), like his father killed by the Parthians at Carrhae.

Caecilius Metellus Delmaticus, L. (cos. 119; cens. 114) Son of L. Metellus Calvus, cos. 142, and nephew to Q. Macedonicus, cos. 143. A little transadriatic campaigning; temple-building in Rome. Ineffectual *pontifex maximus* by 114. No other distinction whatever except his aristocratic blood.

Caecilius Metellus Macedonicus, Q. (cos. 143) Late-born son of cos. 206. Claimed his *agnomen* 'Macedonicus' for his defeat as pr. 148 of Andriscus, pretender to the Macedonian throne. Fathered four sons and two daughters—hence multiple connections and power for the Metelli in later generations. (Cf. his brother L. Metellus Calvus, cos. 142, with two sons and a daughter, similarly adding to the dynastic empire. The daughter was mother to L. and M. Licinius Lucullus, coss. 74; 73.)

Caecilius Metellus Nepos, Q. (cos. 98) Grandson of Macedonicus, son of Balearicus. Co-author with T. Didius of a conservatively orientated law to prevent passing unrelated measures in a single *rogatio*. Otherwise totally undistinguished. A sister married Ap. Claudius Pulcher, cos. 79 and bore the three brothers Ap. Claudius Pulcher, cos. 54, C. Clodius, pr. 55, and the infamous P. Clodius Pulcher—as well as the three sisters Clodiae.

Caecilius Metellus Nepos, Q. (cos. 57) Son of Q. Metellus Nepos, cos. 98. Rowdy tribune aligned with Caesar (pr.) and opposed by M. Cato in 62, perhaps seeking to promote or defend the interests of Pompeius, whom he had served as legate against the pirates and in the East 67–63. For tangled details, see *MRR* 2. 539, 3. 40.

resultant command. Prevented consular candidature of Lollius Palicanus (Pompeian supporter). Took command of Transalpine Gaul where he suppressed an Allobrogan rising; and of Cisalpine Gaul, where he violated citizen rights. Later implacable enemy of C. Iulius Caesar, whom he strove to implicate in the Catilinarian affair of 63.

Calpurnius Piso Caesoninus, L. (cos. 58) Proconsul Macedonia 57–56. Target of Cicero's polemic *In Pisonem*, chiefly because as cos. 58, like his colleague A. Gabinius, he completely failed to protect Cicero against P. Clodius, tr. pl.

Calpurnius Piso, Cn. (quaestor 64 *pro praetore*, Spain) Alleged partisan of L. Sergius Catilina. Killed in Spain, allegedly by partisans/clients of Cn. Pompeius Magnus, perhaps even with Pompeius' consent or on his orders, so some professed to believe.

Calpurnius Piso Frugi, C. Cicero's first son-in-law. Died young.

Calventius Allegedly an Insubrian Gaul who migrated to Rome and insinuated himself into the family of the Calpurnii Pisones.

Cassius, L. Accuser of Milo's henchman M. Saufeius, 52.

Cassius Longinus, C. (cos. 96) Of no known importance whatever.

Cassius Longinus, L. (tr. pl. 104) Passed a law to expel from the senate anyone deposed from *imperium* or condemned by the people.

Cassius Longinus, L. Competitor of Cicero, 64, for the consulship. Later threw in his lot with L. Catilina.

Cassius Longinus Ravilla, L. (cos. 127) Originator of the famous (infamous) advocate's motto '*Cui bono?*' ('Who gains?') in murder trials over which he presided. Special inquisitor (or prosecutor) in the scandal of the Vestals, 114/13, condemning a Marcia and a Licinia, and several others in addition (Ascon. 46C). Earlier as tr. pl. passed a *lex tabellaria* to institute secret ballot in trials before the people in all cases except for *perduellio*.

Cassius, 'P.' (pr. 66) Failed to appear, as appointed, to preside over trial of C. Cornelius *de maiestate* that year. The *praenomen* 'P.' (so MSS of Ascon.) is probably incorrect: *MRR* 2. 152, 3. 51 prefers 'L.', which allows identification with Cicero's rival in the consular elections of 64, later Catilinarian (above).

Causinius Schola, L. Equestrian from Interamna (Nahars—Umbrian/ Sabine), intimate of P. Clodius.

Claudii Pulchri, Appii The transmitted text of Asconius makes them *both* sons of C. Claudius, elder brother of P. Clodius, which makes the *praenomen* look odd if both survived to accuse Milo, as Asconius records. The explanation is that the younger was a son of C. Claudius, pr. 56 but adopted by Ap. Claudius Pulcher, cos. 54. The elder, C. f., the future consul of 38, led the successful prosecutions of T. Milo in 52.

320 *Index of Personal Names*

to embassies from foreign peoples. Then proposed a law to renew ban on exemptions from law except by vote of the people, opposed by optimates through their agent the tr. pl. P. Servilius Globulus. Cornelius' countermoves aroused great opposition on constitutional grounds from the consul C. Piso, and the assembly broke up in a violent riot. In ensuing senatorial debate, Cornelius sought compromise, requiring a quorum of 200 for a senatorial decree to exempt from laws, and a ban on the veto when such a vote was put to the people for ratification. His second proposal was to insist on praetors observing their own edicts in jurisdiction, also unwelcome to optimates. Several other proposals of his were vetoed, amid much dissension. An attempt to prosecute him in 66 *de maiestate* collapsed, but was renewed in 65. Hence Cicero's defence, which succeeded—but Cornelius is not known to have held further office.

Cornelius Cethegus, C. (cens. 194) Cos. 197, when he had triumphed over Insubres and Cenomani. Relatively ordinary censorship, when he and his colleague set aside special seating for senators.

Cornelius Cinna, L. (cos. 87–84) Dominant in Roman politics from cos. I (87) to death as cos. IV in 84. Opposed to Sulla, but probably less extreme than C. Carbo, his somewhat unreliable collaborator.

Cornelius, Cn. Perhaps a moneyer, *c.*100. As pr. 78 L. Sisenna, perhaps a relative, awarded his property to the aristocratic P. Scipio, unidentifiable.

Cornelius Dolabella, Cn. (P. f. L. n.) (cos. 81) Procos. Macedonia, 80–78, indicted by C. Caesar 77 *de repetundis*. Acquitted.

Cornelius Dolabella, Cn. (Cn. f. Cn. n. (?)) (pr. urb. 81) Procos. Cilicia 80–79, indicted *de repetundis* by the younger M. Scaurus in ?78. Convicted.

Cornelius Lentulus Clodianus, Cn. (cos. 72; cens. 70). Jointly responsible with his colleague in the censorship for expelling as many as sixty-four senators, it would seem mostly but not all creatures of Sulla from 81. (They included C. Antonius, cos. 63; P. Lentulus Sura, pr. 63 and ally of L. Catilina).

Cornelius Lentulus Dolabella, P. (son-in-law to Cicero). Married Cicero's daughter Tullia after decease of her first husband C. Calpurnius Piso (see above).

Cornelius Lentulus Marcellinus, Cn. (cos. 56) Aristocratic non entity.

Cornelius Lentulus Niger, L. (*flamen Martialis*, attested 73).

Cornelius Lentulus, P. (son of pr. urb. 81). Joined in dramatic plea to jury for M. Scaurus, 54.

Cornelius Lentulus Spinther, P. (cos. 57) Correspondent of Cicero, instrumental in his recall from exile. Failed in ambition to command in takeover of Egypt from Ptolemies.

Cornelius Scipio Aemilianus, P. (cos. 147; 134) The famous (Younger) Scipio Aemilianus (Africanus Minor). The standard account is Astin (1967).

Cornelius Scipio Africanus, P. (cos. 205; 194) The famous (Elder) Scipio Africanus. The standard account is Scullard (1970).

Cornelius Scipio, P. (cos. 218) Father of Africanus. With colleague Ti. Longus, lost to Hannibal at Trebia (218) but went on to command in Spain with great success until killed on campaign there in 212.

Cornelius Sisenna, L. (pr. 78) The historian, probably best of his day. Wrote what was regarded as the definitive history (from the Roman viewpoint!) of the Marsic/Social War, but most probably included much of the Civil Wars of the 80s. Possibly of Etruscan ancestry, to judge from the name.

Cornelius Sulla, Faustus (quaestor 54) Son of following. Joined in dramatic appeal to jury for M. Scaurus, his half-brother. Pompeian partisan in Civil Wars 49–46. Killed 46.

Cornelius Sulla, L. (dict. 81; 80) The infamous dictator. Modern accounts include *CAH* IX², ch. 6; Keaveney (1982).

Cornelius Sulla, P. (cos. des. 65) Deposed with his prospective colleague P. Autronius after being convicted *de ambitu* during the consular elections. Defended by Cicero on charges of collusion with L. Catilina. Caesarian legate, 48–47.

Cornificius, L. Accuser of Milo, 52, *de ambitu,* and also in his second (nominal) trial *de vi.*

Cornificius, Q. Thoroughly respectable and ineffectual competitor of M. Cicero for consulship in elections of 64.

Curius Dentatus, M'. (cos. 290, 275, and 274) Victorious general against the Samnites and King Pyrrhus in the 3rd cent. BC. Famous as a type of old Roman virtue, frugality, and incorruptibility.

Curius, Q. The damaged MSS of Ascon. 93C appear to make him still quaestorian in 64, so unlikely to be identical with the man of similar name (but perhaps really L. Turius?), who was consular candidate in 65, so pr. by 67. Notorious gambler, later condemned. Probably the quaestorian expelled from the senate by the censors (so in 70), (alleged) betrayer of Catilina's secrets to Cicero through his mistress Fulvia (Sall. *Bell. Cat.* 17; 23 etc.).

Damio (P. Clodius) Freedman of P. Clodius, gangster 58.

Didius, T. (cos. 98) Co-author of Lex Caecilia Didia banning composite rogations covering more than one measure. Lengthy and fairly brutally effective tenure of Hispania Citerior ensued, with a second triumph 93.

Domitius Ahenobarbus, Cn. (cos. 96; tr. pl. 104) As tr. pl. failed in indictments of M. Iunius Silanus (cos. 109) and M. Aemilius Scaurus (cos. 115); passed a law to appoint priests no longer by co-optation within the colleges, but by popular vote of seventeen of the thirty-five tribes.

Domitius Ahenobarbus, L. (cos. 94) Little else known.

Domitius Ahenobarbus, L. (cos. 54) Violent opponent of C. Manilius' law on freedmen's voting as tr. pl. 66, so favoured by conservative senators thereafter. Bitter enemy of Caesar, politically close to his brother-in-law M. Cato. Kept out of consulship by enemies until 54. Attempted to succeed Caesar in Gaul. Hostile presentation in most sources, esp. Caes. *BC*. Killed at Pharsalus, 48.

Domitius Calvinus, Cn. (pr. *de ambitu* 56; cos. 53) Caesarian, commanded centre at Pharsalus, subsequently Asia 48–46. Survived to be cos. II 40, command in Spain 39–36.

Domitius, Cn. Probably son of previous. Joint accuser of Milo 52 *de ambitu*.

Eudamus Slave, gladiator, in Milo's retinue in clash with P. Clodius at Bovillae, 52.

Fabia, Vestal, accused and acquitted *de incesto* 73.

Fabius, L. The inquisitor in the second case of 52 *de vi* against Milo.

Fabius Maximus, Q. (cos. V 209) Major military and political figure during the Second Punic War, nicknamed Cunctator ('the Delayer') because of his promotion of a war of attrition against Hannibal.

Fabricius Luscinus, C. (cos. 282 and 278) Victorious general in the 3rd cent. BC, renowned for his incorruptibility and austerity of life.

Fausta, Cornelia Daughter of Sulla the dictator, brother of Faustus Cornelius Sulla and wife of Milo in 52, present at the 'Battle of Bovillae'.

Favonius, M. (pr. 49) Follower and slavish imitator of M. Cato. Pompeian in Civil War.

Fenestella Historian/antiquarian of ?Tiberian age. Often cited—critically—by Asconius.

Fidius, C. Accuser of M. Saufeius in his second trial *de vi*, 52.

Flaminia Mother of P. Valerius Triarius, accuser of M. Scaurus in 54, close friend of Servilia, half-sister to M. Cato, pr. 54, who was presiding over the court.

Flavius Fimbria, C. Mutinous legate to L. Valerius Flaccus, cos. suff., in expedition of 86 to confront Mithridates in Asia in the Cinnan cause. Connived at or incited Flaccus' murder by his troops, but after important victories in Asia himself succumbed to their mutiny and desertion to Sulla there in 85.

Flavius, L. (pr. 58) Clashed with P. Clodius when Clodius snatched Tigranes, interned prince of Armenia, from his custody.

Fufius Calenus, L. Harried if did not indict Q. Mucius Orestinus (tr. pl. 64) for theft, who begged Cicero to defend him. Otherwise unknown.

Fufius, M. Friend of Milo, and his travelling companion at Bovillae, 52.

Fufius, Q. (cos. 47) In 61 mitigated severity of senatorial decree against Clodius in the Bona Dea affair. In 52, assisted the tribunes T. Munatius Plancus and C. Sallustius Crispus against Q. Hortensius' attempted intervention on behalf of Milo.

Fulcinius, L. (tr. pl. 52) Among M. Saufeius' accusers in his first indictment *de vi*, 52.

Fulvia Wife of P. Clodius, 52. Aroused popular feeling by her lamentations over his corpse at his home before its transfer to the *rostra* and then the senate house. Subsequently gave her evidence in similarly emotive fashion, with her mother Sempronia, daughter of a Sempronius Tuditanus. Quite probably to be identified with the Fulvia who was mistress to Q. Curius (see above) and acted as a double agent in the Catilinarian affair of 63. Certainly later (and famously) wife to M. Antonius, IIIvir, after a brief marriage with C. Scribonius Curio, Caesarian tribune 50, killed in the Civil War in 49.

Fulvius Flaccus, M. (cos. 125; tr. pl. 122) Unreliable, turbulent ally of C. Gracchus as tr. pl. 122. See further *MRR* 1. 510, 512, 517, 521.

Fulvius Neratus, P. Accused T. Milo in 52 *de sodaliciis*, and was rewarded for his success.

Furius Camillus, M. Enormous tally of high offices on record. Legendary military leader, organizer, and commander at close of 5th cent. and early 4th. See further *MRR* 1.

Gabinius, A. (tr. pl. 67) Author of law to establish a pan-Mediterranean command against piracy, awarded to Cn. Pompeius Magnus.

Gallius, Q. (aed. 67; pr. 65) Acquitted *de ambitu* 64.

Gellius, L. (cos. 72) As censor of 70 jointly responsible with Cn. Lentulus Clodianus (also cos. 72) for expelling as many as sixty-four from the senate, including C. Antonius, P. Lentulus Sura, Q. Curius, and perhaps others with later Catilinarian affiliations—as was his own highly disreputable non-senatorial brother.

Herennius Balbus, L. Tried to retaliate on Milo's behalf against his accusers, 52, by demanding production of Clodius' slave household for interrogation.

Hortensius, Q. (cos. 69) Cicero's somewhat older famous rival for fame as an orator. Optimate politics, well-connected. See esp. Cic. *Brutus* (and Douglas (1966)).

Hostilius Tubulus (pr. 142) Notoriously corrupt in presiding over murder trials. On indictment and summons from exile in 141 committed suicide.

Licinius Crassus, P. (cos. 97) Governed Farther Spain 96–93, ending with a Lusitanian triumph. Father of the famous M. Crassus, cos. 70; II 55.

Licinius Lucullus, L. (cos. 74) Most famous Lucullus. See standard accounts. Married first to the second of the three Clodia sisters; then to the elder Servilia, half-sister to M. Cato. Famous (infamous) *bon viveur*, possessed of enormous wealth after his campaigns against Mithridates and his ally Tigranes of Armenia. Of some assistance in suppressing insurgents in Italy 63 while waiting to triumph with some few troops outside Rome. Later lapsed into dementia.

Licinius Lucullus, M. (cos. 73) Brother of Lucius, adopted by a M. Terentius Varro. Average career, unremarkable. Co-author of a law to restore some measure of corn distribution, 73.

Licinius Sacerdos, C. (pr. 75) Lightweight candidate for the consulship of 63 in competition with Cicero.

Livius Drusus, M. (tr. pl. 91) Son of tr. pl. 122, who opposed C. Gracchus. Author of a package of reforms essentially in the conservative interest, 91. No success, assassinated.

Livius (Patavinus), T. Livy, the historian. Still the best overall account is that of Walsh (1961).

Lucceius, L. Historian (recipient of Cic. *Fam.* 5.12), consular candidate 60, indicted L. Catilina *de sicariis* 64/3 without apparent success.

Lucilius The famous satirist. Family later related by marriage to Cn. Pompeius Strabo/Magnus.

Lucilius, C. Agent for his friend Milo in dealings with Pompey. This is quite likely C. Lucilius Hirrus, tr. pl. 53, Pompey's cousin, politically lightweight, but of considerable landed wealth.

Lucius A known plebeian in 52. Utterly unidentifiable.

Lucretius Afella (Ofella), Q. Attempted to stand for the consulship of 80 against the express wishes of Sulla, who procured his assassination—allegedly by L. Bellienus.

Luscius, L. A centurion of Sulla and great profiteer from his victory in the Civil War of 82/1. Condemned 64, probably, like L. Bellienus, for murders at that time.

Lutatius Catulus, Q. (cos. 78) Pillar of the optimate Establishment in the post-Sullan era. Opposed award of large command to Pompeius, 66. Lost election as *pontifex maximus* to C. Caesar in 63. Dedicated Capitol, rebuilt after conflagration 83/2.

Manilius, C. (tr. pl. 66) Passed and rapidly repealed law to allow freedmen('s sons?) to vote in all thirty-five tribes; and to give Pompey enormous powers *extra ordinem* to fight the war against Mithridates. Indicted 65—??*de repetundis.*

Manilius Cumanus, Q. (tr. pl. 52) With colleague M. Caelius Rufus rescued a slave from custody and restored him to Milo.

Manlius, C. Sullan veteran, Catilina's chief agent in 63 in Faesulae and surrounding Etruria—allegedly.

Manlius Torquatus, A. *Quaesitor* 52 for trials of Milo *de vi lege Pompeia* and *de ambitu.* Possibly but only very doubtfully identifiable as L. Torquatus, cos. 65.

Manlius Torquatus, L. (cos. suff. 65) Elected with L. Cotta to replace the deposed P. Autronius, whom he had successfully indicted *de ambitu.* Prospective victim of so-called First Catilinarian Conspiracy.

Marcius Figulus, C. (cos. 64) Of consular descent. Completely unremarkable.

Marcius Philippus, L. (cos. 91) Conservative opponent of M. Livius Drusus, tr. pl. (see above). See further *MRR* 2. 20; 54; 3. 139.

Marcius Philippus, L. (cos. 56) No activity on record at this stage of his career. Later, after Caesar's murder in 44, of some importance as a senior consular and stepfather to the young C. Caesar Octavianus.

Marius, C. (cos. 107; 104–100; 86) The famous C. Marius. See standard accounts.

Marius Gratidianus, M. (pr. 85; 84). Related to both the Marii and the Tullii (Cicerones) of Arpinum. Politically active during the Cinnan regime, author of financial reforms. Brutally killed by L. Catilina (allegedly) in the bloodbath after Sulla's victory, 82/1.

Marius, L. Co-accuser of M. Scaurus, 54, and himself subsequently attacked for *calumnia* (false accusation). Possibly the tr. pl. 62 of that name; or the quaestor 50. Or neither.

Memmius, C. (tr. pl. 66) Hostile to the Luculli 66; pr. 58, hostile to Caesar. Commanded Bithynia/Pontus 57/6. Divorced Fausta, daughter of Sulla, late 55 or early 54. Much involved in intricacies of mid-50s politics.

Memmius, C. (son of previous) Joined in dramatic appeal to jury for M. Scaurus, 54.

Mithridates (VI of Pontus) The Mithridates against whom Rome fought three wars, two of them large-scale. Suicide 63 in the Crimea, his empire by then dismantled by L. Lucullus and Cn. Pompeius Magnus. More in Reinach (1890); Sherwin-White (1984), chs. 5–9; *CAH* IX^2, ch. 5.

Mucia Tertia Daughter of a Mucius, probably Q. Scaevola, cos. 95, and a Metella, daughter of Balearicus. Mother of M. Scaurus pr. 56 before her (third) marriage to Pompey, who divorced her on his return from the East in 62 for notorious infidelity, target of one of Cicero's sharper witticisms.

Mucius Orestinus, Q. (tr. pl. 64) The *cognomen* ought to reveal kinship with earlier consular Aurelii Orestae (coss. 157; 126) and Aurelia Orestilla, wife of L. Catilina. She is not mentioned by Asconius, who presumably when he wrote the commentary on the *Or. in. tog. cand.*, had not yet read Sallust's *Bell. Cat.*, which he probably did later when he came to write his *Life of Sallust*.

Mucius Scaevola, Q. (cos. 95) Co-author with his colleague L. Licinius Crassus of the Lex Licinia Mucia to regulate citizenship in Rome and Italy. Also commanded Asia (97/6 or 95/4) with great credit, probably the first provincial governor to issue an edict for jurisdiction in his command.

Munatius Plancus, L. Mentioned in Asconius as an orator, brother of T. Plancus, tr. pl. 52. Later a correspondent of Cicero, important Caesarian, with a key role 44/3; cos. 42. Founder of the citizen *colonia* at Lugdunum (Lyon).

Munatius Plancus, T. (tr. pl. 52) With his colleague Q. Pompeius Rufus incited the mob to take Clodius' corpse from his house and display it on the *rostra*. Later with M. Antonius at Mutina, 43.

Ninnius Quadratus, L. (tr. pl. 58) Attempted to prevent the Ludi Compitales given by Clodian gang-leader Sex. Cloelius (see above). Also to support Cicero.

Novius, L. (tr. pl. 58) Took cognizance of alleged attempt to besiege Pompey's home.

Numerius, Q. (tr. pl. 57) Allegedly one of only two tribunes to oppose recall of Cicero.

Octavius, Cn. (cos. 87) Extreme optimate, opposed to his colleague L. Cinna. Killed in civil strife of that year.

Octavius Laenas Curtianus, M. Otherwise unknown. Joined in dramatic appeal to jury for M. Scaurus, 54.

Octavius, M. (tr. pl. 133) Attempted opposition to Ti. Gracchus, 133. See standard accounts.

Opimius, L. (cos. 121) Acquitted on indictment by P. Decius Subolo (tr. pl.) before *concilium plebis* (?) for killing Gracchans without trial. Later (110 or 109) condemned by the Mamilian Inquisition, nominally for misconduct in dealings with Jugurtha in Africa, but at least as much for the events of 121.

Pacuvius Claudus, M.; Pacuvius Claudus, Q. Brothers, accusers of M. Scaurus 54, later attacked for *calumnia* (false accusation).

Papirius, M. (*pont. max.* 449) See *MRR* 1. 49.

Papirius, M. Friend of Pompeius Magnus, equestrian *publicanus*, killed in affray with Clodians when sent to recapture the escaped Tigranes of Armenia.

Papirius Maso, P. IIIvir for founding Latin colony at Placentia, 218.

Patulcius, Q. Totally obscure accuser of Milo in his second trial of 52 *de vi* (under the Lex Plautia).

Peducaeus, C. Joined in dramatic appeal to jury for M. Scaurus, 54.

Perpenna, M. (better Perperna) One of nine ex-consuls to support M. Scaurus, 54. This must be the cos. of 92, cens. 86, who died in 49 at the age of ninety-eight.

Phileros Slave to a Cornelius *c.*67–65. A common slave-name.

Philodemus Famous Greek Epicurean philosopher and littérateur, resident in and around Rome mid-1st cent. BC, close and revered acquaintance of several leading Romans. Some fragments of his writings have been recovered from the ashes of Merculaneum.

Plautius Hypsaeus, P. Consular candidate 52 against Milo and Q. Metellus Scipio, supported by P. Clodius against Cicero; also by Pompey, whom he had served as quaestor/ proquaestor (66(?)–61), but later dropped by him. The tribunes of the plebs, T. Munatius Plancus and Q. Pompeius Rufus also supported him against Milo. Probably involved in violence against Milo on the Via Sacra in 53.

Plautius Silvanus, M. (tr. pl. 89 or 88) Author of Lex Plautia *iudiciaria*, on composition of juries, repealed by Sulla, 81.

Pompeius Magnus, Cn. (cos. 70; 55; 52) (Pompey) Standard accounts include *CAH* ix², chs. 7–10; Gruen (1974) (*passim*); Seager (1979); Gelzer (1959).

Pompeius Rufus, Q. (cos. 88) Opposed with his colleague Sulla to P. Sulpicius, tr. pl. See *MRR* 2.

Pompeius Rufus, Q. (tr. pl. 52) Maternal grandson of Sulla. With T. Munatius Plancus his colleague incited the mob to display Clodius' corpse on the *rostra*. Later opposed by M. Caelius Rufus, tr. pl., then with colleagues T. Munatius Plancus and C. Sallustius Crispus continued to foment popular feeling against Milo.

Pompeius Strabo, Cn. (cos. 89) Father of Cn. Magnus (see above). Important role in northern theatre of Social War, and later in civil war of 87, when he lost his life.

Pomponius, Cn. (tr. pl. 90) Probably the correct identification (rather than Cn. Pompeius Strabo, cos. 89) of the man first indicted *de maiestate* under the Lex Varia before courts newly constituted by the Lex Plotia of 89 (Ascon. 79C). See Badian (1969), 465–75.

Pomponius, P. Travelling companion of Milo at Bovillae, 52. Well-known member of the urban plebs.

Pomponius Atticus, T. Atticus, friend and agent of Cicero (and many others). See Horsfall (1989); Millar (1988).

Porcius Cato, C. (tr. pl. 56) Not to be confused with the far more important M. Cato. Defended by M. Scaurus, 54, probably *de vi*, and joined in dramatic appeal to jury in his case shortly afterwards. Strongly pro-Clodian as tr. pl. 56.

Porcius Cato, L. (cos. 89) Killed early in the Marsic War early in his year.

Porcius Cato, M. (Uticensis) (pr. 54) The Younger Cato, archetypal martyr of the Republic in its last days. Moderns: Fehrle (1983); Goar (1987); Afzelius (1941).

Pupius Piso, M. (cos. 61) Careful rather than brilliant orator and lawyer. Politically undistinguished. Contrived a Spanish triumph in 69 as ex-praetor. In 81/80, unlike C. Caesar, had obeyed Sulla's order to divorce his wife.

Rabirius, C. Defended in 63 on a somewhat contrived, politically motivated charge of *perduellio* before the tribal assembly.

Roscius Otho, L. (tr. pl. 67) Author of law to grant special seating to equestrians at games.

Rutilius Nudus According to Fenestella, father-in-law to L. Piso, cos. 58. Very obscure. Probably the legate of M. Cotta at Chalcedon, 74. If so, very likely an ex-praetor by then. See *MRR* 2. 105; 3. 183.

Rutilius Rufus, P. (cos. 105) Infamously convicted by an equestrian jury *c.*92 *de repetundis* for his conduct as legate to Q. Mucius Scaevola (see above) in Asia, either 97/6 or 95/4.

Sallustius Crispus, C. (tr. pl. 52, later historian) See standard accounts, esp. Syme (1964*b*).

Saufeius, M. Henchman of T. Annius Milo Papianus (see above), tried twice under different laws *de vi* 52 after Milo's conviction, twice acquitted.

Scribonius Curio, C. (cos. 76) Once threatened by Lex Varia of 90, but survived as Sullan lieutenant and partisan to reach cos. 76. Still alive in mid-50s, when he wrote at least one pamphlet, probably in dialogue form, against Caesar.

Scribonius Curio, C. (tr. pl. 50) Famous partisan of Caesar in pre-Civil War political machinations. Earlier a partner of P. Clodius in various activities, derided by Cicero (*Att.* 1.14.5) as 'Curio's little girl' (*filiola Curionis*), and with him the target of his invective *Against Clodius and Curio*, of which only a few fragments survive.

Scribonius Libo, L. (aed. cur. 194) With his colleague C. Atilius Serranus provided special seating for senators at the Roman Games.

Seius, M. Possibly (great-?) grandfather of Seianus, Guard Prefect of Tiberius. In 52 accuser of M. Saufeius in his second trial *de vi*.

Sempronia Daughter of a Sempronius Tuditanus. Bore witness against Milo with her daughter Fulvia (see above). Plausibly closely related, conceivably even identical, with the famous *femme fatale* of Sall. *Bell. Cat.* 25.

Sempronius Gracchus, C. (tr. pl. 123; 122) The famous tr. pl. On both Gracchi it may suffice here to mention *CAH* ix², ch. 3; Stockton (1979).

Sempronius Gracchus, Ti. (tr. pl. 133) The famous tr. pl.—see standard accounts. Note also father (cos. 177, 163) and grandfather (cos. 215, 213).

Sempronius Longus, Ti. (cos. 218) With his colleague the elder P. Scipio, lost to Hannibal at the River Trebia, 218.

Sempronius Longus, Ti. (cos. 194) Solid career of public service 200–174. No great fame.

Sempronius Tuditanus Father of Sempronia. Might conceivably be identified with the following, but rather more probably an otherwise unknown son or other younger relative.

Sempronius Tuditanus, C. (cos. 129, historian) Left inscribed monuments of his Illyrian campaigns.

Sergius Catilina, L. Insurgent, 63. See standard accounts and *MRR* 2. 72, 138, 147, 155.

Servilia Granddaughter of Q. Servilius Caepio, cos. 106. Mother of M. Iunius Brutus (see above), half-sister to M. Porcius Cato. Also alleged mistress of C. Iulius Caesar. Second marriage to D. Iunius Silanus, cos. 62. By the 40s, one of the *grandes dames* of Roman political life.

Servilius Caepio, Q. (cos. 106) Disastrously defeated at Arausio by the Northmen as procos. 105. Author of a Lex *iudiciaria* to share juries between senators and *equites*.

Servilius Caepio, Q. (pr. 61) Enemy of M. Aemilius Scaurus. Son of previous, father of Servilia (see above).

Servilius Glaucia, C. (pr. 102; tr. pl. ?101) Author of law on extortion, making the juries wholly equestrian.

Servilius Globulus, P. (tr. pl. 67) Sought to impede the initiatives of his colleague C. Cornelius in the interests of the optimate Establishment.

Servilius Vatia Isauricus, P. (cos. 79) Senior consular by 54, when he spoke in support of M. Scaurus. Major command in Cilicia 78–74 (note length, despite Sulla's legislation). Abortive censorship 55.

Sicinius Velutus, L. One of the first tribunes of the plebs, 493, according to the annalist Tuditanus. See *MRR* 1.

Sulpicius Galba, P. (cos. and. 64) Competitor of Cicero. Patrician blood, little ability.

Sulpicius, P. (cos. 461) Envoy to plebeian secessionists, 449. See further *MRR* 1.

Sulpicius, P. (tr. pl. 88) [*Cognomen* 'Rufus' unattested] Formidable orator. Author of a highly contentious series of laws provoking reaction from the consuls, esp. Sulla, and ultimately the civil war of 88. Killed by Sulla as a result.

Tanusius, L. Alleged victim of Catilina in Sullan reign of terror.

Tarpeius, Sp. (cos. 454) Envoy to plebeian secessionists, 449. See further *MRR* 1. 43, 49.

Tatius, T. Legendary Sabine immigrant King of Rome with Romulus.

Teidius, Sex. Senator in 52, picked up Clodius' corpse and had it transported to Rome. The name suggests Apennine provenance.

Terentia Cicero's first wife. Well connected. Half-sister to Fabia, Vestal (see above). See accounts listed below under Tullius Cicero, M.

Terentius Varro Gibba, M. Joined in the successful defence of M. Saufeius, 52, in his second trial *de vi* (*lege Plautia*). Later quaestor to M. Brutus in Cisalpine Gaul 46; tr. pl. Executed after battle of Philippi, 42.

Terentius Varro, M. Scholar and antiquarian—and much else. Pompeian supporter. For career, *MRR* 2. 625; 3. 204. For intellectual pre-eminence, *oeuvre*, Rawson (1985), index.

Terpolius, M. (tr. pl. 77) Apparently lightest of lightweight tribunes in the years immediately after Sulla's reforms. Apparently fell foul of Q. Catulus, cos. 78, procos. 77.

Trebellius, L. (tr. pl. 67) Opposed the rogation on the anti-piracy command proposed by his colleague A. Gabinius, who threatened to have him deposed, as Ti. Gracchus deposed M. Octavius in 13?. Yielded with one more tribal vote required to unseat him.

Tullius Cicero, M. The orator, politician, man of letters. Modern accounts abound, among which notable items include Rawson (1975); Shackleton Bailey (1971); Stockton (1971).

Tullius Tiro, M. Cicero's freedman and highly trained secretary, manumitted 53. Wrote a Life of Cicero, probably not especially politically orientated, but fairly full, reaching 57 BC by the fourth book (Fr. 2 Peter), yet going on to cover his murder in 43. Apparently lived to a ripe old age: Jerome mentions him under *Ann. Abrah.* 2013 = 4 BC, where he seems to locate his decease.

Valerius Antias Annalist, wrote in or just after Sullan age, or, as some now argue, in the late 50s, early 40s. Major source of Livy, but not particularly reliable user of earlier annalists, over-inventive for his own purposes.

Valerius, C. Accuser of Saufeius *de vi* under Lex Pompeia, 52. Otherwise unidentified. Very possibly a relative of P. Valerius Leo, P. Valerius Nepos (see below), also hostile to Milo.

Valerius Flaccus, L. (cos. 100) Colleague of C. Marius, whom he supported. *Princeps senatus* 86–.

Valerius Leo, P. Hostile to Milo 52, seconded accusation of him *de ambitu*.

Valerius Nepos, P. Seconded main indictment of Milo *de vi* under Lex Pompeia, 52.

Valerius Messala, M. (cos. 53) Elected late, after very lengthy *interregnum*. Political lightweight.

Valerius Messala Niger, M. (cos. 61) Advocate for M. Scaurus, 54. Political lightweight.

Valerius Triarius, L. (pr. 78) *Praenomen* more probably C. rather than L. Commanded in Sardinia 77, opposing M. Lepidus there. Legate to L. Lucullus in East 73–67. Disastrously defeated by Mithridates 67.

Valerius Triarius, P. (son of previous) Accuser of M. Scaurus 54, especially suitable because of his father's connection with Sardinia. Unsafe to identify him with C. Valerius Triarius, Pompeian naval prefect 49–48, but a likely brother.

Valerius Volusi f. (cos. 505) See *MRR* 1. 7.

Valerius Volusi f.-n. Maximus, M'. (dict. 494) See *MRR* 1. 14; 3. 213.

Valerius Volusi f. Publicola, P. (cos. suff. 509; cos. 508, 507, 504) See *MRR* 1. 2; 5–7.

Varius Hybrida, Q. (tr. pl. 90) Author of a *lex* to indict persons deemed to be in collusion with Italian rebels of 91/90. Many prominent men were exiled as a result. Varius himself was ultimately condemned under it and executed.

Vatinius, P. (tr. pl. 59) Notorious author of wide-ranging legislation in 59, most notably the award of a five-year special command to Caesar in Illyricum and Cisalpine Gaul, to which Transalpine Gaul was later added. Later legate to Caesar in Gaul 58(?)–56; pr. 55; Caesarian legate again 51–47; cos. suff. 47 etc. Detested by Cicero, who was forced to defend him in 54. Later reconciled.

Verginius, L. (tr. pl. 449) See *MRR* 1. 48–9.

Verginius Tricostus, A. (cos. 494) See *MRR* 1. 13–14.

Verres, C. (pr. urb. 74) The infamous Verres, accused *de repetundis* by Cicero in 70 for activities in Sicily. See standard accounts of Cicero.

Veturius Cicurinus, L. (cos. 494) See *MRR* 1. 13–14.

Volcacius, C. His deprivation of an inheritance by Cn. Cornelius Dolabella pr. 81 may be inferred from Asconius (74C).

Volcacius Tullus, L. (cos. 66) Refused Catilina's candidature for cos. 65. Otherwise utterly undistinguished.

Volumnius, M. Alleged victim of Catilina in the Sullan reign of terror.

Laws and Rogations in Asconius

LEX/LEGES

Aelia et Fufia *de caelo servando* (?); *de comitiis habendis* (?) Most probably two laws, not one, of *c.*150 BC. See Marshall (1985*b*), 97–8.

Aurelia *de iudiciis privatis*, 75—one of the 'minor' items above, in Ascon. 67C.

Aurelia *de iure tribunicio*, 75, amid minor legislation, by C. Cotta, cos., to restore access to higher office for tribunes of the plebs.

Aurelia *iudiciaria*, 70, by L. Cotta, pr. for tripartite juries of senators, *equites*, and *tribuni aerarii*.

Calpurnia Pisonis *de ambitu*, 67, by C. Piso, cos., to check electoral malpractices.

Cassia *de abactis damnatis*, 104, tr. pl., to expel from senate deposed or condemned officials.

Cassia *tabellaria*, 137, tr. pl., to institute secret ballot in trials in assemblies.

Clodia *de collegiis*, 58, tr. pl., to restore *collegia* disbanded by senatorial decree of 64.

Clodia *de nota censoria*, 58, tr. pl., to regulate censors' condemnation of individuals, in particular expulsions from the senate.

Clodia *de obnuntiatione*, 58, tr. pl., to restrict the declaration of bad omens in order to suspend public business.

Clodia *frumentaria*, 58, tr. pl., for distributions of free corn to the people.

Cornelia *de edicto praetoris*, 67, tr. pl., to require praetors to adhere to their edicts in jurisdiction.

Cornelia *nequis in senatu legibus solveretur*, 67, tr. pl., to require a quorum of at least 200 in the senate for exemptions from the laws by senatorial decree, and to invalidate any veto against referral of any such exemption to the people for ratification.

Cornelia Sullae *de iure tribunicio*, 81, as dictator. In the Asconian context, the ban on tribunes of the plebs holding further office. (Sulla's law on tribunes included much else.)

Cornelia Sullae *de maiestate*, 81, as dictator, on trials for various modes of conduct deemed to breach constitutional law as defined by Sulla.

Cornelia Sullae *de repetundis*, 81, as dictator, on trials for actions *de repetundis* (see Glossary).

Domitia *de sacerdotiis*, 104, to appoint to the major priesthoods by popular election, no longer by co-optation.

Gabinia *de piratis persequendis*, 67, tr. pl., to establish a pan-Mediterranean command to eliminate piracy.

Iulia *iudiciaria*, probably that of Augustus, 17, rather than of Caesar, 46.

Iunia *militaris*, 109, cos., in face of the Cimbric threat, to abrogate recent laws shortening the length of military service.

Licinia Mucia *de civitate (vel sim.)*, 95, both coss., to insist on correct registrations of citizenship for Romans and (Italian) allies. Not a law to expel Italian allies from Rome.

Liviae 91, tr. pl., including *leges agraria* (allocations of land), *frumentaria* (corn subsidies), *iudiciaria* (composition of juries), *de senatu legendo* (selection of senators), *monetalis* (coinage), (*rogatio*) *de civitate danda* (grants of Roman citizen-rights).

Manilia *de imperio Cn. Pompeii* (?), 66, tr. pl., however titled, in effect to grant Pompeius enormous powers to conduct of the Mithridatic War, supplanting L. Lucullus.

Manilia *de libertinis*, 66, tr. pl., to allow freedmen to vote in all thirty-five tribes. Rapidly annulled. Cf. Lex Sulpicia of 88 (below).

Plautia *de vi*, date uncertain, perhaps *c.*70, tr. pl. or pr. Exact content also uncertain, but beyond doubt intended to check violence deemed to be against the public interest.

Plautia (Plotia) *iudiciaria*, 89 (or 88), tr. pl., to appoint all juries from a panel, fifteen per tribe, from 'the best men available'—that is, upper classes, undifferentiated.

Pompeia *de ambitu*, 52, cos., to prevent electoral malpractices.

Pompeia *de quaesitore prodendo* (?), 52, cos., to secure appointment of president for the trial of Milo for the murder of Clodius.

Pompeia *de vi*, 52, cos. Further regulations for trial of cases for public violence.

Pompeia *iudiciaria*, 55, cos. Minor amendments in the composition of juries.

Pompeia Licinia, 70, both coss., to restore all pre-Sullan rights to tribunes of the plebs not yet recovered.

Pompeia Strabonis *de iure Transpadanorum*, 89, as consul, granting Latin rights to all inhabitants of Transpadane Gaul, and access to full Roman citizenship for magistrates of their communities.

Porcia *de provocatione*, probably by M. Cato as pr. 198 or cos. 195, to uphold a citizen's right to immunity from being flogged on orders of a magistrate. However, there may have been at least one other Lex Porcia (later 2nd cent.) of similar import, extending rights of *provocatio*.

Roscia *de spectaculis (vel sim.)*, 67, tr. pl., to allocate special seating to *equites* at the Games.

Servilia Glauciae *de repetundis*, probably 101, tr. pl., to recruit juries solely from *equites*, to recover wrongfully taken assets from ultimate recipients, to enfranchise Latins for successful prosecutions, to provide for adjournments of trials, perhaps other adjustments to previous regulations.

Sulpicia *de libertinis*, 88, tr. pl., to allow freedmen('s sons?) to vote in all thirty-five tribes. Annulled.

Valeria *de loco publice dando assignando* (?), cos., date uncertain, trad. very early in Republic—possibly 509, 508, or 505—if you believe in such things. To assign to the author a site for a house, at public expense.

Varia 90, tr. pl., to set up a court to try persons found to have acted in collusion with Italian rebels in the Marsic (Social) War.

ROGATIONES

Servilia Rulli *agraria*, 63, tr. pl., to appoint a far-ranging and powerful agrarian commission for large-scale agrarian settlement.

Bibliography

Afzelius, A. (1941), 'Die politische Deutung des jungeren Catos', *Class. et Med.* 4, 100–203.

Aigner, H. (1976), 'Zur Wichtigkeit der Waffenbeschaffung in der späteren römischen Republik', *GB* 5, 1–24.

Alexander, M. C. (1981), 'The Legatio Asiatica of Scaurus: did it take place?', *TAPA* 111, 1–9.

—— (1985), '*Praemia* in the Quaestiones of the Late Republic', *CP* 80, 20–32.

—— (1990), *Trials in the Late Roman Republic* (Toronto).

—— (2002), *The Case for the Prosecution in the Ciceronian Era* (Michigan).

Astin, A. E. (1964), 'Leges Aelia et Fufia', *Latomus* 23, 421–45.

—— (1967), *Scipio Aemilianus* (Oxford).

Austin, M., Harries, J., and Smith, C. (1998) (eds.), *Modus Operandi: Essays in honour of Geoffrey Rickman* (London).

Babcock, C. L. (1965), 'The early career of Fulvia', *AJP* 86, 1–32.

Badian, E. (1956*a*), 'P. Decius Subolo', *JRS* 46, 91–6.

—— (1956*b*), 'Q. Mucius Scaevola and the province of Asia', *Athenaeum* 34, 104–23.

—— (1957), 'Caepio and Norbanus', *Historia* 6, 318–44.

—— (1962), 'Waiting for Sulla', *JRS* 52, 46–61.

—— (1964), *Studies in Greek and Roman History* (Oxford).

—— (1965), 'M. Porcius Cato and the annexation and early administration of Cyprus', *JRS* 55, 110–21.

—— (1966), 'The early historians', in Dorey (1966), 1–38.

—— (1968*a*), 'Sulla's Augurate', *Arethusa* 1, 26–46.

—— (1968*b*), *Roman Imperialism in the Late Republic* (Oxford).

—— (1969), 'Quaestiones Variae', *Historia* 18, 447–91.

—— (1983), *Publicans and Sinners*, 2nd edn. (Dunedin).

—— (1989), 'The *scribae* of the Late Roman Republic', *Klio* 71, 582–603.

—— (1990), 'The Consuls, 179–49 BC', *Chiron* 20, 371–413.

Balsdon, J. P. V. D. (1937), 'Q. Mucius Scaevola the Pontifex and *Ornatio Provinciae*', *CR* 53, 8–10.

—— (1957), 'Roman history 58–56 BC.: Three Ciceronian problems', *JRS* 47, 15–20.

Barlow, C. T. (1980), 'The Roman government and the Roman economy, 92–80 BC', *AJP* 101, 202–19.

BATES, R. L. (1986), '*Rex in senatu*', *Proc. American Philosophical Soc.* 130, 251–88.

BAUMAN, R. A. (1967), *The Crimen Maiestatis in the Roman Republic and the Augustan Principate* (Johannesburg).

BENNER, H. (1987), *Die Politik des P. Clodius Pulcher* (Historia Einzelschriften 50, Stuttgart).

BERRY D. H. (1993), 'Pompey's legal knowledge—or lack of it: Cic. *Mil.* 70 and the date of *Pro Milone*', *Historia* 42, 502–4.

—— (1996), *Cicero*: Pro P. Sulla Oratio (Cambridge).

BLOCH, G. (1908), 'M. Aemilius Scaurus: étude sur l'histoire des partis au VIIe siècle de Rome', *Mél. d'hist. anc.* 25 (Bibliot. de la Fac. des Lettres, Paris), 1–81.

BODEL, J. (1994), *Graveyards and Groves: A Study of the* Lex Lucerina (*AJAH* 11 (1986 [1994]), Cambridge, Mass.).

BONNEFOND-COUDRY, M. (1973), *Le Sénat de la République romaine de la guerre d'Hannibal à Auguste* (Rome).

BRENNAN, T. C. (2000), *The Praetorship in the Roman Republic*, 2 vols. (Oxford).

BROUGHTON, T. R. S. (1946), 'Notes on Roman magistrates', *TAPA* 77, 35–43.

BRUNT, P. A. (1957), 'Three Passages in Asconius', *CR* 7, 193–5.

—— (1966), 'The Roman Mob', *Past and Present* 35, 3–27.

—— (1980), 'Evidence given under torture', *ZSS* 97, 256–65.

—— (1982), '*Nobilitas* and *Novitas*', *JRS* 72, 1–17.

—— (1988), *The Fall of the Roman Republic and Related Essays* (Oxford).

—— (1990), *Roman Imperial Themes* (Oxford).

BUCHER, G. S. (1995), 'Appian *BC* 2.24 and the trial *de ambitu* of M. Aemilius Scaurus', *Historia* 44, 396–421.

BULST, C. M. (1964), 'Cinnanum Tempus: a re-assessment of the *dominatio Cinnae*', *Historia* 13, 307–37.

BURCKHARDT, L. A. (1990), 'The political élite of the Roman Republic: comment on a recent discussion of *nobilitas* and *novus homo*', *Historia* 39, 77–99.

BUTLER, H. E., and CARY, M. (1924), *Cicero: De Provinciis Consularibus* (Oxford).

CADOUX, T. J. (1980), 'Sallust and Sempronia', in Marshall (1980), 93–122.

CARANDINI, A. (1986), '*Domus* ed *Insulae* sulle pendici settentrional del Palatino', *Bullettino della commissione archeologica classica di Roma* 91, 263–78.

CARCOPINO, J. (1947), *Les Secrets de la Correspondance de Cicéron*, 2 vols. (Paris).

CARNEY, T. F. (1961), *A Biography of C. Marius* (Proc. African Classical Associations 1, Salisbury).

CARSON, S. (1988), 'Asconius *In Cornelianam* 68.7–69.12 Clark and Roman legislative procedure: a textual note', *AJP* 109, 537–42.

CASTAGNOLI, F. (1977), 'Roma arcaica ed i recenti scavi di Lavinio', *La Parola del Passato* 32, 346–55.

—— *et al.* (1975), *Lavinium II* (Rome).

CAVARZERE, A. (1982), 'Asconio ed il *crimen calumniae*', *Atene e Roma* 27, 164–70.

CELS-SAINT-HILAIRE, J. (1985), 'Les *libertini*: des mots et des choses', *DHA* 11, 331–79.

CLARK, A. C. (1895), *M. Tulli Ciceronis Pro T. Annio Milone: ad iudices oratio* (Oxford).

—— (1907), *Q. Asconii Pediani orationum Ciceronis quinque narratio* (Oxford).

CLARK, P. A. (1991), 'Tullia and Crassipes', *Phoenix* 45, 28–38.

CLOUD, J. D. (1977), 'The date of Valerius Antias', *LCM* 2, 225–7.

COARELLI, F. (1981), *Fregellae: la storia degli Scavi* (Rome).

—— (1985), *Il Foro romano II: periodo repubblicano ed augusteo* (Rome).

—— (1986), *Fregellae 2: il santuario di Esculapio* (Rome).

—— (1987), *I santuari di Lazio in età repubblicana* (Rome).

—— (1989), 'La casa dell'aristocrazia romana secondo Vitruvio', in Geertman and Jong (1989), 178–97.

—— (1997), *Il Campo Marzio: dalle origini alla fine della Repubblica* (Rome).

CORNELL, T. J. (1995), *The Beginnings of Rome* (London).

COURTNEY, E. (1961), 'The prosecution of Scaurus in 54 BC', *Philologus* 105, 151–6.

—— (1980), *A Commentary on the Satires of Juvenal* (London).

CRAWFORD, J. W. (1984), *Cicero: The Lost and Unpublished Orations* (Hypomnemata 80, Göttingen).

—— (1994), *M. Tullius Cicero: The Fragmentary Speeches* (2nd edn., Atlanta).

CRAWFORD, M. H. (1968), 'The edict of M. Marius Gratidianus', *PCPS* 94, 1–4.

—— (1974), *Roman Republican Coinage*, 2 vols. (Cambridge).

—— *et al.* (1984–6), 'Excavations at Fregellae, 1978–84: an interim report on the work of the British team', *PBSR* 52. 21–35, 53. 72–96; 54. 40–68.

—— *et al.* (1996), *Roman Statutes*, 2 vols. (London).

CROOK, J. A. (1967), *The Law and Life of Rome* (London).

DAMON, C. (1992), 'Sex. Cloelius, *scriba*', *HSCP* 94, 227–50.

—— (1993), '*Comm. Pet.* 10', *HSCP* 95, 281–8.

DAVID J. M., *et al.* (1973), 'Le *commentariolum petitionis* de Quintus Cicéron', in *ANRW* 1.3, 239–77.

DEGRASSI, A. (1937), *Inscriptiones Italiae* 13.3 *(Fasti et elogia)* (Rome).

—— (1947), *Inscriptiones Italiae* 13.1 *(Fasti et elogia)* (Rome).

—— (1967), *Inscriptiones Italiae* 13.2 *(Fasti et elogia)* (Rome).

DOREY, T. A. (1966) (ed.), *Latin Historians* (London).

DOUGLAS, A. E. (1966), *M. Tulli Ciceronis Brutus* (Oxford).

DRUMANN, W., and GROEBE, P. (1899–1929), *Geschichte Roms*, 6 vols. (2nd edn., Leipzig).

DYCK, A. R. (1996), *A Commentary on Cicero, de Officiis* (Ann Arbor).

EPSTEIN, D. F. (1986), 'Cicero's testimony in the Bona Dea Trial', *CP* 81, 229–35.

FABRE, G. (1981), *Libertus: recherches sur les rapports patron—affranchi à la fin de la république romaine* (Rome).

FEARS, J. L. (1975), 'The coinage of Q. Cornificius and Augural symbolism', *Historia* 24, 592–602.

FEHRLE, R. (1983), *Cato Uticensis* (Darmstadt).

FERRARY, J.-L. (1983), 'Les Origines de la loi de majesté à Rome', *CRAI* 556–72.

FLAMBARD, J.-M. (1977), 'Clodius, les collèges, la plèbe, et les esclaves. Recherches sur la politique populaire au milieu du 1er siècle', *MEFRA* 89, 115–56.

—— (1978), 'Nouvel examen d'un dossier prosopographique: le cas de Sex. Clodius/Cloelius', *MEFRA* 90, 235–45.

—— (1981), 'Collegia Compitalicia: Phénomène associatif, cadres territoriaux et cadres civiques dans le monde romain à l'époque républicaine', *Ktema* 6, 143–66.

FLAMMINI, G. (1977), 'Marco Emilio Scauro e i suoi frammenti', *Ann. della Fac. di Lettere e di Filosofia dell' Università di Macerata*, 10, 37–56.

FLOWER, H. I. (1996), *Ancestor Masks and Aristocratic Power in Roman Culture* (Oxford).

FOWLER, W. W. (1899), *The Roman Festivals in the Period of the Republic* (London).

FRACCARO, P. (1957), 'Scauriana', in P. Fraccaro, *Opuscula* 2 (Pavia), 125–47.

FREDERIKSEN, M. W. (1966), 'Caesar, Cicero and the problem of debt', *JRS* 56, 128–41.

—— (1984), *Campania*, ed. and suppl. N. Purcell (London).

FRIER, B. W. (1969), 'Sulla's priesthood', *Arethusa* 2, 187–99.

GABBA, E. (1976), *Republican Rome: The Army and the Allies*, tr. P. J. Cuff (Oxford).

GABBA, E. (1984), 'The *Collegia* of Numa: problems of method and political ideas', *JRS* 74, 81–6.

GARGOLA, D. J. (1995), *Lands, Laws and Gods: Magistrates and Ceremony in the Regulation of Public Land in Republican Rome* (Chapel Hill and London).

GARNSEY, P. (1988), *Famine and Food Supply in the Graeco-Roman World* (Cambridge).

GEER, R. M. (1929), 'M. Aemilius Scaurus (Suetonius *Nero* 2.1 and Asconius in Cicero *Pro Scauro* 1)', *CP* 24, 292–4.

GEERTMAN, H., and JONG, J. J. (1989) (eds.), *Munus non ingratum: Proc. of the International Symposium on Vitruvius 'de architectura' and the Hellenistic and Republican Architecture* (Leiden).

GELZER, M. (1959), *Pompeius* (2nd edn., Munich).

—— (1968), *Caesar, Politician and Statesman*, 6th edn., tr. P. Needham (Oxford).

—— (1969*a*), *Cicero: ein biographischer Versuch* (Wiesbaden).

—— (1969*b*), *The Roman Nobility*, tr. R. Seager (Oxford).

GIBSON, C. A. (2002), *Interpreting a Classic: Demosthenes and the Ancient Commentators* (Berkeley).

GOAR, R. J. (1987), *The Legend of Cato Uticensis* (Coll. Latomus 197, Brussels).

GREENIDGE, A. H. J. (1901), *The Legal Procedure of Cicero's Time* (London)

GRIFFIN, M. T. (1973), 'The Tribune C. Cornelius', *JRS* 63, 196–213.

—— and BARNES, J. (1989) (eds.), *Philosophia Togata: Essays in Philosophy and Roman Society* (Oxford).

GRUEN, E. S. (1965*a*), 'The Lex Varia', *JRS* 55, 59–73.

—— (1965*b*), 'The political allegiance of P. Mucius Scaevola', *Athenaeum* 43, 321–32.

—— (1966*a*), 'Cicero and Licinius Calvus', *HSCP* 71, 215–33.

—— (1966*b*), 'Political prosecutions in the 90s', *Historia* 15, 32–64.

—— (1968), *Roman Politics and the Criminal Courts, 149–78 B.C.* (Cambridge, Mass.).

—— (1969*a*), 'Notes on the First Catilinarian Conspiracy', *CP* 64, 20–4.

—— (1969*b*), 'The consular elections of 53 BC', in J. Bibauw (ed.), *Hommages à M. Renard* 2, Coll. Latomus 102, Brussels), 311–21.

—— (1974), *The Last Generation of the Roman Republic* (Berkeley and Los Angeles).

HALL, U. (1964), 'Voting procedure in the Roman assemblies', *Historia* 13, 267–306.

HASELBERGER, L. (2002) (ed.), *Mapping Augustan Rome* (*JRA* Suppl. Ser. 50, Portsmouth, RI).

HENDERSON, M. I. (1950), 'De commentariolo petitionis', *JRS* 40, 8–21.

—— (1963), 'The establishment of the Equester Ordo', *JRS* 53, 61–72.

HORSFALL, N. (1989) (tr. and ed.), *Cornelius Nepos: A Selection, including the Lives of Cato and Atticus* (Oxford).

JONES, A. H. M. (1972), *The Criminal Courts of the Roman Republic and Principate* (Oxford).

KALLETT-MARX, R. M. (1989), 'Asconius 14–15C and the date of Q. Mucius Scaevola's command in Asia', *CP* 84, 305–12.

KEAVENEY, A. (1982), Sulla, the Last Republican (London).

KLEINER, D. E. E., and MATHESON, S. B. (1996) (eds.), *I, Claudia, Women in Ancient Rome* (Austin, Tex.).

KLOTZ, A. (1927), *C. Iulii Caesaris Commentarii*, vol. 3 (Leipzig).

KÜHNERT, A. (1991), *Die plebs urbana in der späteren röm. Republik* (Abh. Leipzig phil.-hist. Reihe 73.1, Berlin).

KUMANIECKI, K. (1970), 'Les Discours égarés de Cicéron "pro Cornelio" ', *Med. Kon. Vlaam. Acad. Belg.* 32, 3–36.

KUNKEL, W. (1973), *An Introduction to Roman Legal and Constitutional History*, tr. J. M. Kelly (Oxford).

LACEY, W. K. (1961), 'The tribunate of Curio', *Historia* 10, 318–29.

LENEL, O. (1927), *Das Edictum Perpetuum* (3rd edn., Leipzig).

Les Bourgeoisies municipales (1983) = *Les Bourgeoisies municipales italiennes aux IIe et Ier siècles avant J.-C.* (Colloq. internat. CNRS 609, Naples, 7–10 déc. 1980) (Paris).

LEWIS R. G. (1988), 'Inscriptions of Amiternum and Catilina's last stand', *ZPE* 74, 31–42.

—— (2001*a*), 'Catilina and the Vestal', *CQ* 51, 141–9.

—— (2001*b*), 'Scope for Scaurus', *Athenaeum* 89, 345–54.

LINDERSKI, J. (1972), 'The aedileship of Favonius, Curio the Younger, and Cicero's election to the augurate', *HSCP* 76, 181–200 = Linderski (1995), 231–50.

—— (1974), 'The mother of Livia Augusta and the Aufidii Lurcones of the Republic', *Historia* 23, 463–80 = Linderski (1995), 262–79.

—— (1984), 'The *genera militiae* and the status of Octavian', *JRS* 74, 74–80.

—— (1995), *Roman Questions* (Stuttgart).

LINTOTT, A. W. (1965), 'Trinundinum', *CQ* 15, 281–5.

—— (1967), 'P. Clodius Pulcher—*Felix Catilina*?', *G&R* 14, 157–69.

—— (1968), '*Nundinae* and the chronology of the late Roman Republic', *CQ* 18, 89–94.

—— (1974), 'Cicero and Milo', *JRS* 64, 62–78.

LINTOTT, A. W. (1977), 'Cicero on praetors who failed to abide by their edicts', *CQ* 27, 184–6.

LINTOTT, A. W. (1999*a*), *The Constitution of the Roman Republic* (Oxford).

—— (1999*b*), *Violence in Republican Rome* (2nd edn., Oxford).

McDERMOTT, W. C. (1969), 'De Lucceis', *Hermes* 97, 233–46.

—— (1972), 'Cicero and M. Tiro', *Historia* 21, 259–68.

MADVIG, J. N. (1828), *De Q. Asconii Pediani et aliorum veterum interpretum in Ciceronis orationes commentariis disputatio* (Copenhagen).

MARSHALL, B. A. (1974), 'Cicero and Sallust on Crassus and Catiline', *Latomus* 33, 804–13.

—— (1975*a*), 'Q. Cicero, Hortensius and the *Lex Aurelia*', *RhM* 118, 136–52.

—— (1975*b*), 'The date of delivery of Cicero's *In Pisonem*', *CQ* 25, 88–93.

—— (1976), 'The date of Q. Mucius Scaevola's governorship of Asia', *Athenaeum* 54, 117–30.

—— (1977), 'Two court cases of the late second century', *AJP* 98, 417–23.

—— (1980) (ed.), *Vindex Humanitatis: Essays in Honor of J. H. Bishop* (Armidale, NSW).

—— (1985*a*), 'Catiline and the execution of Marius Gratidianus', *CQ* 35, 124–33.

—— (1985*b*), *A Historical Commentary on Asconius* (Columbia).

—— (1987), '*Excepta oratio*, the other *Pro Milone* and the question of shorthand', *Latomus* 46, 730–6.

MARTINO, F. de (1975), *Storia della Costituzione romana* (2nd edn., Naples).

MEIER, C. (1968), 'Die *loca intercessionis* bei Rogationen', *Mus. Helv.* 25, 86–100.

—— (1980), *Res Publica Amissa* (Wiesbaden).

—— (1995), *Caesar*, tr. D. McLintock (London).

MICHELS, A. K. (1967), *The Calendar of the Roman Republic* (Princeton).

MILLAR, F. G. B. (1988), 'Cornelius Nepos, Atticus, and the Roman Revolution', *G&R* 35, 40–55.

—— (1998), *The Crowd in Rome in the Late Republic* (Ann Arbor).

MITCHELL, T. N. (1986), 'The *Leges Clodiae* and *obnuntiatio*', *CQ* 36, 172–6.

MOMMSEN, T. (1887–8), *Römisches Staatsrecht* (2nd and 3rd edn., 3 vols. Leipzig).

—— (1888–94), *Römische Geschichte* (4th edn., Berlin), tr. W. P. Dickson as *History of Rome* (London, 1894).

—— (1899), *Römisches Strafrecht* (Leipzig).

MOREAU, P. (1982), *Clodiana Religio* (Paris).

NICHOLSON. J. (1998), 'The survival of Cicero's letters', in C. Deroux (ed.), *Studies in Latin Literature and Roman History* IX (Brussels), 63–105.

NICOLET, C. (1966–74), *L'Ordre équestre à l'époque républicaine (313–43 av. J.-C)*, 2 vols. (Paris).

—— (1967), 'Arpinum, Aemilius Scaurus et les Tullii Cicerones', *REL* 45, 276–304.

—— (1980), *The World of the Citizen in Republican Rome*, tr. P. S. Falla (London).

NIPPEL, W. (1995), *Public Order in Ancient Rome* (Cambridge).

NISBET, R. G. M. (1961), *Cicero, In Pisonem: Commentary* (Oxford).

OGILVIE, R. M. (1965), *A Commentary on Livy Books 1–5* (Oxford).

PAIS, E. (1918), *Dalle guerre puniche a Cesare Augusto* (Rome).

PATTERSON, J. R. (1992), 'The City of Rome: Republic to Empire', *JRS* 82, 186–215.

PEASE, A. S. (1955) (ed.), *Cicero: De Natura Deorum* (Cambridge, Mass.).

PHILLIPS, E. J. (1974), 'The prosecution of C. Rabirius in 63 BC', *Klio* 16, 87–101.

—— (1976), 'Catiline's Conspiracy', *Historia* 25, 443–8.

—— (1979), 'Cicero and the prosecutions of C. Manilius', *Latomus* 29, 595–607.

PINA POLO, F. (1968), *Contra Arma Verbis* (Heidelberger althistorische Beiträge und epigraphische Studien 22, Heidelberg).

PLATNER, S. B., and ASHBY, T. (1929), *A Topographical Dictionary of Ancient Rome* (Oxford).

POYNTON, A. B. (1902), *Cicero: Pro Milone* (2nd edn., Oxford; repr. 1953).

PUCCIONI, G. (1971) (ed.), *Marco Tullio Cicerone: Frammenti delle orazioni* (Milan).

RAMSEY, J. T. (1980), 'The Prosecution of C. Manilius in 66 B.C. and Cicero's *pro Manilio*', *Phoenix* 34, 323–36.

—— (1985), 'The trial of C. Manilius in 65 BC', *AJP* 106, 367–73.

RAWSON, E. (1971), 'Lucius Crassus and Cicero: the formation of a statesman', *PCPS* 17, 75–88 = Rawson (1991), 16–33.

—— (1973), 'The eastern *clientelae* of Clodius and the Claudii', *Historia* 22, 219–39 = Rawson (1991), 102–24.

—— (1975), *Cicero, a Portrait* (London).

—— (1981), 'Chariot-racing in the Roman Republic', *PBSR* 49, 1–16 = Rawson (1991), 389–407.

—— (1982), 'History, historiography and Cicero's *Expositio Consiliorum Suorum*', *LCM* 7, 121–4 = Rawson (1991), 408–15.

—— (1985), *Intellectual Life in the Roman Republic* (London).

—— (1986), Review of Marshall (1985*b*), *Liverpool Classical Monthly* 11, 79–80.

—— (1991), *Roman Culture and Society* (Oxford).

REEVE, M. D. (1983), 'Asconius', in L. D. Reynolds (ed.), *Texts and Transmission: A Survey of the Latin Classics* (Oxford), 24–5.

REID, J. S. (1909), Review of A. C. Clark (1907), *CR* 23, 21–2.

REINACH, T. (1890), *Mithridate Eupator, roi du Pont* (Paris).

RICHARDSON, J. S. (1971), 'The *Commentariolum Petitionis*', *Historia* 20, 436–42.

—— (1998), 'Old statutes never die: a brief history of abrogation', in Austin, Harries, and Smith (1998), 47–61.

RICKMAN, G. (1979), *The Corn Supply of Ancient Rome* (Oxford).

RILINGER, R. (1989), '*Loca intercessionis* und Legalismus in der späten Republik', *Chiron* 19, 481–98.

RIPOSATI, B. (1939), *M. Terenti Varronis, De vita populi Romani: fonti, esegesi, critica dei frammenti* (Milan).

RUEBEL, J. S. (1979), 'The trial of Milo in 52 BC: a chronological study', *TAPA* 109, 231–49.

SALMON, E. T. (1967), *Samium and the Samnites* (Cambridge).

—— (1969), *Roman Colonisation under the Republic* (London).

SCULLARD, H. H. (1970), *Scipio Africanus, Soldier and Politician* (London).

SEAGER, R. J. (1964), 'The First Catilinarian Conspiracy', *Historia* 13, 338–47.

—— (1967), 'The Lex Varia de maiestate', *Historia* 16, 37–43.

—— (1969), 'The Tribunate of C. Cornelius: some ramifications', in J. Bibauw (ed.), *Hommages à M. Renard 2* (Coll. Latomus 102, Brussels), 680–6.

—— (1973), 'Iusta Catilinae', *Historia* 22, 240–8.

—— (1979), *Pompey: A Political Biography* (Oxford).

SETTLE, J. N. (1963), 'The trial of Milo and the other *Pro Milone*', *TAPA* 94, 269–80.

SHACKLETON BAILEY, D. R. (1960), 'Sex. Clodius—Sex. Cloelius', *CQ* 10, 41–2 = Shackleton Bailey (1997), 13–14.

—— (1965–70), *Cicero's Letters to Atticus*, 7 vols. (Cambridge).

—— (1971), *Cicero* (London).

—— (1973), 'Ciceroniana I' (*Atti del I Colloquium Tullianum*, Rome), 23–6.

—— (1976), *Two Studies in Roman Nomenclature* (University Park, Pa.).

—— (1977), *Cicero: Epistulae ad Familiares*, 2 vols. (Cambridge).

—— (1986), '*Nobiles* and *novi* reconsidered', *AJP* 107, 255–60 = Shackleton Bailey (1997), 309–13.

—— (1988), *Onomasticon to Cicero's Speeches* (Oklahoma).

—— (1997), *Selected Classical Papers* (Ann Arbor).

SHATZMAN, I. (1972), 'The Roman general's authority over booty', *Historia* 21, 177–205.

—— (1975), *Senatorial Wealth and Roman Politics* (Brussels).

SHERWIN-WHITE, A. N. (1966), *The Letters of Pliny: A Historical and Social Commentary* (Oxford).

—— (1973), *The Roman Citizenship* (2nd edn., Oxford).

—— (1984), *Roman Foreign Policy in the East* (London).

Sider, D. (1997), *The Epigrams of Philodemos: Introduction, Text and Commentary* (New York).

Solin, Heikki (2003), *Die griechischer Personennamen in Rom: Ein Namenbuch* (2nd edn., Berlin).

Squires, S. (1990) (ed.), *Asconius: Commentaries on Five Speeches of Cicero* (Bristol).

Staveley, E. S. (1954), 'The conduct of consular elections during an interregnum', *Historia* 3, 193–211.

—— (1972), *Greek and Roman Voting and Elections* (London).

Stewart, R. S. (1962), 'The chronological order of Cicero's earliest letters to Atticus', *TAPA* 93, 459–70.

Stockton, D. (1971), *Cicero, a Political Biography* (Oxford).

—— (1979), *The Gracchi* (Oxford).

Stone A. M. (1980), '*Pro Milone*: Cicero's second thoughts', *Antichthon* 14, 88–111.

Stroh, W. (1975), *Taxis und Taktik: Die advocatische Dispositionskunst in Ciceros Gerichtsreden* (Stuttgart).

Sumi, G. (1977), 'Power and Ritual: the crowd at Clodius' funeral', *Historia* 46, 80–92.

Sumner, G. V. (1964), 'Manius or Mamercus?', *JRS* 54, 41–8.

—— (1973), *The Orators in Cicero's Brutus: Prosopography and Chronology* (Toronto).

Syme, R. (1937), 'Who was Decidius Saxa?', *JRS* 27, 127–37 = Syme (1979), 31–41.

—— (1939), *The Roman Revolution* (Oxford).

—— (1955), Review of T. R. S. Broughton, 'The Magistrates of the Roman Republic', *CP* 50, 127–38.

—— (1960), 'Piso Frugi and Crassus Frugi', *JRS* 50, 12–20 = Syme (1979), 496–509.

—— (1964*a*), 'Senators, tribes and towns', *Historia* 13, 105–25 = Syme (1979), 582–604.

—— (1964*b*), *Sallust* (Cambridge).

—— (1970), *Ten Studies in Tacitus* (Oxford).

—— (1979), *Roman Papers*, 1–2, ed. E. Badian (Oxford).

—— (1986), *The Augustan Aristocracy* (Oxford).

Tatum, W. J. (1990), 'Cicero and the Bona Dea Scandal', *CP* 85, 202–8.

—— (1999), *The Patrician Tribune P. Clodius Pulcher* (Chapel Hill and London).

TAYLOR, L. R. (1942*a*), 'Caesar's colleagues in the Pontifical College', *AJP* 63, 385–412.

—— (1942*b*), 'The election of the Pontifex Maximus in the Late Republic', *CP* 37, 412–14.

—— (1960), *The Voting Districts of the Roman Republic* (Rome).

—— (1964), *Party Politics in the Age of Caesar* (Berkeley).

—— (1966), *Roman Voting Assemblies from the Hannibalic War to the Dictatorship of Caesar* (Ann Arbor).

—— and BROUGHTON, T. R. S. (1968), 'The order of the consuls' names in the official lists', *Historia* 17, 166–72.

TREGGIARI, S. (1969), *Roman Freedmen during the Late Republic* (Oxford).

—— (1991), *Roman Marriage* (Oxford).

VANDERBROECK, P. J. J. (1986), '*Homo novus* again', *Chiron* 16, 239–42.

—— (1987), *Popular Leadership and Collective Behaviour in the Late Roman Republic* (Amsterdam).

VASALY, A. (1993) *Representations: Images of the World in Ciceronian Oratory* (California).

VEYNE, P. (1990), *Bread and Circuses*, tr. B. Pearce (London).

VIRLOUVET, C. (1985), *Famines et émeutes à Rome des origines de la République à la mort de Néron* (Rome).

—— (1995), *Tessera frumentaria: Les procédures de distribution du blé à Rome à la fin de la République et au début de l'Empire* (Rome).

WALLACE-HADRILL, A. F. (1996), 'Engendering the Roman house', in Kleiner and Matheson (1996), 104–15.

WALSH, P. G. (1961), *Livy: His Historical Aims and Methods* (Cambridge).

WARD, A. M. (1970), 'Politics in the trials of Manilius and Cornelius', *TAPA* 101, 545–56.

—— (1977), *Marcus Crassus and the Late Roman Republic* (Columbia).

WATSON, A. (1965), *The Law of Persons in the Roman Republic* (Oxford).

—— (1971), *The Law of Succession in the Later Roman Republic* (Oxford).

—— (1975), *Rome of the Twelve Tables: Persons and Property* (Princeton).

WEBER, C. W. (1983), *Panem et circenses: Massenunterhaltung als Politik im antiken Rom* (Dusseldorf).

WEINRIB, E. J. (1970), '*Obnuntiatio:* two problems', *ZSS* 87, 395–425.

WEINSTOCK, S. (1937), 'Clodius and the Lex Aelia Fufia', *JRS* 27, 215–22.

—— (1960), 'Two archaic inscriptions from Latium', *JRS* 50, 112–18.

—— (1971), *Divus Iulius* (Oxford).

WELCH, K. E. (1995), 'Antony, Fulvia and the ghost of Clodius', *G&R* 42, 182–219.

WISEMAN, T. P. (1966), 'The ambitions of Quintus Cicero', *JRS* 56, 108–15.

—— (1967), 'Lucius Memmius and his family', *CQ* 17, 164–7.

—— (1968), 'Two friends of Clodius', *CQ* 18, 297–302.

—— (1970*a*), 'Pulcher Claudius', *HSCP* 74, 207–21.

—— (1970*b*), 'The definition of *Eques Romanus* in the later Republic and early Empire', *Historia* 19, 67–88.

—— (1971*a*), 'Celer and Nepos', *CQ* 21, 180–2.

—— (1971*b*), *New Men in the Roman Senate, 139 BC–14AD (Oxford)*.

—— (1973), Review of Badian, *Publicans and Sinners*, *Phoenix* 27, 189–98.

—— (1979), *Clio's Cosmetics* (Leicester).

—— (1998), *Roman Drama and Roman History* (Exeter).

ZUMPT, A. W. (1865–9), *Das Criminalrecht der römischen Republik*, 2 vols. (Berlin).

Index

Further information on entries with *, ** can be found in the Index of Personal Names or the Glossary respectively. Dates of office are included below to distinguish identical names.

Lightning Source UK Ltd.
Milton Keynes UK
UKOW04f1531071214

242758UK00001B/6/P